Studien zu Lateinamerika | 22

Otto Argueta

Private Security in Guatemala: Pathway to Its Proliferation

Nomos

Die Deutsche Nationalbibliothek lists this publication in the Deutsche Nationalbibliografie; detailed bibliographic data is available in the Internet at http://dnb.d-nb.de.

a.t.: Hamburg, Univ., Diss., 2012

ISBN 978-3-8487-0118-6

1. Edition 2013

Acknowledgments

I would like to express my deep gratitude to all of those who gave me their strength and support, which enabled me to complete this doctoral dissertation: The German Academic Exchange Service (DAAD) for giving me a doctoral scholarship to write this dissertation in Germany. The GIGA German Institute of Global and Area Studies, especially, my supervisor Prof. Dr. Detlef Nolte and the President of the GIGA Prof. Dr. Robert Kappel for supporting my research as well as providing travel grants to present this study at international conferences as well as the research and administrative personnel of the GIGA Institute of Latin American Studies for their advice and support.

I wish to express my gratitude to those persons who supported me in the elaboration of this doctoral dissertation: Isabel Rosales and Nadine Haas for editing and correcting the last version of this manuscript. Dr. Sabine Kurtenbach and Dr. Sebastian Huhn for helping me to make my arguments better and clear, special thanks to Sebastian Huhn, my friend and colleague who "on the other side of the desk" helped me everyday with comments, informal conversations and critics to each chapter. Ana Elisa Rosales and Alexandr Burilkov for correcting the language of different chapters of this work. A very special thanks to Dr. Knut Walter for his comments, language corrections and valuable academic advises as well as for giving me the motivation to initiate and finish my doctoral studies.

My special gratitude reserved to Prof. Dr. Detlef Nolte whose criticism and supervision helped me to improve this work. Prof. Dr. Detlef Nolte gave me always the necessary motivation and confidence to improve my professional skills and expand my networks with other academic institutions and colleagues. I also thank my second supervisor Prof. Dr. Anika Oettler who since the beginning of this study gave me important feedback from her broad knowledge of Central American countries.

During my fieldworks in Guatemala I conducted several interviews with social scientists, state officials, private security entrepreneurs and personnel, civil society representatives and international advisors, thanks to all of them for sharing their knowledge and experience. Likewise, I extend my gratitude to the Guatemalan Historical Archive of the National Police whose personnel guide me to find the necessary documentation, which has been essential for this dissertation. I also received strong institutional support from the Latin American Social Sciences Faculty (FLACSO-Guatemala) who hosted me during my fieldwork. I also thank family Argueta Ramírez and family Pareja Sandoval for hosting me during my different fieldwork trips.

Finally, I would like to manifest my personal gratitude to those persons who have been and are by my side through the different phases of this process. My friends and colleagues Nadine Haas, Sebastian Huhn and Peter Peetz. Knut Walter again for his valuable, unconditional and always constant friendship, Heide and Jürgen Lemmermann for making me feel as if I had lived here forever. I thank for the valuable support of my mother, sister and brother.

Last but not least, I express my deepest gratitude to my wife and best friend María Isabel Rosales, for her emotional and intellectual support over these years and for sharing with me the experience of our doctoral studies and our life together. This dissertation is dedicated to her, for holding my hand every time, for giving me the motivation and the happiness of everyday.

Hamburg, December 2011 OttoArgueta

Table of Contents

List of Figures and Tables

Acronyms and Abbreviations

AFPC	Acuerdo sobre el fortalecimiento del Poder Civil y función del Ejército en una sociedad democrática / Agreement for the Strengthening of Civilian Power and the Role of the Armed Forces in a Democratic Society
AHPN	Archivo Histórico de la Policía Nacional / Guatemalan Historical Archive of the National Police
CCL	Comités Clandestinos Locales / Local Clandestine Committees
CEH	Comisión del Esclarecimiento Histórico / Guatemalan Truth Commission
CICIG	Comision Internatioal contra la Impunidad en Guatemala / International-Commission Against Impunity in Guatemala
COCP	Centro de Operaciones Conjuntas de la Policía Nacional / Joint Operation Centre of the National Police.
COSEHOGUA	Consejo de Seguridad Hotelera de Guatemala / Hotel Security Council of Guatemala
CUB	Comités Ùnicos de Barrio / Neighbourhoods Committees
DNSA	Digital National Security Archive
EMP	Estado Mayor de la Defensa Nacional / General Staff for National Defence
FIL	Fuerzas Irregulares Locales / Irregular Local Forces
GIS	Guild of Security Industries
JLS	Juntas Locales de Seguridad / Local Security Boards
MINUGUA	United Nations Verification Mission in Guatemala
MLN	Movimiento de Liberación Nacional / National Liberation Movement
MMP	Mobile Military Police
MP	Ministerio Público / Prosecutor Office
ODHAG	Oficina de los Derechos Humanos del Arzobispado de Guatemala / Human Rights Office of the Archdiocese of Guatemala
PAC	Patrulla de Autodefensa Civil / Civil Patrol
PDH	Procuraduría (Procurador) de Los Derechos Humanos / *Ombudsman* Office
PNC	Policía Nacional Civil / Civil National Police
PSC	Private Security Companies
PSP	Public Safety Program of the United States
SAIA	Servicio de Análisis e Información Antinarcóticos / Anti-Narcotic Analysis and Information Service
SAT	Super Intendencia de Administración Tributaria / Superintendence of Tax Administration
SSR	Security Sector Reform

URNG	Unidad Revolucionaria Nacional Guatemalteca / National Revolutionary Unit of Guatemala
VAC	Vice Ministry of Community Affairs

1. Introduction

Private security has rapidly proliferated in almost the whole world in the last decades. The diversity of its services, organizations, coverage, and activities characterize the displacement of security functions centred in the state as the main provider of security to a new polycentric perspective of security in which various actors – including the state – interact to provide security. This perspective is characterized by its heterogeneity and the wide range of non-state armed actors operating from the legal and public sphere to a more informal and illegal sphere. From a broad perspective, private security includes both commercial activities such as private security companies (PSCs) and private military companies (PMCs) as well as non commercial forms such as citizens organizations to provide protection and self-defence, the so-called "security neighbourhood committees". The activities of private security can range from a national level of public security to international operations such as the protection of natural resources, war against terrorism and organized crime, among others. In this scenario, there is a noticeable absence of legal frameworks and effective state controls at both national and international levels.

All of the above place private security at the centre of different dilemmas and debates. On the one hand, under effective state controls private security can contribute to improve security against threats and respond to an increasing demand for citizen security both at a national and a global level. On the other, the proliferation of private security implies the substitution of security functions traditionally associated with the state, which are expected to be core aspects of the legitimacy of public institutions. The displacement of state security functions to the private sector also implies transgressions to nation-state sovereignty, inequitable access to public goods, authoritarian practices, vigilantism, patronage (clientelism), and human rights violations. In addition, it is clear that private security contributes to the displacement of crime due the implementation of preventive and dissuasive private tactics.

Whatever the practical issues and concerns identified above, there are academic concerns about the implications of private security and the mechanisms that produce its proliferation as well as its relation with the state and society. Private security is mainly explained as the result of, on the one hand, the increasing threats associated with insecurity and crime both at a national and a global dimension. On the other hand, private security is analysed as a product of the weakness of the state to confront these threats. The problem is that private security has proliferated both in strong and weak states and mostly before an increase in crime became a global concern.

However, there is little knowledge about the influence of contexts and historical processes. It is not the same when proliferation of private security begins through international delivery companies providing security services to states and the consequent implementation of international armed operations as when proliferation begins through national state actors that implement private security operations before, during, and after internal conflicts or an increase in crime. The first among other factors supposes actions of international private actors against the existence or absence of national public institutions, the second suggest an active interaction between private and public actors. These interactions are rooted in the social and political system and interact with historical political processes of state formation and institutional change. Those differences suggest that contexts and processes matter when attempting an explanation. For this reason, the isolation of variables related to crime and institutional capabilities does not answer satisfactorily the central questions of this research: What explains the proliferation of private security in particular contexts? How do context and history interact with the proliferation of private security?

To deal with these questions this study approaches private security as a result of political processes with a strong temporal dimension. From this perspective, historical contexts feature the configuration of security and the social relations that emerge from this configuration. The focus of the research is on the proliferation of private security in a post-war context. The study is defined by both theoretical and empirical objectives. Historical institutionalism is the theoretical basis of this study and it seeks to contribute to the analysis of private security from a wide perspective which integrates security issues and their interaction with given contexts and political and social processes. In addition, the study identifies path dependent processes, critical junctures, institutional arrangements, and self-reinforcing sequences which have led to the proliferation of private security in the case study. Finally, the contextual political analysis makes it possible for the research to observe the relationship between private security and political processes as well as the feedback produced by these elements themselves.

1.1 Private Security in Contextual and Historical Analysis

This study postulates that the proliferation of private security in a post-war society such as Guatemala is an outcome of contextual and historical political processes and formal and informal reproducing mechanisms that have set an institutional pattern of public security displacement to the private sphere. This process has reinforced private security in the social system with dynamic and adaptive functions. The historical displacement of state security functions is a sufficient cause to explain the proliferation of private security. The existence of other factors, such as the continuity of specific social control mechanisms, the presence of internal armed conflicts, the security sector reform, and the dynamics of post-war crime constitute a set of causal mechanisms that, as a result of their interaction within the socio-political context, help to explain the proliferation of private security.

In Guatemala, the transition to democracy produced a formal institutional reform of the security sector that allowed the continuity of both self-defence policing mechanisms and also commercial private security services. Although the proliferation of private security accelerated from 1996 on, the roots of the phenomenon are older. I propose that private security should be analysed as an outcome of self-reproducing mechanisms that overlap in different sequences. The emphasis is on the historic delegation of security functions granted by the State to private security firms (as commercial private security) and vigilante groups (as non-commercial private security). This research underlines that the proliferation of private security has its origins in public security institutions that through the promotion of private policing fulfil the vacuum of public security. The displacement of security functions reinforced the selection of private security given the political context and societal demands. From a contextual political analysis perspective the study presents an analytical model based on a reproducing sequence elaboration. Establishing the initial conditions allow to identify the critical juncture through which private security emerged as a functional option for the social system. It makes a distinction between the origins of the institutional pattern and the mechanisms that reinforced private security in the social system. This distinction is very important to understand the institutional genesis and the institutional change of private security and how historical analysis explains present phenomena as an outcome of institutional trajectories.

Commercial and non-commercial forms of private security interact in the institutional process of public security displacement. In different historical contexts, the state has delegated self-defence and protection policing through a wide range of informal mechanisms of collaboration with the citizenry. Private security companies (PSCs) are one of these that in a particular context were formalized as a result of a modernization process of the National Police. For this reason, the institutional genesis of PSCs is directly linked with the institutional transformation of the state. On the other hand, self-defence policing organizations have been the mechanism through which the state and other actors gained the community collaboration against different alleged threats.

The reinforcing of the institutional pattern of public security displacement assumes that while the structure of the mechanism can change, its function remains constant in different political contexts due its dynamic and adaptive features. The different mechanisms through which private security reinforces its function in the social system, the sequences of this reinforcing process and its relations with the political context characterize the path dependent process of private security proliferation in Guatemala.

1.2 Private Securit y in the Academic Debate

The literature revision allows to argue that private security is more than guards, companies and organized neighbours; it is more than a highly profitable commercial activity as well. Private security is a reflection of how societies address the political challenges that result from wars, political instability, international conflicts, crime and social fear, and a wide range of threats such as drug trafficking, organized crime, terrorism, and other risks not directly related to violence like natural, financial, and virtual risks. The private security sector is a convergence of both non-state armed actors (private security and military companies, mercenaries, gangs, mafia security organizations) and non-armed actors such as security advisors, political consultants, finance managers, and communication and marketing managers of industrial complexes. Private security includes also the non-paid forms of private security defined as community policing and self-defence organisations, among others. All of them offer particular and contextual responses to one or more security demands. In other words, private security shows how social and political orders are structured and reinforced.

The social function of private security is located in the gray zones of the public and private spheres. This refers to the intersection of public (state institutions and actors) and private (individuals, companies and organizations) processes (Johnston 1992). The relationship between threats and the particular responses to them allude to the protection forces of the society and the way in which governments address this relation. However, the formal and informal displacement of core state functions to the private sphere has a long history. In the modern state, those aspects related to the armed forces that protect the society have to remain a state monopoly (Singer 2003: 7; Tilly 2003). This is true at the institutional level of armies and police but at the functional level, private security has been developed parallel to the institutional framework of the state. The explicative model of state formation process that lead to the state monopoly of the use of force is applicable for some particular countries in Europe and in some degree in the United States. In Latin American countries irregular forces have an important role in the state formation process with strong contextual differences with the European context (Pereira 2003).

Nevertheless institutional forces remain public (minimized in many developed countries), while security functions become more and more privatised. In the long history of wars and conflicts, the legitimate monopoly of the use of violence seems to be an exception to the norm of private provision of the means necessary to start or confront a violent threat (Pereira 2003; Tilly 2003). In the modern state, even during the period of more aggressive neoliberal reforms, the means through which the state uses force (both for protection or repression) has been considered a core task of the state (Singer 2003: 7). The current proliferation of private security raises questions about the situation of security provision. For Max Weber, the legitimate use of violence is the basis of the relations established between people through domination (Weber 1969). In fact, in the modern state the effective control over the legitimate means of violence is essential to the power of the state (Giddens 1987: 192). The provision of private security services, both for international conflicts after the Cold War and for public security, illustrates the rebirth of private policing (Johnston 1992) and the break-up of the state's monopoly over the legitimate means of violence. In its place, a growing global private security industry has arisen; in those areas where such an industry is not possible, a wide variety of informal neighbourhood security organizations has spread as an expression of the breakdown of the state's monopoly of security services (Singer 2003: 18; Wulf 2007: 11).

This process presents important variations which are dependent on the contexts and particular state formation processes in each country. As this study shows, it is not possible to argue that private security attempts against state monopoly of violence in contexts where the process of state formation depended on strong links between public and private armed actors in order to legitimate political power (Holden 2004). Consequently, in post-war societies with new democracies and liberal peace building processes, trends of internal security privatisation (private actors assuming crime control tasks) and global state transformation (neoliberal state reduction) interact affecting domestic democratisation processes. In post-war societies, the reform of the security sector involved the transformation of state institutions that in the past dominated national security. Those institutions were powerful armies that assumed a political and ideological role (Koonings and Kruijt 2003). Due to the interplay of internal and external processes, liberal peace building was unsuccessful in many post-war societies (Kurtenbach 2008 and 2010). Those processes generated a power vacuum in public institutions. The relocation of armed actors (former military and police officers, members of paramilitary organizations, ex combatants of insurgent groups) that were involved in internal conflicts as part of the private security sector allowed strong security structures to continue controlling public institutions from outside the state. The development over time of these security structures combined with an incomplete security sector reform explain how the private security sector – both commercial and non-commercial – became a profitable shelter for those actors.

Most security studies address private security from an inside perspective. Thus, issues seem to be analysed as exclusively inherent to the private security sector or as lacks of institutional management i.e. deficiencies in professionalisation and lack of controls and regulations as well as the scope of their operations. Although, it is accepted that the displacement of traditional state functions to the private sector impacts in a negative way on the legitimacy of public institutions, the democratic access to public goods, and the strengthening of the rule of law. However, the proliferation of private security is not linked with state building processes in a historical perspective. Tracing the process back allows the identification of the institutional arrangements that originated self-reinforcement mechanisms and sequences of private security proliferation.

The theoretical challenge is to provide an analytical framework for the explanation of the function of private security in the interplaying dynamics of state building processes and institutional change. Enriching security studies with a historical and institutional perspective provides new analytical tools beyond the risk-threats based on an analytical model where private security is only explained from the point of view of the security providers. This implies researching how private security emerged and how it is embedded in concrete temporal processes and institutional patterns which are shaped by its contexts.

1.3 Delimitation of the Study

Four key aspects define the scope of this study. First, a focus on the explanatory factors of private security proliferation. This identifies the processes and mechanisms that in certain contexts lead to the proliferation of commercial and non-commercial private security. Beyond a description of the current situation of the private security sector, this study seeks to establish the causal mechanisms that produce its proliferation.

Second, a contextual political analysis of private security. For this reason, more than an analysis from inside the sector focused only on regulations, controls, and professionalism –on which there is sufficient bibliography – this study is oriented to identify the political trajectories that lead to the strengthening of private security and the mechanisms that reinforce its functions in the social system. From the wide range of contexts where it is possible to research private security proliferation, a focus on post-war societies and specific societies with recent internal conflicts. The context in this research acquires relevance because the applied theoretical model seeks to establish causal mechanisms that can be contrasted with other context in a comparative perspective.

Third, from the wide range of non state armed actors that interact with private security organizations, a selection of those actors which have a presence in the public sphere with a formally or informally recognized existence and acceptance by citizens and public institutions, open operations in the name of a "lost law and order", and a commitment to protect a given social order. In this research they are commercial private security in form of private security companies and self-defence policing organizations such as *Juntas Locales de Seguridad* (JLSs).

Four, this is a study about private security proliferation in a particular case with theoretical implications for future comparisons with other similar contextual cases.

Based on these criteria, this study centres on PSCs as commercial private security actors and JLSs as non-commercial security actors in Guatemala. There are other non-state armed actors such as gangs and drug trafficking armed bodies that are not included in this study. However, these non-state armed actors interact with private security, even though their operations are outside the formal recognition of state institutions and civil society. It does not mean that the legality of operations is a selection criteria. In fact, many activities of PSCs and JLSs are illegal but nevertheless publicly and formally accepted. The non-state actors that do not have the formal recognition of state institutions and civil society require a different theoretical and methodological approach. Methodologically speaking, the access to empirical data from primary sources is an important criteria to include PSCs and JLSs in this research. Due to the formal and public recognition of those actors it is possible to access primary sources such as state institutional data and interviews of government officials as well as historical databases necessary for the proposed historical analysis. The main characteristic of these empirical sources is its public accessibility that eventually can be contrasted and revised by other researchers.

1.4 Conceptual Clarifications

Private security will be theoretically analysed in depth in the third section of this study. However, it is important to advance some empirical clarifications about the use of the term "private security." As a generic concept, private security means a set of actors, organizations, groups, companies, committees, and boards that implement private policing strategies (Johnston 1999; Jones and Newburn

1998). There are important differences between each level and type of private organizations that will be addressed throughout the study.

Why study commercial private security and civil security organizations under a general concept of private security? One of the most recurrent shortcomings in the literature produced by security studies is a rather limited or circumscribed definition of private security as a commercial activity. In the literature review, I suggest that most studies about private security are undertaken from an insider perspective that focuses on aspects like professionalisation, controls, and regulations. On the other hand, civil security organizations are mostly studied under crime prevention models of neighbourhood security organizations. I identify an absence of explanations that integrates the two dynamics and its interactions. Based on the concept of private policing, this study addresses those interactions as a social function at different levels (commercial, non commercial, formal and informal). An historical analysis shows that both at an initial institutional stage and throughout their institutional development, commercial forms of private security and the wide range of civil self-defence organizations are functionally linked. Just because of those links, the interplay between different forms of private security and state building processes acquires a very strong explanatory perspective about the current situation of private security in post-war societies.

The case study shows that there are different names for commercial private security organizations. This makes it difficult to define the functional nature of private security. In order to bring some conceptual homogeneity to these different organizations and identify their functional features, I define as "private security companies" – PSCs – the wide range of commercial security services that are publicly offered such as protection services, industrial security, private security, private agencies, private security monitoring, private investigation services, private security advisory agencies, security systems companies, personal security agencies, bank security, tourist security, risk management agencies, industry personnel investigation agencies, private intelligence companies, transportation security, and security training centres, among others. The common feature of this wide range of options is the public offering of security services for profit and the implementation of private policing activities such as surveillance, patrolling, and controlling.

Conversely, non-commercial security organizations include all organized civil groups that implement community-based policing strategies and vigilante actions such as neighbourhood security committees, local security boards, and civil security committees, among others. In this study I employ the term *juntas locales de seguridad* (JLSs) as a generic name that refers to those used by non-commercial security organizations. The differences between these organizations will be explained in the course of the study.

1.5 The Study of Private Security in Guatemala

The particularities of private security proliferation in Guatemala allow to research important aspects of private security and post-war societies and from this to identify theoretical implications. On the one hand, the structure and characteristics of private security proliferation in Guatemala and its political processes of state formation and democratic consolidation reveal a strong interdependence of contexts and historical trajectories. On the other hand, Guatemala is a post-war society that after 36 years of internal armed conflict implemented a transition to democracy and a peace building process. These processes were the basis of a complex security sector reform that still has not been completed. The increasing post-war violence speaks to the diversification of crime and social fear as well as to the limits of weak public institutions.

The commercial private security sector in Guatemala is basically local, namely that most of the PSCs operating in the country were organized in Guatemala; there are only two international companies operating in the country. Interestingly, most of the Guatemalan PSCs have extended throughout the Central American region, an aspects that allows for future comparative studies.

Guatemala has 248 PSCs operating in the country. Of these, 147 are authorized by the Ministry of Interior and approximately 101 function without permission.[1] The existing records illustrate the growth of the private security sector. In the 1990s there were between 70 and 80 PSCs. By 2004, 170 active companies were reported, of which only 82 were authorized by the government to operate (Táger and Mérida 2002: 103). It was estimated as well that 31 were illegal PSCs (*Prensa Libre* 01/20/06). The number of authorized security personnel in 2004 was 60,000 but, taking into account the 99 remaining companies pending authorization, the estimated number could have been 106,700 (UNDP 2010a). This would mean that it was five times higher than the total number of officers in the government police force. In 2007 there were 36,000 police and military personnel in Guatemala. From the police point of view, there were 30,000 policemen, of which 4,000 were assigned to administrative matters; the rest were divided into two shifts of 24 hours to patrol the streets. Therefore, only 8,000 police officers were available on a day-by-day basis to bring public security to a population of 12 million Guatemalans (one policeman for 641 inhabitants).[2]

1 Own calculation with data provided by Registro Mercantil de Guatemala, Ministry of Interior and *Superintendencia de Adminstración Tributaria*, SAT.

2 By comparison, in Costa Rica there is one police officer for every 350 inhabitants, in El Salvador for every 332, in Nicaragua for every 557, in Panamá for every 195, and in Haiti for every 1,889 (UNDP 2010a: 232).

The scope and current situation of the commercial private security sector in Guatemala will be addressed in other section but its contents warrant a prior overview. First, the proliferation of PSCs occurred before the increase in post-war crime. Second, the institutional genesis of private security and the paths to its proliferations reflect a strong interplay between private and public actors. Third, the diversification of the private security sector shows that it has adapted either in a formal and an informal way to the changes in context, namely, that it has happened in parallel to the democratisation process and the security sector reform.

Non-commercial private policing organizations in Guatemala also have spread throughout the country during the last fifteen years. At present there are 1,029 authorized JLSs in Guatemala (Office of the High Commissioner for Human Rights in Guatemala 2010). It has been estimated that another 250 JLSs operate without authorization by the PNC. The JLSs were created in 1999 in order to support the PNC and establish collaborative mechanisms between public security institutions and the citizenry in a context of high international support for community policing models. However, after a JLS has been set up the state takes no further interest in its operation, thus allowing for the reinforcement of structures and practices of self-defence policing created during the internal armed conflict. The JLSs were created only three years after the formal dissolution of the civil patrols (PACs) and the network of military commissioners and as this study shows there is a continuity in the functional aspects of self-defence policing created during the internal conflict and the creation of JLSs.[3]

Most of the JLSs operate without state controls or coordination with security institutions. In fact, the existence of "social cleansing" groups operating as JLSs has been documented as well as its participation in collective violence such as lynching. In addition, there is no reliable relation between post-war crime rates and the proliferation of JLSs, either in a geographical or a temporal dimension, as will be discussed in this study. There are areas of the country where crime rates are significantly lower, yet there is a high presence of JLSs; conversely,

3 Civil citizens dedicated to social control tasks and military operations under the directions of military personnel during the internal armed conflict composed the PACs. They were created during the 60s years based on former civil self-defence organizations. However the PACs were formally dissolved in 1996, they continued operating under different names implementing the same actions as they did during the internal conflict period. The network of military commissioners were integrated by civilians linked with the army to produce information about the community and to organize self-defence policing for local security. However both PACs and military commi- ssioners existed before the internal armed conflict, it was during the military counterinsurgent strategy when they were extended to the whole country.

there are department with high crime rates but low presence of civil security organizations.

It is possible to observe in Guatemala the interaction of historical mechanisms and processes to explain current phenomena. The strongly political dimension of private security proliferation points to the need for a wider analytical perspective in security studies. A historical analysis helps to achieve this goal and Guatemala is a good example of the importance of history in current security debates.

Thus, this study analyses private security as the result of political processes with a strong temporal dimension that as a result of its interaction and interdependence with context become path dependent. In Guatemala the first PSCs were given a formal existence during the internal armed conflict but they provided services in an informal way for many years before in collaboration with public security and military institutions. In the past, there have been different collaborative mechanisms between security institutions and organized citizenry in the country. They were specially reinforced during the periods of dictatorship at the beginning of the 20th Century in order to strengthened social control over the population. These mechanisms seem to be reintroduced repeatedly in the social system depending on the context. Regardless of peace-building processes and the implementation of institutional reforms in order to strengthen democracy, civil security institutions were not capable of addressing an increase in crime and the diversification of post-war violence. Contrary to expectations associated with the liberal peace-building paradigm, the end of the war could not be a "critical juncture" for pacification, democratisation, and development (Kurtenbach 2010: 97). This context encourages the study of private security as a result of the aforementioned political processes and questioning about the continuity of strong self-reinforcing mechanisms and the historical lock-in they produce (Mahoney and Schensul 2006: 463).

Under this perspective, the study of private security in the case of Guatemala allows for observation of the continuities and changes in core institutions related to democratic development and security governance in post-war societies.

1.6 Methodological Considerations

This study formulates a theory-grounded explanation of private security proliferation in post-war Guatemala. Historical institutionalism and path dependence analysis are the two constitutive elements of the theoretical framework. This study proposes a sequence narrative to identify the explanatory factors of the outcome (Mahoney, Kimball and Koivu 2009: 123).

Empirical observations of private security in Guatemala showed that the isolation of causal variables such as crime and institutional capabilities do not explain satisfactorily the proliferation of private security in a post-war context. This leads to the elaboration of a single-outcome design, to observe the interaction between causal mechanisms and context in a historical perspective.[4] This is based on the logic of historical explanations in the social sciences (Mahoney, Kimball and Koivu 2009: 124) in which a self-reproducing sequence for the case of study implies that: (1) initial political and social conditions lead to (2) a particular critical juncture in which it is possible to select a particular institutional arrangement among various possibilities. (3) The displacement of public security functions to the private sphere becomes a sufficient cause to produce a path dependent process and (4) a set of causal mechanisms interplays in different temporal sequences that lead to the proliferation of private security and the reinforcement of its functions in the process of state building.[5] This sequence elaboration has a heuristic function: the development of hypothetic explanations of a particular outcome (George and Bennett 2005: 224) In order to bring together sufficient empirical data to test the validity of this analytical model, I use qualitative research techniques i.e. process-tracing. This method permits the observation of a multiplicity of interaction effects surrounding a particular outcome that it is difficult to explain in terms of two or three independent variables (George and Bennett 2005: 206; Ford, Schmitt and Doherty 1989). Complementarily, through process-tracing I identify the causal mechanisms leading to the proliferation of private security and its path dependent process.

4 Single outcome study can be used with explicative and descriptive purposes and to test previous explanations about specific events (Yin 1981: 97; Gerring 2006; Wynsberghe and Khan 2007). It is a variant of case studies and assumes that the unit of analysis is directly linked with the context. Process-tracing method in a single outcome study seeks to identify the intermediate stages of the case therefore, context acquires and important value (George and Bennett 2005: 207). This methodological design attempts to identify the initial conditions of a specific outcome and the existing links between independent variables and the observed outcome (Van Evera 1997: 64). The utility to use a single outcome study design is that it focuses on the causal processes to construct a complete explanation of a particular outcome (Gerring 2006: 716 and 2004). This design makes an extensive use of the necessary and sufficient conditions as determinant paths to understand causal relations.

5 For methodological reasons I use the definition of causal mechanisms proposed by George and Bennett (2005) "…ultimately unobservable physical, social, or psychological processes through which agents with causal capacities operate, but only in specific contexts or conditions, to transfer energy, information, or matter to other entities" (2005: 137). It is important to underline from this definition that the effects of causal mechanisms depend on interactions with other mechanisms that make up the contexts in which they operate (2005: 145). The discussion of causal mechanisms in the logic of historical explanations is presented in chapter III.

The first methodological phase of this study is the general analysis of the nature, dimensions, diversity, and structure of private security in Guatemala, both commercial and non-commercial. This includes the analysis of private security related to crime rates and institutional capabilities. This analysis presents an empirical puzzle whose complexity can only be theoretically explained. There are four factors that will be addressed by process-tracing: 1) the continuity of social control mechanisms; 2) the internal armed conflict; 3) the security sector reform; and 4) the increasing post-war violence. The second phase is the analysis of the self-reproducing sequence elaborated from an historical contextual perspective and in which causal reproducing mechanisms are identified.[6] The third methodological phase of this study identifies other possible outcomes of the path dependent process of public security displacement, namely the role of the militaries in the post-war and the proliferation of vigilante policing (extra judicial executions and lynching).

The application of a process-tracing analysis on those four factors seeks to elaborate a plausible analytical explanation of a single outcome. This study does not seek to formulate generalizations about private security proliferation. On the contrary, the context-based analysis aims to produce explanations susceptible of being compared with other contexts in the same region. This study has a defined unit of analysis that seeks to identify trajectories and processes of a particular outcome. In other words, the method of this study seeks to explain a single outcome for a single case (Gerring 2006: 710). The clear definition of the outcome (private security proliferation) also involves a precise definition of the causal factors to be explored through process-tracing in order to identify the sufficient and necessary conditions of causal relations (Gerring 2006: 716; Blatter, Janning and Wagemann 2006).

This study is located within the debate about the match of explanatory mechanisms and real mechanisms (Demetriou 2009; Tilly 2001a). This is a methodological challenge that implies a heuristic use of explanatory mechanisms that are to be contrasted with empirical data and a context-based approach (Demetriou 2009: 447). In general terms, this study leaves open the question about the explanatory regularities of private security proliferation and its effects on democratic consolidation in a regional perspective.

6 The self-reproducing sequence elaborated for the study of private security in Guatemala is presented in chapter III.

1.7 The Data Sources

One of the main obstacles with research about security issues is the lack of information sources, especially in a context of weak public institutions. This means the absence of systematic records and the reliability of current information. However, this study provides abundant empirical information from primary sources as well as the review of the main literature about the topic.

The theoretical framework was based on secondary sources such as academic books and articles in the field of historical institutionalism, path dependence, historical sociology, sociology of policing, and security studies. The case study is analysed on the basis of both secondary sources (such as the historiographical literature of Guatemala and security and justice reports published by international organizations and national civil society) as well as primary sources (both documentary and oral).

Private security is a field which has not been much researched in Guatemala and Central America. However, there is considerable interest and participation by civil society organizations in the problem. This study analyses the documentary output of these organizations, especially related to security regulations, security policies, budgets, and human rights violations. The office of the Human Rights Attorney produces crime and justice statistics as well as reports on human rights violations that allow identification of the link between private security and violence. I have used the database of the National Commission for the Prevention of Lynching in order to find information about links between vigilante policing groups and lynchings around the country.

Despite the lack of information in Guatemala on security matters, this study presents the results of three moments of fieldwork: February-March and September 2009 and October 2010. Empirical research was conducted in public institutions such as the Ministry of Interior, the Ministry of Defence, the Division for the Supervision and Control of Companies, Entities and Individuals of Private Security (a unit of the PNC), the Division of Crime Prevention of the PNC, the National Commission for the Prevention of Lynching, the Superintendent of Tax Administration, the State Intelligence Secretary, the Vice Ministry of Community Support and various staff members of mayors offices.

The study uses two different historical archives. The first is the National Security Archive of the George Washington University which has declassified intelligence documents from the armed internal conflict in Guatemala. This documentation was very helpful in explaining the links between private security organizations and counterinsurgency structures during the war years and the transition to democracy. The second is the Historical Archive of the National Police in Guatemala which was opened in March 2009. This archive contains the administrative and operative history of the National Police since the late nineteenth century until 1996. The period of most interest for this research was between 1950 and 1996. It includes the institutional genesis of private security and its transformation from informal mechanisms to more formal institutions. The documents consulted are operations reports of PSCs, national police officers working in PSCs, intelligence reports, and neighbourhood organizations created by the national police, among others. These documents permit the reconstruction of the institutional trajectories of private security and its relation with public institutions as well as the security environment in which this relation was developed. In the same way, the historical data shows the activities of international security advisors and PSCs working together with the National Police under the support of the US Agency for International Development.

During fieldwork in Guatemala, a set of 45 semi-structured interviews were conducted with owners of PSCs (most of them former military and police officers), national and international security advisors and experts, members of JLSs, public security officials (from PNC, SAT, Ministry of Interior, Ministry of Defence, Office of the Human Rights Attorney, National Security Council, judiciary), intelligence officers, and civil society actors. In addition, this study incorporates a wide range of primary sources from the Historical Archive of the National Police of Guatemala.

1.8 Organization of the Study

The study is divided into three sections. The first section has two more parts besides this introduction. The second part analyses the state of the art of private security studies and identifies the lack of integral explanations based on the interaction between formal and informal, commercial and non-commercial private security as well as the lack of historical analysis of present outcomes in the field of security studies. The third part focuses on the theoretical framework which highlights the historical institutionalism approach of private policing. This part seeks to establish an adequate theoretical perspective to study private policing together with a historical analysis of the mechanisms and processes of its functional features.

The second section includes the analysis of the current situation of private security in Guatemala it includes both private security companies and JLSs. It analyses aspects related to budgets, regulations, professionalisation, operations, coverage and relations with public institutions and crime rates and the non-commercial private security organizations. This part develops the characterization of private security as the unit of study and is the basis for the main argument as presented in the following section.

Section three includes the trajectories and self-reinforcing mechanisms of private security proliferation, namely the continuity of structures of social and political control, the internal armed conflict, the security sector reform, and the post-war violence. It analyses historical data from 1950 to 1982 and identifies how the path dependent process of displacement of public security lead to the proliferation of private security before the signing of the peace agreements in Guatemala. Subsequently, it analyses the transition to democracy and the peace negotiation and identifies the reproduction of the institutional pattern however political change. Finally, this section analyses two other outcomes of the institutional pattern of displacement of public security namely the role of the militaries in the post-war and the proliferation of vigilante policing such as extra judicial executions and lynching.

The conclusions are organized in four parts. The first summarizes the structure of this study. The second part refers to the main results of the research. The third part deals with theoretical issues identified in the study and the conditions under which they have developed. The final part outlines a research agenda for the future about private security and the issues not covered in this research that are of importance for future research.

2. Dabates on Private Security

This section focuses on the main debates around private security in social science literature since the "boom" of private security studies in the mid-1990s after the international military operations in Iraq. At that moment, concerns were expressed about the high participation of private military companies in international operations. Today, private security is mostly addressed from the perspective of security studies, failed states and private armed actors focusing on the scope, regulation, control, and growth of the private security sector around the world. International activities of Private Security Companies (PSCs) have called the attention of academics and civil society organizations, while non-commercial private security has been addressed in relation to the concepts of civil security and community-based policing. The general trend in security studies is to understand private security as a result of variables related to crime and violence, on the one hand, and to variables related to institutional capabilities, on the other. From a broader perspective, the sociology of policing provides a theoretical framework to understand private security as a set of private policing activities. However both perspectives leave aside the institutional trajectories and mechanisms as well as their relation with the political context. In the Latin American context, the concept of private policing provides an integral perspective about the actors and activities undertaken in the region at a commercial and non-commercial level.

The chapter is organized in five parts. The first analyses the different perspectives to define private security and underlines the necessity of a broad definitions that includes both commercial and non-commercial private actors as well as its functional role in the society. The second part explores the different approaches to explain private security proliferation. The third part remarks the relation between security sector reform programs and private security sector. The non-commercial private security is analysed in part four in which it is linked with community policing programs. The last part explores the perspectives in which private security has been analysed in Latin America.

2.1 The Challenge of a Clear Definition

A clear definition of private security is a challenge to security studies. The wide range of organizations and actors that constitute the sector make it difficult to define its characteristics in terms of the varied services it provides. Another problem is that the informal expressions of private security are context-based and consequently have different names and activities.

From the perspective of contemporary security governance, the definition of private security has been observed in three levels: inside the state, beyond the state and, in what some authors refer to as, "below the level of the state" (Jones 2007: 846). Security studies (SEESAC 2005; Shearing and Kempa 2000; Waard 1999; Weiss 2007) detect the expansion of this autonomy since the end of the Cold War but in fact the autonomy of the private sector is historical (Pereira 2003; Singer 2003). The current autonomy of the private sector increases in a context of no regulations, both national and international. Finally, private security is related to the level "below the state" given its wide range of informal expressions, especially those related to community-based policing organizations.

One of the most frequently used definitions is that which differentiates between private security companies and private military companies.[7] There are few differences between each other but the most important are related to tactical aspects: PSCs are oriented to the protection and PMCs are linked to warfare (Singer 2003; Schreier and Camparini 2005).

The definition of private security also includes the guardian sector (the largest and most visible component in rural and urban areas), electronic security, sensor and surveillance sector,[8] the investigation and risk management sector, and the private intelligence companies (Schreier and Camparini 2005: 27).

Other studies focus on the commercial element of private security in order to come up with a clear definition. A very complete typology is presented by H. Wulf (2002) who establishes five categories that cover a wide range of options: PSCs (oriented to property protection, crime prevention, and correction services), defence producers (weapon production, military assistance), private military companies (consulting, logistics and support, technical services, training, peacekeeping and humanitarian assistance, combat forces), non-statutory forces (rebels, warlords, organized crime), and mercenaries (Wulf 2002). This typology summarizes more convincingly the wide range of actors, services and operations implemented by the private security sector beyond its commercial or non-commercial interests.

Other perspectives address private security from its social origins. One of these studies top-down privatisation processes that occur when a government de-

7 There is an extensive literature about current operations of PMCs focusing on regulations, control mechanisms and legitimation of its actions. See Waard 1999; Cleaver 2000; Singer 2003, Pozo 2007; Elsea and Serafino 2007; Perrin 2006; among others.

8 This part of private security has generated recent surveillance studies. See Lyon 2006 and 2007.

cides to outsource its internal or external security functions to private military and security providers, either domestic or foreign. Conversely, another perspective looks at privatisation from the bottom up when individuals or societal groups – such as self-defence forces, militias and paramilitaries, gangs of organized crime or drug dealers, vigilantes, survivalists, and neighbourhood watches – decide among themselves to provide for their own security or to hire a private military or security firm from their own country or from abroad (Schreier and Camparini 2005: 42; Camparini 2006: 263; Mandel 2001: 137).

The benefits or problems that privatisation of security generates depends largely on state controls over both privatisations paths. In spite of the fact that bottom-up privatisation seeks to protect a certain social order, it is considered a threat to public security because of its vigilante actions. On the contrary, top-down privatisation is considered a formal procedure of the state that could be of benefit to the expansion of state authority (Mandel 2001: 134). This situation is susceptible of wide variations and the problem emerges when in a particular context both processes interact in an informal way. The role of the state in the interaction of bottom-up and top-down private security processes is an aspect that security studies do not explain clearly. In some societies the state informally promotes bottom-up private security parallel to top-down private security. The first can be observed as par of a responsibilization strategy in which the state does no longer act as the responsible (welfare) institution displacing to the subject the responsible for cure social aspects such as unemployment, sickness and lack of security among others (Garland 2005) and the second can be an effective clientelistic mechanism.

When the differences between private security forms are taken into account, some authors direct their efforts to devising taxonomies of the concept of private security (Schreier and Camparini 2005; Wulf 2002; Singer 2003). These include the difference between countries that provides private security services for international operations (normally developed countries) and the recipients (normally underdeveloped countries). The existence of a conflict that the recipient country cannot resolve on its own is the justification for the international operation of PSCs or PMCs. This perspective has opened the discussion about sovereignty and state monopoly of legitimate violence (Mandel 2001: 136). Regardless of the importance of this discussion, from the perspective of international relations, security studies are limited only to those services provided by international actors in the territory of another country. The problem is more complicated when the provider and the receiver are from the same country or when an international provider becomes a local provider. In this context the alleged differences between provider and receiver are diffuse.

The utility of these taxonomies is evident when differentiating between types, operations, organization systems, providers, purposes, and social processes associated with private security and its presence during certain contexts and times. They help to identify the proliferation processes, trajectories, and political dimensions of private security. The dichotomic perspective of national-international, commercial and non-commercial, public-private, and formal and informal becomes very limited. There is a hybrid perspective with wide gray zones where different actors interplay in the social function of private security. A socio-historic perspective allows to observe that different forms of private security and different processes of proliferation are juxtaposed in a political and social dimension of private security. This requires a contextual political analysis of private security which allows for the observation of these interacting dynamics.

2.2 Perspectives on Private Security Proliferation

Nowadays private security can be observed at a global level. The phenomena seem to be homogeneous but in fact it presents a wide range of different outcomes and different proliferation processes. Along these lines, there are three different trends related to contemporary private security proliferation. The first is the deployment of military weaponry among the citizenry and the participation of mercenaries in ongoing conflicts (Mandel 2001: 130). The second is the increasing perception in society that security in a threatening environment should be provided by the people themselves since governments are unable or unwilling to do so (Mandel 2001: 130). This perception increases alongside public fear about an ostensible and uncontrollable increase of crime, social decay, and the remarkable inability of the state to protect the citizenry against the emergence of powerful crime organizations. In this context, private security emerges as a response to the threatened public (Mandel 2001: 132). These considerations are made within a broad definition of private security. The different forms that private security adopts require that the concept cover the informal forms that citizens employ when they do not have the sufficient income to pay for commercial private security.

The third trend attempts to explain the proliferation of private security from the perspective of international relations. In this case, private security is an outcome of the global changes produced by the end of the Cold War, especially the massive downsizing of armies (Richards and Smith 2007; SEESAC 2005). Only in the USA and Europe, more than 7 million servicemen have been thrown into the employment market with little to peddle but their fighting and military skills. Another change was the power vacuum created at the end of the Cold War that removed controls over levels of conflicts while also releasing unresolved tensions and new pressures. At the same time, global economic changes tended to reduce the participation of the state in public services and the opening of arms markets benefited private industry and its participation in international conflicts (Schreier and Camparini 2005: 5). Increasing privatisation policies in all areas of the state together with increasing demand for security services at the international level, especially after September 9/11 in Afghanistan and Iraq, stimulated the growth of the international private security sector (Schreier and Camparini 2005: 10). Neoliberal governance has reinforced the role of private security and produces its politization (Leander and Munster 2007).

These tendencies are deepened by the reduction of personnel, institutional weakness, chronic insecurity, and low quality of the police forces. The increased confidence in the private security sector makes weak states weaker and this leads to an unequal distribution of security and access to public services, creating a false perception of security and distorting an appropriate evaluation of real security needs. This situation weakens the construction of state security institutions and their legitimacy (Holmqvist 2005: 12).

From a governance perspective, the proliferation of private security involves a number of transformations of the concept of sovereignty for example through the intervention of international firms in interstate conflicts or in combating insurgent groups in the name of national governments (Elsea and Serafino 2007; Branovic 2011; Guzmedze 2009; Howe 1998; Isima 2007 a). Based on this, on the one hand, private security erodes state sovereignty because the operation of private security forces in local conflicts weakens state institutions and controls affecting governance and state legitimacy (Abrahamsen and Williams 2007). On the other, some studies observe that private security acts as an extension of state authority because both international operations and the tolerance towards the proliferation of local private security occurs in a close relationship with formal and informal state building processes (Holmqvist 2005). Both perspectives relate private security proliferation to state weakness and the possibility of enhancing or blocking governance.

When private security is perceived as a non-state actor that exerts authority and provides governance, it acquires legitimacy to represent governments and to mediate in international conflicts over local state authority (Abrahamsen and Williams 2007: 238). Instead, this is a power relation where receiving states have few possibilities to demand and implement controls over international private companies that operate in their territories. In local contexts, the recognition of a legitimate role for private security in governance functions implies, in a normative perspective, the displacement of core functions by the state. In a historical perspective, the state shared those functions with formal and informal private security so this means that the alleged state monopoly is contextually relative for many countries. There are countries that delegate state functions to private security companies without losing control over public security. That happens in countries with strong institutions and controls and where shearing functions with the private sector does not imply replacement processes but only complementary mechanisms (Bayley and Shearing 1996). On the other hand, there are countries where sharing functions with the private sector has been a constitutive process of state authority normally for the benefit of private privileges (Holden 1996; Pereira 2003). This produces weak state institutions and a strong private sector with political power over the state. The role of private security will depend on the historical trajectories of sharing processes between public and private spheres.

International relations studies of private security normally neglect the importance of local trajectories and contexts where international processes occur.[9] The transformation of global security governance and the participation of PSCs in international conflicts occur, ultimately, in local contexts. The way in which global security governance affects national processes requires a contextual based analysis.

Private Security and Historical Studies

Different studies seek to trace the history of private security services. They observe the link between private security and the history of the police, the use of mercenaries by small principalities, and the decisions in political systems regarding the police structure to be implemented during the origins of modern states and the expansion of capitalism. These studies are based on a long term perspective and argue that the state monopoly of the use of legitimate violence covers only a short part of modern western states. On the other hand, the long history of the state is strongly linked to the warlike activities of private groups (Lipson 1988; Singer 2003; Davis and Pereira 2003). The expansion of the current private security industry is largely the revival of an old service geared to a new market (Weiss 2007: 1). One important moment in this process was the formalization of historical private security services that existed informally. The United States and most European countries formalized those services in the middle of the nineteenth century (Lipson 1988: 20; Nalla and Newman 1990). The activities of the private security sector were in the background of the omnipresence of the state during the Cold War. After the end of this period, private security companies were strengthened with arms and personnel in parallel with the creation of new security markets (Singer 2003: 37)

9 In this regard Africa is a paradigmatic case of security privatisation in which is possible to observe multiple trajectories of the process. For a more complete comparative perspective see Gumedze 2008 and 2009; Abrahamsen and Williams 2007. For South Eastern Europe see SEESAC 2005. The case of China has been studied as well see Trevaskes 2007.

The importance of historical studies about private security lies in demonstrating the strong links between private security and state building processes, the different trajectories of private security proliferation, and the importance of context. Historical analysis opens up the concept of private security beyond its commercial dimension and the explanations that reduce its proliferation only to recent events such as the increase on post-war crime and state weakness.

Historical studies show that private security proliferates during times of low levels of real conflict but combined with high social fear (Weiss 2007). In developing countries, private security grows in contexts of economic instability and insecurity, namely when collective fear grows and the state is weak. Those conditions are a conducive environment for private security (Weiss 2007: 9). Nevertheless, the concept of private security, as defined in security studies, limits an expansion of its analysis to include a temporal dimension as well as a functional dimension of private security in particular contexts.

2.3 Private Security and Security Sector Reform

The role of private security in peace building processes has been studied from the perspective of Security Sector Reform, SSR, programmes implemented in post-war societies. These programmes were designed in order to generate a change in perspective from improving the state to strengthening the state; in other words, make weak states capable of addressing their obligations (Andersen 2006; Lilly and von Tangen 2002). These programmes were oriented in two directions. On the one hand, they sought to develop institutions capable of delivering security to the citizenry in accordance with human rights and the rule of law. On the other, they attempted to provide the state with an effective system of democratic regulations and controls over security actors (Richards and Smith 2007: 2). Security was understood as a global public good and as a fundamental condition of a sustainable human development (Ball and Brzoska 2002).

Based on this perspective, the security sector is defined under four categories: the core security actors (armed forces, police, gendarmeries, paramilitary forces, presidential guards, intelligence and security services, among others), security management and oversight bodies (executive, legislative, ministries, civil society), justice and law enforcement institutions, and non-statutory security forces (liberation armies, guerrilla armies, private body-guard units, private security companies, political party militias) (Andersen 2006: 7). The implementation of those SSR programmes in different contexts generated different challenges such as addressing the powerful trajectories of security bodies before, during and after internal armed conflicts. There was a lot of tension generated by the continuity of security actors linked with the internal armed conflict and the set of policy reforms included in the SSR. In some particular contexts, such as Central America, there is a tension between the traditional militaristic and authoritarian organization of security and the new perspective of democratic security.[10] In the midst of these tensions were the public security institutions which had problems related to institutional capabilities and institutional experience as well as the so-called "resistance to change" by the former security structures embedded in civil security institutions (Nathan 2004: 5).

Most SSR reports analyse private security from an international perspective and less from a domestic level. In both perspectives, the analysis of commercial private security predominates while non-commercial private security is little included in the analysis of non-state armed actors and private policing. On the other hand, in post-war societies the focus of SRR is on institutional actors and the necessary legal reforms but only at the domestic level. Still pending is the reform of a wide range of non-commercial actors directly or indirectly linked with armed conflicts that could re-emerge in post-war society (Bourne 2002: 18).

Some studies have shown that the different and contradictory international and national pressures on SSR in post-war societies blocked parallel democratic processes such as access to justice and crime prevention (Bernabéu 2007; Andersen 2006; Isima 2007 b). In contexts where peace building is difficult because of the interaction of strong authoritarian structures, weak institutions, and heavy international pressures, SSR programmes and the democratisation project can interfere with each other due to the measures taken to achieve its objectives (for example the extensive use of PSCs or PMCs to improve national security forces) (Bernabéu 2007).

The international private sector in societies with armed conflicts such as Afghanistan show that the extensive use of private security providers by countries that support SSR programmes generates a contradiction between the use of private services and the strengthening of state institutions (Sherman and DiDomenico 2009). The lack of regulations over PSCs and PMCs creates a gray zone where it is difficult to control the private sector, especially when its activities can threat Human Rights. On the one hand, weak states are asked to assume control over their armed forces and security institutions but, on the other, there is an increasing private security sector that it is stimulated by the presence of PSCs and PMCs brought in by international organizations (UN, NATO). The new private security sector that emerges in this context is composed of local private and international firms that create new local markets. The private security sector increases its political power due to the legitimacy the international organizations

10 The concept of democratic security was defined based on the principles of Human Rights and democracy placing the citizen at the centre in contrast to the National Security approach and its militaristic perspective of security (Aguilera 1996).

give to the private security firms. In the local dynamic of these states, the private sector becomes a strong competitor of the public institutions. The proliferation of private security in this context highlights the double problem of a lack of international regulations and lacks of domestic regulation over private security (Sherman and DiDomenico 2009: 7). Shearing and Kempa (2000) argue that while important efforts have been made to reform institutions that where used to support authoritarian regimes, the evidence in transitional democracies is that the transformation processes should not be limited only to those institutional reforms (2000: 205). Evidence in different regions of the world shows that the excessive concentration of transformation processes in state institutions allows the proliferation of private security firms as well as vigilantism organizations due to the possibility of a continue operation of those non-state armed groups. Both outcomes affect new democracies due to the inability to implement efficient accountability mechanisms and to the brutality of some private security actions (Shearing and Kempa 2000).

An excessive dichotomist public-private perspective explains why non-state armed actors did not receive more attention from SSR programmes. From this dichotomist perspective, private security is defined only as the security provided by private actors vs. the provision of public security by state actors. The focus of the definition is on the security provider and not on the social and historical function of security (Bourne 2002; Nathan 2004, Sedra 2007). This explains the normative perspective of SSR that has its main expression in the creation of regulations to deal with the problems and not on the social process of transformation. As Call (2007) argues, most SSR programs in post-conflict societies attempts to take shortcuts to avoid historical contextual processes creating public police forces and revamped judicial systems in a short period (Call 2007: 10).

Controls And Regulations Over Private Security

Most studies of SSR are based on the assumption that private security may be beneficial to public security if there are effective controls and regulations over its operations. However, there are a number of contradictions regarding the need for better regulation. The first one is that international PSCs operate in a non-regulatory international system and SSR programmes require that national states enhance their institutional capabilities to control the local PSCs that emerge together with the presence of international PSCs. International organizations hire international PSCs that at the same time provide security services for the population that state institutions should protect and international organizations support. On the one hand, the international support for institutional strengthening and, on the other, international hiring of PSCs ultimately weakens local state institutions.

SSR programmes have become reinforcement mechanisms for the proliferation of private security services (Schreier and Camparini 2005; Gillard 2006).

Although private security proliferation is inevitable, the function of the state promoted by SSR is to regulate and control this proliferation.[11] Absence of regulations in developed countries is part of the mechanisms through which private security has become an important economic activity with wide margins of autonomy (O'Connor *et al.* 2008). From the perspective of SSR, the legitimacy of public institutions rests on state capabilities to control and regulate non-state security organizations. Efficient regulation of PSCs could contribute to bring public security to societies which lack state security institutions, but it may become an obstacle to the construction of peace, governance, and development in post conflict societies. The current private security sector deepens the lack of governance and accountability, especially when its proliferation entails transferring central tasks from the state (Richards and Smith 2007). One aspect that emerges from this situation is the legitimacy crisis of private security both at a national and international level.[12] For this reason, requirements for an efficient regulation come fundamentally from outside the private sector as a result of the increasing participation of PSCs in international conflicts (Krahmann 2009; Ocqueteau 1993).[13] Another important aspect is that excessive attention on the regulation of PSCs could push aside the explanatory importance of context, for example the nature of post-war societies and the institutional weakness of their states (Isima 2007 a and b).

However, not only is the absence of regulation a concern. The lack of professionalism of private security agents has been the cause of violations of human rights and corruption (Gibson 2007; Perrin 2006). The professionalisation of the private sector is directly linked with its regulatory status. PSCs and PMCs have in most countries no legal obligation to ensure the professional status of their agents. Without a legal obligation to train the agents there is no legal responsibility for the absence of professional training (Moore 1988; Kümmel 2004: 28). An

11 There is a tendency to observe the regulatory role of the state related to private security companies, see Gibson 2007; Isima 2007 a; Holmqvist 2005. However the exce- ssive interest in this role reinforces the idea of the management rather than the social causes of the problem.

12 Recent studies show the high social and economic costs generated by an extensive use of PSCs. In Afghanistan this situation is expressed on the legitimacy crisis of international PSCs as well as the international organizations that hire them such as NATO and UN. See Sherman and DiDomenico 2009.

13 Just few studies have focused on the so-called "pervention of contractors" and the growth of international private security industry and the SSR as well as its relations with states that supports humanitarian actions through the private security sector. For a more complete vision of the subject see Krahmann 2009; Howe 1998.

excessive attention on regulatory aspects leaves out other problems related to private security, including professionalisation and activities in weak states with internal conflicts. More than regulations, professionalisation or whether private security shares some state functions or not, the question is to what extent private security has become a competitor of the public sector (Gibson 2007).

The changes in the state norm of a monopoly of legitimate violence as a result of the proliferation of private security threatens against the expected security governance in developed countries. The question revolves around who should have legitimate authority to use coercion to generate security? The nation state concept implies a legitimate exercise of sovereignty in which security is one of its core functions as conceived by the idea of state monopoly over legitimate violence (Giddens 1987). Historical studies show that nation-state building processes have involved the application of extra-governmental forms of violence as well as different collaborative mechanisms with non-state actors (Tilly 2002; Moore 1966; Holden 2004).

2.4 Non-Commercial Private Security and Community Policing

Citizen participation in self-defence activities is a concern for social research because of its effects on collective life such as the proliferation of vigilante actions. Criminological theory (especially crime prevention) and community policing strategies seek to understand how citizen efforts contribute to a reduction in crime (Skogan 1989; Klein *et al.* 1989; Triplett *et al.* 2003).[14] This perspective assumes that voluntary action by neighbourhood residents can play an important role in maintaining order in a cost-effective and constitutional manner. However, the ability of individuals to act in defence of their community is shaped in important ways by the opportunities for action that are available to them (Skogan 1989: 437). The results of the participation of neighbourhood groups depends on a wide set of available opportunities. These kinds of groups actually may be less common in high-crime places than in safer neighbourhoods; the same factors that generate crime also may erode the social bases for collective action and produce

14 Those programs seek to incorporate community-policing initiatives into a wider national security perspective. However today these claims are public, the informal state controls of non-commercial private security organizations take the form of information exchange. This mechanism was common during internal conflicts and it was part of counter insurgent strategies. Since the eighties in the United States the Neighbourhood Watch Programs have functioned as the "eyes and ears" of the Police reproducing old mechanisms used during the Cold War by intelligence agencies (Garofalo and McLeod 1989: 329). Related to Criminal Intelligence Shearing programs see National Submit on Intelligence 2008.

displacement of crime rather than its prevention (Skogan 1989; Klein *et al.* 1989).

There are two perspectives in collective action approaches about the participation of neighbourhood organizations in crime prevention activities. The first one argues that there is a positive relationship in which crime problems stimulate neighbourhood action. The basis of this argument is that because people live in neighbourhoods with high crime rates and consequently with high social fear, they are stimulated to organize such groups. On the other hand, there is a negative relationship when problems actually discourage constructive responses; in other words, high crime rates and social fear block the collective action of those groups (Skogan 1989; Arriagada and Godoy 2000).

Most studies about community policing organizations have been conducted in the United States, Canada, and the United Kingdom and seek to determine the origins, activities, and scope of neighbourhood organizations. It is important to explain those aspects of the social resources of the community such as income, education, home ownership, and the capacity for informal problem solving.[15] In the United States, the most widespread organizations are those under the model of Neighbourhood Watch; its central idea is to induce people to exercise social control over their own neighbourhoods or communities through surveillance and the construction of a common enemy and the promotion of activities such as security training, prevention, information sharing, and patrolling, in order to strengthen the links between community and public security institutions (Garofalo and McLeod 1989). There are different forms of these models but they all share basic elements: social control and links between state institutions and community. Those organizations emerge and persist most easily in the most cohesive communities, those where residents are bound together by ethnic solidarity, church and family ties, and intimate acquaintance (Skogan 1989: 442). The relationship between neighbourhood residents and the police may be cooperative or conflicting and it will depend on contextual factors as well as historic trajectories (Skogan 1989; Klein *et al.* 1989).

Community based policing strategies, whether formal or informal, depend on context and historic trajectories of mechanisms of conflict resolution. Private policing can be presented as a programmatic model of crime prevention activities but the outcomes will depend on the interaction of context and trajectories as well as the active or passive role of state institutions. The situation can be troublesome in cases where crime prevention models are implemented without considering contextual and cultural factors. In those cases private policing becomes a mechanism to preserve the control of security structures during transitional po-

15 About community policing programs implemented in these countries see Pennell *et al.* 1989; Vindevogel 2005; Schaefer 2008.

litical processes. The main critic to community policing programs is that its theoretical models avoid historical and contextual features of the communities in which they are implemented (Müller 2010). The concept of prevention can be transformed in the construction of a common enemy that normally is not related with the real criminal situation of the communities but with the stigmatisation of cultural minorities such as youth and immigrants (Huhn 2011; Peetz 2011; Savenije 2010). Both in its original contexts (USA, Canada, Britain) but also in post-war contexts in which the model is implemented the delegation of self-protection to the citizenry has lead to vigilante actions.

Security Sector Reform and Community Policing

One of the objectives of SSR programmes in post-war societies is to implement community based policing strategies. Citizen security participative models have been implemented in post-war societies to provide active support for police institution reform. However, the participation of citizens is very important as contextual problems emerge especially when the implementation of these models does not incorporate organizational trajectories of communities and neighbourhoods. Problems arise in the same way when the state has no possibilities for controlling citizen security organizations which lead the way to reproduce practices implemented during conflicts.

Gaining the confidence of the population is one of the challenges of crime prevention models developed in Britain, USA and Canada and is for these countries the future of policing in democratic societies (Bayley and Shearing 1996). But in contrast, in post-war societies the police become one of the institutions that represent an authoritarian and repressive past. This situation has to be faced in parallel with political instability, increased crime, and the consequent demand for security by civil society and international organizations. In this context, there exists a risk that neighbourhood organizations might implement vigilante actions in order to protect social order. This situation is activated by the presence of pre-existing security organizations such as paramilitaries and guerrilla groups that are informally legitimised by the organization of neighbourhood security organizations. Those organizations can evolve into groups of authoritarian local power and political protection (International Crisis Group 2003). Idealistic conceptions of community action do not incorporate the organizational history and the context in which security organizations were created. This study shows that traditional organizations at a particular time tend to replicate in different context and to seek different objectives.

In spite of the fact that community-policing programmes have been implemented for quite a few decades in Central America, there is no evidence of positive impacts on crime reduction in those areas in which these programs were implemented (Savenije 2010; Huhn 2011). Some outcomes of these programmes are not only related to crime prevention but to changes in citizen behaviour and relations with public institutions (Marx 1989).[16] Beyond this, however, when observing the actual outcomes of these programmes it is important to consider the context in which they were implemented, because both citizen behaviour and crime prevention can becoming vigilante when there no important institutional transformation in post-war societies (Marx 1989: 502).

One of the problems when studying the nature of community policing organizations is the homogenisation of the concept, that is, the implementation of its core characteristics such as prevention, civic participation and links with public institutions in isolation from its context. There is considerable difference between community-based programmes driven from a top-down expert model brought in from the outside and those bottom-up models organized spontaneously. The legitimacy component is different in each path, as well as the starting point, and this can lead to different processes and outcomes as well. SSR programmes have implemented community-policing strategies from top-down models leaving aside historical forms of self-defence that persist through social organization.

The participation of individuals in community policing strategies does not happen automatically or only by an institutional invitation to share important social information with the police. Context and available opportunities as well as institutional trajectories may condition the availability of individuals to choose the appropriate way to protect their public sphere. Who participates and how they participate depends on a complex opportunity structure that is different in each neighbourhood (Skogan 1989).

The previous theoretical model of community policing includes a set of social control actions that has been criticized such as the call for denunciation, controlling neighbours behaviour and the stigmatisation of certain alleged criminal groups for example youths and immigrants (Huhn 2011; Savenije 2010; Garland 2005). Among these critical points it is important to state that international community policing programs conducted in post-war societies do not include the context and trajectories of vigilante organizations. On the other hand is the effect of the changes on the role of the police this community policing models promoted. The police institutions in countries such as United States, Britain and Canada became a provider of services in a perspective of resources management (Garland 2005: 278) but in contexts in which the police had an authoritarian and re-

16 About discursive and philosophical aspects of community-based policing programs see SEESAC 2007; Bayley and Shearing 1996; Adams *et al.* 2002; MacDonald 2002; about Central American cases see Neild 2002; WOLA 2009.

pressive role, the expected collaborative relations between community and the police are susceptible to becoming clientelistic or antagonistic (Savenije 2010).

Actions implemented by private security produce a blurred image of its effects on society. Those actions define deviance from an instrumental perspective and integrate themselves into other social activities. The panopticum dynamic it produces is amplified by private policing in which observers and observed coexist in the same community. The integration of private policing into collective life transforms the system of sanctions leading to a more informal set of discipline and control mechanisms (Shearing and Stenning 1983: 504). In particular contexts in which collective violence had an important role in the consolidation of self-defence policing organizations, community policing crime prevention programs could rapidly become vigilante actions.

From Community Policing to Vigilantism

One of the most common problems associated with neighbourhood organization is the emergence of vigilante activities. Vigilantism is considered one of the self-policing forms present at different levels across the social system (Johnston 1992: 160). Self-policing actions are normally understood as the result of the failure of police and other public security institutions. Extreme expressions of vigilantism are embedded in collective violence that entails handling grievances by unilateral aggression (Senechal 1996: 101). It can include a wide range of actions, from hiring PSCs to voluntary and violent patrolling. Vigilante actions tend towards extralegal actions instead of criminal justice authority (Klein *et al.* 1989: 372). In some countries of Africa for example, the concern is that vigilante groups take on policing and justice functions, often using violent means to elicit confessions and mete out punishment. Studies of this phenomenon highlight that these groups in the community are beyond state controls (Sekhonyane and Louw 2002; Gottschalk 2005). Whatever the region, vigilantism has some common characteristics. On the one hand, vigilantism involves acts of severe violence, including serious assault and murder of alleged criminals, punishments that often exceed the crime allegedly committed and are meted out in the absence of any form of evidence; vigilantes also engage in illegal acts such as kidnappings, criminal injury, malicious damage to property, theft, robbery, and sabotage (Sekhonyane and Louw 2002).

Johnston (1996) clearly defines the specific elements of vigilantism. First, vigilantism implies planning and premeditation by those who take part in vigilante actions; second, the participants are mostly citizens that are individually and voluntary involved; third, vigilantism is a type of autonomous citizenship and therefore can become a social movement; fourth, vigilantism uses or threatens to use violence and force; fifth, vigilantism emerges when an established order is under threat of being undermined; and sixth, vigilantism seek to control crime or other social infractions offering security "guarantees" both to participants and to others (Johnston 1996). These characteristics are based on the British and American criminological tradition and identify the results of community policing out of control.

From a collective violence approach, vigilantism is a form of social control through collective violence and a response to behaviours defined as deviant by a specific social group (Weisburd 1988). As collective violence, vigilantism is a unilateral action expressed as lynching, rioting, and terrorism. However, these vigilante activities vary depending on the context where collective violence is generated (Senechal 1996). In this context, deviant behaviour can be more than odd, abnormal, or illegal because any behaviour can be defined as dangerous by those who claim to maintain social order.

Vigilantism is considered a "popularly initiated strategy" arising as a reaction to social deviance (real, threatened, or imputed), whose aim is to offer people the assurance that an established system of order will prevail. Its focus is invariably local and in the majority of forms there is a concern to minimize objective threats to people, property, or social values and to reduce associated fear. The motivation arises from a popular desire of "do something" when formal systems of control are, considered ineffective (Johnston 1996: 231). The voluntary adhesion to vigilante groups can be relative in context of armed conflicts in which those groups occupy a paramilitary dimension with political goals. In contexts in which there were no effective post-war demobilization processes, the post-conflict citizen organizations were often structured on the basis of pre-existing paramilitary organizations that were active during armed conflicts. The adherence to these supposedly new organizations cannot be totally free. In SSR literature, the voluntary adherence is evaluated from an excessively formal perspective in which the historical roots and authoritarian mechanisms are not understood as determining elements.

As a sociological structure, vigilantism is characterized by its organizational structure, which can be formal or informal. Violent vigilante actions implemented by neighbourhood organizations are structured by a functional independence (Senechal 1996: 111). This characteristic allows the continuity of vigilante actions over transformative processes of collective life and make relevant to trace whether vigilantism is top-down or bottom up motivated. Historical trajectories of these organizations show a repeated restructuring that generates social control mechanisms within collective life. There is a process of separation between real security needs of the community and the actions implemented by vigilante groups that claim a self-assigned legitimacy. Functional independence differs from the institutional dependence that SSR seeks to create through neighbourhood organizations.

Critics to community policing programmes emphasizes that social structures such as networks and collective efficacy not only allow the proliferation of self-defence organizations but the expansion of crime as well. Thus, it is possible to explain how some organized communities are at the same time communities with high crime rates (Browning *et al.* 2004). Studies in the United States have shown that confrontations are associated with the proliferation of commercial and non-commercial private security in communities (Kilburn and Shrum 1998). Those who have invested in commercial private security are not willing to pay taxes to strengthen public institutions nor participate in community policing initiatives. On the contrary, those who actively participate in community actions tend to support preventive programmes proposed by local institutions. However, in other contexts this relation does not provide an explanation as to why highly-organized communities with no presence of commercial private security refuse to support public institutions and why, sometimes, collective violence such as lynching is directed against local institutions (municipalities, police, and courts of law, among others).

The different trajectories of community policing organizations show that initially its activities are oriented to crime prevention but end up becoming vigilante actions (Johnston 1992). Theoretically community-policing models expects a set of actions and institutional relations in which citizens take part actively in policing its own community. The problem emerges when these models are implemented in contexts in which vigilantism and lacks of state controls are informal institutions that characterizes private policing. Studies about vigilantism use historical examples to show that the possibility of transforming preventive actions into vigilante actions is highly probable. Even in strong democracies the risk of stimulating active citizenship in security matters is to transform those organizations into autonomous citizenship groups that avoid formal controls.

In the case of Latin America, Waldmann (1995) identifies the interaction of three different forms of vigilantism namely crime-control vigilantism, social-group-control vigilantism and regime-control vigilantism (Waldmann 1995: 68). The first is represented by those groups that based on the alleged inefficiency of state institutions implement "law and order" actions violating the social order they supposedly protecting. When is a social group and not only isolated individuals who are contesting traditional structures of social order and the balance of power then social-control-vigilantism is implemented in order to protect the social order. The third type is the regime-control vigilantism motivated mainly by actors or organizations in order to protect the political order (Waldmann 1995: 69). Latin America and especially post-war societies show how these three types of vigilantism are interrelated in vigilante organizations mostly motivated by state actors. Extra judicial executions and lynching exemplify how vigilantism actions can be oriented to the three types of vigilantism depending on political contexts.[17] Waldmann (1995) emphasizes that vigilantism in Latin America in comparison with vigilantism in the United States differentiates from its state origins, in other words, the responsible of violent vigilante actions are the state security forces both as governmental authorities or implementing informal functions (Waldmann 1995: 73).

Based on the previous arguments, the empirical line between community policing programs and vigilante actions depend on the socio-historic context. As it will be explained in chapter 7, most community policing programs in post-war Central America and specially in Guatemala were implemented by international donors through state institutions avoiding the existence of strong historical patterns of vigilante policing which made diffuse the difference between community policing and vigilante policing.

2.5 The Legacies of Militarism: Private Security in Latin America

In Latin America the interaction of democratisation, neoliberalism, and rising crime stimulate the proliferation of different forms of private security (Ungar 2007). Nevertheless, it is important to highlight that in order to understand the reproduction of historical forms of private policing, a broader definition of private security is required. A definition centred only in the commercial aspect of private security provides a partial explanation of the phenomenon. The other aspect to consider in the Latin American context are the social and political mechanisms through which former security organizations are recycled into new postwar concepts of community policing organizations.

Some studies on private security in Latin America tend to define causes that are outcomes of pre-existing processes; for example, the rise of crime and the institutional weakness of the new security forces (Arias 2009; Fundación Arias 2003). These aspects seem to be more than causes, since they intensify, accelerate, and deepen the proliferation of private security. Crime rates rose during the 1990s while state transformation processes accelerated the privatisation of core state functions and reduced the capacities of state institutions. At that moment private security was already embedded in the social system and worked as a growing functional option. This process has its roots in the historical state delegation of public security and social control functions to the private sphere. Neoliberal models applied both tardily and in weak states generated negative social

17 Chapter VI and VIII analyse the relation between vigilante actions and policing organizations in Guatemala.

consequences to democratic governance and the rule of law (Call 2007). Neoliberal transformations have involved also the requirement for more flexibility and responsibility by citizens with respect to the security of their neighbourhoods which implies the organization for crime prevention. This situation in some countries of Latin America has stimulated the proliferation of self-help organizations and the enlargement of the informal security sector (including private security patrols, vigilante groups, lynching, and social cleansing) as a response to increased crime (Goldstein 2005; Jaramillo 1993; Godoy 2006). This aspect explains the emergence of so-called private justice or vigilante justice which in some countries takes the form of "social cleansing" squads (Goldstein 2005; Godoy 2002). In specific cases, such as Colombia (where there is an ongoing war), community-policing organizations have taken the form of paramilitary or "parapolice" structures (Huhle 2001; Jaramillo 1993). Such organizations include PSCs and armed vigilante associations known as "Convivir". These examples are part of a wide range of non-state armed actors but it is important to note that there are important differences among them.

The criterion applied to study such a range of actors is that policing organizations as well as policing activities change as locations change (Shearing 1992: 423). In other words, context matters in seeking differences and similarities among armed actors.

The proliferation of non-state armed actors in post-war societies, some of them with a military past, is considered a basis for post-war violence and can be analysed as an explanatory factor of the proliferation of private security services as well.[18] The 1990s transformed the military's role to one of security and intelligence advice for civilian governments (Kruijt 2004: 758; Koonings and Kruijt 2004). It is possible to identify the same former military personnel in PSCs. The proliferation of mini-wars and armed urban actors in Latin America is related to the appearance of gaps in formal local government which, in turn, are the result of a long absence of authorities and law and order representatives (Kruijt 2004: 757).

This situation relates with the blurred line between public and private spheres. Arias (2009) suggests that one of the main problems related with the private security sector in Latin America is the emergence of hybrid or mixed spaces between public and private spheres where the functions of public and private security overlap. A clear definition of spaces and functions of private and public security is directly related with the institutional capabilities of the countries (Arias 2009). Historical studies, on the other hand, argues that this dichotomist perspec-

18 There is an extensive literature on non-state armed actors. See Guzmán 1993; Jarami- llo 1993; Salazar 1993; Kruijt 2004; Alba Vega and Kruijt 2007; Kurtenbach 2003; Koonings 2004.

tives lose meaning when they are analysed from a temporal perspective. In doing so, the Latin American contexts show that the continued collaboration between both spheres are part of the state formation process (Holden 2004).

Thus, in Latin America the meaning of self-defence is linked with the trajectories of public institutions, particularly police and armies. In contexts of armed conflict, self-defence puts citizen action in the dilemma of legitimate protection and counterinsurgent collaboration (Huhle 2001). The change on the nature of violence during the last decades has been studied to explain the proliferation of private security in Latin America, especially the increase in urban violence (Olmo 2000; Guzmán *et al.* 1993; Salazar 1993; Gabaldón 2001). Contextual analysis shows that urban violence is an important factor in the proliferation of private security but it is difficult to explain this proliferation in non-urban areas. Rural areas with low crime rates present high incidence of neighbourhood security organization and PSCs. Explanations of private security proliferation as a consequence of increased urban violence are complemented with other aspects characteristic of post-war contexts such as negative security perceptions and distrust of public institutions (Melara 2001). However important their contribution, these studies explain only partially the proliferation of private security because they begin their analysis when private security was already rooted in the society and in the security system. The starting point and the reproducing mechanisms have been scarcely studied until now.

To trace the roots of private security in the political and social system, the link between political context and state security forces must be identified, especially the army and the police. Only few authors emphasize the continuity of pre-existing structures beyond political transformation processes (Holden 2004; Jaramillo 1993: 28; Méndez 2002; Zinecker 1999; Stanley 1996). Those authors ague that the more established the violence, the greater the probability that it might become "structured" violence and, consequently, the actors linked to violence will also operate in a more structure manner.

In the Latin American context, security becomes a political problem determined by the trajectories of public and private security sectors. In some Latin American countries, institutional trajectories have been highly configured by militaristic traditions and authoritarian regimes. At the same time, other aspects such as internal armed conflicts, regional dynamics, and international power relations are part of the historic processes in which institutional patterns emerge. Security matters in this context are related to political considerations (law and order, stability, and democratisation, among others) and economical processes (economic growth, neoliberal transformations) (Zirker and Danopoulos 2004; Serrano 1998; Castellanos 2003).

State-building history in Latin America shows the blurred difference between public and private violence (Holden 2004). The power and authority of the state is highly dependent on local political elites that at the same time depend on its ability to use physical violence and offer protection by hiring private gunmen or assassins that in some cases where part of public institutions (Hurrell 1998: 31). These historic trajectories (authoritarian regimes, internal wars, political instability) are important in understanding the origins of private security services.

The return to democracy and the change of the security paradigm in some countries of Latin America provided the rule of law as guarantor for the protection of civil rights. However, weakness of security institutions coincided with a rise in crime and corruption in the security sector. The corporate response of military and former military personnel in defence of their privileges led them to oppose civilian governance and to boycott the democratisation process of the police (Diamint 1988: 92).

From a temporal perspective, many informal community-policing organizations and other private security forms have varied their mission by adapting to different political contexts. In the same way, the links of these organizations with state institutions have shifted from formal to informal mechanisms that operate under new names but with the same social function. Changes on the nature of the violence influence those formal and informal shifts of private security. The emergence of the so-called "new violence" generated a new constellation of actors and targets of violence. More than forms of violence that not were present during internal conflicts or wars, the concept of "new violence" seeks to identify those forms of violence that emerge after the formal finalization of political violence (Alba Vega and Kruijt 2007). It is important to remark that the concept produces a confusion about the interaction of different forms of violence in different temporal sequences and also that the differentiation of political violence from those non-political violence is weak because its makes diffuse the role of the state in the production or prevention of violence (Kurtenbach 2011).[19]

The consulted bibliography in this chapter shows that there is a concern about the general situation of private security services in post-war societies, especially in their regulation, professionalisation, and control. From the perspective of Security Sector Reform programs there is an attempt to identify the effects of the private sector on post-war societies, especially on the rule of law and the legitimacy of democratic institutions. However, there is a lack of explanations about the continuities and changes of these services, the pre-existing conditions, the importance of social and political contexts, and the reinforcement mechanisms of the selection of private security services. This is especially important related to community policing programs which are implemented without observing the his-

19 The concept does not allow to identify the multiple representations of violence in other social fields. For different perspectives about representations of violence and the perception of its ubiquity. see Haas 2010.

torical trajectories of policing organizations and the socio-political contexts. Whether bottom up or top-down proliferation of self-policing there is a lack or explanations about the reproductive cycles of this mechanisms and its relation with the socio-political context.

3. Private Policing and Historical Institutionalism

In the previous chapter, it was pointed out that most security studies define private security from a commercial perspective. This chapter proposes a broader definition based on the sociology of policing. From this point of view, private security can be seen as a socio-political relation that involves different actors and political processes according to changes in contexts. Policing studies clearly show that the current proliferation of private security can be understood as the rebirth of private policing, in other words, the reproduction of historical processes (Johnston 1992). How these processes reproduce themselves depends on social and political contexts as well as the temporal dimension of social change. To explain them satisfactorily, a theoretical framework is needed that integrates elements such as time, context, and social and political processes. This study proposes an historical-institutional approach to find out how private policing institutions are embedded in temporal processes that configure institutional arrangements. Processes and institutional mechanisms are juxtaposed in different temporal sequences that reinforce certain outcomes. This approach focuses on initial conditions and reinforcing mechanisms of the institutional patterns.

This chapter is divided in two parts. The first deals with the concept of policing and private policing in order to understand the interplay of commercial and non-commercial private security. To deal with this objective the analysis must go beyond dichotomist perspectives based on the public or private nature of security providers. This study perceives private security as a field of socio-political relations with particular functions in the social system. Private security can be defined through the different social control and self-defence actions that private actors implement. Those actions can be implemented both in a commercial and non-commercial, organized and spontaneous, and formal and informal ways.

The second part of this chapter focuses on the construction of an analytical model to explain the proliferation of private security in particular contexts. Because one of the main features of this model is the temporal dimension of reinforcing processes, the model is based on a path dependence approach. It involves the initial conditions and critical junctures of institutional patterns as well as the self-reproducing sequences that allow the outcome under study.

3.1 Private Security and Private Policing

Policing and security are two concepts that have to be differentiated from each other. Security is defined here as a generic concept that involves different forms of policing, including public, private, and popular. It includes the preservation of an established order against internal or external threats (Johnston 1996: 231). Both the established order and threats against it are directly linked with contextual factors. Security can be understood as the aspiration of participants that nothing should happen that changes the status quo within which collective life develops. This desire for "peace" is not possible without assurances of those guarantees that make it possible (Johnston 1996). In this sense, security implies the implementation of strategies directed to offer the guarantee of peace for the participants (Johnston 1996: 231). This liberal approach to peace implies civil guarantees for property, life, and personal integrity, among others.

The debate on the concept of security varies from perspectives centred on the real state of that which is being protected from all threats and dangers (Booth 2005; Beck 1998) to the subjective feeling of safety, which refers to the means to achieve protection (Jones 2007: 844). Other perspectives link the forms of security provision to different levels of security relations (international, regional, global, and local) (Buzan *et al.* 1998). From those perspectives it is possible to distinguish three dimensions of security. The first is the instrumentalist dimension, in which the degree of security is a necessary condition for civic freedoms. The second is the social dimension, in which the security of some depends on that of others. And thirdly, there is a constitutive dimension in which the promotion of security is fundamental to the establishment and sustainability of collective life (Jones 2007: 845).

The theoretical framework presented here seeks to analyse those perspectives and to observe the political component that emerges from their interplay. How security is structured in a particular context explains important developments of institutional and political aspects of the state. Complementarily, private security is a field to which important state security functions have been displaced, reflecting the transformations of the state building process (Camparini 2006: 271).

The term "policing" refers to a socio-political relation exerted by civil society and the state (Johnston 1992). From a broader perspective, the concept of policing is linked with a neoliberal framework about state functions. British criminological tradition refers to policing as the preservation of peace, in other words the maintenance of a way of doing things where individuals and property are free from unwarranted interference (Shearing 1992: 399). Peace as a foundation order is the basis to discuss the link between the concept of policing and security (Shearing 1992). It is the social order of peace (foundation order) that security seeks to keep free of threats, and upon which other orders depend. In these terms, policing is the activity that seeks to preserve this foundation; policing refers to those activities through which an assurance or guarantee is given (Shearing 1992: 400). The difference between security – that state of being free from threats against the social order – and policing – the actions implemented to achieve and sustain that state – is merely heuristic. Its utility lies in the possibility of observing those aspects in a specific context. On the one hand, security is an aspiration involving guarantees of peace and, on the other, policing is carrying out actions to achieve that end.

However, policing has been extensively studied from criminologist perspectives, although the term is not only limited to the criminal justice field.[20] One of the heuristic aspects of the concept of policing is that it defines security as a social relation that involves different levels: public-private, formal-informal and central-local (Johnston 1999 and 1992). From private security perspectives, the policing actions implemented by private actors are historically located on the private-informal-local side of these dichotomic levels (Johnston 1992: 7). The other side, the public-formal-central side, has been considered as an historical phase during which the modern state has tried to monopolize and legitimise the means of violence through public institutions. The historical norm in the modern state has been the coexistence of private and public forms of policing and each context has created the way in which those relations have developed (Johnston 1992).

One of the common features of the actors who participate in these relations is their involvement in social control activities. Policing implies a self-conscious process whereby societies designate and authorize people to create public safety (Johnston 1999: 178). This perspective implies the above discussed foundation order of peace, although contextual political analysis is possible to observe the political aspect of private policing (i.e. power structures, inter-institutional relations, and political change processes, among others).

The central point is that policing is a governmental activity – the act of governance (or rule) directed towards the promotion of security – although it is not an exclusive function of the state (Johnston 1999: 179). Many current private policing strategies can be located outside the state but that does not mean that they are not linked with state institutions or that they are mechanisms to strength state-society relations. On the contrary, the relational character of policing is located between public and private spheres and this is why security adopts a political dimension.

20 However the link between criminal justice and policing is fundamental to understand the modern security governance, there is scarce bibliography about the impacts of that relation on the public opinion, see Brodeur and Shearing 2005.

This study is based on private policing as a concept that allows for an understanding of different forms of private security. As derived from criminological and social control theories, private security can be understood as a social control system with strong similarities to the police in its functional aspects (South 1988). These perspectives address private security beyond the common descriptions of the security sector (scope, operations, and regulations) and propose an exploration of the relations between private security and other spheres of social and political life (state institutions, legitimacy, organizations, and social and political mechanisms and functions). The term "private security" is commonly applied to a specific part of the security sector and the term "private policing" refers to the social function that is implemented through this sector. Thus, private security is a form of social control and a set of social and political relations.

Some authors define private security based on aspects that are beyond the concept of private policing, for example, the industrial characteristics of private security in developed countries (South 1988: 4).[21] This study shows that in post-war societies the industrial dimension of private security has little relevance to explain its proliferation. In those societies national private security companies and informal civil policing organizations predominate.

Although private policing is a concept that evolved in parallel to the interests of academics of observing the changes of modern society after the Second World War. The first wave of policing studies was focused on the commercial aspects or private security. These studies focused on changes on the use of public spaces generated by the proliferation of private security. Along the same lines, the emergence of public-private hybrid spaces extended the concept of private policing beyond the commercial sphere of private security. In recent years the trend has been to observe as part of private policing those non-paid forms of private policing like civil policing initiatives, informal private policing motivated by state agencies or "community policing" programmes, informal systems of criminal justice, and even private policing in global spaces (Kempa *et al.* 1999; O'Malley 1997; Marenin 1982).

Some authors define private policing conducted by civil organizations as an expression of active citizenship or responsible citizenship that varies depending on contexts. Some of these responsible citizenship organizations are created by state institutions and are oriented to implement community crime prevention actions (Johnston 1992: 137). The outcomes of active or responsible citizenship depends largely on state controls over crime prevention actions implemented by citizens. Without effective controls, these forms of citizen action can become autonomous and implement self-policing actions such as vigilantism, social clean-

21 About changes on the security industry see Maguire and King, 2004.

sing, and self-defence patrols, among others (Pepinsky 1989). However, not all state controls can guaranty positive outcomes of active citizenship. The construction of enemies based on perceptions which are legitimised by public institutions can reinforce vigilante actions by active citizenship. This is the case when for example the citizen perception and the official perception stigmatised some particular group as the alleged responsible of a particular criminal situation and it leads to vigilante actions against those groups.[22]

Private policing includes all non-state agencies that consciously participate in the process of bringing about and guaranteeing security (Shearing and Kempa 2000; Shearing 1992). Pluralistic perspectives analyse policing as the provision of security guarantees beyond the differences between public and private. From this perspective, the study of policing suggests a Foucaultian definition of power as not centralized but decentred and embedded in social relations (Shearing 1992: 421; Vaughan 2007). The evolution of the concept of private policing shows how non-paid forms of community crime prevention were incorporated in its definition in order to encompass the multiplicity of actors related to policing activities (Kempa *et al.* 1999: 199). One example of this situation is the proliferation of community policing programmes implemented since the late 1980s. These programmes express the links articulated by the state via the promotion of private policing activities among the citizenry. The criticisms aimed at those programmes point out that they become strategies to extend responsibilities that assume different forms in each context and also that theoretical models of community policing could not prevent vigilante actions produced by the influence of historical trajectories (Garland 1996 and 2005).

Responsibilization strategies generate two displacements. On the one hand, the responsibility of risks is displaced to citizens who have to implement prevention organizations, such as neighbourhood committees, promoted by the state. On the other, the state not only promotes investment in private security but, at the same time, displaces accountability on to the private security sector (Garland 2005). Citizens have to control the quality of Private Security Companies (PSCs) but must pay the consequences of an uncontrolled private sector (Johnston 1999: 189). Responsibilization strategies have in common the aspiration to create collaborative mechanisms between public institutions and private actors to identify and resolve community problems (Kempa *et al.* 1999: 210).

22 Huhn (2011) analysed how in Costa Rica the historical trajectories of the social construction of crime can influence official discourses and consequently community policing organizations when they are promoted by public institutions (Huhn 2011). In this case, active citizenship and the official discourse match in an anti-immigrant explanation of crime. Other examples in Central America are related to anti-youth discourses (Peetz 2011; Huhn, Oettler and Peetz 2006a).

Contextual factors such as organizational traditions, history, and public institution trajectories are powerful causes linked to the emergence of vigilante actions in community policing organizations. From a criminological perspective, private security is seen as the product of a broader shift of governmental practices of governance (Loader and Walker 2001). This reflects the liberal trend to delegate on individuals and families the responsibility for their own security. In response to the wide range of risks and threats in modern societies, individuals seek to find protection in commercial and non-commercial private security (Singh 2005: 154). Through private security services, governments, both in an official and explicit form and through informal and undercover mechanisms, implement disciplinary and surveillance techniques. In this sense, private security is a field in which state and non-state forms of coercion interact, with each assuming both preventive and reactive actions over citizens (Singh 2005: 156).

Private Policing and the Public-Private Debate

The analysis of private security necessarily results in a discussion about public and private spheres that are linked through policing actions. However, the public-private debate is very broad. The important point in this study is how policing can be understood as a field in which the interplay between both spheres is blurred as part of the social relations that surround private security.

From a historical perspective and from the social functions of private security it is possible to observe that the main element explaining its reproduction in different sequences is the political dimension of private policing in which interact self-defence mechanisms with a political context of displacement of public security functions. From this perspective private policing assumes public control functions and in fact intends to reform social order.[23] Private policing allows observation of private security as an interlocking system of social control located in the gaps of the public-private relation (South 1988). From a policing perspective, the liberal state is conceived as the centre of the production of social order, as well as being held responsible for the preservation of that order. In this sense, private policing become also a political mechanism of control in particular contexts (Marenin 1982). Social control finds in policing actions the means to produce and preserve social order. This goal can be achieved through different means, so that the differences between public and private become formal and heuristic. The history of policing shows that the rebirth of private policing is a result of the limits on the monopoly of violence of the liberal state (Shearing and

23 Chapter VI and VIII explain this role of private policing in the case of Guatemala.

Stenning 1987: 11; Kempa *et al.* 1999). Private policing becomes the mechanism through which the state fills the gaps of the private-public relation enabling these spheres to functionally interact in the social system (Shearing and Stenning 1987; Garland 1997). In this perspective the concept of policing has a heuristic utility because it allows for the observation of the social control system within which there is an interplay of both public and private spheres.

Nodal security governance perspectives question the exclusively state responsibility for the production of social order. However, the liberal state's monopoly over legitimate violence presupposes a state-centred production of social order; that is, there are in the social system formal and informal mechanisms of social order production via private policing mechanisms. Currently the liberal welfare that conceives security as a public good is confronted by an extended process of formal and informal privatisation of security (Shearing 1992: 425). The liberal state has attempted to define the line between public and private policing through formal institutions. The creation of the police is an expression of the state institutionalisation of policing as well as the formalisation of historical forms of private security as private security companies. But this process has had to coexist with strong historical and informal mechanisms of policing located in the gaps of private-public relations. Private security penetrates the public sphere not only in a spatial dimension but also in its political relations as corporate interests. At the international level, nodal security governance allows to the observation of the correlation of power emerged after the Cold War. However, at the national level in post-war societies in which the interaction of state and non-state armed actors is a historical *continuum*, the concept helps to identify those interactions in the production of security in different sequences. In other words, the concept helps in an analytical level but its normative implications such as the limited role of the state and the responsibilization strategies it produces should be criticized. Contemporary security governance shows that lack of effective public institutions has lead to wide acceptance of the belief that private security has to be a complement – or in some cases a substitute – of public institutions (Jones 2007: 859; Loader and Walker 2001).

The debate of public-private spheres and policing must be analysed based on contextual limits. Western democracies define specific configurations of private-public relations and consequently the role of policing mechanisms change in comparison with Latin American societies, for example. The different trajectories of state formation exemplify that the irregular forces have had an important role in the formation of the state in other non-central European regions such as in Latin America (Davis and Pereira 2003; Holden 2004).

Gordon (1987) studied the interplay between private and public through policing organizations in Nicaragua. He argues that the "revolutionary vigilance" implemented through the Sandinista Defence Committees is a good example of how an organization created by the state implements private policing to preserve public and private social order. Those kinds of organizations cannot be defined in terms of a dichotomist perspective of public and private. Legitimate self-defence or self-help private armies have their roots in the liberal governance that seeks to create collaborative links between state and citizenry in order to protect a specific social order (Shearing 1992: 407; Stanley 1996). The Nicaraguan example shows that policing should be analysed according to contextual factors.[24] Formal institutional analysis can produce a distorted vision of what is public and private in policing actions which is the case of security sector programs. Most private policing organizations are created as part of a wider state strategy; in other words, they are promoted by the state in order to achieve specific contextual goals. In contrast to community-based programmes in Western democracies that have proliferated in the last years as part of top-down privatisation processes, in Latin America and Africa informal community-based policing predominates, that even when promoted by the state, is characterized by informal organizations that become autonomous and, in many cases, operate as vigilante groups (Savenije 2010; Huhn 2011; Gottschalk 2005). Contextual configurations can transform top-down models of community policing. Communicative mechanisms and asymmetric power relations between police and community can be strong barriers to collaborative relations, especially in marginalized areas (Schneider 1999). The prevalence of informal structures makes this a bottom-up privatisation process in which the state legitimises pre-existing informal policing organizations (Wisler and Onwudiwe 2008).

Based on the previous debate this research observes that the trajectories of policing organisations show that their formal institutional configuration can change depending on contextual factors but the social functions those organizations reproduce remain constant over contextual changes. In this process an organization can transit from formal to informal. For example when the state creates an organization and then decides its formal dissolution, it remains in the social relations as an informal organization. On the contrary, the state legalizes and formalizes traditional informal policing organizations and integrates them into larger transformation processes. For this reasons, the study of private policing has to include more aspects linked with context in order to determine the social function that private policing organizations reproduce in the society.

In addition to the debate about private and public spheres related to policing, contextual analysis opens a window on the diversification of security providers in local communities and helps to understand that all of them – formal and in-

24 Other studies about private policing have shown the heuristic utility of the concept when it is applied in different context such as Africa, see Grant 1989; Kempa and Singh 2008; House 2000.

formal – contribute to the social definition of the threats that justify the implementation of private policing activities.

3.2 *Private Policing and Contextual Political Analysis*

Private security is analysed in this research as a policing function that can be explained as an outcome of political processes and institutional trajectories. The main argument is based on historical institutionalism approaches in which institutions evolve in response to changes in context and political processes, both constrained by past trajectories (Thelen 1999: 387 and 2003). Path dependence analytical models allow the identification of the causal mechanisms that reinforce processes of institutional change (Cappoccia and Kelemen 2007). The interaction of processes and mechanisms is observed in dynamics embedded in historical processes in which social interactions affect each other in time and space (Tilly 2001b).

Private policing is a field in which those interactions can be observed. Different mechanisms interplay in the process through which private security organizations have transcended changes in political contexts. Private policing seems to be a dynamic social function that is capable of adapting to the social system. The links between private security and the evolution of the political system allow for private security as an outcome of political processes that aims to displace security functions to the private sphere.

Tilly (2001b) discusses the concept of political process from a historical analysis perspective and defines it as all social processes in which governments are significant. Governments are conceived as the concentration of coercive means inside a particular and delimited territory and the exercise of them over other organizations operating inside this territory (Tilly 2001b: 570). A strong vision of historical analysis focuses on more than events and processes occurred in the past; it seeks to identify "...ways that when and where an event or process occurs affect how it occurs, why it occurs, and with what consequences it occurs." (Tilly 2001b: 570). This study argues that the proliferation and evolution of private policing (as a category of social processes analysis) varies in relation to context and processes that are not exclusively linked to security aspects. In this perspective, private policing is a social mechanism with long-term effects on the society that has evolved parallel to modern state building. The political process related to this evolution is directly linked with the current situation of private security in certain societies. However, there are differences between states and societies concerning institutional capabilities to concentrate policing activities. Private policing has an important role in those processes and it can range from competitive to collaborative relations between public and private spheres. The formal or informal role of the state in this relation is determinant to understand private security as an outcome of political and historical processes.

The importance of the context as a "partner concept" of causal mechanisms is located in the centre of historical analysis and is necessary to specify its conceptual scope (Falleti and Lynch 2009). From a contextual political analysis perspective, context is made up of those relevant aspects of a setting (analytical, temporal, spatial, or institutional) in which a set of initial conditions leads (probabilistically) to an outcome of a defined scope and meaning via a specified causal mechanism or set of causal mechanisms (Falleti and Lynch 2009: 1152). Thus, both the definition of causal mechanisms and the criteria to define the relevance of the elements of context are the basis of a historic analytical framework.

The first aspect to clarify is the temporal dimension of the context (sequencing, tempo and duration, and initial conditions). When things happen, different sequences (self-reproducing or reactive) are possible. Secondly, there is the question of how long things take. This allows for an observation of the cumulative characteristics of social mechanisms and processes. Third, the initial contextual conditions are defined by the question when things start; those approaches of historical institutionalism define the genesis of particular institutional patterns and avoid the infinite temporal regressions that can occur when a process is traced back (Tilly and Goodin 2006; Mahoney and Schensul 2006).

One of the features of context is its dynamism. Contexts change throughout time and those changes affect outcomes given that they are the result of interactions between context and social mechanisms. Mechanisms change as the context changes but these changes are directed to the reinforcing of a particular institutional pattern and to the new configurations of the context. The dynamic interaction between those aspects characterizes the causality contained in mechanism explanations.

As was mentioned in the previous chapter, security studies focus on explanations of private security based on present manifestations of the phenomena. However, still pending are explanations of the political dimension of private security and its relation to specific contexts (i.e. post-war societies). For this reason, this study is based on the logic of historical explanations in social sciences (Mahoney *et al.* 2009: 124) and is structured around a self-reproducing sequence elaboration that was constructed from empirical data of the case study. From this, (1) initial social and political conditions led to a (2) critical juncture in which one particular institutional arrangement was possible from several options. In this process, (3) the displacement of public security to the private sphere became a sufficient cause from which a path-dependent process was started and (4) a set of causal mechanisms played out in different temporal sequences which resulted in the proliferation of private security in Guatemala. This elaboration is a heuristic tool based on a particular theoretical framework, in this case on historical institutionalism and empirical data from the case study. The separation of different temporal moments of the sequence seeks to identify the factors and mechanisms involved in the socio-historic process.

For Mahoney (2008) once in motion, the mechanisms acquire deterministic properties directed to specific trajectories. The interaction between context and mechanisms produces the outcome when trajectories reinforce mechanisms (Falleti and Lynch 2009). From this, context gains an important explanatory dimension and determines that one mechanism in different contexts can produce both different and similar outcomes. In spite of the fact that critical junctures can start trajectories that reproduce themselves through functional mechanisms, the selection of the mechanisms and the possibility of its functionality depends on the socio-political conditions of the context. Different authors argue that context is the temporal and spatial delimitation of the social world and its relations (Pierson 2004: 171; Tilly 2001b; Mahoney *et al.* 2009) which for the study of private security allows to observe the interaction of political and social processes. The analytical link between the concept of private policing and path-dependence approach aims to provide this study with a contextual and temporal basis to the study of private security.

The Path Dependent Process of Private Policing Proliferation

Private security in a contextual political analysis is understood as an essentially social and political process and therefore it cannot be studied from an isolated perspective. On the contrary, this study is based on the idea that temporal ordering and the interactions of different processes explain certain outcomes (Thelen 1999: 338). In this sense, historical explanation can trace back present outcomes by understanding causality as the necessary and sufficient conditions for the reproduction of certain trajectories and not only as the correlation of contextual isolated variables. Historical studies show that social relations contain multiple causal factors that once combined produce particular outcomes (Mahoney *et al.* 2009).

From an individual level, causal factors are neither necessary nor sufficient, but they are part of a set that in certain contexts produces the observed outcome. As a socio-political relation, private policing presupposes the interplay of multiples elements such as political processes, institutional trajectories, historical and traditional organizations, and political conflicts, in addition to the current crime situation linked to insecurity. From this it is possible to highlight the political elements that in different moments reinforce the displacement of state social functions to the private sphere. The multiple analytical levels those elements represent, describe the complexity of the public-private relations and its complex network of formal and informal organizations and actors. It is possible to observe how reinforcement mechanisms allow the mobility this displacement produces. This means that a possibility exists for the interchange of the formal and informal condition of organizations and actors.

Although path-dependence analysis is based on a set of historical and political science arguments, its origins as an analysis model are from economics. The import of a concept from one disciplinary field to another implies the production of multiple definitions that seek to clarify the scope of the concept in the new cognitive field. There is a common acceptance that history matters in the explanation of politics, which means that particular events in the past can have crucial effects on the future even when those events are located in a distant past (Mahoney and Schensul 2006). Path dependent analysis centres on the study of causal processes with a strong temporal dimension, in other words, the effects of a particular event can be traced throughout time and this becomes an explanatory dimension (Mahoney 2000; Pierson 2004).

The combination of causal factors is produced during a given temporal sequence that influences and defines a path-dependence process. The first element of this perspective is the temporal dimension of the process (Tilly 2001b: 567). It does not mean that the analysis is concentrated only in a specific time frame but, on the contrary, it refers to the way in which the process is affected by time. This allows for the analysis to extend beyond an artificial boundary between past and present. By observing the process from its temporal dimension it is possible to identify how the present is continuously change by the continuity of past trajectories. Path dependence analysis places mechanisms and processes in motion to capture the temporal interaction of outcomes and its constitutive dynamics of change and evolution.

Although there are no clear definitions of path-dependence, it is possible to identify key elements that define the existence of path dependent processes in the social world. First, path-dependence suggests the possibility of observing how the past affects the present. This is a common discussion in historical studies, but the contribution of path-dependence lies in the connection between political science views of present phenomena and the time dimension of social life. The resulting interaction of those dimensions introduces analytical sources to a less present-based explanation of current political phenomena. Secondly, path-dependence analysis can identify the causal importance of initial conditions on the observed process. This is part of the historical institutionalism debate about institutional change and identifies the difference between the conditions in which an institution emerges and the mechanisms through which an institution is reproduced, persists and changes. Third, for some authors such as Mahoney (2000), contingent events are causally important. Although this aspect deserves a broad discussion, the observation of the trajectories of political processes shows how some events generate certain effects that, on the one hand, could not be imagined or anticipated by any theory and, on the other, have deterministic properties (Mahoney 2000). The contingent nature of those events lies in the fact that at the moment they occur it is not possible to identify or observe their future outcomes, which are determined by the sequence and mechanisms that produced them. Fourth, path dependent processes are characterized by a certain lock-in; in other words, the possibility of reproduction of an institutional pattern that becomes historical. The historical lock-in is possible due to the fifth element of path-dependent processes that is the existence of a self-reproducing sequence. The other possibility is the existence of a reactive sequence. The existence of a self-reproducing or a reactive sequence depends on contextual aspects (Mahoney 2000: 457). Although both sequences are characteristic of path-dependent processes, they have important differences. Self-reproducing sequences are characterized by the formation and reproduction of a particular institutional pattern stimulated by the increasing returns it produces (Pierson 2000). Thus, the cost of reversing the selection to the initial conditions increases more and more to the extent that its benefits increase; in other words, preceding steps in a particular direction induce further movement in the same direction (Pierson 2000: 252).

To the study of the self-reinforcing sequence that explains private policing, it is important to mention that the above explanation based on increasing returns focuses on economical aspects that are partially explicative of private security proliferation. There are functional explanations of self-reproducing sequences that match better with the socio-political dynamic of private policing since it is conceived as a set of social and political relations. As will be explained in the following part, this functional approach of self-reproducing sequences is key to a path-dependent process that explains private policing in post-war societies given that it is strongly linked with historical security trajectories that only currently have become high profit economic activities. The continued adoption of private security consolidated a particular institutional pattern in which the functional benefits of private security allowed its reproduction beyond changes in the initial conditions of the institutional pattern. Private policing is a functional mechanism since it undertakes security functions allegedly monopolized by the state. The difference lies on the process and the intensity of the displacement change depending on the context.

The differences in the definitions of path-dependence lie in the importance that they give to one or another of the above elements. Mahoney argues that the most important elements are the constitutive events that produce a sequence that has deterministic properties (Mahoney 2000). On the other hand, Pierson argues that increasing returns or positive-feedbacks that sequences produce are defining aspects of path-dependent processes (Pierson 2000 and 2004). Both perspectives agree that the causal explanation that path-dependence provides is made up of a continuum of contingent events and critical junctures toward more extended and significant processes of institutional change (Mahoney 2000: 536).

3.3 A Functional Approach of Private Policing Historical Explanation

From a historical institutionalism perspective it is important to differentiate two processes. The first is the institutional genesis constituted by a set of initial conditions, critical junctures, and contingent events. The second is the process of institutional reproduction that in the case of private security can be analysed through a self-reproducing sequence in which both mechanisms and processes are in motion and produce an institutional "lock-in". The differentiation of those two aspects is a heuristic mechanism that reinforces the argument that events that occurred in the past affect the present. On the other hand, this differentiation explains that institutions change from their initial conditions and motivations.

Mahoney (2000) argues that from a functional perspective institutional reproduction can be explained through the existence of reproduction mechanisms through which an institution serves a function for an overall system (Mahoney 2000: 517). Functional explanations of self-reproduction of private policing focus on its functional consequences (integration, adaptation, and survival). In the case of private policing in Guatemala, the consequences of its functions in the social system are at the same time its social justification, namely the weakness of public institutions. Private policing is integrated into the Guatemalan security system with the objective of filling the vacuum created through the displacement of public security to the private sphere. The trajectory of private policing shows that in the post-war years when public security became a priority in order to reduce the power of the military, public policing institutions were unable to reduce the increasing crime rate because at the time many of the social functions of public policing were already displaced to the private sphere.

From the perspective of crime prevention, private security is less functional than public security due to the nature of its operations and the absence of effective controls over the sector. However, its proliferation can be explained through the political and economic earnings it produced which increased throughout its trajectory. Based on the arguments of Mahoney (2000) about self-reinforcing sequences, private policing was selected through a set of contingent events after a critical juncture. At this moment, the functional aspects of private security were marginal. Nevertheless, its functional aspects were reinforced through institutional trajectories that produced positive feedback or increasing returns both to the private sector and to the political system. The trajectories of private security show that in the political and social system critical junctures can produce different effects; in some cases they open the possibility of breaking certain historical structures but they can, at the same time, reinforce the continuity of other structures.

The Institutional Genesis: Initial Conditions

The initial conditions of private policing are those events at the beginning of a self-reinforcing sequence. However, the causal potential of those conditions with respect to the outcome is relative in the case of private policing. The initial conditions of the institutional pattern that generated the reproduction of private security can change and even disappear through the institutional trajectory. It is for this reason that the analytical separation of institutional genesis and institutional change is important (Mahoney and Schensul 2006). Thus, the initial conditions define periods of institutional genesis that correspond to critical junctures (Mahoney 2000: 513). At the same time, contingent events reinforce a specific selection that will initiate a sequence. The institutional arrangement that makes possible the emergence of a path dependent process will be generated by the interplay of those three elements: initial conditions, critical junctures, and contingent events. It is important to highlight that these elements interplay in some specific context that changes with and creates the social and political conditions for this interplay (Mahoney 2000). Initial conditions are the periods before a critical juncture and it is possible in this time to observe the wide range of possible outcomes that can be interpreted as possible futures.[25] Only when the critical juncture is over, it is possible to identify why some specific institutional pattern was selected and not another (Mahoney and Schensul 2006).

From historical sociology perspectives, the outcome is a moment in the present that has a temporal explicative dimension in the past; it is a causal temporal dimension. However, initial conditions do not have deterministic properties over the outcome. The outcome will be related to these conditions only when one of the generated options during initial conditions was selected during the following critical juncture. The self-reinforcing sequence generated through the critical juncture will imply a set of causal mechanisms. For these reasons, initial conditions are located outside the path-dependent process; instead, they are located before the trajectory.

25 This study covers the period from 1944 to 1954 in Guatemala as initial conditions. For an extensive study of this period see Argueta 2006.

Both critical juncture and reproducing mechanisms generate a specific sequence of constitutive elements of path dependence in specific initial conditions.[26] Regardless of the existence of multiple definitions, in this study critical junctures are defined by the adoption of one particular institutional arrangement from multiple options in a particular moment in history.[27] There are some key elements of this definition. First, critical junctures are chosen points when a particular option is adopted from among two or more alternatives (Mahoney 2001b). Second, once an option is selected, it is increasingly difficult to return to the initial point in which other possibilities were available (Mahoney 2001b). The critical nature of this juncture is that once adopted, the deterministic properties of the selection make it difficult to turn aside from the trajectory toward a different outcome. The key element of the critical juncture is the possibility to generate a self-reinforcing process, whether to change or to assure the continuity of certain institutional patterns (Capoccia and Kelemen 2007).

There is an important debate about the role of critical juncture in institutional development. Capoccia and Kelemen argue that historical institutionalism has turned its attention fundamentally towards the institutional formation period as well as the period of its reproduction (2007: 342). However, as the authors maintain, both the definition and the utilization of the concept of critical juncture has not been appropriately addressed. The perspective from which the authors address critical junctures are fundamentally based on a relatively short period of structural relaxation that opened the possibility for the decisions of some actors to influence the outcome (2007: 342). This perspective gives the critical juncture period a fundamental importance that goes beyond only the selection of one possibility.

In order to explain the proliferation of private security in Guatemala, this study is based on the historical sociological perspective of critical junctures. Although critical juncture has been considered as a moment of selection and change, it is important to note that change is not a necessary element of critical junctures (Capoccia and Kelemen and Kelemen 2007: 348). In the case of Guatemala, it is argued that there are two critical junctures in the trajectories of political institutions.[28] But specifically to public security institutions whatever the particular selection made during a critical juncture, the institutional patterns that

26 Key studies of these themes are Collier and Collier 1991; Moore 1966; about critical junctures in Central America see Mahoney 2001a and 2001b.

27 For a more extensive analysis see Capoccia and Kelemen 2007.

28 The first is the counterrevolution in 1954 and the second is the Peace Agreements in 1996.

emerged have tended to reinforce pre-existing structures embedded in the political system rather than to change them (Stanley 2007). In other words, during critical junctures the key point is the capacity of actors to affect the outcome that will serve their interest whether they are made in order to favor change or continuity. A critical juncture shows that the effects of actors' decisions are determined by previous institutional patterns and the general context. For this reason some critical junctures are moments of change for some institutional patterns but also they can be non-critical junctures for other institutional patterns.

The private policing development shows how moments in which historical "normality" has been interrupted in some political spheres, in others that interruption has reinforced its functional structures. A given critical juncture of a specific process cannot be a critical juncture from the perspective of another simultaneously process. In this case, some critical junctures can be a contingent event for other political processes. In these cases, contingent events emerge from a critical juncture producing continuity and not change. For Capoccia and Kelemen critical juncture can be defined not only under the perspective of a expected change, but under the possibility of re-stability or re-equilibrium of a specific institutional pattern (2007: 352). A critical juncture opens up the possibility that one of the available options can be the restructuring of a pre-critical juncture status quo. A situation like this can be defined from an institutional change perspective as a "non-critical" juncture or "near miss" case (Capoccia and Kelemen 2007: 352). [29]

Contingent Events

The contingent character of these events lies on the unpredictable nature of a specific outcome under certain initial conditions (Mahoney and Schensul 2006). The functional features of private policing evidence different events that in a specific moment of its trajectory had no importance to the outcome, but due to the accumulative characteristic of self-reinforcing sequences become important to the outcome in the present.[30]

29 Kurtenbach (2010) introduces this question related to the ending of the internal wars in Central America that are widely defined as critical junctures that lead to the democratisation process in the region. In the case of the private policing evolution in the region it is possible to observe that such period leads to the re-equilibration of a historical institutional pattern. See also Stanley 2007.

30 An example of these contingent events is the creation in 1970 of the law that formalized a specific form of private policing. This formalization was of benefit to private actors linked with public institutions. This process implied the formal separation between commercial and non-commercial private security. This formaliza-

Some authors link the occurrence of contingent events to a critical juncture period. These events can be accidental, causal, or have a very short existence. Mahoney and Schensul (2006) argue that the characteristic of these events is that they cannot be explained or predicted by one or more theoretical frameworks (2006: 462). Based on this, it is possible to argue that the trajectory of private policing shows that however contingent events can be linked to a critical juncture period, its occurrence can be repeated throughout the trajectory. Contrary to what Pierson (2000) argued about the possibility of including or not contingent events in the definition of path dependence, private policing shows that contingent events can be an important part of the path dependent processes that explain its proliferation and reproduction.

Self-Reproducing Sequences and Private Policing

One of the main characteristics of self-reproducing sequences is that the observed outcome has been reinforced over time (Mahoney and Schensul 2006). From an economics perspective, this sequence is defined as "increasing returns" and the central argument is the repeated introduction of movements in the same direction (Pierson 2000 and 2004). The introduction of a self-reinforcing sequence in the explanation of private policing is based on the idea that initial conditions and critical junctures constitute the genesis of the institutional pattern that allows the displacement of public security functions to the private sphere. From historical institutionalism this is a problem of institutional evolution because the concept of institutional change does not include the persistent element of some institutions. On the contrary, an institutional development perspective allows the observation of institutional continuity (Pierson 2004). The importance of the sequence is that some institutions or structures persist throughout time in the absence of the processes responsible for its original development (Mahoney 2001: 8).

The functional element of self-reproducing sequences lies in the fact that the effects of an institution are related to the explanatory factors of its emergence and persistence (Pierson 2004: 46). The author emphasizes the utility of identifying these sequences to the extent that they answer the question of why some institutional patterns are persistent despite changes in the context (2004: 52). The author argues also that continuities are a striking feature of the social world (Pierson 2004: 52). It does not imply an invariable vision of the social world. On

tion process reinforced the function of private security in public security. The porosity of the law contributes to an uncontrolled expansion of the commercial private security sector.

the contrary, the dynamic element relies on self-reproducing mechanisms that assure continuity versus change.

There are two perspectives on how self-reproducing sequences are explained. On the one hand, rational choice approaches argue that the equilibrium of a self-reproducing sequence depends on the utilitarian considerations of rational actors (Pierson 2000 and 2004). This argument is based on the increasing returns that accrue to the actors and for this reason they feel impelled to reinforce the same direction in the trajectory. On the other hand, from a historical and sociological perspective, self-reinforcing sequences are a set of social and political mechanisms that produce the stability and reproduction of a pre-existing institutional pattern (Mahoney 2000 and Mahoney *et al.* 2006). Those mechanisms can be functional or mechanisms of power and legitimacy. As was mentioned above, private policing reflects the prevalence of functional mechanisms.

The adoption of an explanatory model based on explanatory mechanisms requires a heuristic definition of the concept. The heuristic key point is the possibility of bringing explanatory mechanisms and real mechanisms closer (Demetriou 2009). Tilly (2001a) argues that the logic of the explanatory mechanisms approach is that explaining the moment of origin of a phenomenon is the same as explaining how the phenomenon is produced and how it affects the outcome of interest. The link between the reproduction and the persistence of a phenomenon lies on the accumulation and duration of its effects. Tilly argues that "mechanisms form a delimited class of events that change relations among specified sets of elements in identical or closely similar ways over a variety of situations" (Tilly and Goodin 2006: 15). This argument is based on an outcome-driven definition of mechanisms that conceives mechanisms as moving to a lower level of aggregation to establish the micro-foundations and the macro effects in political science (Tilly 2001a: 24 and 2008). Explanatory mechanisms arguments seek to find the continuity and dynamism necessary to adapt the outcome to changes in context (Tilly and Goodin 2006). To reach this it is necessary to highlight that, on the one hand, mechanisms are constituted by a limited class of events that have the possibility to change relations between specific sets of elements and, on the other, they occur in similar or identical way in a diversity of situations (Tilly 2001a: 25).

With the aim to bring close explanatory mechanisms and real mechanisms, some authors from a realistic approach propose that the definition of mechanisms is the concatenation of (pertinent) outcomes (Demetriou 2009). In these terms, the mechanism is not an outcome itself but it is the way in which the outcome is combined with other outcomes to account for an explanation. That combination is what constitutes the explanation provided by a mechanism. The heuristic dimension of explanatory mechanisms lies in the diversity of concatenations of outcomes that constitutes a mechanism.

The interaction, combination, and sequencing of mechanisms allows for an observation of the process (Tilly and Goodin 2006: 15). This study addresses the proliferation of private security as the result of a process that involves a set of fundamentally political mechanisms. As an example, Tilly and Goodin (2006) argue that the subordination of the armed forces to civil control was a fundamental mechanism of the state transformation process (Tilly and Goodin 2006: 423). This process is centred on the historical possession of coercive mechanisms for the exercise of political authority. The way in which this coercive concentration process has developed has varied in history. One of the main expressions of this process is the hiring of private agents to carry out war, in other words policing activities. In any case, the mechanism that Tilly and Goodin seek to exemplify is the control over military organizations and it shows how different state transformations can be related to context and history (Tilly and Goodin 2006: 424). However this model explain the parallel existence of private policing in the state formation process, the role and the function that private armed actors had in the state formation process could be contextual and historically different in each region and different are also its outcomes (Davis and Pereira 2003).

3.4 The Self-Reproducing Sequence of Private Security in Guatemala

This is a combination of the above described constitutive elements of path dependence and based on that, this study propose the following empirical argumentative structure to analyse private security proliferation in post-war Guatemala.

A set of initial conditions characterized by a period of state transformations during the decade of 1944-1954 was necessary to generate political and institutional options that competed against dictatorial trajectories. Until then, formal policing institutions were centred on dictatorial social control tasks. Parallel to this, informal civil collaborations were interconnected through informal private policing mechanisms. During this decade there were institutional reforms aimed at modernizing formal policing institutions. However, in 1954 a critical juncture ended the state transformation process and allowed for the emergence of competitive political options (traditional dictatorial policing versus modern police institutions). This critical situation resulted in the selection of an institutional arrangement that reintroduced social control mechanisms in order to stabilize the political order. Some of those social control mechanisms become commercial private security services. The result of the selected institutional pattern was the displacement of some public security functions to private policing, while formal policing institutions were directed to become part of the counterinsurgent strategy during the internal armed conflict with the support of national and international actors. A set of contingent events such as police reform and the creation of new security forces made possible the emergence of private policing inside public institutions. The continuity of social control mechanisms, both formal and informal, such as the *Patrullas de Autodensa* Civil (PAC) and the network of Military Commissioners and the existence of an intense internal armed conflict interacted in the social system to reintroduce private policing as a complementary mechanism of state public security functions in the form of vigilante groups of self-defence. During the transition to democracy, the security sector reforms were implemented that involved the transformation of formal public policing institutions. This reform did not include the control or effective dissolution of private policing organizations created during the internal conflict. These elements in the context of an increased post-war criminality reinforced commercial private security and the implementation of community policing programmes, in other words, the proliferation of private security. In brief, the set of initial conditions is a necessary causes to start a self-reproducing sequence of causal mechanisms that together explains the proliferation of private security as a result of the reinforcing of the institutional pattern of public security displacement.

4. Private Security Companies in Guatemala

Before I will analyse non-commercial private security in the following chapter, the main findings of this section should be shortly summarised and underscored. Summed up, the chapter made clear that private security has to be analysed as a set of private policing actions that result from political and social processes that share a historical trajectory linked with context. Before explaining the trajectories of private security in Guatemala, this chapter describes the current state of commercial private security companies in the country as well as their relation to crime rates. This description aims to explain why private security should be understood as a current outcome of institutional trajectories that has to be explained in socio-historic terms.

Commercial private security grew in a context in which the institutional priorities were related to national security and not to control the proliferation of non-state armed actors operating to produce public security. The historical perspective allows to observe that the current state of institutional controls over Private Security Companies, PSCs, is the product of the long trajectory of autonomy of the private sector. The historical link between PSCs and political processes explain the differences inside the commercial private security sector. Thus the different actors (former police officers and militaries, international security advisors and civil entrepreneurs) that compose the actual private security spectrum are related with the different political phases of the internal conflict and the post-war transformations.

While most bibliography analysed previously explain the proliferation of private security from the perspective of crime rates and institutional capabilities, this chapter shows that on the one hand, crime rates increased after the private sector had the control of some areas of the public security institutions and on the other hand, however the strong link between public and private security services during the post-war, crime rates did not decrease.

4.1 Quantification and Informal Mechanisms

One of the main problems in analysing PSCs in Guatemala is the lack of quantitative data. There is no precise knowledge about the number of active PSCs, hired personnel, firearms, and operations, among others. Official sources present different data because they consider different aspects of a PSC. There are no public institutions that exercise effective control over PSCs and there is no precise definition of a PSC in order to define the aspects that each institution would have to control. Aside from the problem of quantification, the study of different sources allows the identification of a variety of informal mechanisms to create, operate and evade controls, taxes and other legal obligations. The existence of a set of informal mechanisms of functioning is possible through the existence of a strong link between private and public security services.

Secondary bibliography cannot offer precise data and what data they include is not current. There are three studies that address PSCs in Guatemala and only one study that address PSCs from a Central American regional perspective. The first of them was published by the United Nations Verification Mission – MINUGUA – in 2002 and analyses PSCs from a legal perspective. This study reported the existence of 86 PSCs in 1999 and estimated that in the year 2000 there would be 90 authorized PSCs. It also reported the existence of 63 PSCs applying for authorization and 50 PSCs that were operating without any authorization at all (Minugua 2002: 101). Ana Glenda Táger and Mario Mérida prepared a second study in 2002. This study provides some explanatory elements about PSCs in Guatemala. It reports 170 active PSCs, of which only 82 were registered officially; another 45 were applying for authorization and approximately 25 PSCs operated without authorization (Táger and Mérida 2002: 103). The Human Rights Coalition Against Clandestine Structures (CDDHHCEC 2004) prepared the third study. This study addresses PSCs from a legal perspective as well and is basically a description of the existing laws related to PSCs and the different bills that have been presented for consideration in the National Congress; however, it contains no valuable data on PSCs. Finally, a study prepared by the Arias Foundation addresses PSCs from a Central American perspective. This study includes data from the Federation of Guilds and Associations of Security (FEGRASE) and the National Civil Police (PNC). It states that there are 81 authorized PSCs. According to FEGRASE, 30 PSCs were applying for authorization but according to the PNC there were 53. For FEGRASE, the PSCs without authorization to operate or that were applying for authorization added up to 80, but the PNC claimed there were only 20 (Fundación Arias 2003: 113). There is an average difference of 10 authorized PSCs in the three studies, that is, 20 PSCs applying for authorization and 30 PSCs without authorization or application. The variation in the data among the different studies during the period 1999-2003 exemplifies the difficulty of specifying the number of PSCs. In addition, it reflects the confused nature of controls on PSCs and the challenge of research based on primary sources.

This study uses diverse official sources in order to bring together empirical data about the number of PSCs and to explain the problems of quantification. Furthermore, this problem actually benefits PSCs, both those that operate illegally and those that are undergoing an authorization process. This study is based on the idea that the illegal condition of PSCs is relative and depends on the kind of institution from which PSCs are controlled. In Guatemala one PSC can be registered as a security company to pay taxes but at the same time the Ministry of Interior does not authorize it. To avoid the wide range of possibilities that the institutional framework may produce, this study quantifies PSCs in Guatemala on the basis of the public offer of security services. This means that the PSC is active, functional and present in society and operates publicly regardless of whether it is authorized to do so or is applying for authorization or has neither. These conditions have no impact on whether the social function of private security is implemented or not.

Based on the above criteria, this study explores three different sources namely the Ministry of Interior, advertising media and the *Superintendencia de Administración Tributaria* (SAT), the state's main tax office to estimate the number of PSCs. By comparing these sources, a more accurate idea of the scope of commercial private security in Guatemala comes into view. The first source is the data on authorized PSCs provided by the Ministry of Interior. This Ministry is responsible for authorizing and controlling security capabilities of PSCs, for example, the number of hired and active guards, the security services they provide, the stock of firearms, and the organization of the companies. The official data of this Ministry indicates that until October 2010 there were 147 authorized PSCs.[31] This ministry began to register PSCs during the 1960s. At that time, it included commercial forms of private policing that existed before the law of 1970 that created the legal concept of PSC. From 1970 onwards, the Ministry no longer registered informal commercial private policing. Informal commercial private policing companies are required to apply for authorization but the existing law does not forbid their operation without having authorization. On the other hand, the Ministry is required to control only authorized PSCs, thus making possible the operation of PSCs without controls. The number of PSCs operating in this form is difficult to establish. They are called "illegal" PSCs or "ghost" PSCs. For this research, it is important to note that they are not illegal because they are legally registered as companies in order to pay taxes and they are not "ghost" either because they have a public existence and offer security services.

The second source was put together to calculate the number of companies that applied for authorization to operate and those that did not, i.e. the number of PSCs that the official records do not show. A survey of three different advertising media showed the companies that offer security services but are not included

31 Data provided by the *Sub-Dirección Administrativa del Ministerio de Gobernación de Guatemala*.

in official records.[32] The search was conducted around items related to security services, such as private security, industrial security, security service and consulting, surveillance services, and protection services. In this manner, 101 PSCs offering private security services were identified. It was discovered also that one authorization certificate is used by more than one company. In these cases, one of the companies was considered duly authorized and the others as not authorized because this mechanism is considered illegal by the existing laws. This mechanism is called "coverage" (*cobertura*) and is recognized as a common practice in the private security sector (Álvaro Hernández, Security Advisory of the PNC, 03/12/09) For example, under authorization 1666-07 three PSCs offer security services: *Grupo Técnicas Integradas de Protección y Seguridad* (TIPS), *Máximo Control, and Grupo* SEIRH S.A. A similar situation applies to *Agencia de Seguridad Israeli* (ASI) which functions together with *Sistemas Integrales de Seguridad Centinela* and *Monitoreo* Non-Stop under the same authorization number 094-98.

The grouping of more than one PSC under one authorization can be explained variously. On the one hand, one company creates new companies to diversify its services but avoids the bureaucratic process of authorizing the new ones, which involves investments of time and money that the mother company is not willing to make. On the other hand, a company might downsize by splitting up in order to reduce taxes. At the same time, by dividing the company there are fewer controls over labour obligations such as medical insurance and other employee benefits. Another situation along these lines occurs when a company cannot comply with the formalities to be authorized and pays another company to cover for it. This covering strategy is a factor that explains the massive emergence of non-authorized PSCs during the 1990s (Interview with Álvaro Hernández, Security Advisory PNC, 12/03/09).

When taken together, the data from the Ministry of Interior on authorized PSCs and the information on non-authorized PSCs suggests a total of 248 PSCs operating in Guatemala. The analysis of other official data supports this estimate of the number of PSCs. The *Registro Mercantil* of Guatemala is the government institution that records all companies irrespective of the services they provide. This institution reported 189 companies registered to deliver security services.[33] The *Registro Mercantil* is only required to keep records of registered companies

32 The survey was conducted in three publicity Web pages from Guatemala. These Web pages group the companies by type of service offered in the country: http://www.masdetodos.com/quicksearch.php,http://www.paginasamarillas.com/seg seguridadprivada/Guatemala/1_2.aspx;http://www.guialocal.com.gt/Guatemala_gu atemala/tag/seguridad-privada.

33 Data provided by *Registro Mercantíl de Guatemala.*

but not to control them. Once created and registered, the companies can offer different services under their original registry. There are companies registered as cleaning companies but they also offer security services. This is a common situation for those companies registered as communication or technology companies that offer private security services including GPS monitoring, CCTV, alarm systems, polygraph tests, private investigations, and complementarily armed guards. Because the law does not define clearly what is understood by "private security" and its scope, it is even possible for an individual to offer private security by hiring other people. An example of this situation is the PSC "Edwin Manuel Valiente Barahona" or "Dilma Schomer Ortiz".[34] These are private individuals who offer private security services. The first of them is a known former police officer active during the internal conflict in Guatemala that will be analysed in later..

Some companies create their own security service in order to avoid hiring external security companies or be subject to institutional controls. Later, the company begins to offer security services in the market while conserving its original name. This is the case of the *Banco de los Trabajadores, Telgua*, and *Hulera de Exportación* among other companies and institutions that offers private security in the market. This is a practice that started in the 1970s when informal private policing organizations were created to deliver security within companies, institutions, and farms.[35] The first reported company that created a security service is the *Vigilancia de la Urbanización Likin* (AVELIKIN) in 1970 (AHPN 1982/doc2776733). This was a housing project that created a policing group to guard its properties.

Finally, a third source consulted is the Superintendencia de Administración Tributaria (SAT), the state's main tax office. In 2001, the SAT reported 144 companies that were taxed as PSCs; by 2008 the number had risen to 289.[36] During the last ten years this institutions has been strengthened in order to improve tax collection mechanisms. Most PSCs offering security services without authorization are small or medium companies with less than 400 employees. For these entrepreneurs, it is more important to have their tax records in order than authorization to operate because the SAT has stronger control mechanisms. Having tax records in order does not prevent tax evasion by PSCs. Figure 1 underlines two important aspects. First, there are important differences among the institu-

34 More information about these companies http://www.masdetodos.com /quicksearch.php; http://www.paginasamarillas.com/seguridad-privada/Guatemala/1_2.aspx; http://www.guialocal.com.gt/guatemala_guatemala/tag/seguridad-privada.

35 http://www.masdetodos.com/quicksearch.php; http://www.paginasamarillas.com/seguridad-privada/Guatemala/1_2.aspx; http://www.guialocal.com.gt/Gua temala_guatemala/tag/seguridad-privada.

36 Data provided by the Direction of Institutional Planning and Development of the SAT.

tions responsible for controlling PSCs. The Ministry of Interior is less able to keep records of PSCs; there are only 147 PSCs on its records. On the other hand, the SAT has more PSCs registered which means more tax control than security and quality controls. Companies that are illegal for the Ministry of Interior for security matters are legal for the SAT for tax matters. Companies that do not possess a ministerial authorization do have tax documentation to operate as a company and they does not need to record the company as a PSC. The second aspect that stands out is that despite of the fact that the number of registered companies has increased, the taxes paid by the companies have decreased as a percentage of GDP. There are different factors that explain this phenomenon, namely the size of the companies, the way their personnel is hired, the tax revenue mechanisms, and tax evasion, among others. My interest is to show how the variety of mechanisms to create PSCs and the weak institutional capabilities to control them can be strong factors that explain the low tax revenue. Tax evasion contributes to the high profitability of private security businesses and for this reason Guatemala is considered a "paradise of non-regulated PSCs" (*Prensa Libre* 10/10/04).

The SAT Director of Institutional Planning and Development explains that PSCs are taxed depending on the kind of economic activity the companies have. This refers to the fact that, for tax reasons, companies can be registered as a cleaning and repair service company and offer security services on the side, for example. They are not legally required to specify the services they offer. Another strategy to evade taxes is to hire security personnel as free-lancers. Under this arrangement, free-lancers have to pay taxes directly to the State by declaring their income every month, thereby allowing the company to pay less tax and not worry about social security payments. In this manner, free-lancers lose their social security guarantees because this kind of contract does not require the company to have a permanent employment relationship. Often, people working in security companies do not have the necessary educational level to manage the complicated tax documentation by themselves. In these cases, the security companies manages the employee's tax records and can declare less tax to be paid. In addition, if the employee is dismissed, the company may keep the tax file active to use it to cover up other illegal activities, for example the purchase of guns and ammunition (Interview with Manfredo Chocano, Director of Institutional Planning and Development, SAT, 02/19/09).

Figure 1: Number of PSCs and Tax Revenue From PSCs As Percentage of the GDP

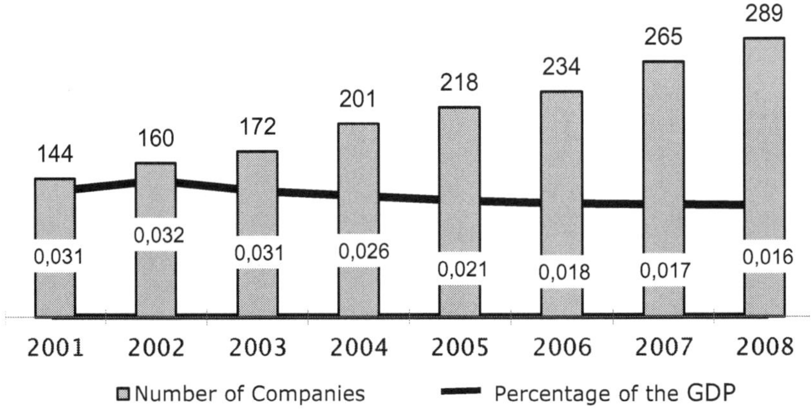

Source: Own elaboration with data provided by SAT. The percentage of the GDP was calculated using the GDP deflactor of 2001 to adjust the tax revenue to the inflation index.[37]

An analysis of the data provided by these different sources provides not only an estimate of the number of active PSCs but also the institutional nature of government controls as well as the different informal mechanisms used by PSCs to operate evading controls. Based on the three sources (Ministry of Interior, *Registro Mercantíl*, SAT and Internet advertising), it is possible to conclude that there are 147 active PSCs that are authorized plus 101 PSCs without authorization. The total cited in this study is 284 PSCs operating in the country.[38]

The number of authorized agents in 2004 was 60,000 but when the 99 companies pending authorization are taken into account, the number of agents has been estimated at 106,700 (UNDP 2010a). According to data of the Chamber of Guatemalan Security, the commercial private security sector generates 136,500 jobs, including administrative and operative personnel.[39] This numbers differs consid-

37 The fiscal deficit in 2008 corresponded to the 1.6 of the GDP. http://www.banguat.gob.gt/ inc/main.asp?id=36512&aud=1&lang=1. The average inflation in 2008 was 11.35%. http://www.banguat.gob.gt/inc/ver.asp?id=/imm/imm01&e=570.

38 The number of PSCs varies depending on controls and regulations. For example in Costa Rica where there are better controls and regulations the number of PSCs is on 664. On the contrary, in Honduras where the controls and legislations are similar as in Guatemala, there are almost 200 PSCs; in El Salvador the number is on 192 while in Nicaragua there are 98 PSCs (Godnick 2009).

39 Data provided by the Chamber of Guatemalan Security 2009.

erably from official data that puts the total at 36,728 authorized agents, a number which represents a monthly average based on reports of 101 PSCs (Interview with Álvaro Hernández, Security Advisory of the PNC, 03/12/09). Figuring out an estimate is difficult for different reasons such as the existence of non-authorized PSCs for which there are no records of personnel and the high level of personnel rotation. One estimate suggests that there are 98 PSCs applying for authorization with 8,134 agents and another 31 "ghost" PSCs with approximately 2,230 agents (Interview with Álvaro Hernández, Security Advisory of the PNC, 03/12/09). In addition, 101 authorized PSCs reported 27,839 firearms in their possession.

Table 1: PNCs and PSCs Agents Indicators 2007

Inhabitants	**13.018,000**
Total officers PNC	20,300
Total guards PSCs	106,700
PNC officers per 100 thousandinhabitants	1,56
PSC guards per 100 thousand inhabitants	8,19
Inhabitants per Km2	119,55
PNC officers per Km2	0,19
PSC guards per Km2	0,98
Inhabitants per PNC officer	641
Inhabitants per PSC guard	122

Source: Own elaboration with data from ENCOVI 2006 and UNDP 2010a.

The differences in the data reflect the uncontrolled situation of commercial private security personnel. If the higher number of private security personnel provided by the Chamber of Guatemalan Security is accepted, it would be five times higher than the total number of police officers in 2007 (when there were 36,000 police and military personnel in service). Police data indicates that there were 20,300 officers, of whom 4,000 were assigned to administrative duties; the rest were divided into two shifts of 24 hours to patrol the streets. Therefore, only 8,150 police officers were available on a day-by-day basis to bring public security to a population of 13 million Guatemalans (one police official for 1,595 inhabitants).[40]

40 As comparison in Costa Rica are 350 inhabitants for each police officer, in El Salvador 332, Nicaragua 557, Panama 195, Haiti 1,889 (UNDP 2010a: 232).

The previous numbers provide a comparative dimension of public and private security in Guatemala. The number of active PNC officers might, in fact, be lower due to constant personnel reduction as a result of programmes of police reform, including the dismissal of corrupt officers. On the other hand, the number of private security agents might be higher.

"Ghost" PSCs

As was mentioned above, the legal or illegal status of PSCs depends on the public institution that determines the absence of a particular requirement. The category of "ghost" PSCs is a media term to denounce the absence of controls by the Ministry of Interior. In fact, these companies offer their services in the public sphere without restrictions. However, their existence reflects not only a problem of governmental controls but also the power struggles within the commercial private sector and the existence of different informal mechanisms to operate outside legal obligations.

From 1970 to 1996, the problem posed by non-authorized PSCs was insignificant. There were only 36 PSCs until 1996. Most of those PSCs were founded by active police officers that exercised control over the authorization process. They were also part of the counterinsurgent strategy by providing information for the army and offering public security to fulfil the security vacuum created by the excessive concentration of public institutions in national security. After the demobilization process, retired police and army personnel gravitated to the PSCs as the most attractive employment option. This produced a glut of private security personnel that endangered the monopoly over commercial private security exercised by former police officers. By blocking the authorization of the post-war PSCs, the result was the emergence of a large sector of non-authorized PSCs fundamentally owned by former military officers. This issue will be expanded upon in the next section of this study.

In spite of the historical trajectories of private security, the discourse of PSCs owners blames the state for the proliferation of illegal PSCs. From the perspective of owners of authorized PSCs, the emergence of non-authorized PSCs is attributed, on the one hand, to the excessive requirements of the Ministry of Interior and, on the other, to rampant corruption. Due to the high demand of private security and the considerable profitability of this commercial activity, the authorization process is both slowed by a powerful sector that controls the institution that extends authorization and complicated in order to require extra payments. For most non-authorized PSC it is better to operate without authorization in order to avoid state controls (Interview with Byron Heredia, President of COSEHOGUA, 02/24/09).

PSCs owners argue that "ghost" PSCs have discredited the old group of PSCs by offering lower prices and providing lower quality services because they pay low salaries and by promoting criminality and corruption within the private sector. They argue that "ghost" companies adapt their services to the needs of the client and not to quality standards (Interview with Jorge Sierra, Grupo Almo, 03/02/09).

For Carlos Maldonado, founder of El *Ebano* in the 1970s and president of the Chamber of Guatemalan Security, the illegality of PSCs is a problem for the authorized PSCs and for the state because it reproduces an idea of private security as an illegal and dangerous activity. He argues that the proliferation of illegal PSCs is caused by the state because the authorization process is flawed. The illegal PSCs stimulate a negative impression among clientele that grows increasingly and that undermined the prospects of the group of authorized PSCs (Interview with Carlos Maldonado 03/10/09).

Most non-authorized PSCs are part of the informal economy in Guatemala. The tolerance towards the informal sector is a reflection of its importance in the overall economy and explains in part the proliferation of PSCs free of state controls.[41] At the same time, labour conditions in both authorized and non-authorized PSCs are defined by the prevalence of informal employment and also by high levels of underemployment.[42] Thus, "ghost" PSCs can be explained in the context of generally depressed labour costs in Guatemala, especially in the predominance of salaries below the official minimum.[43]

The existence of this large informal private security sector reproduces not only an economical dimension of informality but also a socio-political dimension of informal rules[44]. Informal rules are imposed in order to reproduce an institutional pattern that allows the operation of private security in the social system. During the 1990s, informal rules were the mechanisms through which the PSCs founded during the war and the post-war years coexisted and were mutually reinforced. Regardless of the control over the authorization process by the old PSCs

41 During the period 1999-2000 the informal economy in Guatemala represented the 51,5% del GNP. World Bank data Washington D.C. 2002. The informal economy constituted the 75% of the employed population in 2000 and the 71.3% in 2006. The informal sector contributes to the national economy because people employed in the informal sector pay direct taxes (UNDP 2010b).

42 The percentage of underemployed people in Guatemala respect to the total of employed people was 8.4% in 2000 year and 15.2% in 2005 (UNDP 2010b).

43 In year 2000 the 23.3% of the total employed population became less than the official minimum salary. In 2005 it was the 50.1%. In 2000 the 89.1% of the employed population became less than the value of the basic market basket and in 2005 it was the 87% of the employed population (UNDP 2010b).

44 About informal rules see Helmke and Levitsky 2006; O'Donnel 1996, 1997, 2002 and 2004; Lauth 2000; Gel'man 2004.

that attempted to limit the number of new PSCs, informal rules, on the one hand, allowed the private security sector to absorb a large number of former military and police officers and, on the other hand, made possible the coexistence and equilibrium of a growth sector dominated by its own rules. Both sides of the commercial private security sector are competitive but not exclusionary. Commercial private security reflects the dominance of informal rules in the field of security operations as well and this is characterized by secrecy and impunity. Under these terms, the "ghost" characteristic of PSCs should be analysed under the concept of informal private policing activities in which the important element is the trajectory that ends in a functional institutional pattern. These aspects will be analysed in the next section of this study.

Spending on Commercial Private Security

An analysis of spending on commercial private security shows how resources have been displaced from the state, industries, and families to the private security sector. The amount spent in Guatemala on private security in 2005 was 574.3 million dollars (1.8 per cent of GDP) (UNDP 2006).[45] Of this total, family homes spent 29.4% and private companies made up the rest. On the other side, public institutions also spend on private security companies for public buildings such as museums, libraries, hospitals, and ministries and also in public transportation and ports among others.[46] This spending transforms public spaces and collective life; in fact, it is quiet evident the expansion of alarm systems, security walls, lighting, and checkpoints, among others.

Hiring PSCs constitutes the largest category of private spending because they offers a variety of services adapted to the incomes of the clients. During 2005 a total of 5,250 companies invested US$346.4 million dollars in hiring private guards. This amount represents 92% of the total spent on security by companies (UNDP 2006: 39). The remaining 8% went to security measures involving other type of companies such as insurance services. The impact on productivity generated by spending on private security is approximately US$500 million (UNDP 2006: 92). According to a report of UNODC (2007), Guatemala was at the top of the global list of countries that confirmed that crime is a serious obstacle to in-

45 There is no reliable information about following years. Different studies show that Latin American countries invest between eight and twenty five percent of the GDP in private security. In Brazil the invest in private security was calculated on 1,54 percent of the GDP; in Chile in 2005 it was invested the 0.63 percent of the GDP in private security; in El Salvador in 2003 the invest in private security was on 2,8 percent of the GDP (Arias 2009; UNDP 2010a).

46 There are no available data about this spends.

vestment. And 80% of 445 companies surveyed identified corruption as an important obstacle to commercial activities in the country (UNODC 2006: 19). This data reinforces the idea that the private sector does not trust public institutions.

Figure 2: Private Security Services Hired by Companies and Industries, 2005

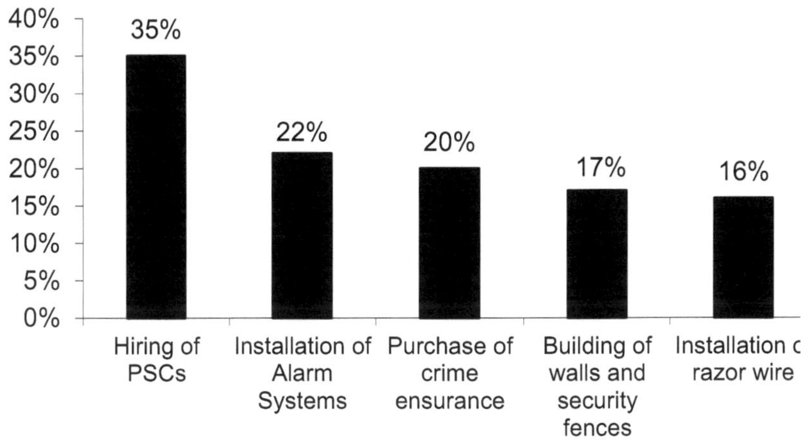

Source: UNDP 2006.

A survey conducted by the Chamber of Commerce of Guatemala of over 1,228 companies in July 2010 showed that 30.1% of the companies hired guard services from a PSC and that 48% hired alarm systems and razor ribbon. At the same time, the study showed that spending on private security and the context of insecurity decreases sales and consequently the competitiveness of the commercial sector in the country. Just fewer than 79% of the surveyed companies said that sales had decreased and 81.1% considered that the insecurity situation in the country affected them more than the global financial crisis (*El Periódico* 07/22/10).

By comparing spending by companies and homes on private security with the government's budget for security, it is quiet evident the displacement process of public security to the private sphere. The total public investment on security is divided between defence (army) and public security (police). The official budget for public security is allocated to the Ministry of the Interior, which is also entrusted with other functions that are not related to public security, such as the government's journal, the public lotteries, and ID documents for the population. The budget assigned to public security in 2005 was US$234.6 million dollars.[47] It was not until 1999 that the internal security budget exceeded the military defence budget and, even so, the tendency was irregular: in 2004 the spending on Defence was drastically reduced due to downsizing of the Army.

Figure 3: Public Spending on Internal Security and Defence (in millions of Quetzales)

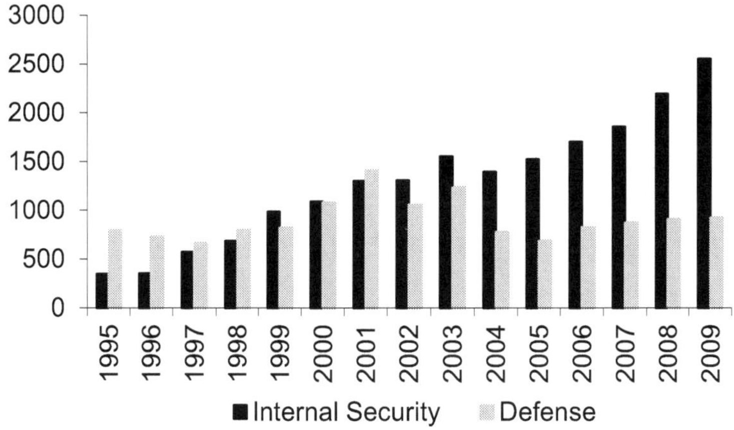

Source: Author's calculation with data from the Ministry of Finance of Guatemala.

The budget allocations for internal security never covered the needs of institutions like the National Civil Police, the penal system, and civil intelligence. The available data show that in 2005 private security spending exceeded the budgets of the Ministry of Interior and the Ministry of Defence.

The comparison between public security budgets and spending on private security provides an objective description of the general economic dimension of private security. Due to the lack of oversight of PSCs, the available data provides only a general description of the situation. It is not possible to calculate the total income of PSCs because there is no oversight of non-authorized PSCs. The available data does suggest, on the one hand, an upward tendency in spending on private security and, on the other, a low level of spending on public security by the state.

47 According to the exchange rate of 2005, available on http://www.banguat.gob.gt /cambio/historico.asp?kmoneda=02&ktipo=5&kdia=01&kmes=01&kanio=2005&kdia1=01&kmes1=12&kanio1=2005&submit1=Consultar.

Figure 4: Ministries Budgets and Spending on Private Security in 2005 (in millions of US Dollars)

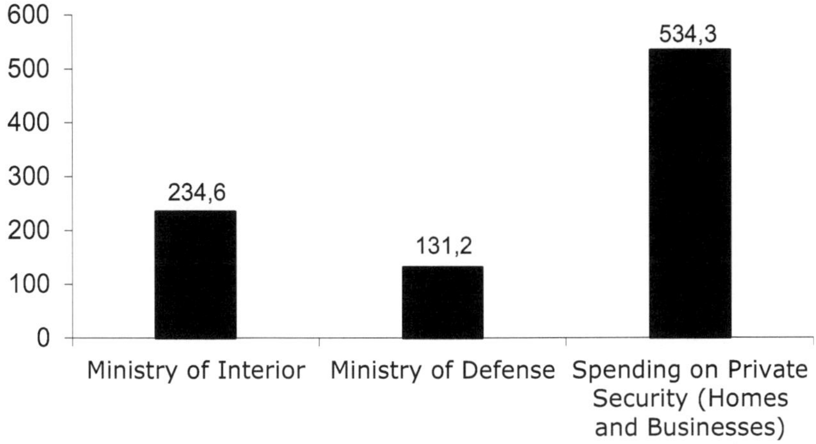

Source: Author's design with data from De León-Escribano and Sagone 2004; UNDP 2006.[48]

4.2 Recruiting and Professionalization

The current legislation on PSCs defines four types of private security agents: watchmen (*vigilantes*) who are not allowed to carry firearms; guards that are allowed to carry firearms; private bodyguards; and private investigators that are allowed to carry firearms as well. However, this classification is at variance with the services offered by PSCs, which often operate beyond the bounds of the law.

From the perspective of the PSCs, there are two different types of guards. The first type is the regular guard with a shotgun who has no experience in security issues and weapons handling. This kind of guard (*guardianía*) has a lower cost and operates much like a watchman. The *guardianía* (or security guard post) is a service widely used by the population. It provides protection of property and life. The man with the large shotgun displaces crime to areas with no guards. This is a deterrence function more than a preventive one. The use of shotguns and rifles has only a demonstration effect in the same way as the presence of military personnel in the streets. The legal and professional restrictions on these types of

48 The currency exchange in 2005 was 7.57 Quetzales for one US Dollar. Information available at http://www.banguat.gob.gt/inc/buscar.asp?query=bcos.

guards limit them to preventive security actions (Interview with Carlos Quintanilla, Owner of SERPROP, 03/17/09).

If the client wants to hire a guard with weapons experience, he must pay for training offered by the same security company. Otherwise, a "VIP" guard generally is a former military officer with full training in security and weapons handling and is the most expensive of all. As a result, "VIP" guards are the minority; the normal guard service is the most common (Interview with Jorge Sierra, Grupo *Almo*, 03/02/09).

The diversity of types of guards is linked to the wide range of services PSCs offer and their adaptability to a changing market. PSCs evolved from an offer of guards inspired by military models to more sophisticated surveillance services. For example, the *Ébano* Group started operations at the beginning of the 1970s as a private security service for the banking sector in response to a wave of bank robberies. This company employed National Police officers, paid their salaries directly to the police chief and gave them company uniforms. Since its foundation, *Ébano* diversified its activities creating different companies for each security area: PROVAL for transportation of high value goods and TRANSVAL for less valuable items. It also has another company that specializes in electronic alarms (*Alarmas de Guatemala* – ADG) and another for monitoring and geopositioning (*Linker Monitoreo*). Other *Ébano* subsidiaries offer private investigation services, consulting in property protection, and rescue operations of people and goods (Interview with Jorge Sierra, Grupo Almo*,* 03/02/09). Police officers and investigators from the Public Ministry[49] work informally in all of these services (Interview with Rodolfo Muñoz Piloña, Owner of the Unidad de Servicios Integrales de Seguridad, 03/17/09).

Ébano offers different types of agents and different prices. The "normal" guard is one who is posted at the access to a neighbourhood, at a shop or a warehouse. This kind of guard has no security or firearms training but he is armed with a pistol or shotgun. Another kind of agent is the so-called "route" guard, who has the same qualification as the "normal" guard but differs in that he guards goods that are transported from one point to another. And still another category is the "chauffeur" guard, with similar qualification but who accompanies the driver when he has to get out of the vehicle (while the "route" guard stays inside). These three types of guards are not differentiated by their professional skills but only by the post they hold. These sectioned security mechanisms are the result of the displacement of crime that the very PSCs produce. Once a section of the business chain is protected, criminality moves on to those which are still unprotected. This then opens a new market opportunity for the PSCs as

49 The Public Ministry is the institutions responsible of the criminal investigation and prosecution in Guatemala.

new security concerns need to be addressed and so on. The clients for these services are mainly shops, industries, neighbourhoods, and public institutions (Interview with Jorge Sierra, Grupo Almo, 03/02/09).

Due to the absence of effective controls over this segmented chain of services, there is a high level of participation by private guards in criminal activities. This problem is only managed by the PSCs but not overcome. The mechanism employed is the rotation of agents, that is, the relocation of suspected guards to new posts. A guard who is suspect has to pass a polygraph test. If he does not pass, he is dismissed but the PSC makes no legal charges. Dismissed guards usually find a new job at another PSC. *Ébano* estimates that private security guards commit 80% of robberies inside companies (Interview with Jorge Sierra, Grupo Almo, 03/02/09).

As mentioned above, another category of guard is the "VIP" or personal guard. This agent has military experience and extensive security training to defend the life of his client. VIP guards are not hired for long by PSCs because once the guard has gained the confidence of his client he ends up being hired directly. Clients for this kind of guard are business managers and government officials. The normal contract is for a given number of hours per day and the salary is approximately US$ 1,000 per month.[50] This arrangement for VIP guards represents about 65% of all VIP guard contracts (Interview with Jorge Sierra, Grupo Almo, 03/02/09).

The diversification of criminal activities creates demands for new security services and thus expands the market. At the same time, a segmented security strategy displaces crime to other non-protected areas. This is the basis for arguing that PSCs contribute to increased crime because their services are reactive and end up displacing crime. PSCs are not conceived to prevent crime but to dissuade; they are not preventive but reactive. The displacement of crime is the basis for the profitability of PSCs because it opens up new markets (Interview with Rodolfo Muñoz Piloña, Owner of the Unidad de Servicios Integrales de Seguridad, 03/17/09).

A marketing study conducted by one of these security companies showed that 89% of the authorized PSCs offer guard services and 26% offer electronic security systems and guards. Nonetheless, 69% of the companies that were studied do not have records of their operations and guard personnel (Interview with Jorge Sierra, Grupo Almo, 03/02/09).

There are two reasons for this; one is that some of the companies are illegal and the other is that some companies started out with no security services and then guard services were added. Because electronic security and investigation

50 The average salary of policemen in Guatemala is US$ 200.

services are offered under the cover of other companies, they are not defined as security services and therefore not controlled.

Security companies offer design, installation, maintenance, production, and sale of security equipment. The companies also offer security services (investigation, recovery, pursuit) against crime detected by electronic systems. These three components – guards, electronic systems, and investigation – are the basis of profitability for the commercial private security sector. State institutions can control only the guards component.

The diversification of private security services, as well as the political processes of institutional change (such as the reduction of the army, the reform of the police, and the abolition of military conscription), have changed the socio-economic composition of the workforce in the commercial private security sector. The scarcity of former military personnel requires that PSCs look for workforce in the agricultural sector. Although there are no trained personnel in the agricultural sector, one advantage for the private security sector is that it can pay these individuals the minimum official salary. In other words, there is a reduction in costs by paying low salaries for untrained personnel. This leads to increasing profitability for PSCs but probably worsens the general situation of security in the country given the countless untrained agents carrying firearms and in need of additional incomes. As pointed out in her study about private security in the northern departments of Guatemala, Dickins (2001) shows how private security became a complement income for rural communities in which agriculture has been the main economical activity however the risks its represents for untrained persons (Dickins 2001).

The process for hiring an agent at *Ébano* can be described as follows (Interview with Jorge Sierra advisor of Grupo Almo, 03/02/09). The company sets up a stand in poor rural communities. Applicants must be between 18 and 25 years old. Selected applicants are then taken to the central offices in the city. First, the company does a background check (personal identification and police records), then runs medical and psychological tests as well as a polygraph test. The applicant must know how to read and write, speak Spanish and be at least 1.65 meters tall. The applicant often must complete the employment application with the help of administrative staff because of his limitations in education and language. Once the above requirements have been met, the applicant receives two days of training on access controls, laws, and weapons.

Both professional skills and minimum age requirements for guards are two important reasons that explain the delay in reforming the law that regulates PSCs, which has been discussed in Congress for more than ten years. PSCs owners reject these reforms when arguing that existing controls are sufficient and that the minimum age to carry weapons must be 18 years (the legal minimum today is 25 years.) In addition, they reject the minimum wage set for guards. A normal guard earns 1,000 Quetzales a month (US$130 approximately) for a ten-hour day (*Prensa Libre* 05/15/06). PSCs owners claim that the ideal agent is a person between 18 and 30 years of age, who is literate and has military training. Company owners further claim that it is increasingly difficult to find young people with military experience and "the mystic and discipline of the army" (*Prensa Libre* 10/10/04). Previously, many people with military experience were hired, but since the abolition of military conscription and the downsizing of the army, these kind of people are scarce. During the 1970s and 1980s, the army was the "training school of PSCs" (*Prensa Libre* 10/10/04).

The military strategy of using massive amounts of armed individuals was transferred to the private sector, which benefited by increasing profitability due to the payment of low salaries. The idea of the soldier who withstands any hardship in order to accomplish his task was adopted by PSCs as part of a twenty-four hour workday without breaks, with little protection against the weather, and low salaries, among others. With the aim of further reducing costs, PSCs require that guards cover areas that exceed the capacity of one individual. While PSCs use one guard to cover what should be done by two, the client pays an amount equivalent to two or more guards (Interview with Álvaro Hernández, Security Advisory of the PNC, 03/12/09). In some security areas where the presence of guards becomes a problem, such as internal vigilance, PSCs offers CCTV services and alarm systems (Interview with Álvaro Hernández, Security Advisory of the PNC, 03/12/09).

Although hiring employees from the agricultural sector is a low cost solution for PSCs, there are problems related to the nature of seasonal work in the agricultural sector. Peasants employed by PSCs work until the harvest season begins, when they resign and return to agricultural work.[51] The scarcity of workers results, on the one hand, in high employee turnover in PSCs and, on the other, a reduction in hiring standards by the companies (Dickins 2001).

PSCs avoid hiring people from the capital or other large cities because their needs are different and consequently they demand higher wages. For the private security entrepreneurs, the supposedly humble personality of the peasant allows for lower salaries and more effective control over them (Interview with Jorge Sierra, Grupo Almo, 03/02/09). On the other hand, peasants create problems for the companies because their cultural environment is quite different from the work environment in urban areas. One of the main expressions of these cultural differences is the racism among middle and upper class people that does not perceive in the peasant an image of security and protection (Interview with Carlos

51 Internal migration is seasonal and depends on the labour market in the agricultural sector.

Maldonado, President of the Guatemalan Chamber of Private Security Companies, 03/10/09).

The high levels of employee rotation make it more difficult to control PSCs and to protect the labour rights of their personnel. During February 2009, the *Golán* Group reported that 535 guards were dismissed and another 384 were hired at the same time. This particular PSC hires on a monthly average 2,935 agents. Due to agent rotation, there were 151 vacancies in one month that were covered by other agents who did double time (Interview with Álvaro Hernández, Security Advisory of the PNC, 03/12/ 09).

Local and Transnational Companies

Most of the security companies operating in Guatemala are local, meaning, they are registered in the country. A study conducted by the Chamber of Guatemalan Security shows that 64% of PSCs were founded in Guatemala and that 7% are transnational companies. About 29% of the PSCs are joint national and foreign capital ventures.[52] Companies of joint national and foreign ownership were usually set up in Guatemala and then they expanded to the rest of the region. Some examples are the following:

1. Corporate Security Consultants, Group CSC. This British company has operations in all countries of Central America. It was founded originally in Guatemala in 2000 but its authorization process was not completed until 2006. In 2003 it began operating in El Salvador, in 2004 in Honduras, in 2005 in Nicaragua, and in Costa Rica in 2006.
2. *Golán* Group is a PSC with national and international investors. Israeli security experts founded it in Guatemala in 1987. The central offices are in Florida, USA. The company has offices in Guatemala, El Salvador, Honduras and Israel.
3. Krypton is a PSC founded in Guatemala in 1990 but its authorization was not extended until 1997. This company has offices in all countries of Central America.
4. Segursa is a Salvadoran PSC with offices in Guatemala.
5. Serprop was founded in Guatemala in 1997. Currently the company is also present in El Salvador, Honduras, and Nicaragua.
6. Inter-con Security Systems was founded in 1973 in the US and started operations in Guatemala in 1997.

52 Marketing Study directed by Jorge Sierra, Cámara de Seguridad de Guatemala.

7. International Security Operations Group, Inc. (ISOG) was founded in Panama in 2003 and also operates in Guatemala. It is an investigation and security agency.
8. COMSI was founded in Guatemala in October 1997. This company started operations offering guards to protect the transportation of goods. A second office was opened in Tecún Umán, one of the main border crossings with Mexico. Through this crossing pass most of the products imported into Guatemala, El Salvador, and Nicaragua. Currently this PSC has 36 offices in the whole of the Central American corridor including Panama.
9. G4S-Wackenhut of Guatemala is the largest international PSC. It was founded in 1980. Currently it has more than 5,200 employees in Guatemala. The company has offices in all countries in Central America.

The fact that most international PSCs were originally established in Guatemala and then expanded to the rest of the Central American region reaffirms the argument that the historical displacement of public security to the private sphere allowed the emergence of a strong commercial private security sector capable of expanding in the region. There are only two companies which are wholly foreign owned (G4S founded in Copenhagen in 1901 and the British Group CSC); the rest are owned by local entrepreneurs or are mixed foreign and local ventures. The small number of transnational companies can only be differentiated from the rest by their name brand. Otherwise, they operate in the same manner as local companies. These companies abandoned international quality standards and reproduce the logic and mechanisms of the local private security market. As one executive put it, "without this rejection, the international companies could not compete in a market with his own rules" (Interview with Jorge Sierra, Grupo Almo 03/02/09). These informal rules are directly related to the situation of the records and controls undertaken by state institutions.

Security Consulting Companies: The Intermediate Category

Within the wide range of services offered by the private sector, the security consulting companies are located in a sort of limbo because they are not included within the legal definition and they are free of any institutional controls, although they are legally established. From a more general policing perspective, consulting companies are part of the private security sector but are located at a different strategic and logistic level.

These companies produce risk studies and intelligence analysis for industries. One of their services is to hire a PSC and control its activities. Some of these companies are grouped in accordance with the commercial and industrial area they serve. For example, the Guatemalan Hotel Security Council (COSEHOGUA) was founded in 1998 to strengthen the strategies implemented by security advisors in the hotel field. Security managers of the hotel sector study the hotel environment and the routes taken by tourist as well as the cooperative work with the community to generate information about risks and threats. The hotel security managers establish links with neighbourhood organization and seek to identify leaders in the community, as well as promoting confidence with the authorities (Interview with Byron Heredia, President of COSEHOGUA, 02/24/09). Hotel security managers often do not trust PSCs because they are aware of their inefficiency and lack of professional standards among their personnel as well as corruption in the private sector in general. These considerations reflect concerns about security risks for tourists because private guards do not have firearms training and their reactions in critical situations are unpredictable. In this context, the hotel sector opted to create its own security system that operates from inside hotels and is designed to protect the interests of the hotel and not to make an additional profit (Interview with Byron Heredia, President of COSEHOGUA, 02/24/09).

The existence of security systems with armed personnel inside companies and organizations lie outside of state controls because these are not constituted as PSCs. The administration of risk is a preventive model based on analysis of valid information about risks and threats related to a specific good, person, or activity that needs to be protected. International companies operating in Guatemala generally hire companies that offer these services. An example of a Guatemalan risk management company hired by international companies is *Empresas y Sistemas Internacionales* (EMSISA). This company is part of the Guatemalan-American Chamber of Commerce that groups the most important US companies in Guatemala including the US Embassy. EMSISA has operations in all Central American countries, as well as southern Mexico, Panama, Colombia, and the Caribbean. It was founded by a former US military officer who arrived in the country in 1987 as part of the US Embassy military team to advise the High Command of the National Defence of Guatemala. Upon his retirement, he founded EMSISA and was simultaneously the country manager for Inter-Con Security Systems, an international PSC with operations in Guatemala since 1997. Currently EMSISA employs a team of former Guatemalan military officers and international advisors (Interview with Edgar Herrera, Security Advisor of EMSISA, 03/23/09).[53]

Consulting security companies recommend the creation of the post of security manager inside the industry or organization they advise. This person will be responsible for the administration of security measures including the hiring of a

53 For more information about this company see http://www.emsisa-consulting.com/index-3.html.

PSC. Edgar Herrera, a security advisor at EMSISA, explains that local companies are reluctant to create this position in their organizational structure. For this reason, local companies delegate the whole responsibility to a PSC (Interview with Edgar Herrera, Security Advisor of EMSISA, 03/23/09). This creates an insecurity problem for companies due to the lack of professionalization of PSCs. They are unable to administer the risks the company faces and to reduce its costs. The logic of a massive presence of armed individuals that PSCs offer does not reduce risks for the client and raises the cost of operation. In other words, PSCs do not ensure the interest of the client; instead, they are concerned only with profit. The organizational structure of local industries that outsource their own security feeds the big market for PSCs in Guatemala. PSCs exploit and stimulate the perception of insecurity in the country because it increases demand for their services (Interview with Alex Valdez, Security manager of ASEGURI, 03/11/09).

In the same way as EMSISA was founded by a former US military officer, other international consulting companies have been set up in Guatemala after providing services to a particular international company. For example, Yantarni Corporation is a British company established in Central America. It was founded in 2002 and advised and provided security to Blue Oil Corporation. Currently Yantarni operates in the whole region and its security advisors come from the UK, Colombia, and Guatemala, as well as security experts from the French Foreign Legion (Interview with Edgar Herrera, Security Advisor of EMSISA, 03/23/09).[54]

Security consulting companies represents the interplay of different rationalities of private policing in the country. These companies interact with local companies that have different perspectives on private policing activities. The existence of these intermediary companies falls outside of the control of the state. In fact, many of these companies were created by the interaction of state institutions and foreign security experts, especially during the armed conflict. The international security experts could foresee the emergence of a large market due to the lack of public security that the displacement of state security functions was producing. The political conditions for a profitable post-war expansion were generated during those years and former international military types were available to participate in this context. International investors deposit their confidence in consulting companies that understand the context of public and private security in the country and are capable of using both as appropriate to ensure their interests. These companies can interact with both public and private security through former military experts who work for them.

54 See http://www.yantarni.com.gt/.

4.3 Laws and Other State Controls

The State in Guatemala has few possibilities to effectively control the private security sector. The law that regulates the private security sector does not contemplate personal private security services provided by a person in coordination with others but not operating as a formal company. For this reason the number of private security companies can only be estimated. The law regulating the activities of PSCs was passed in 1970 and in 1979 the government issued a decree to regulate the activities of state security forces and private banks. However a reform of the law was made in 2010, the laws do not adequately regulate the activities of PSCs today. For example, they do not take into account private investigations, electronic security systems, or database development. The existing laws only cover private entities with structures similar to the police and those companies that offer private security to banking institutions (Táger and Mérida 2002: 105; MINUGUA 2002: 74). During the 1970s, PSC services were mostly concentrated in providing guards. The diversification of services is a characteristic of PSCs in the 1990s, for which existing laws are not adequate.

Existing laws do not establish criteria for hiring agents nor their professionalization and training, and allow PSCs to:

1. Buy more than one gun (including shotguns) under the name of the same person. The person legally responsible for the use of the gun is the person who handles it, not the owner. This situation is especially important in cases when the worker does not know that the gun has been illegally purchased and does not have any experience with guns.
2. Transfer the use of arms to another person to create a group of armed individuals to provide private security services.
3. Guard any kind of property with a gun. When a guard ends his workday he must return the gun to the company. Normally, the company provides transportation but when this is not available, the guard must return the gun using public transportation.
4. Avoid responsibility in case of death or damages caused by their armed employees.
5. Operate with a commercial license only. This requires the payment of taxes but avoids state quality controls.

PSCs are legally authorized to operate when they have acquired a "ministerial agreement". The process for obtaining this document requires a big investment and lots of time to meet the long list of legal requirements. The process may take up to three years, but paying a bribe could reduce it to a few months. The time will depend on the owner's former military rank and on the size of the bribe (Interview with a security advisor of the Division 03/12/09). The law allows the company to operate while the authorization request is in process, but this situation can go on for years if the owner is not interested in completing the authorization process. This condition is actually convenient for an illegal company because it is not subject to state controls or legal responsibilities. A common practice to operate without authorization is to "rent" a Ministerial Agreement from some company that has two or more of them. This mechanism is called "coverage" and generates extra income for these companies. Aside from renting an authorization, illegal companies also rent uniforms, guns, and even agents from other companies (Interview with a security advisor of the Division 03/12/09).

It was not until 2010 that the law was reformed in Guatemala. However the new law requires a set of secondary regulations in order to be effective. One of the main rejections to the reforms was the age of the agents. The new regulations established a minimum of 25 years old to carry firearms which affects the mostly people hired by PSCs. The private sector still seeks to find the way of blocking the efficient implementation of the law (*El Periódico* 04/13/10).

Institutional Controls

The Division for Supervision and Control of Private Security Companies, Entities, and Individuals (*División de Supervisión y Control de Empresas, Entidades y Personas Individuales de Seguridad Privada*, hereafter "Supervision Division") is the only agency within the National Civilian Police with responsibility to control PSCs. To exercise this control, the agency has a staff of fifty, most of them dealing with administrative matters. The Supervision Division is only able to control authorized companies because there are no records for unauthorized companies nor any information on their agents, arms, or services. One consultant for the Supervision Division identified the absence of information on agents and arms as the most pressing problem. For this reason, when the police arrest an illegal agent, he can only be prosecuted for illegal possession of arms. The only loss for the company is the gun, which is subject to confiscation. The company therefore may prefer to buy a new gun instead of providing legal advice to the arrested guard (Interview with a security advisor of the Division 03/12/09). Due to high levels of corruption in the police, PSCs consider that the Supervision Division is a mechanism to avoid state controls. "The control unit is necessary, but, more important, when it is neutralized" (Interview with a security advisor of the Division 03/12/09). This means that the existence of the Supervision Division as a public institution is important as long as its work does not interfere with the activities of illegal private security companies.

Another problem faced by the Supervision Division arises when a control officer tries to carry out an inspection at a PSC. In that case, the owner assumes his former military rank, thereby avoiding real controls and covering up illegalities. Because company owners or higher level employees most often are former military or police officers, they enjoy respect and authority within an informal structure of hierarchies, even though they have retired from the service (Interview with a security advisor of the Division 03/12/09).

PSCs Organizations

Commercial private security in Guatemala is affiliated with various trade organizations that reflect both its interest as a commercial sector and its varied origins. One group of authorized PSCs is associated with the Chamber of Guatemalan Industry, while another is associated to the Chamber of Commerce of Guatemala. The first group of PSCs is organized as the Federation of Guilds and Associations of Security (FEGRASE), that also represents the Guild of Security Industries (GIS), the Association of Security Companies (ASES), and the producers of security supplies (AGIEXPRIVA). Each of these groups represents more than commercial and industrial specialties; they also represent actors and interests. For example, former military and police officers who are owners of active but non-authorized PSCs constitute the Association of Security Companies.

The GIS was affiliated to the Chamber of Commerce in the 1980s and was the first group of private security companies to be established in Guatemala (Táger and Mérida 2002: 107). Until then, the GIS had been concerned mostly about the conservation of the private security market for an exclusive group of PSCs founded during the internal armed conflict. For this reason one of the formal requirements to become affiliated with the GIS is the authorization of the PSC.

Despite these attempts to monopolize the private security sector, the demobilization process of the army and the reform to the police released a large number of security personnel that saturated the security market and demanded the right to offer their services in the face of the old private security owners. The strong links between the first generation of owners of private security companies and state institutions meant that the refusal to authorize more PSCs became a control mechanism of the market and led to the emergence of a large sector of "ghost" PSCs at the beginning of the 1990s (Interview with Rodolfo Muñoz Piloña Owner of the Unidad de Servicios Integrales de Seguridad, 03/17/09). It was in this context that former police commissioners who owned PSCs created the Integral Association of Private and Banking Security Companies (ASIEGSPRIBA) (Táger and Mérida 2002: 107).

As a result of differences between the companies' representatives, there are currently two main organizations representing private security companies: the Guild of Private Security Companies and the Chamber of Guatemalan Security.

The other groups were incorporated into one of these two organizations. The differences persist to this day. The Chamber of Guatemalan Security was founded in 2006 and includes the different groups of authorized PSCs and is directed by civilian entrepreneurs, while the Guild of Private Security Companies (founded in 1998) is made up of PSCs without authorization and is directed by former military officers. Another difference is that the Chamber companies offer all kinds of security services while the Guild companies only provide guards services (Interview with Jorge Sierra, Grupo Almo, 03/09/09). In both cases, the different organizations of PSCs seek to have formal participation in the discussion of the law in the Guatemalan Congress. They also attempt to connect the private security sector with other groups at an international level for example with the Pan-American Federation of Private Security.[55]

4.4 Private Security Companies: A Security Solution?

One of the main justifications for the current existence of commercial private security is the prevention of crime. Regardless of how the law defines the activities of private security as preventive and dissuasive, entrepreneurs accept that security is partially displaced to the private sector (Interview with Rodolfo Munoz Piloña owner of USI, 03/17/09). From the perspective of private security entrepreneurs, the other factor that produces this displacement is the incapacity of public institutions to deliver security (Interview with Byron Heredia, President of COSEHOGUA, 02/24/09). A number of academic studies based on crime analysis and security commonly argues that the proliferation of private security is directly related to an increase in crime and a decline in state capabilities.[56] Those arguments have to be contrasted with the evolution of crime related to the evolution of the private sector. The argument in this study is that the increase in crime is a factor that accelerates the proliferation of private security. In the case of Guatemala, when post-war criminality increased, private security was already strong and functional for the social system. This is the reason why after the demobilization of army and police forces in 1996, private security was an attractive and effective field to continue exercising control over security structures from the private sphere. This was a time when the state had to reorient its institutional organization to provide public security instead of defence and counterinsurgency. It was impossible for the new democratic institutions to change a historical institutional pattern in which the state relegated its public security functions in order to concentrate its security institutions on defence and counterinsurgency

55 See http://www.fepasep.com/.

56 Chapter II of this study shows the main arguments and studies about this theme.

matters. This is the high cost involved in changing the trajectory of a self-reinforced sequence. The timing of the security sector reform was a critical juncture for many social and political processes but it was a "non-critical juncture" in terms of private security proliferation.

Figure 5 shows that from 1962 to 1996 there was a relative stable number of PSCs authorizations per year, the growth was very low in comparison with the years between 1994 onwards. By 1996, there were 37 PSCs authorized in Guatemala, most of them owned by police officers. The military were linked with PSCs through the national police and together militaries and police officers had the control of the private security sector. It was from 1996 onwards that the number of authorizations accelerated. In fifteen years, from 1996 to the present, 113 PSCs were authorized, in comparison to 37 PSCs created during 37 years of internal armed conflict. From the beginning, PSCs concentrated on public security functions while the army controlled all security institutions in order to focus on defence and counterinsurgency operations.

The security sector reform in 1996 committed the state to resume its public security functions. This turning point happened during other important political processes such as the creation of new democratic and civilian security institutions, the demobilization of a large number of army and police forces, and the shift of security concerns from a national security perspective to democratic security. The interplay of these processes produced different outcomes. The creation of new security institutions and the drastic demobilization of former security forces produced a vacuum of security and the consequent increase in crime. At the same time, the incomplete demobilization process released a large number of trained security personnel without state and civil society controls to assure their reinsertion into society. As it turns out, one of the reinsertion strategies was the creation of PSCs. In other cases the reinsertion process led to participation in criminal organizations (Interview with Rodolfo Muñoz Piloña, owner of the Unidad de Servicios Integrales de Seguridad, 03/17/09). Table 2 shows that the most marked increase of PSCs coincides with the three main demobilizations of the security forces in 1997, 2003, and 2004

Figure 5: Annual Authorizations for PSCs in Guatemala

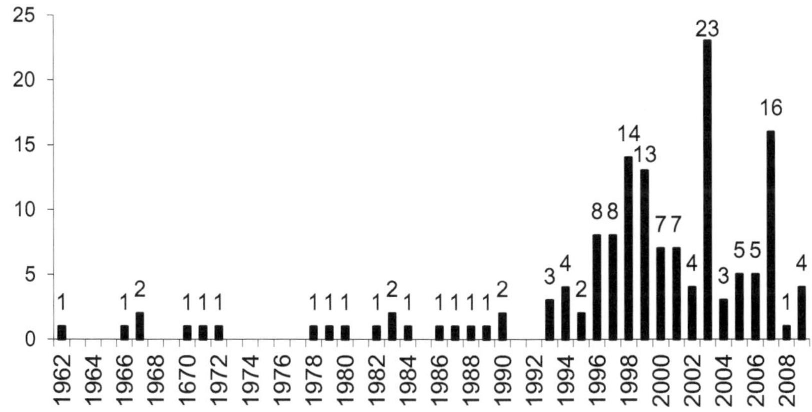

Source: Author's own compilation with data from Ministry of Interior of Guatemala.

In this context there was a significant increase in crime. This increase cannot be only analysed as the emergence of new violence in the country (Kruijt 2004). The criminal structures previously relegated and controlled under the military during the years of counterinsurgency warfare became unrestrained during the transition to democracy in the context of new security institutions without resources and expertise and a private security sector in control of former security structures. The demand for security and the incapacity of security institutions to deliver security reinforced the proliferation of private security companies. The critical point is that, on the one hand, private security has legal limitations to implement security actions: they are restricted to dissuasive activities. On the other, the proliferation of private security companies relied on the incorporation of former military staff trained under authoritarian and militaristic conceptions of security that focuses on the show of force through the presence of armed people in the private sphere.

In the case of crimes that are supposedly covered by commercial private security protection, the tendency is the same. Figure 7 shows how crimes against property and specifically vehicle thefts have increased. These crimes include those committed in homes, industries, and commercial establishments, as well as people who are held up. Private security provides protection for these kinds of goods as well as the protection of vehicles. In 1995 there were 20,633 criminal acts reported, of which 91% were committed against property; in 2000 the proportion was 94% (UNDP 2010a). These figures coincide with the years of decreasing crime; during the years with higher homicide rates, the percentage of crimes against property fell but not so the total number of criminal acts committed.

Table 2: Military Downsizing in Guatemala

Year	Military personnel	Official reduction	%	Remaining military personnel
1997-1998	46.900	15.477	33	31.423
2003	31.423	4.209	8.97	27.214
2004	27.214	11.714	24.97	15.500
Total reduction 1997/2004	---	31.400	66.95	15.500

Source: MINUGUA 2004a.

Homicide rates show that after an important decrease between 1997 and 1999 the tendency points to increasingly higher levels than those reached during the internal armed conflict. From a starting point in 1994 when homicide rates were similar for Guatemala and Latin America as a whole, the general tendency in Guatemala has been toward an increase in murder rates while the average in Latin America remained stable until the last three years. In spite of the fact that private security is not capable to prevent homicides, it is clear that the negative perception of security in the society is directly linked with the rise in murder rates. The social justification for the proliferation of private security is based on the argument that this negative perception of security increases the demand for a response to crime.[57]

The total of criminal acts in 2004 was 34,236, of which 79,44% were crimes against property. In that same year, 23 new PSCs were authorized, for a total of 116. This was the year of the last security forces demobilization. The only year when homicide rates decreased was in 1999; this was the year of greatest support for the new National Police and when the percentage of new police officers was higher than that of officers linked to the old police institutions. During the years between 1997 and 2004 a number of related phenomena overlapped but there is no available data to prove or discard this relation. For example, both homicides and crimes against property increased. Second, there was a proliferation of private security companies. And third, the demobilization process of former securi-

57 All interviewed private security owners coincide with this affirmation.

ty forces continued apace. The facts would indicate that the proliferation of private security companies did not prevent the increase in crime.

Figure 6: Homicide Rates Per Hundred Thousand Inhabitants

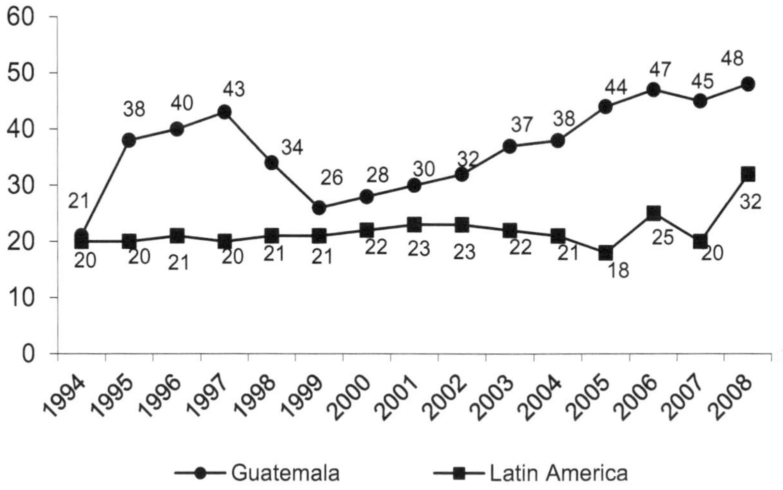

Source: author's compilation with data from UNDP 2010b and UNODC 2008.

Figure 7: Crimes Against Property (in total numbers)

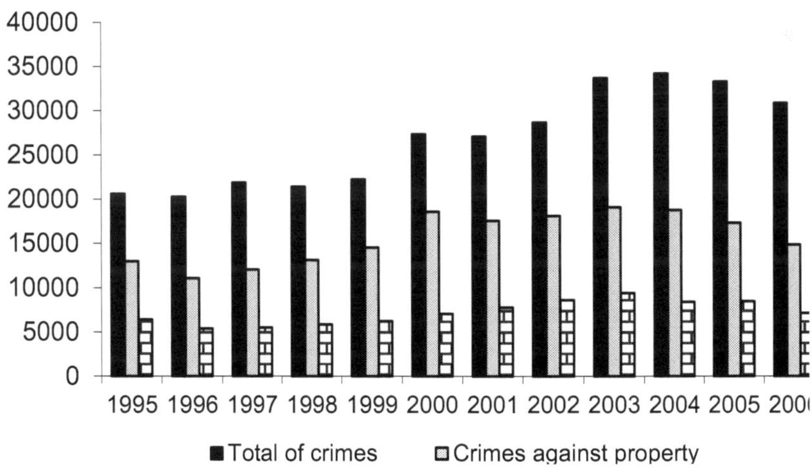

Source: author's compilation with data from, UNDP 2010a.

Nonetheless, there is public support for the state seeking assistance from private security firms to prevent crime. In 2009, the state invested 4 million Quetzales per month to pay one thousand private security guards to protect public transportation in response to an increase in killings of bus drivers (*Prensa Libre* 01/30/09). However, the number of assassinated drivers did not decrease. There were 391 drivers killed from 2007 to 2009 (68 in 2007, 131 in 2008, and 192 in 2009) (*El Periódico* 02/02/10). In 2010, the number people killed while working on public transportation was 178 (GAM 2010).

Criminaliation of PSCs

The links between PSCs and crime is one of the main concerns of civil society organizations in Guatemala and abroad (Godnick 2009; Táger and Mérida 2002; Gibson 2007). This phenomenon is associated with the lack of an effective regulation and the weak institutional capabilities of the unit of control of the PNC (MINUGUA 2002). Other perspectives associate PSCs and crime based on their military past (Táger and Mérida 2002). The fact that former military and police officers discovered in private security an economic activity after their demobilization from public institutions reinforces the perception of links with organized crime (Táger and Mérida 2002; Godnick 2009). This is because there was no institutional control over former military and police officers after their demobilization. At the same time, the lack of proper personnel selection procedures in PSCs does not ensure that they avoid hiring criminals.

It is possible to differentiate between the participation of PSCs in organized crime (for example, drug trafficking, kidnapping, and money laundering) and common crime such as robbery. But there is a third possibility: the participation of PSCs in extra judicial executions. This analysis is based on interviews and newspapers reports because there is obviously no official information about the participation of PSCs or their members in crime.

An example of the participation of PSCs in common crime is that, according to one source, 80% of robberies inside a company guarded by a PSC are committed by guards of the same PSC (Interview with Jorge Sierra advisor of Grupo Almo, 03/02/09). One solution implemented by PSCs to this problem is hiring undercover agents to control the crime network of personnel of the PSC and employees of the company. However, the participation of criminals in PSCs cannot be controlled due to the increased demand for security personnel and the low capabilities of public institutions to control PSCs. The existence of a large number of illegal PSCs is other factor that explains this problem. There are cases in which active private security guards works with kidnapping gangs as a secondary job (*Prensa Libre* 07/16/06). In 2005, the PNC arrested 286 individuals who worked as guards in illegal private security companies (*Prensa Libre* 07/16/06). In 2006, the participation of youth gangs in PSCs was reported (*Prensa Libre* 07/14/06).

Another link with organized crime is the participation of members of PSCs in public institutions that become involved in criminal actions. The owner of SERPROP, Carlos Quintanilla, was appointed in 2008 as director of the Secretariat of Administrative and Security Issues (SAAS), which is the office charged with the personal security of the President of the Republic. After that he was accused and prosecuted for espionage (*El Periódico* 09/08/08). At the same time, a former military officer who owned two PSCs was appointed to direct an anti-kidnapping commando force. In 2008, two members of a special commando of the PNC as well as agents of the Drug Enforcement Administration (DEA) were killed. They were the owners of Global Urban Security (SEGURSA) and were also involved in the killing of seven inmates at the Pavón penitentiary in 2006 (*El Periódico* 06/27/08).

For some analysts the private security sector in Guatemala can be understood as part of the so-called "hidden powers" which are strong political and criminal structures created during the internal conflict (Peacock and Beltrán 2004). Such a perspective is based on the scope and number of agents of PSCs, the number of illegal companies operating in the country, and the criminal activities associated with the commercial private sector (Interview with Fernando Girón. Security Advisor of Myrna Mack Foundation, 03/13/09). From the perspective of the security companies, it is not important who the client is or the nature of the object to be protected; instead, "it is important to provide the service and that is why some PSCs are at risk of being illegal or commit illegal actions" (Interview with Carlos Quintanilla, Owner of SERPROP, 03/17/09).

***

The situation of private security companies in Guatemala is the outcome of the historic displacement of state security functions that place limits on the capabilities of public security institutions in a variety of areas, especially the control of PSCs. The existence of a weak public security sector has contributed to the profitability of private security companies and allows them operate with impunity in a number of illegal activities. As such, it can be seen as an outcome of the historic reinforcing of private security in the social system. The increase in crime since 1996 stimulated the public demand for security and the interaction of processes of political change and reform of security institutions has transformed the private security sector into a mechanism to control security matters as well as to increase its profitability. Problems associated with PSCs, such as lack of professionalization, low salaries, corruption, weak state controls, and inadequate institutions and legislation, among others, can be analysed as the adaptation of private policing activities to the socio-political context. These characteristics reflect the positive feedback that the interaction with the state has produced for the private sector. This situation can be translated as the reinforcing of a private policing function in the social system sustained on the basis of a set of informal and historical rules.

The profitability of commercial private security lies on the possibility of avoid state controls (taxes, quality standards, labour regulations). The state capabilities to control private companies were avoided from the beginning by the first group of private security companies. The lack of state controls has it origins parallel to the emergence of the commercial private security sector based on the strong relation between private and public security sectors.

5. Juntas Locales de Seguridad: Community Private Policing

As was mentioned in Chapter II, security studies have focused on the commercial side of private security, while their analysis of non-commercial security organizations is associated mainly with community-oriented policing from the perspective of international programmes that seek to strengthen the link between police and community. As it was argued in this study, commercial and non-commercial private security are two dimensions of the same process of public security displacement. During this process private policing adopted the form of vigilante actins as a self-defence mechanism. The international models of community policing during the post-war were introduced in a context in which strong vigilante organizations were still active. Community policing reproduced self-defence policing legitimised by the state policies. This situation rapidly lead to the implementation of vigilante actions against alleged criminals, strangers, and even against the state.

Community policing models are based on the idea that collaborative links between public institutions and the society should be created in order to prevent crime based on the assumption that there is a mutual interest in combating threats and risks (Frühling 2003; MacDonald 2002; SEESAC 2007). On the other hand, they can be analysed as responsibilization strategies through which the state delegates on the citizenry the responsible for their own security among other aspects of the social life (Garland 2005). However, the trajectories of private policing and its relation with social and political contexts show how community policing models can be a mechanism to reinforce the reproduction of vigilante actions and self-defence policing. Both international models and also state citizen security policies neglected the historical trajectories of the institutional pattern of public security displacement to the private sphere.

This chapter addresses the current situation of the "Juntas Locales de Seguridad" (JLS) in Guatemala. First, this chapter explains the conceptual use of private policing to analyse the JLSs as part of a private security function in the society. Second, the current situation of JLSs will be described, including its links to state institutions, regulations, controls, and activities. Because one of the main arguments of the research is that the increase and proliferation of private security can be better explained through its historical trajectories rather than its connection with crime rates, the third part analyses the relation between different crime rates and other variables with JLSs. And fourth, the chapter provides an historical explanation of JLSs through the analysis of political violence during Guatemala's internal conflict and the different forms of self defence organizations.

The "Juntas Locales de Seguridad" (JLSs or, loosely translated, "Local Security Boards") are neighbourhood and communal groups organized to protect their living area. Their activities vary from one JLS to another. They can hire private security companies or they can do the policing themselves in possession of illegal weapons with their faces covered. The range of activities implemented by such organizations is very wide. There are different names for civil security organizations in Guatemala. Here the acronym JLS will be used to refer to community policing organizations as a general concept. The term "board" refers to a decision-making group in a community which in some cases is elected and in others is self-appointed. There are, for example, *Comités Vecinales de Seguridad, Consejos Vecinales or Comunitarios de Seguridad* (neighbourhood or communal security councils), and *Comités Únicos de Barrio* (Neighbourhood Security Committees or CUBs). The differences reflect the institutions these organizations are supposedly linked to, which include a wide range of possibilities. For example, there are some organizations linked with the police, others with the Ministry of the Interior through the Vice Ministry of Communal Affairs; in some urban areas private policing organizations are linked to the municipality and others, located in rural areas, are said to be linked with communal leaders or churches.

How they were created or the public institution to which they are linked cannot define the formality or informality of these private policing organizations. There are some organizations created through the initiative of state institutions, others were already created when the state institution made contact with them, while others are associated with non governmental organizations supported by international sponsors, in addition to cases of totally autonomous organizations. The fact that the state in some particular moment created a particular kind of organization does not imply that its social function was formalized. On the contrary, as will be explained later, the state is incapable of controlling and interacting with the large number of organizations that already operate in the country.

For this reasons, in this study JLSs are the generic denomination that refers to the social function implemented by private policing organizations. Empirically defined as community policing organizations, it is important to clarify their relationship with the concept of private policing, on the one hand, and private security on the other.

As defined in Chapter 3, private policing includes all non-state agencies that consciously participate in the process of bringing about and guaranteeing security (Shearing and Kempa 2000; Shearing 1992). This allows for the incorporation of social protection practices into the concept of private security that go beyond its formal and commercial dimension. It includes non-commercial forms or private policing like civil policing initiatives, informal private policing promoted or not by state institutions ("community policing programmes"), informal systems of criminal justice, and even private policing in global spaces (Kempa *et al.* 1999). The non-commercial forms of private policing are associated with particular forms of active citizenship that vary depending on time and context. Generally the bibliography about community policing and private policing make a difference between this active citizenship in the form of community policing models and vigilante organizations. JLS shows how both community policing and vigilante actions are directly linked when international models and public policies do not take into account historical trajectories in which the organizational structure of these organizations can change while its social functions remain constant.

By observing the evolution of social control mechanisms, it is possible to identify how private security companies are the formalization of a kind of informal private policing. In a particular context, it was a bifurcation that created two main levels of private policing, namely the commercial private policing and the non-commercial private policing initiatives. Therefore, the concept of private security has to expand to include those non commercial dimensions of private policing in order to understand the social function of private security instead of the study of a particular sector of private security. It is also noted that non-commercial private policing organizations do not exclude the fact that they are paid activities. The empirical data shows that the inhabitants usually pay community policing organizations for their services. This pay can vary from monetary contributions and food to vehicles and gasoline to patrol the community. In some cases the payment is obligatory under threat of being sanctioned or becoming unprotected (*Prensa Libre* 11/23/05). There are cases in which payment is made through work in the economic activities of the patrollers. Political benefits, clientelism, and patronage are forms of payment in exchange for protection. In this sense, private security refers to social function that produces particular benefits either as a commercial activity or as a voluntary action with secondary benefits. In other words, private policing can easily become an informal sale of protection.

The study of JLSs reflects the ambiguity of public-private bonds. These bonds are determined by contextual dynamics and they change in order to adapt to institutional patterns necessary to carry out social functions. The argument goes as follows: the JLSs are the current adaptation of a historic private policing function that has been reproduced through a particular institutional pattern. Based on what Holden argues for the Central American countries, private policing is a perspective from which to observe how social control mechanisms such as PACs and JLSs are located in the gray zone of collaborative and violent ties that clientelistic states produced (Holden 1996: 442). The JLSs, as structures of civil self-defence, are among many from the wide spectrum of civil organizations that have existed to support social and political controls exercised by the State. Social control and the incorporation of civilian population in security structures is a historical constant which, in the case of Guatemala, has been part of the State since its liberal restructuring during the second half of the 19th century. This process is part of the displacement of security functions to the private sphere. The JLSs were formally created under the Civil National Police (PNC) in the context of the security sector reform after the end of the internal armed conflict and also in the context of ineffective dissolution of former vigilante organizations.

However, the current situation of JLSs indicates that the transition to democracy created a new context for the reproduction of these vigilante relations. Police reform projects included the implementation of community-oriented policing in order to give the new police institution a new image more in line with the concept of citizen security. The process rapidly led to their separation from the state after the creation of JLSs. This does not mean that those organizations already created stopped their activities; on the contrary, they continued operating in many different ways. As an outcome, it is possible to observe that what Garland (1996 and 2005) calls "responsibilization strategies of control" ultimately produced the continuity of social control mechanisms in a new context. This means that the interplay of community policing organizations and the existence of a new police institution with no capacity to control those organizations and to deliver security subsequently reinforced the displacement of public security to the private sector and the collapse of community-oriented policing programmes implemented by the state and international donors. Rather than strengthen the image and the role of the police, the creation of JLSs reinforced the widespread idea that the police is unable to protect the citizenry and that the only option is to implement vigilantism through community policing organizations.

5.2 The Institutional Ambiguity of Community Policing in Post-War

Since their formal creation in 1999, the JLSs were reproduced in many different ways. Three main sources of state-motivated communal organizations can be identified: one created by the Civil National Police (PNC), another created by the Vice Ministry for Communal Affairs (*Vice Ministerio de Apoyo Comunitario* or VAC), and a third group created by the municipality of Guatemala City. Those are three different levels of top-down community policing organizations that coexist in a confused institutional framework. There are some policing organizations that were created before 1999 that do not belong to any institution and there are also others created after this time that remain autonomous. These autonomous groups are integrated into organizations created in the context of the counter insurgency strategy as well as those organizations that were not directly created to deal with policing activities but that during the post-war context were transformed into vigilante groups. As was mentioned, each of these organizations has a different name. The differences between them are important and they will be analysed in depth in this section.

It is important to mention that this process occurred within the security sector reform (particularly the police reform), the dissolution of the former security institutions, and the downsizing of the army and intelligence structures. A new police institution was created and it was endowed with new institutional requirements such as democratic rules and a community- oriented perspective, among others, within a context of accelerated transformations without clear policy orientations. In addition, there were international pressures to accelerate those reforms and to use international financial resources to implement them, including international models of community-oriented policing.[58]

Juntas Locales de Seguridad and the Police: The Origins of Continuity

In July 1999 the National Civilian Police issued a General Order to address public security from a citizen security perspective. The precedent of this initiative was the Neighbourhood Committees for Reconstruction programme established by the Ministry of the Interior in 1998 to support the new police through monetary donations to equip police stations in the neighbourhoods. After determining that those committees were a success, the Ministry decided to create the JLSs (Neild 2002: 18). The general order placed the JLSs within the *Oficina de Relaciones Informativas y Sociales* (Social and Informative Relations Office or ORIS). This order defined the JLSs as a key component of the Public Security Policy to strengthen the links between the police and the community. The Order defined the JLSs as "groups of neighbours of those townships where there are National Civilian Police that aim to collaborate to improve citizen security".[59]

According to the general order, each JLS had to be made up by the mayor or representative and an "honorable" neighbour, in addition to all neighbours who voluntarily wished to join the JLS. At the same time, the general order stipulated that the JLSs also had to have representation of the different sectors and public institutions active in the community like commercial associations, fire-fighters, entrepreneurs, representatives of the Judiciary and Prosecutor Office, and professional guilds. But the general order also stipulated, in somewhat contradictory terms, that "the composition of the JLSs can vary according to the reality and

58 The analysis of the Security Sector Reform will be made in depth in the chapter VII of this study.

59 Orden General Nr. 11.99, Guatemala July 14th 1999.

needs of the locality".[60] Finally, according to the general order the Police recognized the JLSs as informative and collaborative groups but did not stipulate any institutional mechanisms to keep the JLSs in contact with the Police. In fact, there are no control mechanisms over the JLSs in the general order nor any indication about records of persons and activities implemented by the JLSs.[61]

At the beginning, the Ministry of the Interior found in the creation of JLSs a mechanism to promote the new PNC but according to the ORIS there were no public mechanisms to promote the JLSs outside the police. However, in 2002 there were JLSs in 231 municipalities from a total of 331 municipalities in the country (Neild 2002: 18). The Police rapidly created JLSs anywhere based on the idea that the active participation of the community would be important to fight crime. The JLSs were made up of community leaders and in some areas became means to achieve local power due to the creation of clientelistic relations with the PNC (Neild 2002: 18). The police used all traditional and existent organizations to create a JLS. Former paramilitary organizations such as *Patrullas de Autodefensa Civil* and Military Commissioners as well as remnants of the insurgent groups such as *Fuerzas Irregulares Locales* (FIL), were the basis to the creation of many of the new JLSs.

As will be explained in the next section, those paramilitary organizations implemented different actions in the context of the counterinsurgency strategy which involved human rights violations such as killing, kidnapping, and genocide, but also exercised social control against drunks, prostitutes, young people, and strangers. Those organizations were part of the local authorities and remained active despite their formal dissolution. From the beginning of the existe nce of the JLSs, human rights activists denounced their activities in similar terms employed against the PACs and Military Commissioners (Interview with Axel Romero, Chief of Communal Organization of the VAC, 03/12/09). The police were focused on the organization of the JLSs but not on the parallel process of strengthening collaborative bonds. After a few years the organization of the JLSs became spontaneous in response to the inefficiency of the police. This process led to the reactivation of former security structures, this time to defend against crime, either in the form of real dangers or subjective perceptions of crime.

The first period of the JLSs shows that there were high levels of ambiguity in the process of their creation. Among the population the idea prevailed that the JLSs were only a mechanism to generate information for the police (Interview with intelligence analyst of the State Intelligence Agency, 03/05/09). The police used the existing organizations in the communities to hand over responsibility

60 Article 3, Orden General Nr. 11.99, Guatemala July 14th 1999.

61 Article 5, Orden General Nr. 11.99, Guatemala July 14th 1999.

for their own security. This process gave those organizations a free hand to implement any action in the name of their own protection (Interview with intelligence analyst of the State Intelligence Agency, 03/05/09). The result was the restructuring of traditional organizations with a new name and with the delegated authority vested upon them by the state (Interview with Axel Romero, Chief of Communal Organization of the VAC, 03/12/09). In a context of institutional transformation that created a vacuum of security, in addition to highly perceived levels of insecurity and strong legacies of the internal armed conflict, the JLSs reactivated the meaning of self defence based on a concept of survival and protection of persons and goods that justified the use of violence as a response to the inefficiency of the legitimate authority to prevent criminal acts and to deliver justice. Self defence was a result of the functional inefficiency of the security and justice chain (Interview with Col. Mario Mérida, former Vice Ministry of Interior, 05/05/09).

The failure of the JLSs to implement democratic community policing and collaborative links with the police was a result, among others, of the fact that they were used from the beginning only as an information source. This led not only the reactivation of former structures with the same informative function but also the delegation of public security to the population in a non democratic way. When the police received information but did not implement efficient preventive actions, the population preferred acting without the participation of the police (*Prensa Libre* 09/27/05 a). After the JLSs proliferated without control, the Police started the process to recover its institutional role. During the first years of being functioning there was no control or coordination with the JLSs. The new police institution had no institutional capabilities to strengthen collaborative links with the population. Additionally, there were high levels of public distrust towards the police and other armed forces. One state intelligence officer argued that the JLSs degenerated with regard to their original objectives when formally created in 1999 because they were used only as source of information by the Police (Interview with intelligence analyst of the State Intelligence Agency, 03/05/09). Since the police historically planted informants in the communities and neighbourhoods, the population quickly rejected the work of the JLSs and the desired collaboration with the Police was impossible. Nevertheless, the JLSs were organized and are still working without formal links to the Police (Interview with intelligence analyst of the State Intelligence Agency, 03/05/09).

Against the background of the first years of JLS´s existence different efforts were made to strengthen the community-policing oriented actions of the Police. In 2002, the *Oficina de Coordinación Comunitaria de la PNC* (Coordination Office for Community Policing of the Civil National Police) was created. It was part of the operative units of the Police so its function was merely reactive. The Office received the information generated by the JLSs to implement security actions (PNC 2009). Since the Office had no institutional support, it was necessary to seek international support. After a short training course about community policing, 500 police officers were introduced to the philosophy of community policing (PNC 2009).[62] The problem was that the trained officers were scattered across the country under a hierarchy of police officials who rejected the new policing model. It was not until 2005 that the *Subdirección General de Prevención del Delito* (General Crime Prevention Directorate) was created to coordinate and supervise the activities of the JLSs. As part of the *Subdirección General del Delito*, the Division of Communal Affairs of the PNC initiated a process to identify the JLSs. In the first report produced by this Division in 2008, a preventive perspective of the work implemented by the JLSs was incorporated. That year an effort was begun to register existing JLSs (Interview with a police officer of the *Sección de Intervención en Relaciones Comunitarias* of the PNC, 10/22/10). At that moment there were 677 JLSs identified in the whole country but even then the police had no contact with most of them (PNC 2008). In 2009 the same office was transformed from a "division" to a "section" under the name *Sección de Intervención en Relaciones Comunitarias*. This change meant a lower category in the institutional hierarchy, as well as fewer personnel and financial resources.

However, this institutional measures produced the first data about JLS. In 2009, the PNC reported the existence of 1,037 active JLSs in the country (PNC 2009). This information evidenced that an improvement in the institutional capabilities to register existing JLSs was not necessarily proportional to an increase of new JLSs. The data was put together only based on information from the police stations in the country but it did not mean in any way that the police had control over the increasing number of JLSs or that the police worked together with them (Interview with a police officer of the Sección de Intervención en Relaciones Comunitarias of the PNC, 10/22/10). On the contrary, until 2010 the PNC had registered data – such as the names of coordinators and addresses that appear on registration documents – for only 469 JLSs (PNC 2010). This means that there were at least 568 active JLSs without control of the PNC. Although there has been international financial support, the records of the PNC show that no JLS has received training on preventive security issues (PNC 2010).

This first stage of the post-war non commercial private policing produced two effects. On the one hand, the reproduction of vigilante actions and authoritarian and informal social control mechanisms that are part of a historical continuity of private policing functions; on the other hand, the creation of JLSs generated a set of contingent events counterproductive for the democratic process, such as lynching of suspected criminals, vigilantism, delegitimation of the police, rele-

62 About community policing programs see chapter II.

gitimation of the army, a contraction of public spaces, and stigmatisation and criminaliation of young people, among others (Huhn, Oettler and Peetz 2006a and 2006b; Huhn 2011; Peetz 2011).

Complementarily, the introduction of a community oriented policing model in the police created a weak institutional framework to accomplish international requirements.

The Beginning of Formal Institutional Ambiguity

The *Vice Ministerio de Apoyo Comunitario* (Vice Ministry of Communal Affairs or VAC) was created in 2004 as part of the Ministry of Interior with the aim to strengthen links between public security institutions and community organizations. The new institution sought to gain control over the large number of JLSs created since 1999. The idea of the VAC was to convert all kinds of neighbourhood organizations into security committees linked to each level of communal organization and with a special focus on JLSs in order to convert them into the new "Security Commissions" framework (Interview with Axel Romero, Chief of Communal Organization of the VAC, 03/12/09). The new Vice Ministry received support from international financial institutions but not much support from the state.[63] The first year of the Vice Ministry was ineffective due to the political instability at the Ministry of Interior and the lack of clear policies and programmes. The institutional instability continued from 2005 to 2011, when there were approximately seven different Vice Ministers and a large period without one at all (Interview with Ivan García and Arturo Matute, Citizen Security Programme, UNDP, 05/24/09).

The VAC is the result of the importance that the concept of democratic security and citizen security gained in Guatemala in the post-war years. Through the project called "*Hacia una Política de Seguridad Ciudadana*" (Towards a Citizen Security Policy or POLSEC), implemented with the support of international donors, it was possible to establish the basis of a preventive security perspective with emphasis on community-oriented policing programmes (FLACSO 2002; Arévalo 2002a). In order to gain control over the JLSs, the VAC created a new institutional framework into which the JLSs had to be inserted using the system of development councils and the post-war reforms of the municipalities through which local governments gained autonomy and resources. The communal system

63 In May 2006 the Inter-American Development Bank approved a loan of US$ 29 millions to be conducted through the Vice Ministry of Communal Affairs. Document of the Inter-American Bank, Programa de Prevención de la Violencia (GU-0163). See also Benavides 2010.

of development councils includes three levels: *Consejos Departamentales de Desarrollo* (Departmental Councils of Development), *Consejos Municipales de Desarrollo* (Municipal Councils of Development) and *Consejos Comunales de Desarrollo* (Communal Councils of Development). These councils, made up of representatives of civil society, were created after the Peace Agreement and they work together with local authorities to improve infrastructure and services. They are part of the decentralization process of the state.

Three institutional processes constitute the basis of the reform proposed by the VAC: the new Municipal Code, the Development Councils Law, and the General Decentralization Law.[64] These institutional reforms allowed the municipalities to create Municipal Police operating under the authority of the mayors and other prerogatives linked with security matters.[65] The structure of the municipalities in Guatemala thus allows for a conservation of traditional local power structures. The Municipal Councils have the support of the Auxiliary or Communal Mayors, which are traditional figures that originated during the colonial period. The community designates the Auxiliary Mayor, who is legitimised by the communal leaders, or the "council of elders" of the community in the case of municipalities with majorities of indigenous populations.[66]

Thus, the idea of the VAC was to use this organizational structure to create at each level a security commission and, in those areas where there were already JLSs, to transform them or to integrate them into the structure of the VAC. Nevertheless, political instability made it impossible for this Ministry to achieve its goals; on the contrary, it represented an institutional competition with the police. At the same time it provoked confusion in the communities about the institution to which the JLSs belonged. As a Vice Ministry, the VAC had a higher institutional hierarchy as opposed to the Police. It produced conflicts between both institutions and a competition for resources for community-oriented programmes (Interview with Ivan García and Arturo Matute, Citizen Security Programme, UNDP, 05/24/09).

When this institutional structure is analysed, it is clear that the only operational and extended level is that of the JLSs. At the same time, the JLSs are the only organizations with participation by the population and direct contact with them. The other levels of this institutional structure do not have a direct presence in the country. In 2010, the PNC identified only 43 municipal security commissions and five departmental security commissions (PNC 2010). The lack of departmental commissions is explained by the fear of accountability the mayors have.

64 Código Municipal, Decreto Ley 12-2002; Ley de los Consejos de Desarrollo Urbano y Rural, Decreto 11-2002; Ley de Descentralización Decreto Ley 14-2002.

65 Article 259, Constitution of the Republic of Guatemala.

66 Article 55 and 58 of the Código Municipal, Decreto Ley 12-2002.

On the contrary, the municipal commissions are controlled by them and have no accountability mechanisms (Interview with a police officer of the Sección de Intervención en Relaciones Comunitarias of the PNC, 10/22/10).

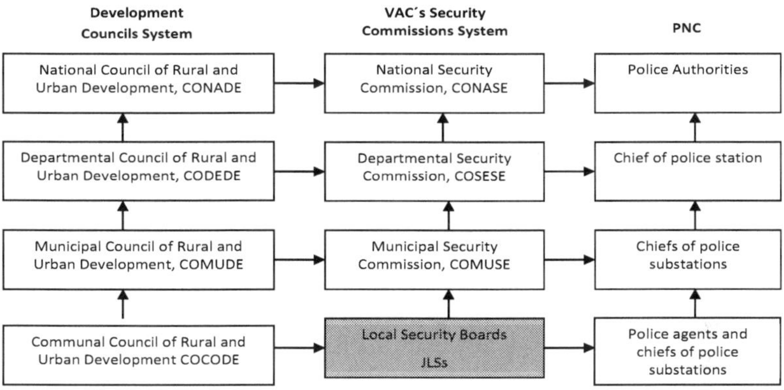

Source: FNUD 2008.

Table 3 shows the number of JLSs and Security Commissions created by the VAC. The big difference between JLSs and the security commissions means that there is no formal integration of JLSs in the local power network. The autonomy of the JLSs remains an accountability problem and the Police have collected information from only 443 JLSs. The figure shows also the territorial distribution of communal security organizations. The national territory is organized around the jurisdiction of each police station. Thus, the main concentration of JLSs registered by the police is in the jurisdiction of Police Station No. 42 that includes the department of San Marcos. Of the 272 JLSs registered by this Police station, only 86 JLSs have some documentation. In second place is Police Station No. 51 that covers the department of Alta Verapaz with 132 JLSs, of which only 38 have some documents. There are Police Stations – such as No. 43 in Huehuetenango – that have registered 44 JLSs without the corresponding documentation.

Contrary to the aims of the VAC, the introduction of JLSs in the local institutional structure reproduced the problems this institutional framework had suffered for decades. It is important to mention that the model of institutional decentralization was a reproduction of a previous interinstitutional structure created by the army during the internal armed conflict under the name of "*Coordinadoras Interinstitucionales para el Desarrollo*". This institutional structure was created in order to gain control over local power holders through a centralized institutional structure directed by the army. One of the effects of this structure was the reinforcement of local caudillos, most of them former military commissioners or chiefs of PACs (Schirmer 2001). With this background, the integration of the JLSs into the system of development councils resulted, on the one hand, in the legitimation of the activities implemented by JLSs (whether violent or not), and on the other, the delegation by the police of security functions on the local organizations.

Due to the lack of police coverage, the police officers that have direct contact with the population, and consequently with the JLSs, are constantly moved from one police station to another. The result is a citizen distrust towards the new officers. At the same time, the training in preventive security provided by international donors is mostly oriented to officers posted in urban areas and not to those posted in rural areas where most of the JLSs are organized (Interview with a police officer of the Sección de Intervención en Relaciones Comunitarias of the PNC, 10/22/10).

Table 3: Number of Community Policing Organizations in Guatemala in 2010

Police Station	JLS	COMUDE	CODEDE
11 (Department of Guatemala)	19	0	0
12 (Department of Guatemala)	39	0	0
13 (Department of Guatemala)	14	0	0
14 (Department of Guatemala)	10	0	0
15 (Department of Guatemala)	24	0	0
16 (Department of Guatemala)	28	0	0
21 (Department of Jutiapa)	13	4	0
22 (Department of Jalapa)	15	0	0
23 (Department of Chiquimula)	30	0	0
24 (Department of Zacapa)	10	3	0
31 (Department of Escuintla)	63	0	0
32 (Department of Santa Rosa)	29	0	0
33 (Depart. of Suchitepéquez)	41	5	1
34 (Department of Retalhuleu)	15	3	1
41 (Depart. of Quetzaltenango)	28	0	0
42 (Department of San Marcos)	272	2	0
43 (Depart. of Huehuetenango)	44	2	1
44 (Department of Totonicapán)	12	1	0
51 (Department of Cobán)	132	0	0
52 (Department of Salamá)	25	0	1
53 (Department of El Progreso)	31	0	0
61 (Department of Izabal)	17	1	0
62 (Department of Petén)	12	3	0
71 (Department of Quiché)	80	0	0
72 (Department of Sololá)	11	8	1
73 (Depart. of Chimaltenango)	19	10	0
74 (Depart. of Sacatepéquez)	10	1	0
Total	**1043**	**43**	**5**

Source: PNC 2010

Another related problem is the lack of police officers. In 2006 there was one police officer for each thousand inhabitants in the country (OCAVI 2008). The system to distribute police personnel also is not based on the cultural and linguistic features of the officers with regards to the area where they are assigned. The

VAC became the receiver of citizen demands for more police officers as the solution to the problem of insecurity. The JLSs argued that they will do anything in order to protect their communities or neighbourhoods because the police were either insufficient or were corrupt (*Prensa Libre* 07/07/05). The participation of the citizenry was conditioned to the participation of the Police and the actions of the JLSs became a threat in the sense that they began to argue: "if the police do not reduce crime, we (the JLS) will do it no matter how" (*Prensa Libre* 07/27/05). The proliferation of JLSs, whether created by the police or by communities, instead of strengthening the ties between police and community, produced a conflictive relationship in which the police delegated its functions to the populations without any controls, but due to institutional instability it rapidly lost citizen acceptance created after its foundation in 1996.

Officials of the VAC argue that the JLSs detracted from the original meaning of citizen participation by implementing repressive and vigilante actions (Interview with Axel Romero, Chief of Communal Organization of the VAC, 03/12/09). In this context, the challenge of the VAC was to recover the original sense of community-oriented policing (Interview with Axel Romero, Chief of Communal Organization of the VAC, 03/12/09). However, as was mentioned above, the interinstitutional network of local authorities has serious problems of coordination and competitiveness. Likewise, the long tradition of caudillism and clientelism embedded in the local power structures makes it difficult to implement a concept of preventive and democratic security. Another problem identified by the VAC was that the prevention model was only part of some particular programme in the Police but it was not part of the whole institution and its doctrine (Interview with Axel Romero, Chief of Communal Organization of the VAC, 03/12/09).

Prevention as concept should be analysed based on a contextual and historical perspective. In fact, during the internal conflict, self-defence policing implemented a set of preventive measures against insurgents, criminals and the army. The failure of crime prevention in the context of community policing models was to avoid the historical meaning of prevention and the consequent actions it implies.

Given the large number of different communal organizations, the VAC seeks to adapt the Security Commissions to existent organizations in the communities. This fact highlights the inherent contradiction of the VAC, which is to control the activities of the JLSs and to adapt its programmes to the existent organizations. Parallel to this, the police discovered in the Security Commissions of the VAC a control mechanism over its activities, which was something that never occurred with the JLSs because the police created them and because they were autonomous (Interview with Axel Romero, Chief of Communal Organization of the VAC, 03/12/09).

The institutional confusion produced by the VAC dates from the beginning of its existence. The first measure of the VAC was to announce that it did not authorize the citizenry to patrol communities and neighbourhoods; on the contrary, it said, the function of the JLSs was to generate and transmit information to the Police, the same function delegated to the JLSs since 1999 (*Prensa Libre* 09/27/05 b). Institutional changes in the VAC made clear that the population had been working alone through the JLSs and that the population have high levels of distrust and fear towards the police institution (*Prensa Libre* 01/19/06). In 2009 the VAC started to identify violent and problem-ridden JLSs. For example, they identified 117 JLSs acting without controls in San Pedro Sacatepéquez in the department of San Marcos and another eight neighbourhood groups in Guatemala City. In response to the increasing number of violent actions by the JLSs, the Unit of Communitarian Prevention was created (*Prensa Libre* 04/29/09). Despite all institutional changes and a modicum of political support for preventive actions implemented by the VAC, the conceptual and administrative confusion persisted until 2010. Public documents of the Ministry of Interior (to which the VAC belongs) continue to present the security commissions the VAC creates as organized groups that seek to recover their environments through processes of pacification and governability and the definition of local security agendas. It is noteworthy that the documents define JLSs under the same terms. The idea of the Ministry is not to support JLSs any longer because they have become "parallel groups"; instead, the Ministry seeks to transform neighbourhood organizations into security commissions (Ministry of Interior 2011).

In summary, a double institutional framework was created; on the one hand, the JLSs created by the police from 1999 onwards and, on the other, the Security Commissions under the Vice Ministry of Communal Affairs. The first one organized the population without any other institutional link than the police. The other one pursued the organization of the population through the institutional framework of local power holders. Neither institutional level had any control over the JLSs that already operated in the country.

Comités Únicos de Barrio

However complicated the institutional overlap created by the Ministry of Interior and the Police, still other institutional actors were created. This time, the Municipality of the City of Guatemala created in 2001 its particular form of community policing organization: a large network of *Comités Únicos de Barrio* (Single Neighbourhood Committees or CUBs). The original project pursued the creation of 600 CUBs; currently there are more than 783 CUBs (MUNIGUATE n.d.). These organizations sought to create their own system to centralize the administration of resources. The participative structure of the Municipality of Guatemala City is a copy of the above mentioned Urban and Rural Development Councils and projects an image of a "mini state" within the state of Guatemala.

The administrative structure of the Municipality of Guatemala provides the CUBs with more autonomy than the rest of the country's administrative local authorities. It incorporated the JLSs created in 1999 but at the same time created other institutional levels beyond the existing one. Even though the organizational structure is the same, the main difference with the rest of JLSs is the role played by military officers in its activities as an extension of the combined patrols program (Army and Civil National Police). These patrols have been widely criticized because they are mechanisms where military personnel continue participating in national security tasks. Each Neighbourhood Committee is said to have a military representative collecting information for the Army, not for the Police (Interview with Priscila de Narciso, Auxiliary Mayors, 03/18/09).[67] The metropolitan districts 9 and 1 of Guatemala City total approximately one million inhabitants and have 200 Neighbourhood Committees. These organizations prefer having military rather than police support because they place more trust in the Army and expect the Army to solve the criminality problem with an "iron fist" (Interview with Rubén Darío Martínez, Auxiliary Mayor, 03/23/09).

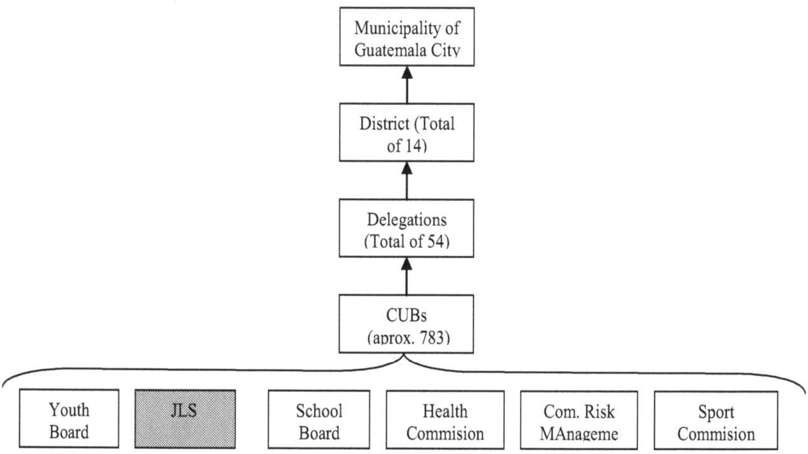

mostly non-indigenous. The areas where these neighbourhood committees are organized have medium income levels and can hire PSCs. The hiring of PSCs and the self-organization in committees is a double mechanism to protect against

67 About combined patrols see chapter VIII.

criminality. There are cases where a security neighbourhood organization is sponsored by a PSC or, on the contrary, the CUB hires PSCs as advisors or as protection providers. In other cases, PSCs sponsor neighbourhood organizations through the CUBs located in commercial urban areas of Guatemala City. The Hotel Security Council of Guatemala sponsors informal organization of neighbourhoods around tourist areas and has representatives in each security committee to collect information about criminal activities (Interview with Byron Heredia, Consejo de Seguridad Hotelera de Guatemala, 02/24/09). In 2008 the CUBs of zones 10 and 14 (high income residential areas) organized 45 JLSs and hired an Israeli security company to implement a security plan named "*Plan Petate*" with the aim of creating hundreds of JLSs in those zones and generating a system of information to be collected by the security company and then transmitted to the police or the army (*Prensa Libre* 10/22/10).

Due to the particular socio-economic level of some participants of the CUBs, their demands and interests are linked to private and individual protection schemes and the enclosure of public spaces, among others. In 2005, there were approximately 500 CUBs in the metropolitan area of Guatemala City and most of those organized into JLSs to close public streets and install checkpoints (*Prensa Libre* 06/28/05). One of the main security projects supported by the Guatemala City Municipality is the plan *Vecino Vigilante* (Vigilant Neighbour) which consists of a list of citizen security recommendations, such as putting together lists of neighbours, organizing a neighbourhood commission, creating alert systems between neighbours, and surveillance of domestic help and service personnel in houses and offices, among others (MUNIGUATE 2000). Through more than 200 security measures, the document insists in the importance of surveillance of the "other" and closing off public spaces.

5.3 The Reproductive Cycle

This section identifies the different phases through which the JLSs became vigilante self-defence policing organizations during the post-war. A number of reactions in the communities towards the JLSs can be identified. Based on empirical data and as an exercise of sequencing the reproductive cycle of social control and self-defence it is possible to distinguish the following sequence. First there prevailed a sense of distrust because JLSs recalled the recent PACs; second, the functional benefit of self defence started to generate acceptance; third, JLSs proliferated; fourth, they executed violent actions such as lynching, vigilantism, and a variety of aggressions; fifth, they deepened public institutional distrust; and sixth, the empowerment of JLSs as repressive and uncontrolled organizations generated fear in the population. Although this is a heuristic resource, it is important to mention that the stages are not independent. On the contrary, there is an interplay of processes and a wide range of effects that this section attempts to summarize with empirical examples.

In Quiché, the department with most human rights violations during the internal conflict, the reaction provoked in 2000 by the JLSs was negative because the population was reminded of the *Patrullas de Autodefensa Civil*, PAC, created by the army and the police to control communities. Even though the General Order prohibited the use of firearms, different groups in this department made it known that the JLSs used firearms, committed abuses, and acted as judges in some cases. These acts were defined as a risk that reproduced the abuses committed by the PACs. The population that integrated JLSs argued that they had the support of the community to prosecute criminals and apply customary punishments (*Prensa Libre* 05/16/00 and 05/29/00). Five years later, in 2005 it was reported that the population organized in JLSs organized patrols and exercised controls in the communities (*Prensa Libre* 05/04/05). In the same year, communities in Baja Verapaz, Quiché, and Totonicapán denounced that the JLS were implementing a system of patrols to fight crime produced by youth gangs, as well as problems in families and the lack of actions by the PNC (*Prensa Libre* 09/07/05). Those departments are considered part of the indigenous region with stronger organizational structures some of them created during the internal conflict (Interview with intelligence analyst of the State Intelligence Agency, 03/05/09).

The JLSs were rapidly incorporated into the social control dynamics of the communities because of their ambiguous nature and functions and because JLSs were organized based on the existing communal organizations. At the same time, the concept of community participation created a mechanism of impunity under violent collective action, such as lynching (which will be analysed in depth in another section of this study). Likewise community policing organizations were used to prevent investigations of crimes committed during the internal war. This is the case of the community of Pocohil in the department of El Quiché, in which the auxiliary mayor who created the security commission was also the former chief of the PAC and the current pastor of one of the evangelical churches. In May 2009, there was an exhumation conducted to find victims of the internal conflict. The population was alerted through traditional security mechanisms that outsiders described as "*guerrilleros*" were threatening the auxiliary mayor. The population directed by the auxiliary mayor threatened to lynch the people who provided support for the exhumation (UDEFEGUA 2010a). These examples show that the organization of JLSs was made, among other factors, to reproduce different functions directly linked with the local political needs and not for crime prevention.

JLSs have been used for profit and have a planned system of trials and punishments. In 2006 various communities of Chimaltenango and Sacatepéquez complained that the JLS together with communal leaders and the evangelical pastor patrolled the community and charged dwellers for each time they patrolled. When a suspect was detected, they activated their security mechanisms such as ringing the bells of the church in order to alert the community and catch the suspected criminal. After an improvised trial, the suspect could be sentenced to death by lynching. The community justifies the lynching based on a distortion of the social order produced by bad attitudes among youth and corruption in the police (*Prensa Libre* 05/06/06). One of the punishments implemented by the JLS was the expulsion of suspected criminals and their families (*Prensa Libre* 09/27/06). Trial and punishment systems implemented by JLSs are reproduction of actions committed by PACs in order to protect the community against insurgents and alleged criminals. The continuity of PACs members in JLSs allowed this reproduction.

However more than the continuity of the actors, self-reproducing policing was the continuity of function in the collective life. In 2007, reports spoke of the existence of a JLS created by former PACs and military commissioners in the village of Los Cimientos in the department of El Quiché. The leaders had been active since 1982 and they renamed themselves as "communal leaders". They were heavily armed, never changed their modus operandi nor structures, and never stopped killing suspects and intimidating the community. They took control of the Communal Development Council and forced the population to patrol and pay for the protection service. The people who were unable to pay were forced to work on the properties of the communal leaders. The violent activities of the Civil Patrol's former members forced more than 50 families to leave the community and prevented the investigations that the police and prosecutor's office wanted to undertake to find weapons (*Prensa Libre* 05/21/07).

The first JLS in Sololá was reported in 2000 when different communities protested against abuses committed by ex-PAC and former military personnel who made up the new security organization. In 2008, the population together with communal leaders announced the intensification of patrols and the publication of lists with new control regulations (*Prensa Libre* 05/13/08). A few days later, members of the security commission blew whistles to alert the community in order to catch two suspected criminals. A "communal judge" appointed by the security committee sentenced the suspected criminals to be burned alive. One of them was rescued by the PNC but the other was killed (*Prensa Libre* 05/16/08).

Santiago Atitlán in Sololá was one of the municipalities strongly affected by violence during the internal conflict. There were PACs as well as military commissioners and a strong presence of military units. In 1990, one of the cruellest massacres in the country was committed in Santiago Atitlán by military forces. After this a security and development committee was created that required that military personnel be expelled from the community. The security committee worked as a community policing organization by setting up patrols and protecting the church and other communal institutions. They defined a traditional system of informal social control based on the knowledge of each member of the community (Murga 1997). Once the state (represented by the army) withdrew, the post-war transformations required the state to recover its presence in communities affected by the war. Thus, traditional organizations were confronted with changes in formal institutions, especially police and judges. Wherever the new democratic institutions were present in the community, they were required to reconcile the differences between traditional and formal security and justice systems and to meet communal demands. The result was the existence of parallel systems of policing. More than ten years later, the situation seems to be different. Since 2006, more than 20 people were killed by social cleansing groups that previously published the names of their victims. The people killed were previously accused by those groups of involvement in corruption, drug trafficking, matrimonial infidelity, and rape as well as witchcraft. The members of the social cleansing groups were dressed in military uniforms and armed with military weapons (*El Periódico* 09/24/07). In 2009, the municipality called on the community to take part in neighbourhood surveillance with official sanction. At the same time, the security commission demanded that the justice system and the police start to catch criminals. The security commission announced also that they would prevent criminals from having the support of lawyers and any judicial defence. After all these measures, the population publicly declared its support for neighbourhood watches, which were considered a plus for the community (*Prensa Libre* 10/16/08; 03/27/09 and 06/10/09). These examples show how community policing organizations allowed the continuity of former vigilante actors and the reproduction of its violent and social control actions.

Other characteristic of JLSs is the high level of autonomy because these organizations define the local threat against which they are supposed to fight. This leads to the stigmatisation of some particular social groups, in this case, youths. In the department of San Marcos, the JLSs, with the support of the municipalities, implemented violent actions against youth gangs suspected to come from Guatemala City. The JLSs in this department are completely beyond the control of the police. They created their own coordination mechanism named "*Coordinadora de Seguridad Ciudanana Marquence*" in 2002 and refuse to have contact with public institutions (Interview with a police officer of the Sección de Intervención en Relaciones Comunitarias of the PNC, 10/22/10). Violent actions against suspected youth gangs were also organized in San Juan Sacatepéquez (only 40 kilometres from Guatemala City) by the JLSs. After the lynching of two gang members in 2007, the population intensified patrols and controls as well as demanding more accountability over the PNC. They demanded that youth accept the rules of the community, leave, or risk being lynched. They even planned to uniform youth and make them work in the streets. One of the measures imposed by the JLS was a curfew beginning daily at seven p.m. (Escobar 2008). After imposing the curfew, there were five lynchings in the municipality and some other people were killed for violating the curfew (*Prensa Libre* 11/07/07 and 12/12/07). The situation became so violent that the President of the Republic declared a state of emergency in the region in order to recover control (*El Periódico* 02/14/08). However not only high levels of autonomy explain the stigmatisation of youths. The definition of local threats was part of the community policing models that produced violent actions against alleged criminal groups.

Another example of the role of JLSs as protection of the established social order against suspected foreign influences is the community of San Pedro la Laguna in Sololá. This community was characterized by its strong social organization before and during the internal armed conflict. After the war ended, it became an attractive tourist destination for drug consumers. There were hotels and restaurants set up by foreigners who decided to live in the country. The community became known as "the little Amsterdam". The differences between the commercial activities of foreigners and locals were rapidly visible. In addition, the increase in drug consumption by local youth who participated in parties and activities organized by foreigners raised concerns among local leaders. The strong leadership of an evangelical mayor led to the organization of surveillance patrols and the Ministry of Interior authorized them. The JLS started to persecute drug consumers, alcohol drinkers, noisy people, and other "criminals". The JLS and judicial authorities started drug raids on hotels owned by foreigners where they found different drugs and a clandestine drug production laboratory. An alcohol ban was imposed beginning daily at 11 p.m. and raids were carried out to find illegal tourists. More than 50 tourists were captured, as well as many local youth identified with the "western" way of life (*El Periódico* 08/22/10).

The same situation was experienced in other communities such as Panajachel in Sololá, where the presence of tourists increased the conflict between modern activities and traditional values. External influences were perceived as a distortion of the established social order and the JLSs assumed a protective role. However, most economic activities in the region depend on the tourist industry and the activities of the JLSs tend to produce a conflict between different groups of the community because tourist feel threatened (*Prensa Libre* 01/08/11). These examples show that the alleged protection of the social order through vigilante actions and the stigmatisation of particular groups were motivated the introduction of community policing organizations in a context in which those actions were part of strong self-defence organizations created during the internal conflict. In this context, concepts such as prevention, identification of local threats and citizen protection reproduced the actions committed during the internal conflict with the additional absence of institutional controls and increased crime.

There are also JLSs linked with extra judicial executions. These JLSs started as community policing organizations and then became vigilante groups due to the high levels of autonomy they have and the legacies of former "death squads".[68] An example of this situation is the department of Escuintla, which currently has high crime rates and a presence of drug trafficking (UNDP 2007). In 2006, a JLS was created in the municipality of Palín and two years later some of the members joined social cleansing groups such as "*Comando de la Muerte*" (Death Command) and "*Ejército Secreto de Ejecución*" (Secret Execution Army). These groups published the names of suspects and then killed them. At the beginning, people of the community saw these actions in a positive light but later those groups turned to extortions and threats in exchange for their protection services. They controlled some roads and it was reported that they were involved in drug trafficking (*El Periódico* 11/14/08). The situation continued in 2009 when reports from the region indicated that the JLSs were armed that they published lists with the names of suspected criminals, and that they carried out their own investigations, judgments, and punishments. The Human Rights Office concluded that the JLSs in the region were totally out of control (*Prensa Libre* 08/11/09).

There are strong links between JLSs and local power authorities that lead to clientelistic relations and abuses of power. The control of local institutions can be observed as a result of the reproductive cycle of self-defence policing. An example of the reproductive process is San Juan Cotzal in Quiché. This is one of the three communities of the so-called "Triángulo Ixil" (Ixil Triangle) that was an area strongly affected by violence during the internal armed conflict. The strong legacy of the PACs and organizations created by insurgent groups marked the organizational structure of local authorities in the region. After the Peace Agreements there was a strong presence of state institutions and international organizations to reconstruct social networks and to strengthen peace processes. The municipality is characterized by its high poverty rates and in 2001 there were various complaints of corruption in the municipality (*Prensa Libre* 09/20/01). The first organized actions to check crime were reported in 2003 when the population beat up a suspected criminal. In 2005 complaints were received that the JLSs patrolled the community with firearms and threatened young people with long hair, tattoos, or other suspect markings with arrest (*Prensa Libre* 09/07/05). In 2008, these groups were formally organized under the model of JLSs in San Juan Cotzal and other communities in Quiché. The municipality provided them with firearms and support to continue patrolling. It was determined that the main security problem of the community was youth gangs. That year, the municipality

68 Chapter VI analyses "death squads" and other vigilante groups during the internal conflict.

and communal leaders accused 20 youths of being part of criminal gangs; they were subsequently arrested and sentenced under Maya rules to force labour in the municipality and assisting at the church. The sentence was based on supposed criminal actions characteristic of youth such as drinking, dressing in Western style, or being part of gangs (*Prensa Libre* 12/12/08 and 01/04/09). In April 2009, the existence of 65 JLSs in four communities of the region (including San Juan Cotzal) was reported. There were claims of abuses committed by patrolmen with firearms. For this reason, an investigation was launched by the PNC over the activities of these JLSs (*Prensa Libre* 04/28/09). In November 2009 a young man was arrested by the JLS accused of being a "*roquero*" (rocker). He was beaten and imprisoned in the municipality. His father was a police agent in a neighbourhood community and tried to release his son. The JLS arrested his father too and proceeded to beat him in the park. The community was called to the park and after a "Mayan" judge arrived at the scene, the police officer was sentenced to be burned. A human rights defender tried to avoid the lynching but he was beaten as well by the JLS. The police undertook an investigation of the facts and the auxiliary mayor was held of responsible for the death of the police officer. To date the mayor remains a fugitive (UDEFEGUA 2010b).

Other violent JLSs were identified in San Martín Jilotepeque in the department of Chimaltenango. In this community the JLS captured two suspected criminals in 2007. The punishment was that they had to fight each other until one of them died, upon which the survivor would be pardoned. In October 2008 the JLS beat two suspected swindlers. In February 2009 five men and one woman were accused of stealing a car, after which they were set on fire until they died. In November 2009 the JLS lynched a police officer accused of extortion by a bus driver who had been discovered without a driver's license by the police officer (*Prensa Libre* 11/11/09). JLSs can be a mechanism to reproduce authoritarian practices even under the form of traditional indigenous justice systems.

These examples show that JLSs became a mechanism to implement violent solutions for any problem that threats the local authority. That includes the organization of collective violence against other state institutions such as police and judicial offices. In 2002 in the village of Chupol, Huehuetenango, one police officer was lynched and the whole police institution was expelled from the village. After that the JLS took over control of security by implementing patrols and other surveillance mechanisms. In 2009 after a "popular trial," two suspects of kidnapping were lynched. The JLS rejected all intervention by any public institution (*Prensa Libre* 12/04/09). In March 2010 there were reports that more than 600 JLSs operated in Huehuetenango but only 78 were registered with the PNC. The authorities recognized that the JLSs in the department were out of control: they frightened the population with firearms, conducted many of the 28 reported lynching during that year, and took over social development projects, among other violent actions. The municipalities provided them with identification papers and also gave them the authorization to carry out their actions (*Prensa Libre* 03/01/10). The examples show that the organization of JLSs in a context of weak transformation processes lead to the legitimisation of vigilante and authoritarian actions and to the delegitimisation of the police. In other words, the introduction of community policing in this context produced the opposite outcome of the ideal of collaborative relations between police and community.

The reproductive cycle of the JLSs produced other effects such as the relegitimisation of the militaristic security solution. The organization of JLSs generates the acceptance of the role of the Army in public security. This process transforms the image of the army, from perpetrators of human rights violations to the only solution to the problem of criminality. Insofar as the PAC and military commissioners were organized by the army and became the organizational basis of the JLSs, after more than fifteen years of reproducing social control mechanisms in post-war society those structures became a legitimate mechanism for the post-war role of the army. In the same way that the CUBs in the metropolitan area of Guatemala City promote the hiring of PSCs and the participation of military officers in public security, in those areas where it is not possible to hire a PSC the remaining option is to demand the presence of the military. This process is reinforced by the fact that the Police organized the JLSs but afterwards they delegated public security to the communities and their organizations. The lack of public institutions, the presence of corruption in the police and justice system, and a growing perception of insecurity led to the acceptance of military presence in the public sphere. Since the military has legal restrictions to implement security operations and arrests, the acceptance of the military lies in its image of a disciplined and incorruptible institution.

In 2005 the JLSs of El Petén requested the installation of a military base because they believed the police were no longer able to protect the area from drug trafficking and other criminal activities (*Prensa Libre* 09/01/05). The same situation occurred in both poor neighbourhoods and exclusive residential areas in Guatemala City where the JLSs requested a permanent military presence to protect the community. A characteristic of this request is that the military personnel assigned to protect high income areas is not linked with the police while in other areas the military patrol together with the police (*Prensa Libre* 08/20/06; *El Periódico* 10/26/08). In 2008, the Ministry of Defence received more than 45 requests for military patrols in different departments and Guatemala City. JLSs, Auxiliary Mayors and Community Councils made the requests (*El Periódico* 12/12/08). In May 2010, the JLSs requested military personnel to implement joint patrols in Huehuetenango; as a result, 200 soldiers were assigned to patrol the city and its villages (*Prensa Libre* 05/11/10). The previous examples showed that the JLSs are the continuity of a collaborative relation between militaries and communities created on the basis of fear during the internal conflict.[69]

Regardless of the institutional efforts that were made to create and then control the proliferation of community policing organizations in post-war society, it still has to be argued that their existence as mechanisms of social control follows the path set by previous experiences. One intelligence officer mentioned that JLSs are not a product of the call for organization made by the police in 1999 (Interview with intelligence analyst of the State Intelligence Agency, 03/05/09). The JLSs were created by their own structure and community and neighbourhood history, especially in those areas with very violent activity during the internal conflict (*Prensa Libre* 05/11/10). That explains why regions with low crime rates reflect high communal organization for security and even violent actions such as lynching. The homogeneous design of JLSs does not take into account the cultural traditions and historical conflicts of each community because they are organizations that are created by the central administration of the security institutions (Interview with intelligence analyst of the State Intelligence Agency, 03/05/09).

The existence of violence, organized crime, youth gangs, drugs and human trafficking, among others, generates a perception of insecurity that allows the civilian population to justify its organization as a response to the absence of state security institutions. However it cannot provide a general explanation for the causes of this proliferation. Usually, the population organizes itself before having contact with state institutions or high crime rates. As was mentioned before, the proliferation of such organizations produces negative effects on the rule of law and reduces confidence in the judicial system because "private justice" is applied, normally, in the form of lynching or extra judicial executions. However, the positive or negative actions of the JLSs depend largely on the historical organizational culture of the region.

The role of self-defence in the production of protection has to be explained in historical terms. The state formation process in Guatemala is based largely on collaborative relations between local elites, state institutions and vigilante organizations. Peace building programs and security sector reforms did not include these historical trajectories. The ideals of state monopoly over the use of force, the rule of law and more specific, the principle of in *dubio pro reo*, for example, should be examined in this historical perspective not only to understand the failure of community policing programs but also to explain the effects of vigilante actions on those democratic ideals.

69 Chapter VIII will analyse the role of the militaries in public security during the post-war.

5.4 Crime Rates and Community Policing

As mentioned in the literature review, the proliferation of security neighbourhood committees is commonly associated with the increase in crime and the absence of public institutions. Simultaneously it is argued that crime rates in poor regions lead to collective violence in the form of private justice through communal organization. The results of this study show that in the case of Guatemala, the continuity of control mechanisms and self-defence policing is a stronger explanation for the proliferation of such security organizations due to the low correspondence between socio-economic and crime indicators and the presence of JLSs.

The analysis of homicide rates and JLSs reveal two important aspects: first, the low homicide rates in indigenous communities, and second, the absence of a clear link between poverty rates and homicide rates.

Figure 8 shows the distribution of homicide and poverty rates per department. The higher the poverty rate, the lower the homicide rate, especially in those areas where indigenous populations represent between 76 and 100 per cent of total population, that is, in Totonicapán, Quiché, Sololá, Alta Verapaz, Huehuetenango, Chimaltenango, and San Marcos (UNDP 2010a). There are also departments with high poverty rates, low indigenous population, and high homicide rates (Jalapa, Santa Rosa and Chiquimula). The extreme case is the metropolitan area of Guatemala City, with lower poverty rates and high homicide rates. While Guatemala City is the only department in the country located between 0.828 and 0.660 according to the Human Development Index, Alta Verapaz and Quiché are located between 0.516 and 0.306 and Totonicapán and Huehuetenango are located between 0.571 and 0.517 (Human Development Index).[70]

While homicide rates are not related to poverty, extreme social inequalities produce situations of serious social tension (UNDP 2007; 2010a and 2010b).[71] One implication of this situation is the high level of perception of insecurity. Insecurity is the principal social problem identified in Guatemala City and only in part it is related to the real situation of criminality (UNDP 2007). Numerous studies have attempted to explain that the perception of insecurity and the reactions that it provokes are based on different social discourses that are related to

70 *"The Human Development Index (HDI) is a summary measure of human development. It measures the average achievements in a country in three basic dimensions of human development: a long and healthy life, access to knowledge and a decent standard of living. The HDI is the geometric mean of normalized indices measuring achievements in each dimension"* (UNDP 2010b).

71 According to UNDP 2007, Guatemala is one of the most unequal countries in Latin America (2007: 10).

political and social phenomena not directly linked with the causes of violence (Huhn, Oettler, and Peetz 2006a and 2006b).

The question now is if the homicide rates as well as poverty rates and ethnic characteristics explain the presence of JLSs in a certain area. Figure 8 shows that there is no clear correspondence among those factors. There are departments with high homicide rates and a majority of non-indigenous population that report only a few JLSs (Petén, Izabal and Chiquimula). On the other hand, departments like San Marcos, Alta Verapaz, and Quiché have low homicide rates, mostly indigenous population, and a high number of JLSs. The rest of departments with a majority of indigenous populations and high poverty rates (Totonicapán, Sololá, Huehuetenango, Baja Verapaz, and Chimaltenango) have a regular number of JLSs.

If homicide rates show a clear inverse trend when related to those departments with higher proportions of indigenous population, it obviously differs when compared with other crime indicators and its linkages with JLSs. Figure 8 and 9 show that there is no specific trend that links those departments with mostly indigenous population and crime rates. The National Human Development Report (INDH) uses data provided by charges the population made to the PNC (UNDP 2010b). However, there are intervening factors such as language, access to police stations, institutional trust, literacy and also collective historical experiences, that influence a citizen's decision to report criminal acts. For this reason, the number of criminal acts which are not reported may produce different results but the data, nonetheless, allows for a description of general perspectives. In comparison with the number of robberies and assaults in Guatemala City (8,274 in the year 2008), the departments with more indigenous population do not present such high rates of these crimes; Sololá and Totonicapán in fact present the lowest number of these crimes. The same situation occurs with data of injured people, which number 54 in Sololá and 39 in Totonicapán while the highest numbers are located in Guatemala City and Chiquimula with 3,511 and 385, respectively. On the other hand, the two departments with the highest levels of indigenous population present some of the highest numbers of reported cases of domestic violence: San Marcos and Huehuetenango with 230 and 203 cases and Guatemala City with 226 cases. Domestic violence is even more difficult to estimate because these events are hardly ever reported due to cultural and social constraints (UNDP 2007; PDH 2004; ODHAG 2010)

Figure 8: Homicide and Poverty Rates in Guatemala 2008

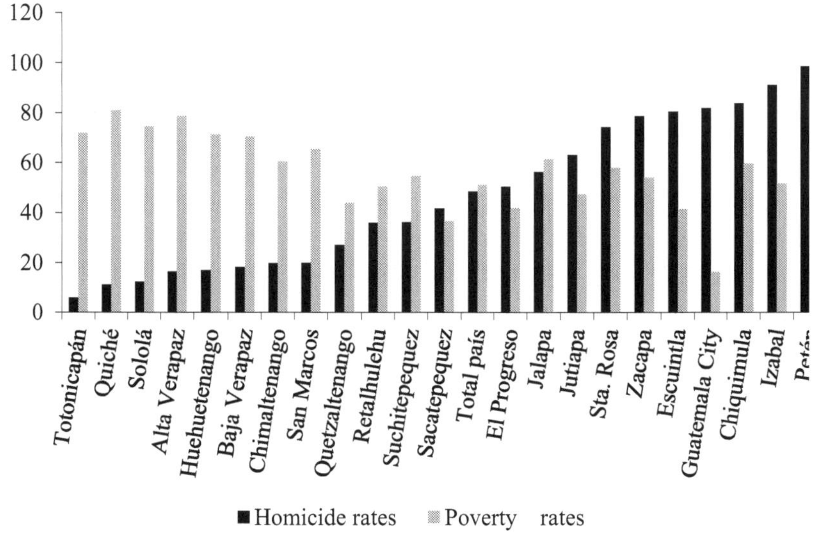

Source: Own elaboration with data from PNC Guatemala 2008 and ENCOVI 2006.

While criminal rates show low correlation with the ethnic composition of the populations, the same situation seems to be present with JLSs. As was mentioned, there is no observable relation between low homicide rates and the existence of JLSs. In the case of other criminal acts such as robbery and assault, there is no direct relation, either. The higher numbers of JLSs are located in San Marcos, where the number of robberies and assaults is lower in comparison with Guatemala City and Escuintla which have, conversely, a low number of JLSs. Another case is Totonicapán, where the number of robberies, assaults, injuries, and domestic violence are the lowest of the country but the number of JLSs is significantly high (134 JLSs). It is possible to conclude from this description that crime rates and the composition of the population do not show a clear relationship with the existence of community policing organizations.

Figure 9: Homicide Rates and JLSs in Guatemala 2008

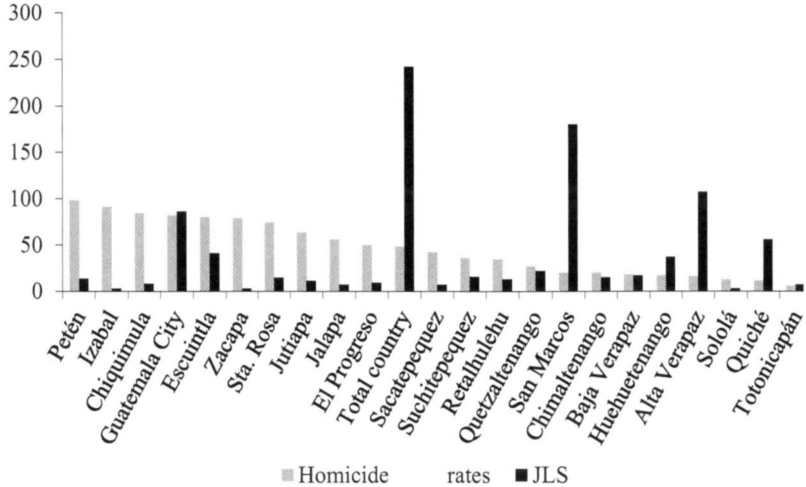

Source: PNC 2008.

The presence or absence of state institutions is used as an explicative argument about the proliferation of community policing organizations. It assumes that policing organizations are the result of institutional weaknesses. The INDH includes an index of state density that examines the territorial action and distribution of the state based on three dimensions, namely physical presence, bureaucracy (number of public employees), and financial resources. It measures how state institutions, bureaucracy, and financial resources are distributed across the national territory (UNDP 2010 b: 122). The data was collected for the period 2008-2010. This is a quantitative description that reflects the quality of public services. The index measures state density in a range from 0 to 1 in which 1 represents high relative density and 0 represents low relative density (UNDP 2010b). The value of each department is the average of all its municipalities. Within each department, the differences between the administrative centres (*cabeceras departamentales*) of each department could be important. For this reason the data of the average of each department is included as well as the higher value that corresponds to the *cabecera* and the lower value that corresponds to a municipality. The use of an index of state density identifies those areas where the state is concentrated and those where there are serious deficiencies of coverage by public institution. The INDH observes that the *cabeceras* of each department have a high average density and of these, Guatemala City has the highest state density. This high centralization of state presence presupposes that a large part of the national territory has to find alternatives to supply core state functions such as health, education, and security.

There is not sufficient information to explore at a national level the different strategies the population employs to supply the lack of state services. As it is argued in this research, private security became a substitute for state public security functions through a historical process of delegation of those functions to the private sector, whether through private security companies or community policing organizations.

Table No. 4 shows that state institutions, services, and resources are concentrated in the *cabeceras* of each department. The five departments with highest levels of indigenous populations are ranked at the national average or sometimes a few points higher. Only San Marcos and Huehuetenango are ranked under the national average, but their *cabeceras* are highly ranked. When comparing crime numbers (robberies and assaults, injuries, and domestic violence) and state density, there seems to be no observable link between them. Guatemala City, with the highest average of state density, experiences the highest number of crimes. The departments with a departmental average that is only one point under the national average are within the average of such crimes. The situation of Totonicapán is different in that it is ranked two points above the national average of the index but the number of reported crimes is very low.

Table: 4: Crime rates, JLSs and State Density Index in Guatemala[72]

Department	Robbery and Assault	Injured	Domestic Violence	JLSs 2010	State Density Index		
					Average	Highest Value	Lowest Value
Guatemala	8,274	3511	226	12	0.37	0.75	0.14 (San Miguel Petapa)
Escuintla	1305	280	130	80	0.26	0.23	0.17 (Palín)
Sacatepequez	702	170	72	11	0.23	0.57	0.14 (Sn. Bartolome Milpas Altas)
Quetzaltenango	672	228	136	132	0.26	0.52	0.14 (Almolonga)
Chimaltenango	512	170	91	44	0.22	0.36	0.13 (Parramos)
Suchitepéquez	436	183	144	25	0.23	0.44	0.11 (Sn. Juan Bautista)
Huehuetenango	428	143	203	19	0.21	0.45	0.14 (Sn. Juan Atitán)
San Marcos	281	161	230	272	0.21	0.56	0.12 (Ocós)
Petén	269	233	73	28	0.25	0.49	0.20 (Sn. Andrés)
Izabal	223	219	33	15	0.28	0.49	0.21 (Livingston)
Alta Verapaz	215	249	96	41	0.24	0.43	0.14 (Sn. Juan Chamelco)
Retalhuleu	198	110	57	10	0.29	0.45	0.17 (San Sebastian)
Zacapa	196	184	36	31	0.30	0.48	0.19 (La Unión)
Chiquimula	176	385	47	15	0.29	0.48	0.21 (Esquipulas)
Jutiapa	172	130	55	13	0.29	0.43	0.14 (Sn. José Acatempa)
Quiché	167	139	101	29	0.22	0.42	0.16 (Sto. Tomás Chichi.)
Santa Rosa	161	142	33	10	0.24	0.57	0.17 (Barberena)
El Progreso	123	53	35	63	0.27	0.55	0.21 (Sanarate)
Jalapa	83	163	49	30	0.30	0.41	0.16 (Sn. Pedro Pinula)
Baja Verapaz	77	55	35	17	0.27	0.46	0.20 (Cubulco)
Sololá	71	54	92	12	0.25	0.41	0.15 (Sta. Catarina Palopó)
Totonicapán	61	39	76	134	0.22	0.35	0.15 (Santa Lucía la Reforma)
Total Country	14,802	6,938	2,050	1,043	0.22	0.47	0,17

Source: UNDP 2010b; PNC 2010.

The question is if this data on crime rates and the index of state density contributes to explain the proliferation of JLSs. Table 4 also shows that those departments with a high average of state density do not have a high number of JLSs. The first case is Guatemala City, with only 12 registered JLSs. The fact that it is possible through other sources to identify more JLSs than those registered by the Police is a sign that no matter how high the presence of the state is, there is also high institutional weakness to control such organizations. Guatemala City is characterized by high levels of citizen distrust over public institutions which

72 Departments in gray have mostly indigenous population.

have an impact on the low number of registered JLSs. There are other alternatives in urban areas to implement protection measures without relying on community organizations (for example, commercial private security). Another case of high state density is Zacapa, which is ranked eight points over the national average but only has 31 reported JLSs. The contextual characteristics of this department can better explain this situation: Zacapa is an eastern department with mostly non indigenous populations, high homicide rates, and low robbery and assault number. In the last two decades, there has been a proliferation of local drug cartels and a large number of people linked to security structures of organized crime. Traditionally, this department supplied state security forces at the direction and command levels as well as intelligence structures. Local authorities have traditionally accepted the use of firearms, which is one of the idiosyncratic characteristics of the region.

On the other side is San Marcos that has reported 272 JLSs and is ranked one point under the national average of state density. The other sources presented in this study show the existence of a large number of JLSs in addition to the ones registered by the police. San Marcos has a mostly indigenous population and low crime rates (between 0.00 and 2.00 homicides per 10 thousand inhabitants) except in two border municipalities. Neither crime rates nor state density explain the proliferation of JLSs in this border department. The contextual aspects of the department show a strong tradition of communal organization and the legacy of a strong activity of organizational structures created during the internal armed conflict.

The differences between *cabeceras* and municipalities are very important due to the centralized model of state administration. As mentioned, the highest level of state density in the country is in Guatemala City while its lowest level in its municipalities is located in San Miguel Petapa (0.14). Taking the level of the *cabecera* of each department, Escuintla has the lowest level (0.23) but its position in the departmental average is six points over the national average. The lowest value in this department is in the municipality of Palín (0.17). The department has high homicide rates specially related to drug trafficking. The pattern of high state density in the *cabeceras* and low density in the municipalities is reproduced in all departments in the country. While the departmental average of state density allows for some identification of trends related to homicides, the differences between *cabeceras* and municipalities permits an exploration of this phenomena in detail.

Whatever the causes of criminal violence are – which is not the central issue of this study – the data shows that state density does not explain higher or lower crime rates in the country. The quality of state institutions could explain its relationship with violent crime and its social reactions. In other words, if the level of state presence cannot explain the existence of high or low crime rates, it also may not be able to explain alleged social reactions to crime such as private security. The official data presented by the police about the presence of JLSs is only a general reference but it reflects the low state capacity to control JLSs and the fact that private policing fulfils those areas where the state is not present.

When the index of state density is related to the state public security presence in the country, the five departments with highest indigenous population (Alta Verapaz, San Marcos, Huehuetenango, Chimaltenango, and Totonicapán) are ranked at a low level of the index between 0.00 and 0.05. On the other side are Guatemala City and other eastern cities in the country that were ranked between 0.64 and 0.99. The index takes into account the number of police officers in each municipality to measure state density related to public security actors (UNDP 2010b: 140). From a state centred perspective, it can be argued that more police presence means more security conditions. However, as was mentioned, low state density does not mean higher crime rates. On the contrary, those areas with low state density (between 0.00 and 0.05) have low crime rates as well. Guatemala City shows again that even though it has the highest state density related to security institutions (between 0.64 and 0.99) it also has the highest crime rates. Other departments such as Escuintla, Izabal, and Petén have relatively low state density (between 0.06 and 0.19) but high homicide rates. There are some border municipalities with high homicide rates located in departments with low state density (San Antonio Huista and La Democracia in the department of Huehuetenango). The department of El Petén indicates that homicide rates increase as the distance to the Mexican border decreases. Border municipalities are regions of high commercial activity and drug trafficking, as are the departments located in the route of the drug to the north. This is also the case of Escuintla and Izabal, where two main ports are located.

For this reason, police coverage in the country is not a strong indicator of the presence of JLSs because, despite the absence of a standard rule about the adequate number of police officers in a country, police coverage in Guatemala is low in comparison to the population (UNDP 2010a). In 2006 there were 20,999 police officers in Guatemala, which means 1.56 police officers per 100,000 inhabitants or 0.19 police officers per square kilometres (OCAVI 2008).[73] Most of the police officers are concentrated in the metropolitan area of Guatemala City, where there are many JLSs and high homicide rates. In regions like Quiché and Alta Verapaz, there is low police coverage, low homicide rates and high presence of JLSs. In other areas like the metropolitan area of Guatemala City, there is high police coverage and a regular number of JLSs.

73 The data provided by the Civil National Police of Guatemala do not distinguish between those agents dedicated to administrative work and operative agents.

Another perspective to analyse the connection between community policing organizations and crime and violence in the country is through insecurity perceptions and victimization rates. In 2010 the perception of insecurity measured by the Latinobarómetro in Guatemala was about midway (40%) when compared with other cities in the continent such as Perú (53.8) and, on the other hand, the USA (22.5) as a country with the lowest insecurity perception rates in the continent (Azpurú 2010: 76). Guatemala shows a decreasing trend from 2004 (45.5%) to 2010 (40%) with regards to insecurity perceptions. However, this data contrasts with the increasing crime numbers that place the country at the top of the most insecure countries in Latin America. In this sense, the differences between rural areas and urban areas are important because a feature of violence in the country is its focalisation. Some 30.3% of people in urban areas were victimized in the last twelve months in contrast with only 17% in the rural areas. In 59.2% of the crimes, the victims reported that the incident occurred in residential areas in both rural and urban territories (Azpurú 2010: 81). In 2009, 58.21% of the victims of criminal acts were located in non indigenous municipalities and 15.78% were located in indigenous municipalities (UNDP 2007: 25). If only the victims of the metropolitan area of Guatemala City (40.7%) are taken into account, the country could be placed at the top of the list of more victimized countries in Latin America while, as a whole, the country is located in a lower position. The victimization by criminal acts shows that crime in Guatemala is mainly an urban phenomenon that occurs in people's own residential area while the perception of insecurity impacts the whole country.

As it was described, the fact that the main state density levels are located in the *cabeceras* of each department corresponds with focalisation of crime in urban areas. Rural areas, most of them with high percentages of indigenous population and high poverty rates as well as low levels of state density, are less victimized by crime. The focalisation of crime and state presence in urban areas does not explain why community policing organizations are present and active in the whole country and why the range of their activities varies in each context.

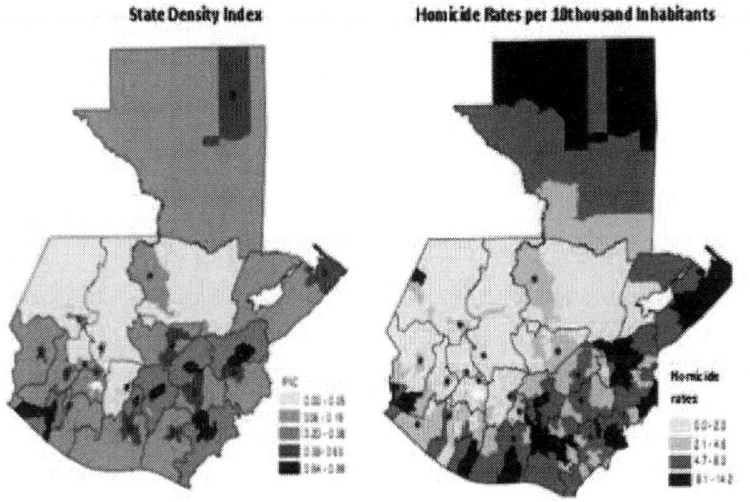

Source: UNDP 2010b.

To sum up, the chapter proves that common explanations based on the lacks of state capabilities and crime rates do not explain adequately the proliferation and reproduction of non-commercial private security in Guatemala. Since this analysis is based only on the reported JLSs, one can argue that the proliferation of non-commercial private security is not directly caused by the increase in crime, ethnic characteristics, poverty rates, or security institutional coverage. In this sense, the continuity and change of social and political mechanisms of control and the organizational history of certain areas are stronger explanatory factors for the existence of JLSs as the most important form of non-commercial private security.

5.5 The Historical Explanation of JLSs

For some Central American countries, including Guatemala, Holden (1996) argues that the process of state making required the state to absorb the protective function of the caudillos of the 19th century. The limits of official violence were amplified in order to protect elite and political interests (Holden 1996: 441). The author also argues that this process was not a pure division between state and subaltern actors. On the contrary, bargaining between them was a common practice that reinforced the continuity of violence and collaboration as mechanisms of state power relations (Holden 1996: 441; Brachet-Marquez 2001). Finally, the author stresses that the "military never acted independently of other, non military agents of the state, and none of those agents has ever acted independently of civil society" (Holden 1996: 452). The basis of this argumentation is that the use of violence in politics is not necessarily concentrated in the actions of one particular institution (armies or police) but in the social relationships the state institutional framework reproduces (Holden 1996: 452).

Private policing is a field where different social and political relations interplay, from state sponsored community organizations or state formalization of commercial private security activities to traditional and historical forms of self defence. The displacement of public security functions to the private sphere is the necessary process that propels this relational mechanism.

As has been argued, the historic continuity of security collaboration mechanisms – formal and informal – promoted by the State vary with regard to its structures and forms of organization. Nevertheless, they reinforce the tendency to displace the state security function to the private sphere. This displacement could be in a substitutive or complementary form and depends on different factors such as the organizational culture of the region and the presence of former members of control mechanisms, among others.

The social control mechanisms created with particular political interests in a particular moment in the past, reinforced the collaboration mechanisms required by the state in order to preserve its political power. The social control relations between state and citizens have been characterized by the creation of social organizations that can be violent and repressive against those identified as undesirable but that at the same time assume a protective role towards the same populations they control as justification for the continuity of a particular established social order. The kind of protection or the alleged threat against this protection is offered according to the political context.

From this perspective this study argues that the existence of collaborative and repressive social control organizations and the intensity and characteristics of state violence explain the reproductive process of the JLSs. After concluding that the relationship of variables such as crime, ethnicity, and state presence with JLSs does not explain satisfactorily their proliferation, its worth looking into the link between state violence during the internal conflict, the presence of PACs and Military Commissioners, and today's existence of community policing organizations.

State Violence and Community Policing Organizations

The areas with highest indigenous populations are the areas where there was more violence during the internal war and where there was a strong tradition of communal organization. Approximately 83.3% of all victims of human rights violations during the internal conflict belonged to a Maya ethnic group (CEH 1999b). Due to the high levels of violence and its characteristics and objectives, scholars have argued that an ethnocide was committed, that is, a combination of massive murder and the destruction of the cultural identity of the enemy (Oettler 2006b: 22). Those populations represented a threat for the military due to the historical culture of communal resistance and organization and the possibility that they might constitute the social basis of the insurgency.

Figure 10: Percentage of Human Rights Violations in Guatemala (1962-1996)

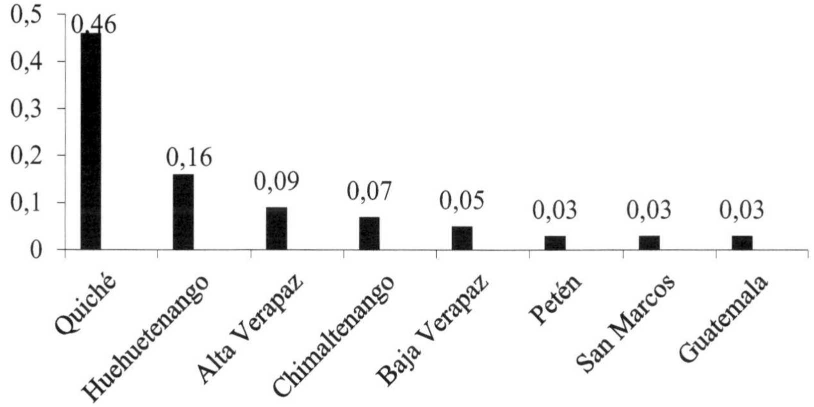

Source: CEH 1999c.

The counterinsurgency strategy required the implementation and reactivation of stronger social control mechanisms inside the communities (Schirmer 2001). Due to the belief that the indigenous population had a secret and dangerous side (Oettler 2006b: 22), the social control mechanisms functioned from inside the community. In this context the figure of the "alien", whether it meant persons, symbols, activities, institutions, or ideologies, became a risk factor to be reduced through the combination of social organization and community policing. During the internal conflict the strongest social control actions of PACs and Military Commissioners and insurgent organizations were located in the north-western part of the country. Most frequent human rights violations during the internal war were committed in areas with majority of indigenous population and structural poverty.

Figure No. 11 shows that 54% of the population organized into a PAC was concentrated in the seven departments with highest indigenous population.[74] It is important to mention that not only PACs where organized in the communities in the context of war. There were also organizations created by the insurgents to gain social support. These organizations were the Local Irregular Forces, FIL, and the Clandestine Committees, CCL, in strategic areas of the country. The capacity of the insurgents to organize the communities was no match for the institutional coverage of the army. These organizations were organized and functioned inside the community and they functioned as a self defence organization (Brett 2007: 51). FIL and CCL did not use firearms but in many cases they supported the insurgent military activities (Brett 2007: 52). The main functions of these organizations were information gathering about the army and the defence of the community. Against this, the counterinsurgent project reinforced community policing through a "civic action" component of the military actions (Ball *et al.* 1999). The nature and functioning of the PACs, Military Commissioners, FIL, and CCL will be explained in the next section of this study.

Figure 11: Number of former PACs who requested compensation (2003-2004)

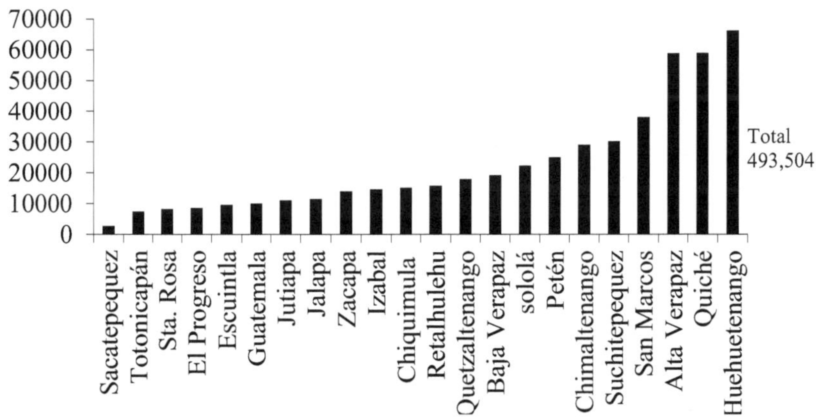

Source: Own elaboration with data from Sáenz de Tejada 2004.

The operations and organization were different in each region. It began with the divergence of social control mechanisms between rural and urban areas. There were PACs, Military Commissioners, and insurgent organizations in urban areas but their characteristics were different from those in rural areas, which meant

74 This percentage was calculated based on the number of people that in 2005 required payment for its services as PAC (Sáenz de Tejada 2004).

that they were adapted to the traditional and cultural forms of organization. The case of Totonicapán is an interesting exception because due to its historical and strong organizational culture, the community refused to participate both in the PACs and the insurgent organizations, and nowadays there is only a small number of JLSs in the department. Nevertheless it is possible to identify some concentration in particular areas.

Likewise, the percentage of human rights violations committed by paramilitary structures like the network of Military Commissioners was especially high in those areas with a majority of indigenous populations. As was explained earlier, the Military Commissioners had been activated due to different reasons at given moments in Guatemalan history. During the internal war, they were responsible for organizing PACs and controlling the activities of the community and the implementation of military activities. Due to their direct link with the military, they were considered responsible for the security of the community against threats such as insurgent groups or criminals. With the exception of Zacapa, the remaining departments match the departments with high rate of human rights violations and presence of PACs and are nowadays departments with high number of JLSs.

As it was mentioned before, the explaining factors of criminality in the post-war period seem to be different from those that explain private policing proliferation. In other words, the link between crime and community organization seems to be weak. What seems to be strong is the social organization for self defence both in the context of the internal conflict but also during the rise in crime after the war. Non-commercial private security reinforces historical mechanisms of self-defence against new threats, either real or potential. Nowadays the high perception of insecurity and the existence of historical citizen security mechanisms without State controls lead to private responses that, in the case of JLSs, can result in violent and authoritarian practices.

Figure 12: Percentage of Human Rights violations committed by Military Commissioners (1962-1996)

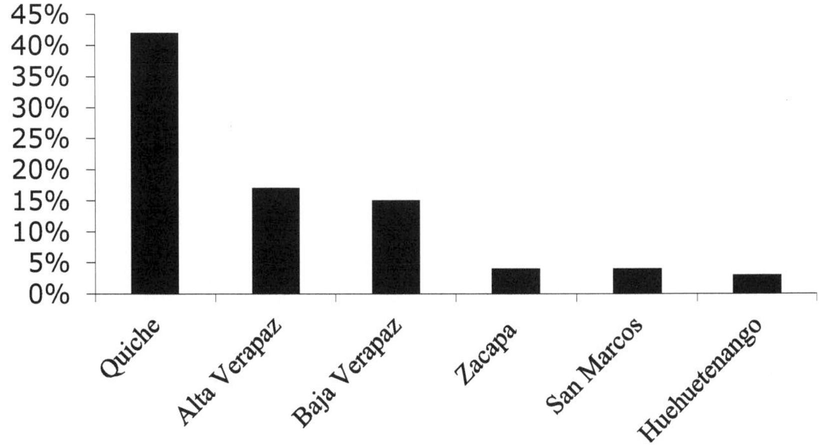

Source: CEH 1999c.

Political violence during the internal conflict is linked with the existence of self-defence policing organizations. The data shows that there is a relation between the existence of vigilante organizations and the presence of JLSs. More than the search of the continuity of the same actors, the emphasis here is on the continuity of vigilante actions as a self-defence policing function which was reproduced in the post-war context. The historical analysis presented will show the continuities of the functioning of these mechanisms as an explicative perspective of the proliferation of private policing.

***

After analysing the origins and institutional transformations of the post-war community policing organizations, the following aspects might be underlined. First, the creation of the JLSs in 1999 occurred in a context in which the former social control mechanisms created during the war were only formally dissolved but remained functionally active. In fact, they became part of the formal and informal local institutions. This situation presented a risk when transferring the operations of those social control structures into the new post-war organization. Second, the new police institution found in the creation of JLSs a way to delegate its security functions to the neighbourhood organizations. This happened, on the one hand, because of the lack of agents, training, and other institutional capabilities and, on the other, due to the persistence of criminal organizations in the police and the failure of a post-war police reform.

In the case of Guatemala, this persistence was produced through the process of agents "recycling" from the former security structures into the new police. At the same time, the creation of multiple and competitive institutional levels led to a gradual separation of the community policing organizations and the public security institutions. This separation did not mean the end of its activities; on the contrary, community policing organizations became autonomous and outside of state control. International models and public policies did not observe the strong historical trajectories of self-defence policing that rapidly reproduced vigilante actions of preventions and protection against alleged criminals.

Parallel to this, the creation of JLSs reinforced the role of the army in public security matters as well as PSCs in urban areas. During a first stage, the JLSs reproduced the sense of self defence which was created largely by the military during the internal armed conflict. But in a second stage, the JLSs found in the army a substitute for the police. The army offered an iron fist and an image of discipline and incorruptibility when compared with the police. This reinforced the social function of military officers in public security as well as violent and vigilante actions implemented through community policing initiatives such as lynching, extra judicial executions and public punishment.

Crime rates as well as demographic and territorial state institutional presence do not explain satisfactorily the proliferation of community policing organizations. In this chapter a description was given of the strong link between violence during the internal conflict, the more affected areas, the perpetrators, the victims, and the presence of social control mechanisms. The next section of this study will be continued by a description of the self reproducing sequence that explains the proliferation of both commercial and non commercial private policing from an historical perspective

6. Public Security and The Emergence of Private Policing

This chapter addresses the evolution of the institutional pattern that explains the proliferation of commercial and non-commercial private policing in Guatemala. The argument follows the logic of an historical explanation in which a set of initial conditions, encompassed within the decade of 1944-1954, created the context for the irruption of a critical juncture in 1954 during which competing political projects (reformist and counterrevolutionary fought over control of the state. The result was political stabilization based on a repressive anti-communist policy that led to the construction of public security institutions geared to prevent the re-emergence of reformist governments. The chapter focuses on the functions of security institutions that emerged from this critical juncture under the argument that the concentration of national security tasks by those institutions – which basically means fight against communism – initiated an institutional pattern of displacement of public security functions in which public security and traditional policing functions were marginalized. As a consequence of this marginalization, private security and mechanisms of social control took over public security functions. Commercial private security appeared in parallel to the National Police in matters of national security. On the other hand, informal social control groups directed by security forces implemented vigilante actions in the name of anticommunism and the fight against crime. In summary, it is necessary to understand the trajectories of the state in order to explain the proliferation of private policing. To do this, this chapter describe in detail historical information in order to recreate the many different paths that constitutes the historical displacement of public security.

The chapter describes the decade of 1944-1954 and the events that marked the end of the reformist government. In order to explain the institutional pattern of public security displacement, this section focuses on the trajectories of the National Police, the vigilante groups, and the private security services until 1986. This analysis will be undertaken, on the one hand, from the perspective of the influence of the United States in the reform on the National Police and other security forces. Documents of the Digital National Security Archive (DNSA) show that the inclusion of Guatemala in the Public Safety Program of the United States reinforced the security forces for the fight against communism while traditional police functions were marginalized. On the other hand, documents of the *Archivo Histórico de la Policía Nacional de Guatemala* (AHPN) evidence the parallel creation of private security services by police and military officers as well as private security companies created by international security advisors. The chapter also analyses the trajectories of non-commercial private policing through the reinforcement of self-defence organizations and vigilante groups.

As a complement to the perspective of U.S. influence and internal institutional dynamics, the analysis of the political context is included throughout the study. The context is marked essentially by the political instability of the governments and the emergence and intensification of the armed conflict.[75]

6.1 Initial Conditions and the Rupture of 1954

The end of the reformist decade of 1944-1954 has been largely studied as a time when the country underwent a particular sequence of events that explain the history of the rest of the twentieth century.[76] For this study this period is consedered the initial conditions of a path dependent process.[77] The events of 1954 represent, on the one hand, the end of the reformist period that resulted from the crisis of the liberal oligarchic state (Tischler 2001). On the other hand, different political forces confronted one another in order to gain control of the state, such as those conservative social groups seeking to reimpose political stability via state coercion and elimination of the opposition,[78] and on the other hand, the reformist groups (young military officers, students, urban professionals) that sought the return of democratic guarantees. The deep roots of the authoritarian state and the conservative and anti democratic make up of the economic elites, plus the support of the United States, provided for political stabilization based on repression of all form of opposition under an anti communist policy in which the armed forces (and specially the military) were the core of the state terror apparatus (Gleijeses 1991; Jonas 1981). As a critical juncture, the overthrow of the government of Jacobo Arbenz in 1954 not only defined the trajectory of the state for

75 Annex 1 and 2 provide a graphical explanation of all institutional transformations and processes described in this chapter.

76 Gleijeses (1991) analysed the scope and limitations of the revolutionary process, the agrarian reform, the Guatemalan communism; Schlesinger and Kinzer (1982); Cullather (2002) and Jonas (1981) analysed the role of the United States and the CIA and the counter revolutionary process. Vela (2008) analyses the ideological elements of the counter revolutionary actions and constituted the basis of the following state terror. García Ferreira (2010) analyses the context of the Cold War and the political process in Guatemala and Latin America.

77 Initial conditions are the set of events at the beginning of a self-reinforcing sequence. They are the previous context of the path dependent process and are not determinant to the outcome. Initial conditions can change and even disappear through the institutional trajectory, they constitute the period of institutional genesis that leads to a critical juncture (Mahoney 2000; Mahoney and Schensul 2006).

78 This political movement was know as the 'Counterrevolution'.

the next decades but also placed in motion different reinforcing mechanisms under the institutional pattern of public security displacement produced by the concentration of the security forces on national security (anti communism and counter insurgency). Under this perspective, private security is the result of a broader historical political process that has state security institutions at its core.

From Reformism to Anti-Communism

After a long period of economic crisis and dictatorships in Guatemala, important changes were made during the years 1944-1954 in order to expand economic productivity, increase social benefits, and open the political arena. Reformist transformations occurred in most countries of the region motivated as a reaction to dictatorships and economic stagnation as well as the international context favourable to democratic transformations after the Second World War (Bulmer-Thomas 1989).[79]

However, the drive for democratic reforms was limited by both the increasing international polarization produced by the Cold War and the opposition of local elites to radical transformations in the political and social spheres.[80]

In this context, the social and political changes initiated in Guatemala by two reformist governments between 1944 and 1954 were strongly opposed by local elites which interpreted those changes as a risk to their social and political status and also by the United States that considered those changes as the result of the influence of international communism in the country (Gleijeses 1991; Jonas

79 In May of 1944 in El Salvador the dictator Maximiliano Hernández Martínez were overthrow by a movement composed by young officer, university students and middle class protesters. In Honduras, Tiburcio Carías was confronted by an increased opposition that produced a political transition in 1947; in Costa Rica were made important reforms through different political alliances avoiding strong political confrontation. However different attempts to overdraw the regime of Anastasio Somoza in Nicaragua, its regime could support the reformist wave in the region and the economic power of the Somoza´s family was strengthened (Rojas Bolaños 1994; Walter 2004; Dunkerley 1988).

80 The different trajectories of each country prior to the reforms of the 1940s explain the outcomes of this reformist period. As Mahoney (2001a) argues, three different reformist experiences occurred in the region. First, reformist liberalism in Costa Rica that allowed for long-term democratic transformations without violent confrontations. Second, aborted liberalism that in the cases of Honduras and Nicaragua ended in the failure of domestic transformations of political and social institutions. And thirdly, radical liberalism that in the cases of Guatemala and El Salvador allowed for both the existence of powerful economic elites and dictatorships and also urban opposition groups capable of overthrowing authoritarian regimes and promoting deep social transformations (Mahoney 2001a).

1991).[81] The main changes initiated by those governments aimed to abolish a set of laws that allowed the use of coerced labour (such as personal services, the so-called *servicio personal de vialidad*) and the law against vagrancy. In addition, the army was constitutionally separated from civilian power, investment in education and heath was increased, and social security and labour laws were implemented, among others. These changes allowed for an increase in the participation of social sectors traditionally excluded from the political arena, such as unions, peasant and student organizations, and political parties. The economic transformations aimed to increase the productivity of the agro-export sector in order to reduce the high dependence on those products (such as coffee) dominated by traditional elites and to reduce the privileges of international monopolies such as the United Fruit Company (Bulmer Thomas 1989; Guerra Borges 1994). The agrarian reform[82] was the centre of the political project of Jacobo Arbenz in 1950 combined with the discourse of modernisation and social justice (Guerra Borges 1994: 61).[83] These measures affected the traditional privileges of local elites and U.S. companies strongly rooted in Guatemala: the United Fruit Company (UFCO) and its subsidiary, the International Railways of Central America (IRCA).[84]

The discussion about authoritarian regimes in Guatemala has centred on the relation between the military, the domestic dominant classes, and the United States influence. It is mostly said that the military acts as a tool for the dominant classes and the interests of the United States (Tischler 2001; Jonas 1991). However, as Mahoney (2001a) argues, the military was a more powerful and autonomous actor that came to power in reaction to democratising movements and the inability of the old liberal model to sustain itself (2001a: 237). The formal separation of the military from civil administration occurred during the years 1944-

81 This period is named the 'Revolution of October' due to the overthrow of the dictator Jorge Ubico in October 1944.

82 In 1952 was promulgated the Decree no. 900, the Agrarian Reform Law which stipulated the delivery of properties to peasant, increase financial credits to peasant and farmers, the supply of working cattle, fertilizers, seeds and technical assistance; the restitution to the indigenous communities of those properties in conflict with private individuals and municipalities (Guerra Borges 1994: 63).

83 There were three main objectives of its government, first to transform Guatemala in an economically independent country; second, to transform the economy in order to achieve the status of a modern capitalist country which meant industrialization and agrarian reform, and finally, to increase the living standards of most population (Rojas Bolaños 1994; Gleijeses 1991).

84 The government also proposed the construction of infrastructure that facilitates the creation of an internal market and the promotion of private investors under the condition of full respect to labour laws, no privileges over local investors and no intervention in national politics (Rojas Bolaños 1994: 99).

1954 with the aim of modernizing the armed forces and avoiding the use of military power by personalistic governments, as was the case of the dictator Jorge Ubico (1931-1944). In an attempt to protect the Army from manipulation by a sitting president, the new Constitution of 1944 created the *Consejo Superior del Ejército* (the Supreme Council of the Army). This Council was responsible for the technical and organizational aspects of the Army while the Ministry of Defence represented the Army in the executive's cabinet. The separation of the Army into two institutional branches, one technical and organizational and the other political, is considered a desperate measure of the young officers of 1944 to gain control of the Army (McClintock 1985: 21).[85] The modernization of the Army was complemented with the strengthening of military education, especially for the officers. The rationale for these changes was to avoid the direct interference of the president in military issues but it gave the military sufficient autonomy to become a powerful institution in itself.

The police functions (under army control previously) were transferred to a Civil Guard, which had its own police school, radio station (named "The voice of the Civil Guard"), magazine, radio studio and cinema (McClintock 1985: 21). Although these were outwardly formal changes, the most important measure was a clean sweep of the old police system, with few former National Police personnel permitted to join the Civil Guard. The secret police created by Ubico was transformed into the Judicial Police with only formal changes (PGDH 2009).

The reorganization of the Army and the formal changes in the Police were circumscribed to the political administration of the government and to the urban areas where the police were present. The most important change in the rural areas was the abolition of the administrative structure of social control created by the dictatorship. The territorial representatives of the central government during the dictatorship of Jorge Ubico (1931-1944) were the *jefes políticos* who were named directly by the President in each department and were at the same time the head military officer (*Comandante de Armas*) (Tipografía Nacional 1937).

Their functions were to ensure order and tranquillity among the population under their authority and provide security to persons and property by patrolling the roads, pursuing criminals, and dissolving any meeting that might disrupt public order, among others (Tipografía Nacional 1932). The next administrative level was the municipality, within which the *intendentes municipales* occupied the

85 The constitution of 1945 established that the Council was elected by army heads and officers while the Chief of the Army's Council was to be elected by the Congress of the Republic from a slate of three officers chosen by the Army's Council. The President of the Republic appointed officers to political positions, such as ministers of defence, communications, and interior as well as to serve as departmental governors and diplomats (McClintock 1985: 21).

highest post. For each *Intendente Municipal* there was a *Comandante de Plaza* or Local Commander, who was the military authority in the municipality. The *Jefe Político* appointed them and their functions were linked to social control mechanisms through the recruitment of the civilian population for specific tasks. They were responsible for the inscription of the male population into the local militias, the organization of military schools of primarily education, investigation and political control, military intervention in cases of rebellion or riot, conflict management, organization of patrols and appointment of military commissioners, and organizing the military service, among others (Tipografía Nacional 1932). Due to the system of Military Assimilation it was possible for civilians to assume military roles.

However, there were no important changes on the civil social control network created during the dictatorship. This network incorporated civil population into social control mechanisms grouped into the so-called *Auxilios Civiles* (Argueta 2004: 177). Part of the civilian collaborators was the Military Commissioners created in 1938 under the authority of the Local Commander. This administrative system was put together in order to guarantee the political stability of the dictatorship through repression of all kind of protest and also to ensure the provision of a workforce for the agricultural sector (Gleijeses 1991; Tischler 2001).

The combination of economic and political transformations and the attempt to regulate the excessive privileges of U.S. companies deepened the crisis in Guatemala. An international campaign against the country was initiated with the support of local elites and the U.S. government. The support of the military to the government decreased and an elaborate plan of intervention was implemented by the Central Intelligence Agency (CIA) (Gleijeses 1991; Jonas 1991). The government of Guatemala was accused of being manipulated by international communism and lost international support in the face of actions by the United States. In a short military and psychological operation, the government of Jacobo Arbenz was overthrown through a combination of an international blockade, a group of mercenaries trained by the CIA and led by colonel Castillo Armas, air attacks and the refusal of the army to defend the government. Jacobo Arbenz turned over the presidency to a military junta on June 27, 1954, and Carlos Castillo Armas was appointed President of the Republic on June 7 of that year (Cullather 2002; Jonas 1981).

Mahoney (2001a) focuses on the importance of domestic factors in the events of 1954 arguing that even in the absence of the United States intervention, the 1944-1954 reform period might have failed due to the pre-existing patterns of state militarization and class polarization which made it extremely likely that military authoritarianism would develop. The Guatemalan military would seize power if any government attempted to alter the class structures in the countryside in ways that empowered lower rural classes (Mahoney 2001a: 213). Within this perspective the transformation potential of the reformist period did not alter the social structure of the country but the moderate reforms related to the property of land benefited significantly the peasant sector and introduced the political participation of actors such as the communist party.

The combination of benefits for the peasants and the participation of the communist party generated the idea that international communist directed the government and that it would attempt to alter the status quo of the local elites (Gleijeses 1991). The economic and social reforms did not represent a risk for the interests of the United States; in fact, U.S. policy towards Central America through the Alliance for Progress pursued the same goals but without the political component which in the context of the Cold War represented a security threat (Mahoney 2001a: 214).

On the other side of the debate, the reformist period of 1944-1954 is considered revolutionary because the emergence of new political actors was the expression of a revolutionary subjectivity that transformed the subjectivity of marginalized actors to confront the liberal domination model and U.S. imperialism (Tischler 2001). This argument is built on the basis of the active participation of different actors in the urban areas such as students, teachers, unions, and the communist party, in other words, the political component of the reform period. This political component would explain the following insurgent development and the reaction of the local elites and the United States because the revolution of 1944 liberated the core of a transformed society (Tischler 2001: 275). The problem with this argument is that the situation in the countryside shows that power relations were not drastically transformed during the 'revolutionary period'.

The events that occurred in 1954 show the interaction of competing projects and the accumulated tensions among different actors. First, the military and the economic elite would tolerate, even with the presence of a communist party, reforms in the urban sector especially aimed to improve the social situation of workers and professionals, including the military. Second, the attempt to reform the agrarian structure of the country activated the historical defence of the privileges of dominant and traditional groups as well as the international private investors. This meant the possibility of losing the guarantees that an unchanged model provides. Third, this situation opened two possibilities for the armed forces: whether to support the modernization process centred in the urban areas as well as the government and its attempts to change the agrarian structure and confront dominant economic groups and the United States; or resume its traditional role of political protection even when it meant the emergence of internal conflicts between young reformist officers and others who were conservative or extreme rightists. Fourth, the role of the United States was to speed up the process of elections in support of the economic elites and the military and generate the necessary conditions for a short and successful operation to overthrow the presidency of Jacobo Arbenz.

The end of the reformist period triggered anticommunism as a mechanism that reinforced the guarantees of the social structure of the oligarchic state. Due to the crisis of this oligarchic model, a set of ideas emerged in 1954 that constituted the ideological foundations of subsequent state terror policies (Vela 2008: 94).[86] The military were located at the core of this process and operated in parallel with the police forces to counter actions by displaced actors such as labour unions, students, political parties, and young military officers, especially in the urban areas. The U.S. Guatemala General Plan of Action in 1953 stated that the only organized element in Guatemala was the army. "The police force was made up of 3,500 individuals, which could neither defeat an army coup, nor itself overthrow the government without support of the army" (DNSA 1953). All reformist actions were homogenized under the concept of communism and consequently treated as a security problem. Mass arrests were conducted regardless of the individual's real political leanings.[87]

The critical juncture of 1954 initiated the institutional pattern that placed national security as the primarily function of the security forces and public security, while traditional police functions were sidelined. Immediately after the triumph of Castillo Armas (1954-1957), the Committee Against Communism made its appearance and took control of all records of the previous government as well as lists of collaborators and members of political parties, unions, and student organizations, among others. Committee processed all of this information and created a long "black list" of approximately 70,000 individuals who were suspect of being communists. The list was a powerful instrument to identify potential subversives during the next decades (McClintock 1985: 33).

The constitutional reform in 1956 prohibited communist and related activities. Parallel to the new constitution, the necessary institutional reforms were introduced and the Committee Against Communism was transformed into a Department of Defence Against Communism as part of the National Security Council.

86 This ideology was rooted in radical anticommunism and national conservatism, racism and a fear of indigenous rebellion, the defence of private rural property (the *"finca"* or large landholding), radical Catholicism, and an international perspective linked to the doctrine of national security, all of these merged into an overall doctrine of anticommunism which justified the extensive use of state violence against those defined as communists (Vela 2008: 94).

87 Immediately after the overthrow of Jacobo Arbenz, the Civil Guard and the military identified more than 4,000 prisoners as being communist. A CIA report stated that these alleged communist leaders showed no communist indoctrination or links with communist supporters (DNSA 1954).

After this constitutional reform, the Committee for National Defence Against Communism was no longer justified according to the new constitution.[88]

The new National Security Council was defined by the United States as an agency to coordinate activities of investigation and police services. It functioned under directions of the Ministry of Interior and had jurisdiction over the National Police, as well as authority to investigate both political and common crimes. It was organized into four departments: judicial, juridical, security, and administrative.[89] The establishment of an institutional framework to bring political stability through the use of force against all forms of political opposition defined the concept of public security as the defence of the social order against political threats, placing crime prevention and investigation on a secondary plane.

In this situation, private security emerged separate from both police functions and from national security strategies. Commercial private security evolved out of the precarious situation of the National Police (low salaries and lack of training, leadership, and clear functions) and from the vacuum of formal policing actions, while non-commercial private policing is derived from the logic of self-defence and vigilante actions introduced by the military. The support of the United Sates, as will be shown, was on the one hand, to support the centralization of national defence within the military (including the police institution) and, on the other hand, to support the active participation of civilians in counter-terrorism organizations.

6.2 The Role of United States

The United States support for Guatemalan governmental security forces began in 1881 when the country was setting up its "Model Police" which included involvement in security, health, and public cleanliness in substitution of the former Civil Guard (PGDH 2009: 4). The New York City police provided security assis-

88 This Committee had semi-judicial powers such as holding communist or alleged communist under detention for six months without trial in the interest of national security.

89 The security department was charged with investigating and preventing political crimes and consisted of a section of secret services and a section for the defence against communism (DNSA 1956a). This department was organized along lines of the U.S. Secret Service and had 36 members that acted as a security escort of the President. In fact, it was the resurrection of Jorge Ubico's secret police or *judiciales* (McClintock 1985: 35). The judicial department investigated and prevented common crimes in accordance with the criminal code. The juridical department provided legal advice to the General Director for interrogating prisoners and preparing charges for presentation to the courts (McClintock 1985: 35).

tance. The main objective was to organize the 150 men of the new police according to the style of the New York police. The police concept introduced by the police of New York was abandoned when the dictator Manuel Estrada Cabrera (1898-1920) created a secret police and subordinated the old police to this new corps, especially in urban areas (McClintock 1985: 12). From the former police force characterized by urban patrols and citizens' assistance, the new secret police was rapidly transformed into a political police to defend the regime under the direction of Estrada Cabrera.[90] In the countryside different informal organizations normally linked to the army implemented policing activities through the system of military detachments (*Comandancias de Armas*) in each department. It was not until 1925, five years after the overthrow of Estrada Cabrera, that the police was reorganized and declared a civil institution. Its new functions were maintaining public order, protecting people and property, and co-operating with the courts in the prevention and investigation of crime (McClintock 1985: 13).

Before becoming the next dictator, Jorge Ubico was one of the first of Guatemala's rising officers to benefit from US training and was an important actor to transform the organization of the army into the model of the United States. As president in 1932, Jorge Ubico transformed the police into an "auxiliary army" with the primary objective of protecting his own person. In order to weaken the potential and strength of the police, Ubico removed the investigative unit from its structure and created an autonomous agency called the Judicial Police (also called Secret Police), which was an intelligence unit (DNSA 1956b). The efficiency of the Judicial Police as a mechanism to control communist activities was well evaluated in different US intelligence reports (McClintock 1985: 19).

During the reform period of 1944-1954, foreign training for young military officers was instituted. Almost 80 officers were sent to the United States and the Panama Canal Zone.[91] As mentioned, the police was reformed and renamed "Civil Guard" and the secret police of Ubico was converted into a new Judicial Guard. The changes were focused on personnel changes, such as denying the incorporation of former Ubico police into the new police force (PGDH 2009: 6). In order to build up the new police corps, President Arévalo (1945-1951) turned to the United States for technical support; the United States responded by sending an instructor from the Federal Bureau of Investigations at its own expense (McClintock 1985: 22).

90 For an historical analysis about the Police during the nineteen century in Guatemala, see Riekenberg (1996).

91 The Latin American Ground School (a predecessor of the School of the Americas) was created in 1946 in the Canal Zone where since 1939 the United States trained Latin American military personnel (Gill 2005: 46).

Despite this support by the United States for the security forces of Guatemala, its political influence was mostly directed at the dictators, especially in the case of Jorge Ubico. The reformist period of 1944-1954 made clear for the United States the importance of strong security institutions to avoid the alleged influence of international communism. The intensification of the Cold War redefined the role of the security forces and consequently the influence of the United States. From the perspective of the United States, the social and economic conditions of some countries in Latin America were the optimal context for the expansion of communism.[92] It was clear that the end of the reformist government was not sufficient to reduce the risk of the re-emergence of pro-Communists groups in the country (Kumar 1981: 58; Jonas 1981). In this context, Guatemala together with Bolivia, El Salvador, and Ecuador were included within the Public Safety Program (Davis and James 2001: 16). This situation and the existence of ambivalent support of some young officers of the Guatemalan army toward the anticommunist government installed in 1954, led to the implementation of extended programs of technical and financial support to the security forces.

The U.S. Public Safety Program and the Political Context

The Guatemala Public Safety Program, PSP, started in 1956 when David Laughlin, a retired Captain from the Indiana State Police, arrived in the country. The Program formally terminated in 1974.[93] The declared goal of the PSP for Guatemala was to assist in the overall improvement of the National Police, the Judicial Police, and the Border Police (Guardia de Hacienda). A permanent staff of security advisors provided vehicles and communication equipment, as well as participant training in Guatemala, the United States, Puerto Rico, and Panama (Davis and James 2001: 16). Before the PSP started U.S. advisors wrote some important

92 After the overthrow of Mossadeq in Iran in 1953, the overthrow of Jacobo Arbenz in Guatemala was the second successful covert action of the CIA and the first in Latin America (Kumar 1981: 58).

93 The military assistance was conducted through the Military Assistance Program, MAP, which was a separated program from the Public Safety Program. However they shared some important tasks such as some civic actions and the development of intelligence capabilities. The main objectives of MAP trainings were to increase the capability of the Guatemalans for internal security and civic action. Secondary or longer range objectives were the acceptance of US doctrines, the preservation of US position as the predominant foreign military influence, the promotion of democratic concepts and the fostering of pro-US sentiment among military personnel (DNSA 1966g).

country analysis that described the general situation of the police and the political context of the counter-revolutionary government of Castillo Armas.[94]

The Public Safety Program was part of the Office of Public Security, a worldwide police training program established by the International Cooperation Administration (the precursor of the Agency for International Development, AID). After a report on the National Police of Guatemala made by Fred G. Fimbres, a detective of the Los Angeles County Sheriff's Department, Guatemala became the first Latin American beneficiary of the Program in 1956 (Doyle 2007: 61). The report stresses the military character of the police and its centralized control.[95]

Despite of the fact that the report stated clearly that the police did not achieve the public policing goals expected of it, the program made no provision for reinforcing those functions in the National Police due to the primacy of the military and its counterinsurgent functions: "The National Police is actually geared to security against subversive activity and communist attack, with the primarily police function taking a secondary role" (DNSA 1956b). The report listed the administrative deficiencies of the police such as lack of professional training, unwieldy control mechanisms, absence of good executive management, poor budgeting practices, poor personnel administration coupled with a lack of human relations in management, very low morale and lack of esprit de corps, improper deployment of field personnel, lack of adequate and centralized police records, inadequate office equipment and housing facilities, and lack of preventive maintenance and care of motorized equipment (DNSA 1956b). The report concluded that

> "U.S. technical and material assistance be provide the Government of Guatemala for the purpose of strengthening its internal security by increasing the effectiveness and level of service of its national police force." (DNSA 1956b).

The U.S. PSP initiated in an instable political context. The counterrevolutionary government of Col. Castillo Armas (1954-57) has been defined as a personalistic regime with low legitimacy and supported by the conservative local elites and

94 The Outline Plan of Operations for Guatemala reported that the new government confronted a critical situation: a looted treasury, a badly disorganized government structure, economic dislocation resulting from the revolutionary period of 1944-1954, and the recent decline on coffee prices, as well as the inexperience of the new authorities (DNSA 1955a).

95 The manpower of the police forces was estimated at over 3,000 agents, one-third of them assigned to the Capital. The Guardia de Hacienda had 663 agents, the Security Department (the political investigative unit of the General Office of National Security) had 36 agents, the Judicial Police had 184 agents, and the Section of Defence Against Communism had 30 agents (DNSA 1956b).

the United States (Mahoney 2001a: 239).[96] The first measures of this government were to dissolve the political organizations of the previous period and to repress all kind of opposition. The government concentrated on avoiding the emergence of insurgent movements while the concern of the United States was the re-emergence of communist leaders and a possible reinstatement of a reformist government. The immediate U.S. assistance was made in order to preserve the Castillo Armas government in power. The U.S. sought to encourage political stabilization through consultation, prudent exchange of information, and individual and collective actions against communist or other anti-US subversion or intervention in any American state (DNSA 1955a). At this point, the United States also was concerned with the emergence of similar communist movements in the Central American region. To deal with this, the U.S. proposed to help Guatemala strengthen its security agencies against any communist subversion in the country with special attention given to technical and ideological training of the police force (DNSA 1955a).

However, the core of the U.S. program should be the army, because of its institutional role and because at that moment the only threat to the government of Castillo Armas were the dissatisfied groups in the Army, as expressed in the confrontation between the "liberation" faction and the "regular" faction. For this reason, the army was neutralized during the first years of the Castillo Armas regime. In the second place, threats to the government were perceived to come from university students, professionals, and the press (DNSA 1955b). The report stated that there was a general sentiment on the part of virtually all "politically-conscious Guatemalans" that the time has come for President Castillo Armas to drop the emergency "dictatorial" authority which he assumed after the fall of Arbenz and to return to the democratic-nationalistic principles of the 1944 revolution (DNSA 1955b).[97]

In this context, the U.S. support focused on the three primary internal security forces concerned with the suppression of subversion: the National Police (Civil

96 The success of the counterrevolutionary movement was based fundamentally on the refusal of the Guatemalan army to defend the government of Arbenz and the use of air power by the United States rather than the military force led by Colonel Castillo Armas. He was killed in July 26, 1957 and his case was never solved. (McClintock 1985: 28; Jonas 1981).

97 The government of Castillo Armas was confronted with a number of protests by social organizations created during the revolutionary period, especially in May and June of 1956 (Rojas Bolaños 1994: 117). The situation was controlled by the excessive use of violence – the police and the military killed five students – and a state of siege was imposed (DNSA 1956c). The political instability and the fragmented situation of the army justified the request made directly by the President for urgent financial and technical support from the United States to the Police (DNSA 1956d).

Guard), the Committee for National Defence Against Communism, and the Military Intelligence Section of the Army. All lacked trained men and there was no clear definition of their respective responsibilities.[98] The Plan recognized that in Guatemala there was no control over border territories and over travellers, which left the country open to agents of international communism (DNSA 1955a).[99]

This was the general situation of the police forces that supported the regime of Castillo Armas. There were no institutionalised repressive structure and the actions of the police forces were centred on torturing and exiling communist supporters. The political challenge for Castillo Armas was to control the army and to avoid the emergence of civil militias conscious of what had been lost. The abolition of the most important reforms undertaken during the Arévalo and Arbenz period produced a general administrative vacuum that was filled by the army (McClintock 1985: 31).

After a period of political instability and conflict within the different fractions of the anti-Communist movement, Miguel Ydígoras Fuentes, a less radical anti-Communist and a former minister in Jorge Ubicos's government, won the elections and took office in March 1958.[100] High levels of corruption characterized the government of Ydígoras. At the same time, the Civic Action Program of the Army was initiated with the support of the United States Agency for International Development (USAID). After a military rebellion in Zacapa and Puerto Barrios which was rapidly stifled, a state of siege was decreed and a large number of political opponents were sent into exile. It was in this context that the first guerrilla groups were organized (ODHAG 1998b: 23).

An evaluation team of the Public Safety Program reported in 1959 that three U.S. advisers were needed for the Police Department to support the role of the police in an unstable environment and to prevent the eruption of subversive vio-

98 The Outline Plan of Operation for Guatemala in 1955 states that the director of the Civil Guard and subordinate officers were customarily selected from the corps of active and retired army officers. The Guard was under the Interior Ministry but usually received instructions directly from the President. The judicial police were a plainclothes squad concerned with political security and the detection of criminals; the Treasury Guard prevented smuggling while Municipal Guards were posted in smaller towns in rural areas (DNSA 1955a).

99 A report emphasized that the International Security Program aimed to strengthen the anti- subversive and anti-Communist capacities of the police, not to increase the efficiency of Latin American police forces. Guatemala was considered one of the countries of Latin America with high risk of communist activity and with the weakest police force (DNSA 1957). The U.S. Program gave importance to the "special investigation work" to identify unlawful organized underground activities. This included methods of investigation, following up undeveloped leads, and training in physical and technical surveillance, among others (McClintock 1985: 35).

100 See Annex 1.

lence. It proposed that the U.S. strengthen the non repressive functions of the police so as not to be accused of only supporting the repressive aspects of the police (DNSA 1959a). The local characteristics of the political context and the personalistic nature of the Presidency of Ydígoras required constant reorientations of the U.S. Program, as the report stated, due to the "patronage efforts on the police" by President Ydígoras (DNSA 1959a).

The traditional clientelistic behaviour of the political authorities increased due to the large financial support of the U.S. programs. The excessive amount of monetary support led to a negative attitude by politicians and the president. The technical cooperation continued only because of the danger of a communist takeover of the Government (DNSA 1959b).

Ydígoras was disenchanted with U.S. policy because the U.S. preferred to support his opponent, who described him as "lackey of the U.S." (DNSA 1961a). Support for the security forces was required to permit the government to finish its period.[101] For the United States, this situation increased the possibility of a guerrilla insurgency or an external attack. The police comes across as badly trained and organized and incapable of delivering internal security (DNSA 1961a).[102] One problem mentioned in the report was that most agents were concentrated in the capital. The police outside of Guatemala City were more symbolic than deterrent. The report thus emphasized the need to strengthen the intelligence capabilities of the armed forces. For this reason Guatemala was one of the two countries in Latin America that had an assigned and accredited intelligence advisor from the U.S. Army Mission working together with the units of military intelligence (G2).[103]

During the months of March and April 1962 a crisis was provoked by high school student protests and high urban dissatisfaction with the Ydígoras government. Both the student movement and dissatisfied military converged in this crisis to demand the restoration of the democratic regime of 1944-1954 (Pinto Soria 2010).[104] The goals of the movement were to move the state along the path of

101 U.S. reports stated that the participation of the government of Ydígoras in the Bay of Pigs operation increased political instability in the country caused by communist-inspired efforts and the actions of political "outs" and military dissidents.

102 The report stated that the activities of armed communist groups could not be checked due to the lack of mobility and communications of the Police and military forces that prevented them from effectively controlling guerrilla movements in the country (DNSA 1961a).

103 From 1951 to 1961, a total of 58 Guatemalan participants were send to the U.S. and Puerto Rico for training in public security (DNSA 1961a).

104 One important characteristic of these protests was a combination of socio-economic and political demands to overcome the crisis produced by the political ambiguity of Ydígoras expressed in the opening of political spaces, corruption, and electoral fraud. See Annex 1.

democracy, economic opening, and national dignity. The announcement of the participation of Juan José Arévalo in the next presidential elections and the rebellion of some military units, increased the level of political and social crisis. The radical rightist *Movimiento de Liberación Nacional* (MLN) blamed the government for the crisis due to its weakness in controlling the protests (ODHAG 1998b: 29).

This context and the ideological confrontation against communism unified the oligarchy, the army, and the United States to defend the regime (Pinto Soria 2010). The return of Juan José Arévalo was the main concern of the U.S. Embassy as it believed it opened up possibilities of a communist takeover of the Government. The proposed solution was to find a successor to Ydígoras in accordance with U.S. interests (DNSA 1962c).[105]

The protests in March and April of 1962 expressed the force of social movements and the beginning of guerrilla actions; at the same time, they revealed the inability of the Government of Guatemala to control these expressions of increased discontent. The situation was complicated by the violent and repressive response of the police forces to the protests. The judicial police, headed by a military officer but made up of civilians, was used as a goon squads during the protest and "created ... widespread resentment among the population by the brutal and crude tactics which it employed" (DNSA 1962d).[106]

The new USAID public safety advisor, Desiderio Crisostomo, prepared a detailed report on the situation of the Public Safety Program in 1962 in Guatemala and showed that the constant reorientation of the program to deal with contextual necessities had put aside the traditional activities of a modern police force. The report stated that the Police had an uncontrolled diversity of police-type organizations.[107] The emphasis of the National Police was on "security against subver-

105 Anticipating a political crisis, on February 10, 1962, the government of Guatemala requested military equipment and assistance from the U.S. in order to improve the anti-guerrilla capabilities of the government in light of the military rebellion (DNSA 1962a).

106 Soon after the protests, the USAID provided a month training curse for 40 Guatemalan police and security officials in riot and mob control techniques (DNSA 1962b).

107 The national police (2,980 agents reporting to the Ministry of Interior); the judicial police (185 agents reporting to the Ministry of Interior); the department of special investigations (38 agents reporting to the presidential staff); the immigration police (40 agents reporting to the Ministry of Interior); the rural guard (164 agents called the "*ambulante*" adjunct to the National Police); the border patrol (647 agents reporting to the Ministry of Finance); the forestry police (56 agents only in Petén reporting to the Ministry of Defence); the military police (192 agents reporting to the Ministry of Defence); and the secret service (number unknown, charged with protecting the president) (DNSA 1962d).

sive activity and communist attack with the primarily police function taking a somewhat secondary role" (DNSA 1962d). The top officers were military men appointed by the President, and most of the police officers were poor and drawn from the local lower social strata. Salaries were extremely low, so that many individuals were forced to take outside jobs; low salaries also made bribery of police officers a common problem. The report also stated that as the result of U.S. training the police did undertake some patrolling activities (DNSA 1962d).

Regardless of the socio-economic situation of the police personnel, the focus of U.S. support continued in the techniques of riot and disturbance control while the strengthening of public security functions and institutional capabilities was displaced to a secondary place. In fact, the traditional institutional models inside the police were constantly reformed in order to reinforce the counter insurgent orientation of the police.[108]

President Ydígoras finally was overthrown by a military coup led by Colonel Peralta Azurdia on March 31, 1963.[109] The government of Peralta Azurdia (1963-1966) defined the role of the military as that of direct leadership of the government; his government also marked clearly the beginning of the armed conflict.[110] Peralta's policies were focused on combating anti-government activities and reducing crime and delinquency. At that moment, the guerrilla groups were not considered a serious internal security threat:

> "Both the army and the police are considered to have an adequate capability in both counter-insurgency and riot control techniques to handle any current insurgency threat" (DNSA 1963e).

The U.S. Embassy recommended the formal recognition of the new military government soon after the coup due to its honest and effective attempt to avoid a communist takeover (DNSA 1963a). The United States supported the coup after assuming, together with the military and groups on the extreme right, that an Arévalo candidacy would receive extensive support in the country. The U.S.

108 For example, the Department of Special Investigations was the only office with the formal and specific responsibility of combating subversion. While the other police forces did not had the formal responsibility for this function, they nonetheless implemented counter insurgent actions based on the definition of public security as the struggle against communism (DNSA 1962d).

109 See Annex 1.

110 The Peralta government program consisted of six points: complete eradication of the possibility of an extremist government, governmental honesty, measures to help the neediest classes, promotion of a climate of effective democracy "so the people will be able at the proper time, to freely elect the person who should guide the destiny of the country, without any kind of pressure", respect for international commitments, and turning over power to a freely elected successor upon fulfilment of these objectives (DNSA 1963d).

Embassy also agreed with the plans of the military government to postpone the elections for two years in order to dissuade an Arévalo candidacy.[111] In more general terms, the anti-Communist goals of the Peralta regime were a message to the other Central American countries and the rest of Latin America that the U.S. government would support any attempt to stop international communism (DNSA 1963b and c). The U.S. Embassy considered the coup as a transitional period that supported the Alliance for Progress and U.S. public safety goal:

> "The immediate primarily objective of our Internal Defence Plan was effectively implemented. But this has not resolved our basic long term objective of promoting the growth of a vital, progressive democratic society in Guatemala with a government friendly and co-operative with the United States" (DNSA 1963e).

During the coup, a U.S. army mobile training team conducted a five-week instructor course in anti-guerrilla training. This was the third U.S. training group used to train Guatemalan instructors. The objective of the new U.S. support included overall training and communications mobility, especially for rural and border coverage (DNSA 1963f).[112]

U.S. support rapidly increased after the coup. Until 1957, the Military Assistance Program had invested US$750,000. In January 1963, the investment made by this program was US$1,667,000. During the two months after the Peralta coup, the amount spent by the Military Assistance Program increased to US$2,524,000 (Pinto Soria 2010: 202). However, there were still inconveniences for the U.S. Embassy because the Peralta government was especially prone to seek military-type solutions and appeared unwilling to come to grip with more complex and relevant matters such as planning for economic and social development (DNSA 1963g). To this point, both U.S. PSP and the context of political instability created the basis of the institutional displacement of public security. The police was placed in the path of an institutional political function reinforced by riot control and cover and over operations with the support of the United States.

Complementarily, one of the changes made in the Public Safety Program during the Peralta government was the strengthening of its Civic Action component. It served for internal and external defence and development objectives. Civic action was especially designed to gain the confidence of the people. It was implemented also for intelligence collection regarding insurgent operations and pro-

111 A U.S. Embassy report stated that the best chance for U.S. interests was to work together with the new government: "Certainly, Guatemala is in many respects more dangerous politically than economically" (DNSA 1963d).

112 Around 10 police officers completed training at the Interamerican Police Academy. Over 100 police agents received special training in riot control in Guatemala from U.S. training teams. Guatemala had at that moment six riot control units of 30 men each trained and equipped (DNSA 1963e).

moted development or "nation building" through the establishment of community relations councils, support for literacy training , school lunch programs and related support, road and bridge construction (especially in Petén), and medical assistance in the form of mobile medical units and medical missions, a report stated that

> "The development of community relations councils made up of civilian and military men in localities throughout the country may appreciably strengthen the institutions of local government and development" (DNSA 1963h).

Although this component was present since the beginning of the program, it was in the context of the emergence of insurgent groups that it was reinforced.

During the next two years the Public Safety Program focused on police reform and the expansion of the public safety program to enable the police to deal more effectively with insurgency problems, with primary emphasis on urban areas but also including rural activities (DNSA 1964 and 1965a). However, the last year of Peralta's government was marked by the beginning of overt actions by extreme right wing death squads which increased the number of killings and kidnappings. At the same time, military actions by insurgents increased as well.

In November 1965, a public security advisor visited the country to assist law enforcement authorities on techniques and methods for combating terrorism, kidnapping, and extortion tactics. A number of meetings were held with the directors of the National Police, Judicial Police, and Treasury Police. The recommendations that came out of the meetings pointed to both overt and covert means, like the methods implemented in Venezuela. After some meetings it "became obvious that because of rivalry, non-cooperation, and distrust between these three agencies there was in fact no coordinated plan or cooperation" (DNSA 1965c). To solve the problem, a suggestion was made to go to the very top government level. Thus, the order to implement all actions recommended by the U.S. advisor came directly from President Peralta. The plan was as follows:

> "a. Overt-Immediate: combined, uniformed police raids in Guatemala City, together with surprise road blocks.
>
> The idea behind this was to force some of the wanted communist out of hiding and into police hands, as well as to convince the Guatemalan public that the authorities were doing something to control the situation.
>
> b. Overt-Long Range: To have a day to day U.S. advisor to give operational advice to the authorities: "Future ability of U.S. advisors to influence police operations in Guatemala is, in my opinion, a "must".
>
> c. Covert Immediate: set up of a safe house to which all information concerning extortions and kidnappings was to be sent: "All police agencies are penetrated by the communists" (DNSA 1965c).

This is an important change in the characteristics of U.S. support. On the one hand, the police assumed counter insurgent operations in urban areas. On the other hand, institutional mechanisms were created that led to the emergence of autonomous security structures inside the police. The coordination mechanisms between military and police were improved and joint operations were initiated.[113] These events reinforced the displacement of public security due to the concentration of public security forces in anti-communist and counter-insurgency operations.

The increase in violent actions by rightist groups and the increase in military actions by the insurgents resulted in a loss of confidence in the Peralta regime which resulted in the possibility of a coup to block the next elections. Of concern to the United States were the insurgents groups located in the north east of the country, which acted with total impunity but they had not gained the support of the peasantry. Kidnappings and extortions increased the sense of fear among the financial and business elites. Another problem was the economic crisis then gripping the country. In this context, the U.S. objective centred on the prevention of a communist take-over of Guatemala by supporting the military in the government.[114]

The process of military reorganization and centralization initiated during the presidency of Peralta Azurdia would not be halted during the new presidency of Méndez Montenegro (1966-1970).[115] Although a civilian president was now in office, this government rapidly became a façade for the military due to the political power of the army, the violent actions of the rightist groups, the U.S. support for anti-communist initiatives, and the increasing military actions of insurgent groups (Pinto Soria 2010: 202).[116]

The presidency of Méndez Montenegro represents the consolidation of the National Security doctrine in the Guatemalan state. Although the central component of this doctrine were the counter-insurgent military actions, it also involved

113 National and judicial police forces were coordinated with the army (military police) both in collection and analysis of intelligence and in actual operations. Security forces were conducting joint large-scale "sweeps" of suspect urban areas (DNSA 1966a).

114 The military again requested a U.S. team to provide advice and training in riot-control, counter-guerrilla warfare, and anti-terrorism tactics for both army and police units. The condition stipulated by the Embassy was that army and police work together (DNSA 1966d and 1966e).

115 See Annex 1.

116 Méndez Montenegro was identified to some degree with the political aspirations of the revolutionary period of 1944-1954. Even though the military accepted the result of the elections, they forced Méndez Montenegro to sign a formal agreement by which the army preserved its autonomy and continued its military counter-insurgent operations (Kraft 2010: 213; Jonas 1991: 60; ODHAG 1998b: 48). Méndez Montenegro offered a general amnesty to any armed group that laid down its arms but the insurgents rejected it and, instead, increased their military operations. It was in this context that the army implemented its first counterinsurgent offensive.

support for structural transformations in order to avoid the social and economic causes of communist insurgency. That is, modernization was presented as the alternative to revolutionary change. To achieve this objective, the U.S. implemented the Alliance for Progress and civic action programs (Kraft 2010: 208). In the case of Guatemala, the counterinsurgency doctrine proposed by the United States was reinterpreted and adapted to the local context and to the authoritarian tendencies of the army and the rightist groups. From the perspective of the United States, the Army was the only state institution capable of implementing both military actions and the modernization process. The initiation of military counterinsurgent operations in the northwest regions of Guatemala was a clear sign of the willingness of Méndez Montenegro to delegate in the Army the conduct of counterinsurgency (DNSA 1966f).

While the military were gaining political power and credibility in the eyes of the United States, the police remained a problem. In 1963 the relation between USAID and the Government of Guatemala was unstable due to the negative attitude of the Government with respect to the civil police.[117] A commission of the Public Safety Program arrived to evaluate the situation of the police. The report stated that the police has been limited by the general context in which the guerrilla activities began in 1960; subsequently, during the Peralta Azurdia government urban terrorism began in Guatemala City and the police were not prepared to deal with it. Police corruption and inefficiency, governmental indifference, and military control contributed to prevent implementation reforms which the U.S. believed were essential for an effective police force (DNSA 1966g).

Another important aspect the report underlined was that the program to support the police was under the administration and goals of the overall military assistance program which had larger goals and financial support (DNSA 1966g).[118]

117 In 1964 the USAID reported the woefully inadequate budget, endemic inefficiency, and overall inefficient administration in the police (DNSA 1966g).

118 The military assistance program aimed to develop an armed force which, in conjunction with a civilian police and other national security forces, would be capable of maintaining internal security, controlling the clandestine movement of arms and men across the borders, assisting in economic and social development through civic action, patrolling and exercising surveillance of adjacent maritime areas, performing OAS and UN peacekeeping functions, maintaining the U.S. position as the predominant foreign military influence, promoting democratic concepts and fostering pro-U.S. sentiments among military personnel, and achieving agreements between Guatemala and the U.S. on the nature and extent of the internal security threat which Guatemala faced.

Training courses were focused on command techniques for disturbance and riot control and were given by USAID public safety advisors (DNSA 1966g).[119]

The USAID advisor proposed a plan to reorganize the police of the government of Guatemala that aimed

> "To strengthen internal security by improving organization of the national police and by training in better methods of investigation and subversive control; improve national police methods of crime detection and prevention by modernizing the crime lab and training personnel and improve traffic control." (DNSA 1966g).

The plan USAID presented to the Government of Guatemala that year generated little enthusiasm. USAID proposed to press for the reorganization of the Police in order to continue the public safety program in the year 1968. In the interim the USAID provided only courses in the U.S. to the investigative units.[120]

The report identified the little importance of the police to the military governments and stated that

> "Since the end of the regime of General Jorge Ubico, government, under heavy military influence, have treated the police body as an orphan child and have consciously or inadvertently prevent it from becoming a professional and competent force." (DNSA 1966g).

It was clear that the intention of the governments was to put the army in a better position vis-à-vis the police, both in relation to its political role and also to receiving international support: "No program showing a promise of developing an effective civil police force would have had the support of either the government or the military" (DNSA 1966g). This situation produced a gradual reduction of U.S. funding for the police by focusing only on particular areas such as investigation units that were key operational structures within the counterinsurgency strategy.[121]

The success of the counterinsurgency offensive set in motion different mechanisms which were reinforced by U.S. support such as the militarization of public

119 Up to 1966, five thousand police personnel had been trained locally, sixty-two police officers had been trained in the U.S., in Puerto Rico, or at the Inter-American Police Academy in Panama (DNSA 1966g).

120 The plan was to extend the program until 1970 in four main areas: crowd (riot) control training, utilization of modern technology in police operations, improvement of police investigative techniques, and improvement of administration and organization (DNSA 1966g).

121 “Withholding of commodity support would have slowed improvement in the seriously inadequate material resources of the police and they would provably have deteriorated. Whatever influence we possessed in the police program would have diminished and improvements in organization and training noted over the past three years would have been jeopardized. The program was very small in terms of money and was more tolerated than welcomed by the Government of Guatemala. The Military Assistance Program, on the other hand, was ten times larger and was welcomed by the Government of Guatemala" (DNSA 1966g).

security, the strengthening of vigilante groups (death squads), and placing the police in an auxiliary position in military operations, all of which left the police institution in an underdeveloped institutional situation.[122] A general plan for the reorganization of the security forces was presented by USAID. The core of the reorganization plan was the army:

> "The Guatemalan Army is the only force capable of sustained field operations against guerrilla forces. For this reason, and because of its dominant political role, it must be considered in as many aspects of the development process as possible. At the same time, the civilian police force must be better prepared to meet a relatively well organized, urban-base insurgent force with a modus operandi paralleling that of organized crime. Civilian services (police) should be stressed and developed within the Army." (DNSA 1968f).

The most important recommendations of the reorganizations plan were to improve coordination between police units by establishing direct lines of communication, establishing a joint training facility, establishing a National Police Academy, improving joint records and identification facilities (including photo lab and crime analysis units), and improving coordination between military and police units through the establishment of a Joint Operation Centre (JOC) in Guatemala City with communications links to all department capitals.[123] As it will be explained later, this recommendation led to the creation of the Centre of Joint Operations (COC) in the Police and the General Staff for National Defence *(Estado Mayor de la Defensa Nacional*) of the army.

In 1970, the presidential election was won by the rightist military officer, colonel Carlos Arana Osorio (1970-1974) (known as the "Butcher of Zacapa" for his role in the 1966-1968 anti-guerrilla campaign in the eastern part of the country).[124] The election was held under conditions of extreme terror. Arana was responsible for the organization of armed civilian groups to cope with the guerrilla in the northwest departments of Guatemala. His government represented the reaction of extreme rightist organizations against the weakness of former President Montenegro in fighting insurgents and the inauguration of a middle term military project which included the next decades (Jonas 1991: 60; ODHAG 1998b: 73).

The government of Arana was characterized by increased political violence, death squad actions, and prolonged states of siege; the budget of the army was doubled during the first year of his government and there was press censorship. The objective of the military strategy was to destroy the urban structures of the

122 The police was considered incapable of controlling and containing the insurgent threat, a situation that was interpreted as an urgent need to support the investigative units of the police (1968b).

123 As recommended, the creation of a JOC was to serve intelligence purposes, should not be publicized, and the salaries and administrative expenses for its operation should be paid from confidential funds (DNSA 1968f and 1969).

124 See Annex 1.

guerrillas.[125] Parallel to the repressive actions of the military, the government of Arana established a development plan which included financial support for small farmers, expansion of the agricultural market, and the promotion of crafts and tourism.[126]

During the last four years of the Public Safety Program, support was channelled to strengthen elite police corps to deal with the increasing crime.[127] The idea was to support a major reform of the police once an effective core organization was functioning. This initiative was defined as in the best interest of the U.S. (DNSA 1970a and 1970b). Parallel to this support, the USAID created a Rapid Police Development Program to support president Arana's efforts to restore internal peace in Guatemala and to improve police capabilities over the long run because "Guatemala's internal security is seriously threatened by left wing guerrillas and terrorist and right wing counter terrorists" (DNSA 1970e).[128]

Despite support by this program for the police, the preference of the military was to strengthen the police capabilities of the military forces instead of strengthening the institutional capabilities of the police. One of the measures taken by the military was to expand the role and mission of the Mobile Military Police (the *Policia Militar Ambulante*, MMP) in certain police activities.[129] The MMP was allowed to maintain public order in urban and rural areas and to prevent felonies and to pursue and arrest offenders. Other duties of the MMP included contraband control, protection of railroads and telephone/telegraph lines, forestry services, traffic law enforcement, and control on highways and roads. The justification was that after the creation of the MMP in 1965, it had assumed duties of the National Police in rural areas and there was a need for close coordination between the MMP and the Police so that MMP investigations receive legal recognition (DNSA 1971d).

During the next years other police forces controlled by the military became involved in police functions. This was the case of the Treasury Police also controlled by the military in 1974 (DNSA 1974b). U.S. officials commented that

125 During this period, an estimated total of 724 people were killed and 562 were kidnapped in politically motivated actions in the country (ODHAG 1998b: 76).

126 It included also programs to improve infrastructure, education, and health, the redistribution of social investment, and the concentration of population in urban centres to facilitate access to public services (ODHAG 1998b: 80).

127 Arana requested in March 1970 that the U.S. support the creation of an elite police corps of 30 to 50 men. USAID provided training, equipment (electronic surveillance equipment, automobiles, etc.), and a permanent advisor.

128 The program included in-country resources, crash projects with USAID support, long-term projects for continued development of the three police forces, and the introduction of "vigorous patrolling" both with vehicles and on foot (DNSA 1970f).

129 See Annex 1 and 2.

> "Further within the military circle there is a feeling that the police agencies are poorly organized and equipped, that they lack central organization and training sufficient to make them effective. Yet within this same circle there is also strong resistance for a better trained and equipped civil police, better leadership or greater numerical strength which would be comparable to the military." (DNSA 1971d).

The report concluded clearly that the reluctant attitude of the military as reflected in their resistance to develop police strength and power was typical of Latin America where there was fear by the military of developing a potentially competitive armed group (DNSA 1971d). In this context the conclusion of the Public Safety Program was contemplated by the U.S. Embassy when it argued that this program was the largest in the region and that at the time there were seven full time Public Safety Advisors working inside the police (DNSA 1971e).

In 1971 an evaluation was conducted to determine the end of the program. After the Rapid Police Development Program, the report proposed a next stage called the Police Self-Sufficiency Program which included, for example, the construction of the Academy, providing 2,000 revolvers, the creation of a planning and research unit in the National Police, and overall training (especially in riot operation in Guatemala City).

The excessive support by Arana to the interests of the U.S. was interpreted as an opportunity to press for swift development of the Guatemalans' own capability for coping and an opportunity for the U.S. to reduce the high level of advisory and commodity support furnished to the Police (DNSA 1971f). Regardless of the insurgent threat, the opinion of the U.S. team was that common crime in Guatemala was not a problem: "it did not represent a serious threat to the economic well being of the country" (DNSA 1971f). The idea was to prevent the remnants of the rebels in the cities to mount enough kidnapping and robbery operations that would enable them to "obtain sufficient founds to recuperate in terms of weapons and recruits over time" (DNSA 1971f).

The limited success of the Public Safety Program in strengthening the police institutions was not a failure to the overall counterinsurgency strategy.[130] On the contrary, due to the relative success of Arana in combating the insurgency it was necessary for the U.S. to find an appropriate candidate for president in order to continue the security measures and the relation with the US. This candidate was General Kjell Laugerud who was the Minister of Defence in Arana's govern-

130 The report stated that the public safety program had not made great gains in Guatemala for the first 13 years and six months of its existence. It repeated that one of the causes of the this situation was the traditional loathing of the army to any improvement of the Police. There was a belief by the U.S. advisors that this tendency changed during Arana's government. The support given by Arana to a greater unification and professionalism of the police, coupled with additional financing, provided the opportunity to continue U.S. support for the next four years (DNSA 1971f).

ment; Laugerud won the 1974 election through fraud.[131] From the U.S. Perspective, Arana did more than any other Guatemalan government to combat common crime and to improve the national police in spite of continuing abuses by the security forces (DNSA 1973b).

The Public Safety Project ended in 1974 and left a police institution controlled by the military and with low public security capabilities. Instead, a number of coordination mechanisms between the army and the police were created to conduct counterinsurgency activities. From 1956 to 1974 there were 23 directors of the National Police, all of them military officers.[132] The socio-economic situation of the agents did not improve (they continued to receive low salaries and had no labour advantages) so many were forced to seek secondary jobs to meet their personal needs, for example, working as private security agent.

The next period was marked by an increase in the armed conflict, the extension of political violence in the countryside, and an increase of civil participation in military and social control activities. U.S. support was concentrated in the military program for the next four years. However, the legacies of the U.S. Public Safety Program were the strengthening of the military role in public security and the relegation of police functions which were concentrated only in counterinsurgency operations.

The U.S. PSP was part of a mechanism that reinforced the institutional pattern of public security displacement. However its goals were related to strengthen the political function of the police, it produced a set of effects on the reinforcing of private security.

6.3 The State Roots of Private Security

U.S. support for the police force reinforced an institutional trajectory that defined the functions of the police as mechanisms of political and social control. The combination of U.S. support to prevent the emergence of communist organizations and the authoritarian structure of the army resulted in a set of institutional changes that aimed to strengthen the specific areas of the police institution such as investigative and coordination units. But U.S. support for covert operations implemented by the army and the police encouraged the emergence of autonomous rightist structures that implemented vigilante actions as counter-terrorism

131 The only real opposition came from Guatemala City's mayor Colom Argueta (DNSA 1973a; ODHAG 1998b: 80).

132 From 1957 to 1973, a total of US$ 4,425,000 were allocated to the public safety program in three major areas: technical advisory services, commodities, and participant training (DNSA 1974b).

tactics. Both police investigative units and vigilante organizations were integrated into the counterinsurgency strategy.

The excessive concentration of the security forces in the counterinsurgency led to a displacement of the public security function of the police. Private security, both commercial and non-commercial, emerged as an outcome of this process. On the one hand, commercial private security services emerged as a sideline for police and military officers. From the beginning of the anti-Communist period of the National Police in 1955, its institutional mechanisms reinforced private security services provided by the police, namely the Special Service of Surveillance. Linked to the Special Service of Surveillance, different forms of commercial private security companies were created, such as those run by military and police officers, security companies owned by civilians, and security companies owned by international advisors. On the other hand, non-commercial private security developed from the different mechanisms of incorporation of the civilian population in security groups to undertake vigilante and social control actions such as military reserves, military commissioners, urban and rural civil patrols, irregular forces of the insurgency, and death squads.

Police Organization and Social Control Function

During the Revolutionary period of 1944-1954 the name of the National Police was changed to that of National Guard. The Constitution of 1945 defined the civilian character of the new Guard and stipulated that only under a state of public calamity or state of war could the police be militarised. These measures attempted to reduce military interference in the police institution. However, the internal structure of the police was not modified (Drouin 2009: 12).

The most important transformation of the National Police was in the context of anticommunism. As was mentioned, the creation of the National Committee Against Communism in 1954 placed the police in a subordinate position in which its investigative functions were directed from outside the police institution.[133]

As part of the new structure of the National Police, a unit named Special and Confidential Services was established by which members of the National Police were assigned to particular security services, most of them paid by private indi-

133 A law was issued under which communist activities were prohibited and in 1955 the new Law of the National Police abolished the former Civil Guard and created the new Detective Corps responsible for all criminal and political investigations.

viduals. This unit was also referred to as Special Vigilance Service (PRAHPN 2009: 35).[134]

During the first years of the counterrevolution, the relation between the police and the army was a difficult one and underlined the ambiguous difference between the Civil Guard and the Army. It is within this context that the institutional differentiation between policy and army was initiated in parallel with the functional supremacy of the army over civil security forces.[135] As part of this process, a military census was organized in October 1954 to identify all active military personnel in the country and also to organize the military reserves.[136]

It was not until 1965 that a constitutional reform set the basis for consolidation by the military as the control centre of national security and, at the same time, the police initiated its role as an auxiliary of the army in the anti-Communist drive (Drouin 2009: 20). That year the District Headquarters (*Jefaturas de Distrito*) were introduced, whose authorities were appointed directly by the army; their functions included police activities and military instruction of police agents. Also established was a Model Division (*Unidad Modelo*) responsible for riot operations and protest control in urban areas (Drouin 2009: 20).

The reform of the police at the beginning of the 1970s expanded police presence in urban areas. As explained before, the Public Safety Program for the National Police made it clearly that the police would not be strengthened given the military's supremacy over national security. In this context, the recommendations talked about improving the investigative functions of the police and coordination with the army for security operations.

134 See Annex 2.

135 In July of 1954, soon after Arbenz's overthrow, the Chief of the General Staff of the Army sent an order to the Chief of the Judicial Guard to prevent members of the Judicial Guard from interfering in the actions of the military, in addition to stop arresting members of the army whom the Judicial Guard suspected of being part of the officers allied with former President Arbenz (AHPN 1954/ doc1760054). On August 18, 1954, the Army ordered the Civil Guard to avoid using military uniforms to perform police functions because public opinion attributed the abuses committed by the police to the army (AHPN 1954/doc1760054).

136 The reserves included all males between 18 and 30 years of age with or without previous military service experience. In each department of the country a Departmental Delegation of Military Reserves was created, under a chief who became the main military authority and the representative of the Commandant of the military zone. All military commissioners and their assistants remained subordinated and controlled by the Chief of Military Reserves. As part of the military reserves, the population received military instruction, literacy classes, and military credentials. There was a control file for each member of the military reserves which was administrated by the military commissioner of the locality and his assistants. On January 11, 1956, the Ministry of Defence ordered the Director of the Police to include all police personnel in the military reserves (AHPN 1954/doc1760054).

In 1972 the Centre for Joint Operations of the Police (COCP) was created upon a recommendation of the USAID from 1968.[137] The main function of the COCP was to analyse the information of all units of the police and coordinate operations with other security forces, while responsible, at the same time, for the organization of police personnel (PRAHPN 2008: 34).[138]

The COCP was responsible for controlling police personnel assigned to the so-called *Servicio Especial de Vigilancia* (Special Guard Service) and the security organizations of industries and banks. The COCP was also responsible for producing information on the activities of private security services when the army made a request.[139]

Because of the different nature of private security services, the COCP requested information both from private security companies as well as industries and companies which had their own security organizations.[140] When the person worked for a private security company, the COCP requested information directly from the director of the security company. This was the case in 1979 when the second in command at COCP requested information from Valiente Téllez, director of the private security company Los Vigilantes, about a person who had worked two years previously for the company (AHPN 1979/doc2773753). PSCs were considered part of the security plans of the police and described as "friendly forces" (PRAHPN 2008: 41).

The COCP was responsible also for controlling private security contractors hired by the police for specific services.[141] The information collected by COCP covered all public and private institutions related to public security. It even included the fire department, which had to provide reports of its activities (AHPN 1982/doc2776364).

137 Four police headquarters were created in the metropolitan area of Guatemala City. This reform included new requirements for aspiring police agents, such as prior military service. In 1978, riot control and special operations were brought together in the Reaction and Special Operations Battalion (BRODE), and in 1982 the Special Operations Unit was created (Drouin 2009: 54).

138 As an intelligence unit, the COCP also kept records on non-state armed forces, such as private security companies (PRAHPN 2009: 34).

139 In 1982 for example, an officer of the General Staff of the Army requested information about private security agents employed by the *Banco del Café* (AHPN 1982/doc 2776896). The same situation occurred with the private security personnel of the Montúfar Commercial Centre (AHPN 1982/doc2776868).

140 For example, in 1979 the second in command at COCP requested information from the *Los Tarros* sugar mill about some individuals who allegedly belonged to the security team at the mill (AHPN 1979/doc2773756).

141 Information about private contractors are analysed in this chapter in the section of International Security Advisors and Private Security Companies.

The COCP also received information on the activities of the civil patrols and military commissioners. The civil patrols reported two times a month, both to the COCP and to the military headquarters of the region. The communication went through the departmental chief of the police. The reports were put together by the mayor of the municipal government and the chief of the military commissioners (AHPN 1983/doc2774148). In those areas where there were no civil patrols, it was the mayor's responsibility to prepare and send the situational report to the COCP (AHPN 1982/doc2774139).

When the COCP needed information about specific individuals, it sent a request to the chief of military commissioners through the departmental chief of the Police. Those types of requests were made in different departments in the country and for different reasons, including alleged insurgent activities, common crimes, and participation in private security services, among others (AHPN 1980/doc2774071).

The investigative functions are fundamental in the historical trajectories of public security and police. From 1925 to 1997, the investigative units of the police were reorganized according to the political context and the internal policies of the police. These units changed their names but their organization and functions remained the same:

1925: Section of Investigations
1937: Security Police
1944: Judicial Guard
1956: Judicial Department
1968: Judicial Police
1970: Detectives Corps
1982: Department of Technical Investigations
1986: Brigade of Special Investigations and Narcotics
1988: Department of Criminological Investigations (Drouin 2009: 67).

From its beginning, the investigation units were characterized by the persecution of political opponents. This function was reinforced in the contexts of anticommunism and counterinsurgency moments. Thus, the investigation units were linked with the creation of paramilitary groups that conducted covert operations, including active participation of armed groups of civilians.

Both coordination and investigative units are important in understanding the role of the police and private security services. On the one hand, the function of the police as an auxiliary of the army explains its displacement from public security functions. On the other hand, coordination and investigative functions were developed by both commercial and non-commercial private policing organizations such as private security companies, civil patrols, military commissioners, and vigilante groups. These investigative units were characterised by a high degree of autonomy and the absence of institutional controls over its operations.

The Special Surveillance Service

The Special Surveillance Service (*Servicio Especial de Vigilancia*) was the most important unit in the National Police for understanding the proliferation of commercial private security services.[142] Among other functions, this unit was responsible for controlling the allocation of police officers in surveillance activities at the request of particular individuals, industries, banks, commercial enterprises, embassies, and public institutions. The officers were part of the National Police but the person or institution that requested this service paid for them. They used the uniform, weapons, and other identifications of the police and were under the control of the General Director of the National Police. This unit also posted agents in strategic locations for collecting information on political leaders, students, and alleged insurgents, among others.

Empirical data reveals that the Special Surveillance Service increased its services in tune with the process of centralization of the National Police as part of the counter insurgent strategy. In other words, the more the National Police were integrated into counterinsurgency actions and subordinated to the Army, the more the public security functions, understood as the prevention of crime and the protection of the citizenry, were displaced to private services and covert actions provided by this unit, namely, the private hiring of state police officers.

The Special Surveillance Service was a dynamic unit that changed according to increased requests for its services. Individuals and institutions proposed the hiring of security personnel, which the National Police then authorized and incorporated as National Police agents assigned to special surveillance services. In this process, private security companies requested and used agents of the National Police to provide the security services they contracted.

Due to the low salaries of the police officers and poor institutional guarantees, the Special Surveillance Service provided additional employment that helped the officers increase their income. A report prepared by a U.S. advisor in 1971 mentioned some factors that contributed to the low morale of the National Police, including attacks by insurgents which sometimes resulted in the killing of police officers on guard duty.[143] Other factors that contributed to low morale were the

142 See Annex 2.

143 These attacks sought: a) to demonstrate that the police were incapable of protecting themselves, and therefore were incapable of protecting the public; and b) to undermine police morale and to secure additional weapons. Another possible objective

pay scale and allowances below subsistence level, absolute lack of job security with little or no opportunity for advancement, insufficient budget support for the institution, and excessively harsh disciplinary actions under military commanders (DNSA 1971c).[144]

As explained before, the army had expressed an historic reluctance to strengthen the police institution. The interplay of contextual factors, such as the increasing intensity of the armed conflict, the centralization of state security forces around the army, and the poor and weak institutional situation of the police, created the conditions for the emergence and proliferation of private security companies alongside state institutions.

The importance of the Special Surveillance Service as explanation of the proliferation of commercial private security services is that its creation represents the formalization of a security service that existed before as an informal practice. On the one hand, it meant the formal displacement of public security to private services under the auspices of state institutions. On the other, it reflected the differentiation between formal commercial private security services in the form of private companies and the wide range of informal private security, both commercial and non-commercial, in the form of private policing organizations.

From Contingent Event to Formal Service

The Special Surveillance Service was created as part of the National Police in 1955 in the context of the reorganization of the institution after the revolutionary period of 1944-1955. As was explained before, this reorganization was undertaken in the context of the beginning of the Public Safety Program of the United States and the anti-Communist functions of the Police. The Organic Law of the National Police issued in 1955 established the unit initially as Special and Confidential Services (PGDH 2009: 11).

The first officers transferred by the National Police to the Special Surveillance Service were assigned to the banking system.[145] A contract was signed in which

was to use these assassinations as "training exercises" for new recruits. In the opinion of the U.S. advisor, the impact on the morale of police personnel was threefold: the reluctance to be assigned to an exposed fixed post, a seeming tendency not to take action when a fire fight developed, and difficulty in recruiting qualified personnel together with high rates of attrition (DNSA 1971c).

144 In 1967, fifteen policemen were killed; another 15 in 1968; 22 in 1969; 26 in 1970, and in the first two months of 1971, 15 policemen were killed (DNSA 1971c).

145 On October 23, 1957, an officer was assigned to *Crédito Hipotecario Nacional of Guatemala*, specifically to the finance department. Such assignments were reported as personnel on duty (*altas*) in the institution's records (AHPN 1959/doc1742190).

the person or institution that hired the services was obliged to pay the salary of the officer in the same amount that was paid by the National Police. At the same time, the contracting institution had to provide the necessary equipment, specifically firearms, while the national police provided identification (credentials, breast plate, and cockade). The agent assigned to a special surveillance service was subordinate to the General Direction of the National Police (AHPN 1957/doc1770813). The departmental branches of the banking system also used the Special Service of Surveillance, as did the international banks operating in Guatemala (for example, the Bank of London and South America Ltd. that in January 1959 requested this kind of services) (AHPN 1959/doc1742190).

The Special Surveillance Service worked under similar arrangements when it was hired by other public institutions. In all cases, the agent remained within the National Police but the salary was paid by the other public institution.[146]

The number of requests for the special service of surveillance did not increase during the first years after its inclusion within the structure of the National Police. Its clients were essentially the same institutions: banks (such as the *Banco Industrial*, the *Banco del Café*, the *Crédito Hipotecario Nacional*, the Bank of London and South America, the *Banco de Guatemala*, and the *Banco Hipotecario*), some public institutions (such as the *Dirección General de Cartografía* and a number of public hospitals), and some farms and sugar mills.[147]

It was not until 1969 that small businesses started to hire agents from the Special Service of Surveillance. On April 11, 1969, the restaurant *Casa de Hierro* requested one agent for the surveillance of its property. The terms of the contract were the same but with one difference: the agent was incorporated into the police at that moment, in other words, he was a private individual proposed by the owner of the restaurant who was subsequently accredited as national police officer serving in the Special Surveillance Service. A similar situation occurred that year when the Biltmore Hotel of Guatemala requested agents for the surveillance of its buildings (AHPN 1969/doc665327).

The first period of the Special Surveillance Service introduced the institutional practice of hiring out security agents to private individuals and corporations. As mentioned, this was the formalization of a common practice that had been provided informally. During this period the records show that the range of institutions hiring this service was not wide and that only a few small businesses used

146 On February 10, 1958, the National Railways Company requested an agent for its terminal in Puerto Barrios. The same situation occurred with the Social Security Institute which in January 1958 requested two agents (AHPN 1958/doc1747670).

147 On February 5, 1960, the service was requested by the owners of *El Obraje*, a farm in the department of Escuintla, to protect the perimeter of their property (AHPN 1960/doc592911).

the service. This situation changed alongside the emergence of private security companies that started offering the same service and also used the same institutional mechanisms. The agents of the National Police in the Special Surveillance Service had the same functions as other police agents except that their post was in a private area and that they were paid privately.[148]

The Special Surveillance Service and Private Security Companies

The relation between the Special Surveillance Service of the National Police and the emergence of private security companies shows the interplay between the state and the private security sector. In the context of increased political destabilization and political violence, the supremacy of the military over other security forces, the weak institutional situation of the police, and U.S. support to convert the police into an anti-Communist force, the provision of private security services both from the public sector and from private companies filled the vacuum of public security.

On October 15, 1970, the Law of Private Police Forces (*Ley de Policías Privadas*) was issued by legislative decree 73-70.[149] The law stated that there were a number of private police agencies operating only under the authorization of a public official in the Ministry of Interior without any other regulations or institutional controls. In the first article of this law, private police were defined as those private entities with a similar disciplinary organization as the National Police, including the designation of its board of directors and administration. The law established a list of requirements for the companies such as periodical reports on personnel, arms, and activities. The law stipulated also that the National Police could authorize the inclusion of expelled National Police agents into private security companies. At the same time, the law required that the uniforms of the private police would have to be different from those used by the army, the National Police, and other state security forces.

As will be shown, during the 1970s former police and military officers who used national police agents to provide private services controlled the private se-

148 In March 1982, a complaint was filed concerning a uniformed agent of the National Police assigned by the Special Service of Surveillance to a bus terminal in Guatemala City who was imposing fines on people who refused to pay a special tax to enter the terminal with their cars. The agent argued that the fines were authorized by the Department of Motor Vehicles of the National Police in the person of a military officer who supervised the agents in the Special Service of Surveillance. The agents were allowed also to arrest alleged criminals and to request personal identification papers from any citizen (AHPN 1982/doc2776521).

149 See Annex 2.

curity sector. One of the most important characteristic of the relation between public and private security services was that the private services provided agents who used the uniforms and credentials of the national police because these carried the image of authority and respect that the client needed. The lack of controls by the police allowed the private sector to grow with support from a state institution.

However, the control of the private security companies was delegated to the COCP as well as the director of the Special Surveillance Service. Aside from some attempts to regulate the use of uniforms and other administrative issues, the COCP did not exercise any real control over the private security companies. On the contrary, the COCP strengthened the use of both the Special Surveillance Service and private security companies as sources of information.

One of the effects of the law was to authorize companies that offered services in an informal way. The first companies were mostly directed by police officers such as Manuel de Jesus Valiente Téllez, owner of the private security company *Policía Privada de Investigaciones Valiente "Los Vigilantes"*. The legal authorization for this company was issued on August 3, 1971, and stated clearly that the owner was obliged to reorganize the company in accordance with the new law but could continue to offer its services (Tipografía Nacional 1971). In the same year, the Organization of Private and Police Services (OSPIP) was authorized to continue offering its services (Tipografía Nacional 1971). On February 22, 1972, the Private Office of Investigations (OPI), owned by Pedro Cuevas Bethancourt, was registered as a firm that had offered private security services since 1961. This was also the case of *Alarmas de Guatemala*, which had been offering private security services since 1967 (AHPN 1985/doc2765346).By 1985, fifteen private security companies were registered with the National Police.[150]

These private security companies constituted the core of the business during the armed conflict and provide a view of their operation. These companies emerged from the Special Service of Surveillance.[151] First, there were the services provided by the Police through the Special Surveillance Service. This was the basis of the private security sector during this period and provided agents to private security companies, public institutions, industries, individuals, small businesses, and embassies, among others. Second, there were private security companies owned by police or military officers such as *Los Vigilantes, Vigilancia e Investigaciones Privadas* (VIP), *Organización Servicios Policiales e Investigaciones Privadas* (OSPIP), *Oficina Privada de Investigaciones* (OPI), *Seguri-*

150 Three of them had been operating since the 1960s, seven of them were authorized during the 1970s, and the rest were authorized during the 1980s (AHPN 1985/doc2765346).

151 See Annex 2.

sa, Servicio de Investigaciones Privadas Policiales (SIPP), and Scorpio. Third, there were private security companies founded by civilians such as *Alarmas de Guatemala, El Ébano,* Wackenhut of Guatemala, and *Vigilancia Particular Comercial* (Viparco). Fourth, there were private security companies founded as security groups within an industry to provide it with protection but then expanded to offer security services outside the original industry, for example the banking system which created its own security services. This is the case of *Proa-Cadena de Servicios, Policía de la Urbanización Likin* (Polikin), *Rentalarmas,* and *Aralva.* Fifth, there finally was the group of private security companies founded by international advisors such as Consesa.[152] Together these companies reported in 1982 a total of 1,724 agents (AHPN 1982/doc2776733; /doc2776805; /doc2776800).

Parallel to the emergence of private security companies, the Special Service of Surveillance increased its activity during these decades; even the Army through the Ministry of Defence authorized security corps as special surveillance services (AHPN 1982/doc2770953). As became especially visible, small businesses and private individuals requested the authorization for their agents as members of the National Police in special service of surveillance. The requests were made with attached lists of agents to be incorporated in the special service of surveillance.[153] The approximate total of agents who were attached to the special service of surveillance of the national police was 2,510 in 1985; it included the 13 private security companies created during the 1970s and also individuals, banks, small businesses, sugar mills, big industries, restaurants, public institutions, and the U.S. Embassy (the other embassies are not included in the records of 1985).[154] Thus, the activities of the special service of surveillance resulted in both the assignment of agents of the National Police to private contractors and the inclusion of private agents into the National Police (AHPN 1984/doc2762837).

152 See Annex 1.

153 On April 13, 1982, the Industrial Company of Food, S.A. reported 59 agents accredited as National Police agents in Special Service of Surveillance (AHPN 1982/doc2773268). In 1985, the U.S. Embassy requested 51 agents in Special Service of Surveillance to protect U.S. citizens living in Guatemala (AHPN 1985/doc2767767). During March, April, and May of 1985, *Alarmas de Guatemala* requested the authorization of 171 agents in special service of surveillance (AHPN 1985/doc2767786); on January 22, 1985, *Cementos Progreso* presented a list of 114 agents of its security group who were to receive credentials as agents of the National Police in special service of surveillance; on February 2, 1985, the private security company *El Ébano* presented a list of 151 agents (AHPN 1985/doc2767903); on April 22, the Bank of Guatemala requested 67 agents (AHPN 1985/doc2767815).

154 The total is the sum of requested agents in 81 documents from 1985 located between document number 2767664 and 2767767 of the AHPN.

The Special Service of Surveillance was not regulated by any specific law and created a hybrid service that was public and private simultaneously. This situation was widely tolerated by police authorities, the military, and even the U.S. advisors.[155] However, the U.S. ambassador in 1964 mentioned it as one of the causes for the low capacity of the police to retain its personnel. The ambassador was concerned because:

> "The rate of retention in the police force of officials whom we had sent for training abroad was exceptionally and disappointingly low… too many of the returned trainees left the police soon after being trained in order to set up their private police (guard) business. In the case of military students a formal commitment to stay in the army a certain number of years was required." (DNSA 1963h).

However, in 1984 the chief of the Security Office of the U.S. Embassy wrote to the General Director of the Police about the use of agents of the National Police in Special Service of Surveillance. The document shows that during the years when general German Chupina Barahona was director (1978-1982), there was a formal agreement between the U.S. Embassy and the Police to extend the Special Service of Surveillance by including former members of the National Police or the Army.[156]

Another characteristic of the Special Service of Surveillance was its constancy, meaning that the same agents were posted in an institution, commerce, or industry during years. This resulted in bonds of confidence between the agents and their contractors, who then opposed any decision by National Police to move the agents. In 1984 the *Contraloría General de Cuentas* requested the Director of the Police not to reassign the police agents which during ten years were contracted by this institution (AHPN 1984/doc2773122).[157] The assignment of public agents to the private sector and the incorporation of private agents to the police show the reproducing mechanisms of the institutional pattern of public security displacement.

155 In 1977, the General Director of the National Police issued an order to avoid a conflict of interest by officials in the police force who also occupied executive positions in private security companies. It was reported that this order only affected the security company Los Vigilantes, owned by the Director of Investigations of the National Police who one year after the order was issued continued at the head of his company (AHPN 1977/doc2765087).

156 The use of uniforms of the National Police and other identification by those agents was also authorized (AHPN 1984/doc2773354). Agents of the Special Service of Surveillance were allowed also to provide their services as plain clothes men (AHPN 1982/doc2773398).

157 Traditional guards hired informally by small businesses were incorporated as members of the National Police in Special Service of Surveillance (AHPN 1982/pro004 6; 1984/doc2777132; /doc2777049).

The Police and Police's Private Security Companies

Private security companies owned by police and military officers were cloned along lines reminiscent of the Police, especially with regards to institutional controls, the socio-economic situation of the agents, and the use of symbols of authority. The use of police agents to provide private services and the inclusion of private agents within the police force became a common practice (AHPN 1984/doc2777096). In general, both police agents and officers found in private security services a secondary job which was in increasing demand.[158]

A clear example of the strong links between the police and private security companies is Los Vigilantes, the yet mentioned private security company owned by Manuel de Jesus Valiente Téllez.[159] On September 05, 1978, Manuel de Jesus Valiente Téllez was appointed head of the Detectives Corps of the National Police; his brother, the head of personnel of Los Vigilantes, was killed on September 4, 1981, together with a private security agent of the *Pollo Campero* restaurant chain (AHPN 1981/ref4111). Links between companies and state security forces were reinforced also by the exchange of information. In 1979, the chief of the COCP had a fluid exchange of information with the owner of SIPS, colonel Edmundo Lopez (AHPN 1979/doc2773802).

The private security companies founded by civilians also were linked to military and police personnel. This was the case of *Alarmas de Guatemala* (founded in 1967) and *El Ébano*.[160] Both companies hired police and military personnel but their administrative organization did not reproduce that of the National Police because, as a product of their origins in the banking system, they tried to avoid the militaristic outlook of the security companies owned by police and military personnel. Since its foundation, *El Ébano* diversified its activities creating subsidiary companies for each security area: PROVAL for high value and TRANSVAL for low value transportation and *Linker Monitoreo* for monitoring vehicle movements using GPS.[161]

158 National police agents assigned to special surveillance services for individuals and for private security companies were both subject to the disciplinary rules of the National Police (AHPN 1976/doc2773170).

159 The company involved his whole family: the General Director was himself, the Deputy General Director was Ruben Alberto Valiente Téllez, and the head of personnel was Carlos Valiente Téllez (AHPN 1985/doc2765022).

160 The *El Ébano* group started operations in 1979 as a private security service for the banking sector in response to a wave of bank robberies and insurgent group attacks. This company employed National Police officers of the Special Surveillance Service. Today, *El Ébano* is one of the largest private security companies in Central America and continues to hire police officers and investigators from the government.

161 These subsidiaries were not registered as private security companies.

Initially, *El Ébano* only provided guard services, but it diversified later on to offer private investigation services, consulting in property protection, rescuing kidnapped individuals, and recovering stolen goods (Interview with Jorge Sierra, Grupo Almo, 03/02/09).

During the 1980s there were also attempts to regulate the use of uniforms of the National Police by private security companies and the extended use of agents assigned to special service of surveillance. In 1984 the Director of the National Police issued an order to enforce the law that regulated private security services. The U.S. Embassy and the Guatemalan-American Institute complained about the orders issued by the General Director of the National Police concerning the use of uniforms by special service of surveillance agents assigned to those institutions as well as by their private security groups (AHPN 1984/doc2773354 and doc2773360; AHPN 1984/doc2764806; AHPN 1984/doc277350).[162]

The special service of surveillance assigned to public institutions since ten years before was reduced during the 1980s (AHPN 1984/doc2770950). This attempt to control private security services aimed to differentiate the services provided by the police and those provided by private security companies. There was no clear public/private difference between commercial private security services. The proliferation of private security companies was based on the set of informal rules promoted by public institutions.

The increased controls over private security companies could be explained also by the emergence of non-authorized companies. The core companies created during the 1970s possessed a degree of monopoly both over the commercial private sector and also over relations with the National Police and the prerogatives this relation gave them. On August 1, 1983, the owner of Segurisa, Rodolfo Rosito, who was also the founder of the Guild of Private Security Companies of Guatemala, requested that the General Director of the Police to apply more controls over non-authorized private security services (AHPN 1983/doc2766782).

The attempts at controlling private security companies during the 1970s can be considered mere formalities while the controls in place during the 1980s can be analysed within the context of the beginning of the transformation of the police before the end of the internal armed conflict. On the one hand, the reorganization of police personnel from 1984 onwards was evident. On the other, this

162 On January 17, 1987, the manager of the American-Guatemalan Institute requested authorization for agents of special service of surveillance to continue using the uniforms and identification of the National Police because that way people respected the agents (AHPN 1987/doc2773360). Private security companies thus continued using the name and agents of the National Police. On November 12, 1989, *Alarmas de Guatemala* requested that the General Director of the National Police assign 18 agents to provide security services the company had contracted with *Hotel Dorado Americana* (AHPN 1984/doc2773434).

was the beginning of the creation of a new group of private security companies owned by former military officers demobilized during the security sector reform together with an increase in non-authorized private security companies.

International Security Advisors and Private Security Companies

The origins of private security companies established by international security advisors can be explained along three lines. In the first place, during and after the U.S. Public Safety Program and the Military Assistance Program, some advisors found that the weak situation of the national police offered an opportunity to continue providing security services to the U.S. Embassy and U.S. companies. While the main service offered by these security companies was private investigations, they expanded soon after to provide guards and patrol cars. Second, when the U.S. Public Safety Program ended, international private security companies offered the same training courses the Public Safety Program had offered before. Finally, when the United States stopped military assistance to Guatemala at the beginning of the 1980s, the government of Guatemala sought new providers, both for arms sales and for military advisors.

As was mentioned in chapter IV, international private security companies do not play an important role in the current formation of private security in Guatemala. Their presence in the private security market is limited and its main characteristic is the adaptation of its mechanisms and structures to the dominant rules of the local private security companies. While during the 1970s the private security sector was dominated by a small number of local companies owned mostly by police and military officers, during the 1980s there appeared a few international private security companies directly linked with the police.

For example, On March 16, 1982, authorization was extended to *Consultores de Seguridad Internacionales* (Consesa), represented by Hugo Alvarado Chavez but owned and directed by U.S. citizen Carl William West (AHPN 1985/doc2765346). Carl West was an officer of the U.S. Army who served in Central America.[163] He came to Guatemala in 1977 under an agreement with the Government of Guatemala. His first credential with the National Police of Guatemala was issued in 1978. In Guatemala, he founded his company as a private investigation firm but also requested authorization to offer the service of patrol cars (AHPN 1982/doc2776670). The company also benefited from the assign-

163 During the 1960s, he founded a private investigation office named American Protection System in San Juan, Puerto Rico; he then worked as a director of counter intelligence for a private security firm called Security Association International in Houston, Texas.

ment of agents in Special Service of Surveillance (AHPN 1985/doc2767792). It was reported that Carl West went constantly to the United States to buy firearms and then to sell them to different private security companies in Guatemala, especially to Manuel de Jesus Valiente Téllez, owner of Los Vigilantes and former Director of Investigations of the National Police.

As part of his private security services, Carl West was hired by the National Police to provide training courses for police officers. In 1981, before founding his company, Carl West was accredited as a technical advisor to the National Police together with his partner Vincenzo Mascolo, who also received the same accreditation (AHPN 1983/ref4245). The range of services Carl West provided to the National Police was very wide. In November 1980, he prepared an evaluation of the situation of the explosives depot of the National Police and suggested organizing a training course on the adequate use of explosive materials.[164] At the same time, he informed about a private investigation conducted for the national police; he had taken down witness statements and asked for authorization from the General Director to proceed with the investigation (AHPN 1980/04GX9-101a).[165]

On June 16, 1982, West conducted a course on investigations attended by women detectives of the National Police. While he provided training, West was hired by the National Police to deactivate explosives. In a detailed report Carl West prepared for the General Director of the National Police, Hector Rafael Bol, he listed the deactivation of approximately 35 bombs by request of the Army and the National Police between 1980 and 1983, besides different training courses on bomb deactivation, riot control techniques, and crime investigation, among others (AHPN 1983/of1163).[166]

164 He concluded that the situation was dangerous due to the neglected state of the explosive material and the incompetence of the personnel (AHPN 1980/04GX9-101a).

165 After this report, a 45-day course on explosives management was organized under the direction of West for 22 agents of the National Police (AHPN 1980/04GX9-101b).

166 There are other examples of the relation between the police and private contractors. In April 1979, the Wackenhut Corporation, based in Florida, U.S.A., presented an offer to organize a training course in techniques and special arms (SWAT) to the National Police of Guatemala. In a note to the General Director of the National Police, German Chupina, the COCP recommended that the offer not be accepted due to its high costs (AHPN 1979/doc1028660). In October 1979, Charles Wilson, president of Pro-Ex International Inc., a private security company based in New York, presented an offer to the General Director of the National Police of Guatemala to train the security guard of the President of the Republic, Romeo Lucas García. The training was geared to covert and overt operations and to military and paramilitary agents. The personnel of the company was made up of former green berets, navy

The proposed contracts show how international private security companies offered to provide the training courses given previously by U.S. government personnel to military and police agents in areas such as anti-terrorist teams, anti-guerrilla operations, counter-insurgent operations, commando and covert operations, intelligence operations, and interrogation techniques (AHPN 1979/pro.31 8).[167]

Other mechanism that increased the foundation of PSCs by international advisors was the number of providers of military equipment to the Guatemalan Army. Since 1974, the relation between Guatemala and Israel had also been marked by the sale of firearms and military training. After the suspension of U.S. military aid, Israel was one of the most important suppliers of arms to the Guatemalan Army (Kurtenbach 2008: 16).[168] When public opinion rejected U.S. intervention, Israel became a full-fledged covert partner for the U.S. in promoting counterrevolution in the third world. Israeli intelligence agents, military officers, and arms dealers have supplied training and weapons to Chile, El Salvador, Guatemala, Haiti, South Africa, and the Nicaraguan Contras (DNSA 1976a).

Between 1978 and 1982, Israel delivered 17 Arava aircraft, 10 RBY armoured personnel carriers, three Dabur class patrol boats armed with Gabriel missiles, light cannon, machine guns, and at least 15,000 Galil assault rifles (Bahbah 1986; Beit-Hallahmi 1985). In 1983, reports indicated that during the presidency of Lucas García (1978-1082), Israeli advisors set up a factory to produce Galil rifles in the department of Alta Verapaz and trained Guatemalan military personnel to run it.[169] In 1984, Israel sold to Guatemala 12,000 rifles to arm the Civil Defence Patrols and Israel computer technology was delivered to upgrade the ef-

Seals, marine force recon, police SWAT instructors, army airborne rangers, French Foreign Legionnaires, and Rhodesian light infantry, among others (AHPN 1979/no.6019).

167 Aside from the contracts, there were other prerogatives gave by the police to international PSCs. There were U.S. private security firms that were not included in the records of 1982 but were active nonetheless, as Marine Security Guards and Special Protective Security Agents, for example. In a confidential communication of August 2, 1985, orders were sent to not include these companies in the records of the National Police (AHPN 1982/doc3151861).

168 There were other suppliers such as Belgium, Portugal, South Korea, Switzerland, Yugoslavia, and Taiwan (DNSA 1980b).

169 The expectation of President Lucas was to produce enough arms to supply the Guatemalan army and the Salvadoran and Honduran, as well. The creation of the factory was marked by corruption and graft. The contract was proposed by Pessah Ben-Hor, a representative for Eagle Exports of Ashdod Imgo Sa. The first investment of the government would be US$21 million for a seven years contract (DNSA 1988). The Galil was the official weapon of the Guatemalan Army during the internal conflict.

ficiency of the police and military. This equipment was used to track the activities of the guerrillas and to coordinate all of Guatemala security forces.[170]

The Guatemalan Army also recruited Israeli military at the beginning of the 1980s as military advisors and police trainers. It was reported that in 1983 there were 300 Israeli military officers working as advisors in Guatemalan security and military intelligence structures. During these years the private military company Tadiran trained intelligence military personnel in subjects such as encoding, radio jamming, and monitoring. The equipment was designed and produced by Degem Systems, a company that was one of first ones to use Computer Assisted Instruction in military technologies for developing countries during the 1970s (Bahbah 1986; Beit-Hallahmi 1985).[171]

Israeli security advisors created security systems in farms located in areas where there was armed conflict. They passed on knowledge to Guatemalan military officers on Israeli counterinsurgency tactics (Hunter 1987: 36). Business groups also hired Israeli security advisers (Beit-Hallahmi 1985). As it was a good business opportunity, the Israelis set up private security companies offering security systems based on their war experience. Israeli security companies and gun shops have a large share of the security market in Guatemala.[172]

International advisors were benefited with the institutional pattern of public security displacement, on the one hand, because the counterinsurgent strategy created a demand of equipment and training for the national security forces and, on the other hand, the vacuum of public security created a productive field for commercial security.

The Military Service of Private Security

Parallel to the existence of commercial private security services in the police, the military created also its own private security service.[173] The Mobile Military Po-

170 One computer was located in the old military academy and was used to organize the movements of units in the field. Another computer was located in an annex of the National Palace and was the control centre of the G-2 (military intelligence office) (NACLA 1987).

171 More about this company in http://www.degem.com/index.php?option=com_content&viewarticle&id=6&Itemid=9&lang=en.

172 This was the basis for the creation of a large chain of Israeli private security companies, of which Grupo Golán became the largest and oldest Israeli private security consortium in Guatemala with approximately 3,000 guards and a large number of investigators and security advisors and operations in different countries of Central America (Interview with Edgar Herrera, Security Advisor of EMISA, 03/23/09).

173 See Annex 1 and 2.

lice (MMP) offered a private security service similar to the Special Surveillance Service of the National Police. It was hired by the banking system and in the countryside to protect farms and industries. This corps was originally part of the reformed National Police in 1955. At that time it was named Mobile Police and had four platoons organized in mobile groups to cover the countryside. The Mobile Police could be mobilized easily because its had no specific jurisdictional limit (AHPN 1955).

The functions assigned to this corps were the same as the rest of the police but it had the specific task, in case of emergencies, of assisting the owners of properties in the countryside and to inform of all activities which might exacerbate tensions among the peasant population and when necessarily to repress them (PGDH 2009: 12).

Peralta Azurdia authorized the incorporation of the Mobile Police into the Army in 1965 as the Mobile Military Police under the administrative direction of the Defence Ministry to support the National Police and to maintain order in rural and urban areas (PGDH 2009: 32). In 1971 President Arana expanded its role and mission by allowing the army to coordinate certain police activities and authorized the MMP to operate in both urban and rural areas. The first two duties of the MMP were to maintain public order in urban and rural areas and to prevent felonies and pursue and arrest offenders. Other duties of the MMP included contraband control, protection of railroads and telephone and telegraph lines, forestry services, traffic law enforcement, and vehicle control on highways and roads.[174] In 1990 the MMP was assigned to lead anti-narcotics operation inside Guatemala in coordination with Mexican and U.S. officers and assisted by the National Police and the Treasury Police.[175]

The Mobile Military Police consisted of two different tactical units. The "ordinary" MMP had a typical military structure and was part of the counterinsurgency strategy. Private companies, farmers, and members of economic elites hired the "special" MMP. Hiring of the Special MMP was made directly through field officers. The MMP were hired by industries and farms that risked being targeted by the insurgents or by the labour union movement.[176] The *Embotella-*

174 The reason given for the expansion of its duties was that after the creation of the MMP in 1965, it had assumed duties of the National Police in rural areas. The army argued for the need for close coordination between the MMP and the Police and that MMP investigators should have legal recognition (DNSA 1971d).

175 This was an operation conducted in San Marcos and Huehuetenango against poppy production (DNSA 1990a).

176 This unit had an important role in the counterinsurgency strategy with the consequent perpetration of different human rights violations (CEH 1999a). In 1980 members of the MMP hired by the *Pantaleón* sugar mill killed a member of the company's labour union (CEH 1999a: 321).

dora Guatemalteca (EGSA-Coca Cola) hired the services of the MMP after a labour union was formed within the company. At the same time military personnel were hired by the company to organize the internal security corps (CEH 1999a: 113). In 1997 the MMP had 2,421 agents and, according to MINUGUA, after its formal dissolution, some MMP agents were reinstated within the National Civil Police and the prison system. Most of the rest were hired by private security companies (MINUGUA 1997: 26).

The MMP was also hired as personal security in plain clothes for businessmen and landowners. In 1976 the bodyguards of a member of an economically powerful family, Jorge Kong Vielman, were members of the MMP hired privately. The bodyguards killed two of three brothers of another economically powerful family after Kong shot one of them in an incident in a restaurant. A U.S. report stated that "This is a common procedure here and completely legal" (DNSA 1976b).

The institutional trajectories of the National Police showed how commercial private security was reinforced as consequence of the institutional pattern of public security displacement. However, non-commercial private security was also reinforced by the state armed forces and the political context.

6.4 Private Policing and Civil Participation

Aside from the institutional trajectories of the Police that reinforced the emergence of private security services, the different mechanisms of incorporation of civilians in security and self-defence organizations in the context of anticommunism and counterinsurgency explains the emergence of non-commercial private policing.

From 1955 onwards, civilian participation was reinforced through the reorganization of military commissioners, urban and rural civilian patrols, military reserve units, vigilante groups, and irregular forces of the insurgency. Self-defence worked as a security *dispositif*[177] (Foucault 2003) against communism, insurgents, military forces or common crime that activated different mechanisms of social control and surveillance. On the basis of self-defence, private policing was embedded in the social and cultural dynamics of the population and its adaptive characteristics allowed its reproduction in different sequences and contexts. The following civilian participation mechanisms interacted with state institutions such as the police, the army, and the municipalities, while the levels of compulsory participation were varied. Likewise its usefulness was different depending on the region, the time, and the intensity of the violence. For this reason there

177 *Dispositif* is understood here as the socio-technical system or mechanism that reinforces power and social control relations.

were some organizations under tight control while others operated with high levels of autonomy.

Military Commissioners

The military commissioners were first created under Jorge Ubico in 1938 on the basis of the former *"encargados militares"* and were active before being charged with the control of the militias (AGCA 1933). The military commissioners were civilians with military authority and had responsibility for organizing militias in their own region. They also were responsible for the control of the community and the investigation and arrest of alleged criminals as well as executing all orders issued by the local commander or the departmental governor (the so-called *"jefe político"*) (AGCA 1938). On October 11, 1954, the Department of Organization, Instruction, and Training of the Military Reserves of the Army was created under which the military commissioners were integrated as military authorities over all citizens in their localities (AHPN 1954/doc1760054). The military commissioners were defined as a "bridge between the Army and the civilian population" (CEH 1999b: 159).

The inclusion of the military commissioners in political repression occurred during the presidency of Méndez Montenegro after 1966 and paralleled the increase in political violence.[178] During the first military offensive against insurgent groups at the end of the 1960s, the army gave firearms to the military commissioners. This resulted in the death of several innocent people given the impossibility of controlling the large number of armed military commissioners (CEH 1999b: 160). During the government of Arana (1970-1974), the military commissioners and their assistants acquired a number of privileges and greater power under the auspices of the army.

During the internal armed conflict, the military commissioners participated in military operations in areas of high insurgent activity. As military representatives, the commissioners acted with impunity. Both military authority and impunity allowed some military commissioners to commit criminal actions.[179]

178 See Annex 1.

179 In May 1973, it was reported that a criminal gang integrated by former military police agents and military commissioners in Chiquimula sold firearms to alleged insurgents and at the same time stole from the population and killed some people. The head of the gang was identified as a military specialist working at the *Mariscal Zavala* military base; this person reportedly delivered the money to three bodyguards of a congressmen (AHPN 1973/doc1926161). In 1990 it was reported also that military commissioners and chiefs of civil patrols were involved in opium poppy cultivation in the departments of San Marcos and Huehuetenango (DNSA

As of 1981 the counterinsurgency strategy gave the civil patrols and military commissioners a central role in the organization of the civilian population. The chiefs of the civil patrols were normally military commissioners as well. Social control was the main function of military commissioners and their assistants and it meant that all deviant behaviour was defined as pro-insurgent or criminal. A report of the U.S. embassy stated that aside from their information and recruiting functions, the military commissioners appeared to act as a law unto themselves (DNSA 1979b). In 1989, army headquarters issued numerous identification papers to military commissioners and their assistants and tasked them with rounding up criminals and undocumented persons. The commissioners worked on a rotational basis, with certain individuals patrolling the streets one night per week using their own personal vehicles. Once an individual was arrested, he was turned over to headquarters for processing (DNSA 1989a). Due to the subordination of local civil authorities to the military, the military commissioners became the local authority, superseding the elected mayor (CEH 1999b: 166). In rural and isolated areas, the military commissioners acted as the de facto mayor and law enforcer (DNSA 1995a).

Military commissioners and civilian patrols were part of the human intelligence sources for military intelligence. Until 1995, the functions of the military commissioners were to ensure compliance with military conscription, assist with local security, control weapons issued to civilian patrols, conduct limited military-style operations, and coordinate civil affairs matters, as well as providing information for the police and the military (DNSA 1994). Military commissioners assumed police functions against alleged criminals in their communities; this was one of the formal tasks that reinforced the idea of self-defence through communal organization:

> "The military commissioners or their assistants with information about individual or collective suspects in their jurisdiction should take the necessary security measures and immediately inform the immediate superior military authority." (CEH 1999b: 172).

This was a formal delegation of private policing and social control activities and the fact that they were directed by the army reinforced the exclusion of the National Police in public security. However, the COCP had fluid communications with the military commissioners of each locality in collaboration with the mayors to generate security information (AHPN 1980/doc2774071; /doc2774089 and /doc2774098). Likewise, some military commissioners were hired by farmers and industries to protect private property (CEH 1999b: 178). Whatever the prerogatives the military commissioners had (such as protection by the army, mili-

1990a). In 1993 several military commissioners were identified as members of criminal gangs ; one of them was "the *Churuneles*" in Sololá commanded by a former military commissioner (DNSA 1993b).

tary credentials, firearms, and impunity), there were cases in which the collaboration of civilians as military commissioners was imposed by the military (CEH 1999b: 167). It was calculated that in 1995 there were 25,000 military commissioners in the whole country (DNSA 1995c).

Military Commissioners represent an important reproducing mechanisms of private policing and social control functions. Aside from its military functions the military commissioners were the responsible for local security.

Vigilante Groups

While military commissioners were an extended network of civilian informants and representatives of the military authority that implemented private policing in their communities, vigilante groups – which appeared after 1960 – have implemented "social cleansing" both of persons linked to political organizations and activities as well as alleged common criminals. These groups were known as death squads and were made up of both civilians and police and military types. The groups were the result of covert anti-Communist operations conducted by military and police personnel with the support of U.S. advisors. After decades of activity, different death squads fought against different alleged threats. During the 1960s they were used against communism, during the 1970s and 1980s they targeted political leaders linked to insurgent groups, and during the post-war period death squads were finally organized to fight against criminality.

On November 24, 1965, the Government of Guatemala requested a U.S. advisor to help create a unit to combat kidnapping and extortion using the same tactics used by alleged communist groups, such as torture, annihilation, and deportation (DNSA 1965b). The request was evaluated by the chief public safety advisor in Venezuela, John P. Longan, who arrived in Guatemala on November 27, 1965. In his report to the chiefs of military and police forces and President Peralta Azurdia, he recommended that both overt and covert measures be implemented like those employed in Venezuela (DNSA 1965c).[180]

The high level of distrust the government of Mendez Montenegro generated in extreme right-wing political groups and dissatisfied military officers provided opportunity to take control of these groups and implement vigilante actions

180 As part of the overt immediate actions, a safe house should be set up and all information concerning extortions and kidnappings centralized there; a special unit of selected agents would conduct field investigations in plain clothes (DNSA 1965c).

against alleged communist, while the army and the police denied any direct participation in them (Jonas 1991: 60; McClintock 1985: 83).[181]

To avoid the political instability created by violence, the government of Guatemala requested in 1966 additional U.S. support to strengthen covert training for special squads that sought to kidnap certain individuals in Guatemala City considered key men in communist-inspired insurgency and terrorist activities who would then be exiled.[182]

Rightist "anti-communist" organizations were identified as phantom groups, established and maintained to mask the army's role in vigilantism, and anti-Communist organizations were the propaganda fronts for the army.[183] They were young, well trained, and highly motivated military personnel under the direction of high-ranking military officers (DNSA 1967a). The report also stated that the existence of these groups probably reflected military distrust of the police and the courts as effective agents in combating terrorism. The definition of "communist" as employed by these units was extremely loose and a number of moderate leftists, including non-communist and anti-Communist individuals, had been singled out for action by the vigilantes.

In rural areas, especially those with insurgent activity, the military commissioners were linked to the death squads and were at the same time members or supporters of the MLN and expressed a virulently indiscriminate anticommunism. "It is unlikely that the comisionado's definition of a "communist" is any less subjective than that of their urban confreres in MANO" (DNSA 1967a).

From a special unit created inside the armed forces, the death squads proliferated as private vigilante mechanisms supported by the local military. In 1968, president Méndez Montenegro attempted to disarm the civilian armed groups but this was rejected by the military and the armed civilians who argued that without

181 From 1965 onwards, a rash of kidnappings and killings proliferated in urban areas; in January 1966, the government of Guatemala made kidnapping a crime punishable by death and the unit for covert and overt operations against this crime started formal operations (DNSA 1965e and 1966a).

182 A number of U.S. Government agencies in Washington strongly recommend that the U.S. embassy should fully support current police improvement programs and initiate military psychological warfare training and additional counter-insurgency operations training (DNSA 1966h).

183 The most prominent anti-Communist organizations were: MANO (*Mano Blanca – Movimiento Nacionalista de Acción Organizada*), the New Anti-Communist Organization (NOA), the Guatemalan Anti-Communist Movement (MAG), CRAG, and RAYO. Apparently only MANO was independent of army control it was directly linked with the extreme rightist party *Movimiento de Liberación Nacional* (MLN) and was defined as the armed unit of this party; the others were cover for clandestine army commando units which operated as armed forces execution squads (DNSA 1967a).

weapons they could be helpless against criminality (DNSA 1968d; 1968e).[184] Contrary to the formal intentions of the government, new death squads appeared, such as *Ojo por Ojo* (in 1970), a rightist counter terror organization that executed several Guatemalan leftists; the victims were tortured before being killed and notes were left on their bodies. This organization was made up of former members of the Special Commando Unit of the Guatemalan Army. Civilian cooperation and participation and the internal security situation allowed for a mix of political murders with personal and private vendettas (DNSA 1970c). On the one hand, paramilitary groups increased violence which, on the other hand, reinforced the idea that the police was unable to protect the citizenry and delegitimized the civilian government. This situation and other political factors described before prepared the scenario for the next set of militarised governments (DNSA 1967e; 1968a).

During the 1970s the public justification for the action of the death squads combined the fight against common criminality with the incapacity of the police to protect the population (DNSA 1974a). During this time, the military transferred the responsibility of the death squads to the national police and the government confirmed that they were a smoke-screen for police extra-legal activities while arguing that the military had the responsibility of protecting the population and strengthening public security due to the weakness of the police (DNSA 1974a). In 1979 this transfer was complete when Colonel Chupina, General Director of the National Police, created several "social cleansing" units within the force, especially in the Fourth Corps (DNSA 1979a; PRAHPN 2008).

Between 1963 and 1980 there were 35 different death squads operating in Guatemala in addition to a large number of civilian armed groups (Rojas Bolaños 1994: 122). The role of the death squads was, on the one hand, to eliminate alleged communists and insurgents and, on the other, to play an important political role in destabilizing the government that in turn justified the militarization of the state (CEH 1999b: 342). In the long-term perspective, the death squads reinforced "social cleansing" and armed response as a self-defence mechanism against alleged threats. The evolution of the death squads shows that they began as part of the armed forces and developed as a vigilante mechanism within civilian groups. Their targets ranged from politically prominent individuals to alleged criminals as defined by their own civilian leadership. Simultaneously, the displacement of the responsibility for public security from the police to the army reinforced the idea of the ineffectiveness of the police and the need for military control over public security as well as private responses to crime.

184 Colonel Arana Osorio, who became president in 1970, organized civilian vigilante groups in the northwest departments of the republic and gave them arms, transforming the groups into irregular militias (DNSA 1967b; 1967c; 1967d).

Civilian Self-defence Policing

Civilian self-defence policing is a social function that constitutes the basis of non-commercial private security organizations. Different trajectories reinforced this mechanism in the collective life of Guatemalan society. Patrolling, information sharing, surveillance, denouncing, arresting, and in some cases, extortion, torture, and killing of alleged threats are part of the vigilante actions of these organizations. The initiators of these organizations vary according to context and history. There were, for example, civilian organizations created during the dictatorships of the first half of the twentieth century to reinforce state's authority. During the anti-Communist period, civilian organizations were part of the civic action programs of the army with support by the United States to avoid the re-emergence of communist political organizations. During the years of counterinsurgency strategy by the army, self-defence organizations became a key mechanism to weaken the social basis of the insurgent groups. Aside from their organizational and structural characteristics, these organizations share a self-defence function against threats. For this reason, this study argues that their functions were reproduced again in post-war society under the form of community policing organizations against crime.

The most studied of these organizations are the Civil Self-defence Patrols (*Patrullas de Autodefensa Civil* or PACs), created during the internal conflict.[185] However, there were other self-defence and policing organizations that despite their objectives and institutional supporters implemented, at different levels, the same self-defence policing function. Examples are the Urban Self-defence Patrols, the School Patrols, and the irregular forces of the insurgent groups.

The organizational structure and activities of the PACs during the internal conflict were different in each region of the country. In some regions, they voluntarily collaborated to protect the community; in others, they were forced to participate in the military. Yet in other regions they generated information and were part of the human intelligence sources of the army. Participation in the PACs was formally obligatory for all men between 18 and 60 years of age and most PACs were armed and trained by the military. The training aimed to create a sense of military discipline and loyalty to the army (Remijnse 2002; CEH 1999 b: 128). As a subordinate organization of the army, PAC members were subject to military punishments, that in some cases went as far as the killing of PACs members who refused to take part in military actions against their own communities (ODHAG 1998a: 169).

185 See Annex 1.

One of the main functions assigned to the PACs during the internal conflict was watching and denouncing people, daily facts, and situations that were perceived as suspicious. (Sáenz de Tejada 2004: 50; CEH 1999b: 182). Civil patrols laid the basis of an authoritarian communal organization and reinforced the idea of self-defence as a platform for policing activities.[186]

The number of PAC members formally demobilized in 1995 was put at 274,215 by the CEH (Sáenz de Tejada 2004). Ten years later, after their reorganization as a social movement requesting economic payments from the government, the number of former PAC members had been grown to 493,504. Other sources such as ODHAG reported the existence of approximately 900,000 individuals in the PACs between 1982-1983 (ODHAG 1998b: 119). Despite their formal dissolution in 1996, their members were reincorporated into the new structures of local power in the last twenty years as communal and religious leaders and mayors, among others (Táger and Mérida 2002: 93). The weakness of the state to establish limits and controls over demobilized armed actors resulted in the active continuity of such groups after the end of the social conflicts that formally justified their creation (Fumerton and Remijnse 2004).

Although the PACs were formally established in 1983, their activities already began in the 1960s as part of the civic action programs of the Army (Arias 1988). For the Army, the PACs played an important role in reducing the social base of the guerrillas and providing additional human intelligence sources. The members of the PACs were familiarized with the military because most of them had done their military service or were part of the military reserves (Schirmer 2001: 157). The PACs of the 1980s were the result of a long involvement of civilians in social control and surveillance linked to the military and other state authorities that adapted to changes in the political and social context.

The delegation of social control and security functions gave the heads of the PACs an informal authority that became formal through local institutions such as mayors or development councils, and in other cases remained as informal power structures of social control and security. In some cases the organization and continuity of PACs transformed the traditional community authority systems (CEH 1999b: 183; Schirmer 2001: 164).

Although the organization of the PACs was motivated or imposed by state security forces, some heads of PACs assumed a stronger attitude against alleged

186 The PACs played a violent role in the counterinsurgency strategy and were involve in human rights violations and the cultural transformation of the collective life in the communities (CEH 1999b; Brett 2007; Remijnse 2002). The CEH estimated that PACs committed 18 per cent of human rights violations during the internal conflict (CEH 1999a: 109; Centro para los Derechos Humanos Robert F. Kennedy 1994; CIDH 1996).

insurgents or criminals than the army (Schirmer 2001: 164). In some communities the self-defence policing activities conducted by the PACs produced a sense of protection against different threats, including the repressive actions of the army and insurgent groups (Schirmer 2001: 167; Brett 2007; AVANCSO 2002). Self-defence policing produced autonomy that could be used in an authoritarian and repressive way or as an exercise of local active citizenship and leadership. This is the basis of its functional reproduction through community policing organizations in the post-war.

In a long term, the PACs were more than an counterinsurgency instrument of the army. They redefined collective life on the basis of community policing for self-defence in which patrolling and information sharing became key mechanisms of social control and surveillance. The construction of enemies changed over time: just as the stranger, the communist, the soldier, and the insurgent were identified as military threats during the war years, so a criminal threat was perceived in the post-war years as expressed in the loss of traditional values, the deviant behaviour of youth, and the spread of morally degrading activities such as drinking liquor, consuming drugs, prostitution, infidelity, modern clothing, and imported music. The continuity of these mechanisms of social control are based on the reproduction of the surveillance and social control functions delegated to the PACs (Remijnse 2002: 27).[187]

The PACs were organized also by the National Police, not only by the army, as most studies argue. This is an important fact because the roles played by the military institution and the Police together reinforced the displacement of policing to the private sphere. It is also important because in the post-war years the police again supported community-policing organizations which created a perception of the reproduction of the PACs in post-war times.[188]

187 The reports of the civil patrols sent to the COCP from the northwest departments of the country show that the main actions they implemented were associated with social control. Reports were sent every fifteen days and the main problems identified related to disrespect for authority, drunkenness, and scandalous behaviour in public places (AHPN 1982 /doc2774144, /doc2774135, /doc2774133, and /doc2774139; 1983 /doc2774145).

188 On August 20, 1981, the departmental chief of the National Police in San Marcos reported that there were PACs in the municipalities of La Reforma and San Pedro Sacatepéquez that included 60 auxiliary mayors and military commissioners (AHPN 1981/doc2774125). On October 3, 1981, the departmental chief of the National Police organized a total 40 individuals in a PAC in the village of Bracitos in the department of Suchitepéquez (AHPN 1981/doc2774131). In November 1982, a total of 431 men in Antigua Guatemala, department of San Juan Sacatepéquez, had been organized in 10 platoons of PAC (AHPN 1982/doc2774137). The departmental chief of the same department reported the organization of 42 platoons in Sumpango with a total of 1,680 men (AHPN 1982/doc2774136).

Less studied are the Urban Patrols organized by the National Police. They fulfilled the same functions of the rural civilian patrols but, as is known, without military actions, in other words, their function was geared to patrolling, surveillance, and information sharing about insurgent and criminal activities.[189]

The mechanisms of patrolling and surveillance embedded in collective life through civilian organizations even invaded the school system. Since the 1960s, the police had initiated a program to organize school patrols with students of both private and public schools. Originally they were created only to control the traffic around the school area and to promote civic values (AHPN 1971/882301 923102007). Nevertheless, the activities program of the school patrol training also included basic orientations on security and protection of students and installations as well as identification of threats. The patrols functioned during the school year, at the end of which there was a ceremony in the presence of authorities of the police and the Ministry of Education to formally end the activities of the school patrols and swear in members (AHPN 1982/doc2762896). In 1970, a total of 128 schools had patrols in operation in the department of Guatemala (AHPN 1970/doc852624).

During the 1970s, the school patrols were organized in support of the school system but during the 1980s, when the counterinsurgency strategy was extended to other areas, the security component was incorporated into the program of school patrols under a new name, the School Security Patrols (AHPN 1982/doc2 762896). This was an important change because the patrols were charged with surveillance and information-gathering within the student movement. The members of the school patrols wore uniforms – blue pants and a sky-blue shirt as well as a white belt similar to the uniform of the National Police – and carried a wooden baton. The members patrolled the school to control student misconduct and even set up a room to lock up those accused of immoral behaviour in school (AHPN 1982/doc2762896). More than a mechanism to produce security, the school patrols were part of an integral system of collective policing in which surveillance and patrolling had a central role.

Self-defence as motivation to organize policing actions not only was reinforced by state security forces. To a lesser extend, insurgent groups created a civilian organizational mechanism to ensure logistic support, such as food and sleeping quarters as well as information about the actions of the army. These groups also were organized as civil self-defence against the actions of the army in those communities that supported the insurgents. There were two main civil-

189 In 1983, the Third Corps of the National Police (*Tercer Cuerpo de la Policía National*) reportedly organized 85 urban patrols in zones 1, 5, 6, 13, 16, 19, and 21 of Guatemala City (AHPN 1983/doc2774156). The Second Corps also organized urban civil patrols headed by 14 individuals (AHPN 1983/doc2776352).

ian organizations promoted by insurgent groups between 1979 and 1980: the Local Clandestine Committees (CCL) and the Irregular Local Forces (FIL).

The CCLs and the FILs were the social base of the *Ejército Guatemalteco de los Pobres* (EGP). A number of CCLs made up a district, a number of districts made up a region, and a number of regions constituted a guerrilla front. Each CCL and FIL had a chief but they were badly armed (if at all), even though they were defined as the self-defence of the community. The CCLs were the bridge between the population and the insurgency (Brett 2007: 51). The leaders of the CCLs were chosen by the guerrilla and were charged with the organization of the community. One of their functions was recruiting and training the members of the FIL (Brett 2007: 51).

The FIL were directed by the CCLs and some of them were armed. They were responsible for warning communities that an army incursion was imminent. They also received training from the guerrillas on basic security measures and those who showed high personal capabilities were enrolled as combatants while the rest took part in the self-defence of the community. The military actions in which the FIL participated were sabotage and ambushes. (CEH 1999b: 293).

Due to the limited military capacity of the guerrillas to defend their social base and the strong response by the Army against civilians, the population organized in CCLs and FILs remained helpless. After the repressive military operations of the Army to destroy the social base of the guerrillas, the remaining male population was organized as PACs under the control of military commissioners in those areas in which CCLs and FILs had operated (Schirmer 2001: 98; CEH 1999b: 298). The self-defence techniques of the CCLs and FILs included the installation of traps around the community and alarm systems with speakers, bells, whistles, and fireworks, among others, to alert the community and the neighbouring communities of approaching danger (CEH 1999a: 339).

One of the consequences of the presence of CCLs and FILs was the creation of new communal leaderships that displaced traditional authorities. This was a situation also produced by the PACs and the presence of the army in rural communities. Contrary to the traditional system of leadership elections based on experience and communal service, the presence of self-defence policing organizations for security and self-defence with militaristic characteristics introduced a system of leadership based on the level of involvement and confidence of its leaders with the military or the insurgents (CEH 1999c: 175).

***

As explained in this chapter, the interaction of different mechanisms reinforced the proliferation of private policing organizations, both commercial and non-commercial. On the one hand, the institutional trajectory of the police, influenced by the goals of U.S. advisors and diplomats and the political power of the army, was displaced to a role of auxiliary of the army in the national security strategy. Under this perspective, the public security functions that the police were expected to undertake were marginalized in order that the police institution might concentrate on repressive actions against political leaders, especially in the urban areas. The limited institutional capabilities, the high levels of corruption, and the precarious socio-economic situation of the police force allowed for the emergence of private security services under the aegis of the police institution.

At the beginning, these services were only contingent on a vacuum of public security, but due to interaction with the political context and increasing political violence, other actors were involved in the security business on the basis of prerogatives provided by the police institution. The private security sector increased proportionately as the police concentrated on counterinsurgency actions and neglected its weakened public security capabilities. The armed conflict positioned the army as the only institution capable of delivering public security; second, it strengthened the commercial private sector; and third, it weakened the police institution. The trajectory of the first two reinforced the displacement of public security into the hands of the military and the private sector and neutralized the institutional capabilities of the police to produce public security.

On the other hand, civilian participation in vigilante and self-defence organizations reinforced a set of violent policing mechanisms that defined the fight against crime as one of the main justification for its actions. Aside from the institutional promoters of these organizations and the contextual goals they pursued, they share the vigilante actions and the self-defence organization as security *dispositif* that produced social control and surveillance mechanisms as the content of community policing. The process of reproduction and change of these structures is related to temporal sequences that interplay with a more general political and social context. While the form and structure changed, the function of self-defence and surveillance was reproduced. As a complement, civilian participation was characterized by a very militaristic and authoritarian content. However the enemy was defined, the response tended to be violent, both in the case of those defined as a threat and those who refused to participate in communal policing organizations.

Self-defence policing and private security companies in the context of anti-communism, counter-terror, counter-insurgency, and insurgency were reproduced as a consequence of the institutional pattern of displacement of public security. What changed and what continued during the transition to democracy?

7. Private Policing and Democratic Transition

Guatemala initiated the transition to democracy in mid 1980s after a high intensity armed conflict. The 1986 election of the first civilian president marked the beginning of reform of the main institutions of the state, starting with political institutions, political parties and electoral mechanisms. Specific reforms came a decade later, after the Peace Agreements were signed in 1996. The reform of the security institutions was established through the Agreement for the Strengthening of the Civil Power and the Function of the Army in a Democratic Society (AFPC); this includes a list of reforms of the main security institutions such as the National Police, the army and the intelligence agencies. Prior to the signing of these Agreements, the network of military commissioners and civil patrols was formally dissolved; PACs followed suit a year later. Aspects related to the commercial private security sector were included only due to the necessity of legal reform.

However, the end of the internal conflict was crucial for initiating a new phase in the political trajectories of Guatemalan society. Continuities in the security sector blunted the formal post-war transformations. To identify these continuities, this chapter focuses on police reform, the process of dissolution of Civil Patrols and Military Commissioners and the adaptation of the concept of citizen security to the social and political context.[190] Within this perspective, the chapter shows that excessive concentration on formal institutional reform outside of the process led to an unconstrained and rapidly expanding private security sector; meanwhile, implementation of foreign models of community policing paved the way for the re-emergence of vigilante groups.

The end of the war and the following political transformation created the context for a long-term democratic peace building process. In the political arena, this process represented a change in the formal political trajectory of the country. However, the situation is different with respect to the security institutions, especially to private policing. While the transition to democracy fostered key changes in some spheres such as public opinion, political parties system and civil society participation, for the private policing sphere the failure of the most important transformations in the security sector, coupled with increased post-war violence, reinforced the function of private security in the general security system. As it

190 There are other important approaches to explain these continuities for example the work on transitional justice and policies to deal with the past. For a more in-depth analysis see Oettler 2004 and 2006a.

was mentioned in the theoretical section of this study, a critical juncture does not necessarily mean change; on the contrary, it can reaffirm patterns of continuity in some specific areas depending on the context.

7.1 The Political Context

The model of Security Sector Reform (SSR) included in the Peace Agreements in Guatemala was based on the dominant paradigm of the Development Assistance Committee of the Organization for Economic Cooperation (OECD) (Call 2007). The overall objective of SSR is to create a secure environment that is conducive to development, poverty reduction and democracy as the foundational elements needed to sustain peace (OECD 2005). Several authors (McCandless and Abu-Nimer 2007; Sedra 2007; Isima 2007b; Pearce 2006) emphasized that much of the limited success of SSR in different conflict and post-conflict societies has to do with the contexts within which SSR projects are implemented as well as with the proclivity of SSR designers and implementers to focus largely on the state (McCandless & Abu-Nimer 2007: 1). This international perspective supported a set of institutional reforms in Guatemala that were implemented by local authorities depending on specific historical trajectories shaping the political context in which the reforms were made. A set of concepts such as preventive security, citizen security and community oriented policing emerged as objectives for the new police institution in a transitional period characterized by a security vacuum and increased crime. The nature of police reform and the marginalization of non-state armed actors of the SSR programs led to a reproduction of former self-policing organizations and to growth of the commercial private security. As Kurtenbach argues, the termination of war is an opportunity window for the liberal peace-building paradigm; the transformation process of pacification, democratization and economic liberalization in Central America shows the dominant influence of path dependent patterns that limit the alleged outcomes of the transformation process (Kurtenbach 2010). The context of the democratization process explains the consistency of institutional patterns that reduce the scope of the transformation process.

Democratization in Guatemala began at the peak of political violence in Central America. Democratization in post-war societies implies a set of different challenges in generating the minimal democratic conditions of a democratic electoral system and parallel processes of reconciliation that transform violent conflicts into non-violent, as well as other post conflict elements absent from transition to democracy such as demobilization, reintegration of ex combatants into social life, refugees and displaced people, reconstruction of economies damaged by the war, and the reconstruction of democratic institutions and civil societies destroyed by the war (Azpurú 2007: 16; Karl 1995). Other aspects such as policies to deal with the past that include compensation and restitution of victims as well as transitional justice policies constitute basis to overcome past atrocities (Oettler 2006a: 9).

The electoral process that culminated with the election of civil governments was considered to be limited free and free of fraud; the participation of international observers gave the process a high level of legitimacy (Torres-Rivas 1994: 20). The democratization process began due to a high degree of political discredit of the army, economic crisis and changes in international support for Central American countries. From this it is possible to identify different possible explanations for the democratization process. First, the end of the political predominance of the military was part of a strategy to win the war (Schirmer 2001; Jonas 2000). In this perspective the military delegated the administration of the government to civilians in order to exclusively concentrate on warfighting. The return to political life at the beginning of the eighties was promoted by the military as a consequence of the intensity of the war and international pressure (Torres-Rivas 1994: 20). This process created the institutional context of democratization and covered the two governments instituted as products of the military coups of Efraín Rios Montt in 1982 and Oscar Mejía Víctores in 1983. Second, the peace is the result of the initiation of the transition to democracy (Torres-Rivas and Aguilera 1998: 78; Trudeau 1993).

Hence, two political processes interacted in the Guatemalan democratization process. On one hand, the intensification of military action against insurgent groups, including civilian participation in PACs and extended violence against the civilian population; on the other hand, the strengthening of political parties and electoral institutions as well as the participation of organizations of the civil society and international organizations. In this perspective, the peace-building process produced changes in political life because this was the sphere the military relegated to the civilian power. On the contrary, the security institutions remained under the formal control of the military until the peace was signed in 1996. This process has been analysed through the concept of low intensity democracy (Wilson 1993).

It is not the intention of this chapter to analyse the entire democratization process, but rather to stress aspects that clarify the difference between political change and security function continuity. This difference is clearer if it is analysed from the perspective of the political trajectories. As Torres Rivas argues, some political changes can be analysed as the liberation of the regime, but in fact they represented the exhaustiveness of authoritarian political processes, thus the authoritarian exhaustiveness and the democratic weakness produce juncture vacuums (Torres-Rivas and Aguilera 1998: 87). This trajectory explains the limits of the liberal peace-building approach mentioned by Kurtenbach (2010). In Guatemala, the critical junctures produced by the combination of war and democratization resulted in the implantation of weak democratic governments against military power (Torres-Rivas and Aguilera 1998: 87; Jonas 1990).

During the period of 1982-1985 the most important changes in the political infrastructure were made, such as the law of the Electoral Record, the creation of the Supreme Electoral Court and the law of Political Parties. In 1985 a new Constitution was issued, supplanting the Constitution of 1965 which included the framework of the National Security Doctrine. However, Constitutional reform did not change the central role of the army in public security.

The first civil government in 1986 had an extended electoral majority (86 per cent). However, the intensity of political violence and the struggles inside the military weakened the government of Cerezo Arévalo (Figueroa 1994: 55). Until the middle eighties the insurgent groups suffered high pressure due to extensive military action; simultaneously, the military faced international pressure to end the armed conflict. In this context the government did not had the intention of resolving the armed conflict through military action. On the contrary, both the insurgent groups and the military continued military action in order to initiate negotiations for a political solution of the armed conflict (Torres Rivas and Aguilera 1998: 89; McCleary 1999).

It was during the government of Cerezo Arévalo (1986-1991) that the doctrine of National Stability created by the Army produced its main results. In this doctrine the army was defined as a guarantor of some national objectives related to the democratic regime. The strategy combined the intensity of military counterinsurgency with social and political programs controlled by the army and extended civilian participation through the Civil Patrols. The different phases of this strategy from 1983 to 1987 led the army to neutralize the political and military operations of the insurgency; likewise it led the army to give civilians control over some areas of the state (Torres-Rivas and Aguilera 1998: 81; CEH 1999c: 258).

The end of the first civilian government was characterized by its political failure in combining the military project of National Stability and the neoliberal adjustments required by the private sector. This created political instability to the next presidential period. Contrary to the government of Cerezo Arévalo, the next president had only the 24.9 per cent of the electorate, only ten seats in Congress and only 3 per cent of the municipalities. During the government of Serrano Elias (1991-1993) the process of negotiations continued despite intense political instability in the government and struggles inside the military due to the inevitable transformation of the state and the finalization of the armed conflict. The government of Serrano Elias was characterized by persistent rumours of military coups, high levels of public corruption, increased crime and political violence and strong international pressure to continue the negotiations between military and insurgents. This period of political instability ended with the attempt to a self-coup of Serrano Elias in May 1993, analysed as a case of a failed undemocratic presidential interruption, meaning the violation of the democratic rules (Bjune and Petersen 2010).

Serrano temporarily suspended the Constitution and ordered the dissolution of the Congress, the Supreme Court, and the Public Prosecutor's Office and the Office of the Human Rights Ombudsman. The attempt to involve the army in the coup created a strong division inside the armed forces regarding support for Serrano's plan. In the end, the opposition to the self-coup by the side of a notable faction of the army had a decisive effect on the failure of Serrano's plan (Bjune and Petersen 2010). A key alliance between the economic elite and military softliners limited the effects of the self-coup of Serrano Elias; they favoured civilian rule but wanted to preserve the power of the army as an institution (Azpurú et al 2010: 308; Bjune and Petersen 2010). The solution to the Serrano crisis had a negative effect on the democratic process not only through its attempt to implement an authoritarian rule but also through the way the crisis was resolved. Bjune and Petersen argue that the crisis was not resolved within the system of civilian political institutions but outside democratic institutions (Bjune and Petersen 2010).

In June 6, 1993 the Congress of the Republic appointed Ramiro de Leon Carpio as President of the Republic and the peace negotiations were reinitiated after a short interruption due to the political crisis. However, one of the main obstacles to the peace negotiations was the question about dealing with the past. The URNG supported the demand for a truth commission. On the other side, there were differences about this inside the military. It was in 1994 when the "Agreement on the Establishment of the Commission for the Historical Clarification of Human Rights Violations and Acts of Violence Which Have Caused Suffering to the Guatemalan People" was signed becoming the only instrument of transitional justice provided by the peace agreements (Oettler 2006a: 5).

During this government there was an important advance in the peace negotiations as well as some important transformations related to the paramilitary forces like the military commissioners. During this government international pressure increased and the direct participation of the United Nations in the negotiations accelerated the process. The result was the creation of the United Nations Verification Mission in Guatemala (MINUGUA) effective January 1994. In its first reports between 1995 and 1996 MINUGUA clearly identified the precarious situation of the judicial administration and the existence of legal and illegal security actors and private security groups linked with criminal activities such as drug trafficking, car theft and the theft and smuggling of wood with the tolerance of state agents (Azpurú 2007: 335).

The presidential elections of 1995 are analysed as the rearrangement of the main political forces such as the military, political parties and the private sector following the political crisis of the previous years. In this perspective, the negotiated peace, the reform of the army and economic modernization were the main goals expected by the new government (ODHAG 1998b: 344). During the new government, the peace negotiations ended and a ceasefire was declared between the army and the insurgent groups. The Peace Agreements were signed in December 29, 1996.

The sequence of events between 1985 and 1996 opened up the debate about democratization in Guatemala. For the United States, democracy in Guatemala was achieved following the 1985 elections and it declared the country as "post-transitional" (Trudeau 1993: 4). For others, the democratic process in Guatemala was a façade through which the military won the war and only superficial institutional changes were made, without meaningful change for society (Jonas 1990). From the transition to democracy approach, this period sees the creation of electoral structures as the first step in a transition to a more democratized polity (Torres-Rivas and Aguilera 1998; Gills *et al.* 1993).

Following Sereseres (1998), the process can be summarized as follows. First the process of Guatemalan democratization since 1982 was guided by military leaders and in the late eighties became a tacit partnership between civilians and the military. During this period the military was the dominant institution in the democratization process. At the beginning of the nineties the political context changed. The rebels continued fighting and the counterinsurgency strategy of the army increased political violence, however the diversity of political actors grew and sparked increased public discussion of possible negotiated resolution of the armed conflict. As a reaction to the increased civilian participation and the international pressures, the private sector also initiated its participation in the process. After the political crisis between 1993 and 1994 the United Nations Verification Mission arrived to Guatemala and provided an additional dimension to the political opening. Human rights observation increased; this includes the importance of a truth commission.

In general the context of transition to democracy in Guatemala created the basis for change in civil-military relations, decentralization and the emergence of local community organizations and power and for the expansion and diversification of Guatemalan political leadership and institutions (Sereseres 1998: 208). The transition to democracy in Guatemala was the result, among other factors, of the balance of power between the elites, the military and the organized private sector. After a trajectory of agreements and disagreements these two elites set the context for a negotiated peace and the subsequent peace agreements without deep state transformations (McCleary 1999).

The post-war trajectories show the scope of outcomes of this process. While this period created the basis for an institutional transformation of some areas of the state, the possibility to define this as a critical juncture depends on the elections that the political actors made. In this sense, the security sector presents a particular set of possibilities opened by the Peace Agreements but the process of implementing these reforms also shows how the election was made in order to allow some continuity including private security functions. Although this perspective limits the scope of the peace agreements related to the security sector, it is possible to list some important contributions made by the peace negotiations to the democratization process. First, the peace negotiations limited the political project of the military and instead of a tutelary democracy (such as during the governments of Cerezo and Elías) it was possible to establish a functional and participatory democracy which included social, political, economic and cultural rights as a minimal condition (Azpurú 2007: 330). Second, there was an opening of the public debate on important social and political themes with the active participation of the organized civil society and other relevant actors such as the private sector, churches and universities (Azpurú 2007: 330; Torres-Rivas and Aguilera 1998).

7.2 Civilian Power and Armed Forces in a Democratic Society

This section analyses the main aspects of the Peace Accords that explain why the security sector reform did not represent a critical juncture in the trajectories of the public security institutions, and how the continuity of displacement of public security to the private security sector was reinforced during this phase. The analysis centres on the reform of the national police and the formal dissolution of the military commissioners and the PACs.

The peace agreements signed by the government of Guatemala and the *Unidad Revolucionaria Nacional Guatemalteca* (UNRG) created a set of institutional reforms that largely depended on the willingness and capacity of key actors as well as the process of strengthening public institutions and civil participation. While the Peace Agreements cover a wide scope of social and political spheres such as indigenous population, education, health, agrarian situation and human rights among others, the aspects related to security institutions were included in the Agreement for the Strengthening of Civilian Power and the Role of the Armed Forces in a Democratic Society (AFPC). This Agreement was considered the decisive shift in the historic civil-military relations in the country (Schirmer 1999; Stanley 2007; Call 2000).

The main areas to be reformed through the Agreement included a reduction and reorganization of the Army, a reform of the National Police, the creation of a civil intelligence system and a Legislative Oversight Commission. Other aspects regarding public security were included, such as the creation of a new Academy of National Civilian Police, the dissolution and demobilization of the Mobile Military Police and the eventual creation of programs for the reinsertion of the demobilized into civil society. Apart from the reforms made in order to reduce and limit the role of the army in external defence operations, the implementation of this Accord included the dismantling of the network of 33,000 military commissioners, all Civil Patrols and the Mobile Military Police.

The AFPC is organized in three categories, the first is demobilization, disarmament and reintegration (DDR); the second is Security Sector Reform (SSR); and the third is the Democratic Oversight of the Security Sector. All of this was slated for implementation between 1997 and 2000. In the case of the DDR the formal demobilization of the Military Commissioners and the PACs took place prior the signing of the peace accord; this introduced the problem of civilian oversight of the demobilization process (Schirmer 1999; Petersen 2007). The demobilization of the Army was carried out by the military with total control of the process, thus obstructing a proper verification by the United Nations. At the end MINUGUA stated that there was no possibility to verify the demobilization process because there was no government information regarding the number of demobilized soldiers and recollected weapons as well as paramilitary lists and its weapons (Petersen 2007: 35).

The first reduction of the army was made between 1997 and 1998 when it was reduced to 33 per cent (15.477 personnel) from the prior total of 46.900 personnel. The second was made in 2003 with a reduction of 8.97 per cent (4.209 personnel) and the third in 2004 with a 24.97 per cent (11.714 personnel). After these reductions the Army was composed of 15.500 personnel (MINUGUA 2005). The reduction of the army was not made on the level of officers that graduated in the military academy and this allowed the powerful part of the military structure to remain intact (Sieder 2002 and 2003; Petersen 2007). One important aspect that reinforced the role of the army in public security was the outcome of the Constitutional Reform of 1999. In this referendum, 55 per cent voted against the reforms and consequently the main reforms proposed in the AFPC were not implemented (Jonas 2000: 199).

The aspects related to the reform of the police were included in the section on public security. The proposed reform aimed to convert the police to the only institution responsible for public security, meaning the institution responsible for guaranteeing the freedom and rights of the population, preventing and fighting crime and keeping public order, with jurisdiction throughout the entire national territory. At the same time the AFPC established that the police would have to be directed by civilian authorities and its organization would have to be multiethnic and pluricultural related to recruitment, training and territorial deployment. Also included was a provision that the salaries of the agents would have to be increased and it would have to include a plan of social safety net for them. The police reform would have to be financially supported by the international cooperation and technically supported by MINUGUA.

It was planed in 1996 that by 1999 the new Civil National Police (PNC) should be working in the entire national territory with a minimum of twenty thousand agents, meaning an increase of eight thousand new personnel within three years. Complementarily, the investigation capabilities and information techniques as well as the coordination mechanisms with other security and justice institutions should be strengthened. The budget of the police had to be increased by 50 per cent of the GDP in relation to the per cent of the GDP assigned in 1995. In addition, the new institution should encourage communal participation in the assignation of agents and in the promotion of a peace culture and human rights respect. Complementarily a civilian intelligence unit for crime investigation should be created inside the Ministry of Interior. The reform of the national police should be made based on the previous experiences in El Salvador, Nicaragua and Haiti (Byrne *et al.* 2000).

In general, the Peace Accords defined a model of police reform according to the general context of police reforms in Latin America which were strongly influenced by democratization processes, increasing crime and general changes in the structure of Latin American states produced by neoliberal reforms and economical crisis (Frühling 2007; Dammert 2010). However, there are important national trajectories that explain the rapid failure of the process of police reform related to that expected in the Peace Agreements.

As it was explained in the previous chapter of this study, the National Police was an institution strongly influenced by the context and especially by the political power of the army reinforced by the influence of the United States public safety program. The public security function expected from such institution was displaced in order to strengthen its role as political protection against the alleged enemies of the state in the framework of the counterinsurgency strategy. Analysing the security sector reform and specifically the police reform as a non-critical juncture of the institutional trajectories of the public institutions, it is possible to identify different outcomes. On one hand, the strengthening of private security services; on the other hand, the transformation of the police from its function of political protection to what Tilly (1985) defined as protection rackets; in other words, the use of the police pursuant the elimination or neutralization of rivals of the state within its territory (the internal enemy) and the use of the police for the elimination or neutralization of the enemies of the clients of the state.

Until 1996 the trajectories of the national police were strongly marked by constant institutional reform, whether motivated by personalistic presidents, the army or international agencies. Each change in the police was oriented to fit the institution to the requirements of the context, and because the changes were mostly concentrated on the investigative functions, it produced different autonomous and secret units within the police linked with repressive and violent actions (Sieder 2002: 11; Peacock and Beltrán 2004). The challenge in the Peace Accords was to overcome this trajectory or at least to avoid its reproduction in the democratic society (Byrne *et al.* 2000).

The trajectories of the police reform in 1996 show how the reproduction sequence was in motion again in order to reinforce the institutional pattern of public security displacement. The commonly observed outcome of this displacement is the process through which the army recovered its role of protector of the public order (Arévalo 1997: 29; Gutiérrez 1998). Nonetheless, this study argues that private security was the other reinforced outcome of this reproducing process. On one hand, the army fulfilled the state institutional vacuum of public security produced by both the reform of the national police and the reduction of the army. On the other hand, commercial private security became the labour market for demobilized armed forces and it also continued providing the security services previously covered by public security institutions.

The Post-war Police Reform

As was mentioned before, the police is an institution that constantly changes in order to fit its institutional framework to the dynamics of the political context. The reform of the nineties showed that despite a strong institutional reengineering, the conjuncture of the peace agreements did not allow the institution to avoid the reproduction of its institutional pattern of public security displacement.

The police reform was initiated before the signing of the peace agreements during the unstable period between 1993 and 1996. During this period the military took control of the reforms of the police and so created a military team to work together with international advisors in the National Police (Glebbeek 2001: 4). The inevitable reform of the security sector, motivated by advances in the peace negotiation and international pressure initiated a struggle within the army to keep the control of the police institution.

In order to limit the control of the military over the police, the government of Serrano Elias ordered the withdrawal of military personnel from officer positions in the police. During the next government the Hunajpú unit, a joint operations unit of military and police, was dissolved (Glebbeek 2001: 4). Parallel to the military struggles to retain the control of the police, the necessary institutional reforms that allowed for the continuity of the military in the public security sphere were instituted.

Before the signing of the Peace Accords the government of Alvaro Arzú (1996-2000) delegated the reform of the Police to the Spanish Civil Guard. This decision was not consulted with the organizations of the civil society that participated in the reform process of the security sector. The main criticism by the organizations of the civil society was that the Spanish Civil Guard had a militaristic organization (Byrne *et al.* 2000; WOLA 2009; Castillo 2002).

Despite the struggle to retain military control over police reform, the Peace Accords created the political context to make changes in the security sector. As Schirmer (2001) argues, the political change of the military after the peace agreements can be explained by the necessity of improving the international reputation of the armed forces as the basis of its new role in post-war society. While the military gave the civilians control over some important areas of the state, the security institutions were considered a strategic part of the role of the military (Schirmer 2001). Based on this, it is possible to argue that the government of Alvaro Arzú instituted police reform according to specific political requirements such as to avoid the massive dismissal of former police agents and parallel to the liberalization of police investigative and intelligence units linked with the military. For the military it was important to preserve some degree of control over those structures in the post-war society, same as the situation of the military commissioners and the PACs (DNSA 1995e).

Thus the central areas of the police reform were recruitment mechanisms, selection and training of agents, police leadership, internal controls and disciplinary mechanisms, crime investigation and community oriented policing (WOLA 2009). In order to accomplish the requirements established in the Peace Accords there were formal reforms such as the "recycling" of agents, consisting of the reintegration of agents of the former National Police and the Treasury Guard into the new Civil National Police, PNC after having completed and passed a three months special course. Those agents who did not pass the course were assigned to the penitentiary guard or to administrative tasks in the new PNC. At the same time there were no efficient investigations into violations of human rights and corruption (WOLA 2009; Neild 2002; Byrne *et al.* 2000).

The new agents of the PNC were subordinated to the authority of former police officials. The same situation occurred in units responsible for internal control and criminal investigations (Byrne *et al.* 2000). The potential of institutional change inside the Police was rapidly blocked by limiting the scope of new agents, internal controls and specially crime investigation. Likewise, the expected multiethnic recruitment mechanisms and personnel selection were weakened by the low budget of the police and the prioritization on fighting increased crime (WOLA 2000 and 2009).

Although, the operative capacities of the new police model were rapidly overcome by rising crime. Justified by the inexperience of the new civil authorities, the government of Alvaro Arzú once again implemented joint police-military operations and instead of creating the unit of civil intelligence included in the Peace Agreements, the solution was to strengthen the use of military intelligence units to fight common crime (WOLA 2000 and 2009). These political decisions rapidly delegitimized the civil police institution and reinforced the role of the military in public security and as it was mentioned before in the chapter IV of this study, this was the period during which commercial private security began to increase rapidly in comparison with the low increase of the private security sector during the internal conflict.

During the following presidential period (2000-2004) the police reform was limited by the presence of military in leadership positions and the emergence of powerful criminal structures inside the police. The crisis of the reform process was especially strong in the professionalization of the agents, low scholarly levels, lack of labour guaranties and the discredit of the public image of the police (WOLA 2009). This period was characterized by the incorporation of the military in the Ministry of Interior and in the police. There were four Ministers of Interior, two of them were former military and both were linked to public corruption. One of the decisions taken by those authorities was the suspension of the norm that mandated that the General Director of the PNC was to be a civilian authority with police trajectory. Thus, there were eight general directors of the PNC, three of them were lawyers and one even a congressman. Consequently, the chain of command was broken and the functions of the police expected in the Peace Agreements were limited at the same time as organized crime structures operated also in other security institutions such as the army, migration offices, airports and customs.[191] These structures are defined as the "hidden powers" of Guatemala in which corrupt and criminal networks are linked with actors in the traditional private sector, emergent economical actors, police and military and common delinquency all of them interacting corporative mafia (Peacock and Beltrán 2004: 6).

The structures of organized crime consolidated its control over some areas of the police institution. For example, the Department of Anti-Narcotics Operations (DOAN) was considered a "Central American cartel". After members of this unit stole 600 kg of cocaine from a police warehouse, the unit was dissolved and transformed in the Anti-Narcotic Analysis and Information Service (SAIA), without efficient vetting of personnel, some of whom were part of the former anti narcotic unit. In 2005 the director of this unit was captured in the United States for drug trafficking and in 2006 other agents from the same unit were captured for theft of cocaine from a police warehouse (*Prensa Libre* 03/10/08). In addition

191 About corrupt networks in migration and custom institutions see Rosales Sandoval 2011.

the PNC was used for political goals when in July 2003 during a number of violent protests supporting the official party the police was ordered to remain inactive against the protesters despite violence in the streets (Hernández 2005: 535). During this period there were approximately 1,600 denounces of police corruption and the internal control mechanisms were not strengthened and corrupted agents worked in the police without sanction or penal prosecution (WOLA 2009).

During the next years the process of police reform focused only on the depuration of allegedly corrupt agents. Approximately 1,200 agents were expelled from the police without effective investigations and penal prosecution (WOLA 2009). The government of Oscar Berger (2004-2008) made no important changes to improve the institutional situation of the National Police. On the contrary there were new leaders without experience in security institutions. There were three Ministers of Interior and three General Directors of the PNC, one of them was appointed at 34 years old and hired a team of external advisors who participated as police officers (WOLA 2009). External individuals controlled the police and the institution was involved in drug trafficking, violent evictions and the existence of alleged structures of extra judicial assassination or "social cleansing" groups.

For instance, in September 2006 the National Police executed a security operation to take the control of a penitentiary centre; involved were approximately three thousand personnel from the police and the military. As a result seven prisoners were killed by the state security forces. Since then the killings were denounced as extra judicial assassination conducted by "social cleansing" groups operating inside the PNC (CICIG 2011).

Likewise, on February 19, 2007, three Salvadoran members of the Central American Parliament and their chauffeur were killed in Guatemala. As a result of the preliminary investigations four police officers of the PNC that participated in the killing were captured; one of them was the Director of Criminal Investigations of the PNC. Five days after the agents were captured an armed squad killed three of them inside the penitentiary centre. Later an investigator of the PNC and a prosecutor of the Prosecution Ministry investigating the case were also killed. Two external security advisors and owners of a private security company hired by the General Director to work inside the Police were also killed (*El Periódico* 06/27/08).

Parallel to the strengthening of criminal structures inside the police, during this period the police was involved in a number of violent evictions of farms occupied by peasants as protest. In April 2006 members of the PNC and agents of a private security company shot the members of the *Movimiento Campesino en Resistencia Pro Justicia Finca Nueva Linda* (Amnesty International 2009; Rights Action 2005).

The political instability produced by the operation of criminal and "social cleansing" structures inside the Police forced the resignation of the Minister of Interior, Carlos Vielman (on trial in Spain since 2010 for extra judicial assassinations), the General Director of the PNC, Erwin Sperisen (on trial in Switzerland since 2011 for different crime including extra judicial assassinations) and the Director of the Penitentiary System (prosecuted in Guatemala since 2009) (CICIG 2011).

With respect to the relationship between the PNC and the private security sector, the Peace Agreements mentioned only the need to reform the law that regulates private security services. This was not included in the plan of implementation of the AFPC in 1996. There were different attempts to reform the law of 1970 but it was not until reality until 2010 when Congress issued a new law that regulates private security services. The efforts of the post-war governments and international cooperation were oriented towards downsizing the army and police reform; the commercial private security sector was outside of the political agenda. However, it was during this period that the commercial private security sector grew in both formal and informal ways.

The analysis of the police reform shows that the expected transformation proposed by the Peace Accords was made only on a formal level, producing the institutional reengineering similar as the number of previous institutional changes made to adequate the police to the changes in the context. As was shown, the period defined as the democratic transition produced changes in the political sphere but the security sector was only formally reformed.

The failure of the police reform had multiple consequences. First, the reinforcement of the institutional pattern of public displacement to the military and the private sphere; the police captured the attention of public opinion and to it was delegated the political responsibility for the failures of the general security sector, thus accelerated the discrediting of the institution. In this context, the military strengthens its role as the only public institutions capable to guarantee public security and the private sector became the solution that individuals chose to reduce the feeling of insecurity produced by the increased crime and the discredited PNC. Second, the lacking internal controls and investigative capabilities of the police allowed secret structures that operated during the internal conflict to become active criminal organizations inside the new PNC.

The Peace Agreements and the liberal peace-building program in Guatemala did not represent a change in the institutional trajectories of the main security forces. On the contrary, as a non-critical juncture, the end of the internal armed conflict created a social and political context in which the main decisional actors (military, organized private sector, international cooperation) concentrated on the necessary institutional reform to guarantee the end of the armed conflict and the political stabilization of the country. From a functional perspective, the security institutions were reformed without changing their historical functions in the security system. Although during the internal conflict the commercial private security sector had a secondary role in public security and filled the areas that the security forces did not cover due to their focus on counterinsurgency, during the transition to democracy the commercial private security sector became a powerful actor offering a wide range of security services justified by the increased crime and the discredit and inefficiency of the PNC.

Commercial private security was not the only aspect that remained marginalized during the transitional period. By 1996 the self-defence policing organizations created during the internal conflict, such as PACs and military commissioners, were also formally dissolved but not effectively demobilized. The lack of institutional mechanisms of control over the participants in vigilante organizations and the fact that in 1999 the PNC again organized policing organizations under the concept of citizen security reinforced the continuity of self-defence policing that rapidly transformed into vigilante organizations.

7.3 Marginalized Actors in the Security Sector Reform

Military Commissioners and PACs were defined as self-defence policing organizations that in the context of the internal armed conflict were oriented towards implementing vigilante and social control actions against insurgents, the military or alleged criminals. Even though they were formally dissolved during the Peace Negotiations they remained active and were reintroduced to the security system in the form of community policing organizations. The lack of controls over these organizations and the reinforcement of past trajectories of self-defence policing rapidly led to vigilante actions. The excessive state-centric design of the SSR did not include informal and non-state security actors and in the context of fragile states this lead to the failure of institutional reform processes (Andersen 2006; Nathan 2004).[192]

The large network of military commissioners recreated during the internal armed conflict was formally dissolved in 1995. It was estimated that there were approximately 30,000 persons acting as military commissioners or assistants of military commissioners (DNSA 1995c). According to the CEH (1999b) the mili-

192 This chapter focuses on the institutional mechanisms that reinforced the continuity of private policing. However, there are other important explanations to the post-war strengthening of PACs, for example, that lack on effective polices to deal with the past led to the inexistence of a clear dividing line between victims and perpetrators. Consequently some memories (which include actions and symbols) were strengthened (Oettler 2006a: 10).

tary commissioners were responsible for 6,878 human rights violations during the internal armed conflict, 13 per cent of these violations were committed independently while the rest were committed in collaboration with PACs or military forces, 6 per cent were committed in Guatemala City and the rest in the rural areas (CEH 1999b: 181). As it was mentioned before, the main function of the military commissioners was to generate information from within the communities and to organize security and auto defence operations in coordination with the PACs and other local or military authorities.

The announcement of the dissolution of this network was made at the end of the transitional government of Ramiro De León Carpio and the military struggles for the control of the transitional process in 1995. For the military, the dissolution of the network of military commissioners was a problem for two main reasons. The first was the disbandment of its main human intelligence source and the second was the risk that important information about human rights violations implicating military officials remained uncontrolled and at large (DNSA 1995e). Integrating the commissioners into the reserve system was understood by the military as too transparent and likely to leave the military open to attacks from human rights activists and international watch groups (DNSA 1995e). For these reasons and as a preventive plan, the military initiated the demobilization of the military commissioners some years before and they were reduced from approximately 77,000 to 35,000 in 1995 (DNSA 1995c). Even though this originated from the formal order of the President of the Republic, the military sought the possibility to kept the control of this network (Schirmer 1999: 12).

The demobilization plan proposed by the military included the authorization to the former military commissioners to carry out firearms and the issuance of identification to continue using the Military Commissary and the Officers' Club as well as access to the social security institute (*Instituto de Prevision Militar*) (DNSA 1995b). A U.S. report stated that the plan included that:

> "All military commands were directed to develop the necessary activities that would allow a continued relationship between the Guatemalan Army and the military commissioners after their demobilization through organizations that would protect the environment, regional shutting clubs, sport activities, artistic activities, among others." (DNSA 1995b).

The first option was to incorporate the military commissioners into the military reserves but this option was substituted with the creation of a new category of military collaborators. The idea of not incorporating the military commissioners as reservists was done in order to avoid accusation that only the name was changed but not the function (DNSA 1995e). It was calculated that approximately 25,000 military commissioners were incorporated in this role. The order was that each G-2 officer had to make two lists, one with the commissioners who provided some intelligence information and the second, with the commissioners that were involved in human rights violations (DNSA 1995c). The order stated that:

> "The directorate of intelligence (D-2) at the national defence staff will maintain a master roster of all collaborators. While these individuals will no longer be identified as military commissioners, they will be recognized as army collaborators and will continue to have an invisible role within the army." (DNSA 1995c).

The role of the military commissioners as representatives of the army transformed them in many isolated communities into the local authority. The announcement of dissolution produced in different communities a shift in the local power relations, resulting in many cases in the reproduction of the figure of military commissioner under a different local authority name (AVANCSO 2002: 360; DNSA 1995d and e). Likewise, in urban areas economically powerful and influential individuals were part of the commissioners system. As a result, military commissioners opposed the president's decision based on their belief that the civilian government cannot maintain public safety and security (DNSA 1995e).

The demobilization plan reported that about 15 per cent of the Military Commissioners had firearms, which were their own property and therefore did not had to be turned in to the Army. If the owners wanted to continue to carry their arms, they had the possibility to apply for a license from the Department for the Control of Arms and Munitions (DECAM), otherwise they could keep them in their residences only (DNSA 1995f).

Moreover, in 1996 it was reported that former Military Commissioners were hired to work for the DECAM. From the approximately 40,000 military commissioners it was reported that 5,000 of them worked as "collaborators" for the D-2 (Military Intelligence Unit) via their respective intelligence officers in each separate military zone only. The DECAM issued them a military license to continue carry out their firearms and to retain their military privileges (DNSA 1996).

The demobilization of the military commissioners was a double-layered process. On one hand the formal dissolution made by the President Ramiro De León Carpio and on the other hand the internal attempts by the military to retain some degree of control over the network of informants. At the local level the military commissioners and the PACs found a way to retain their political power. In some cases they avoided the participation of the population in any human rights organization or other civil society initiatives in order to both avoid any denouncement or investigation of past human rights violations and also to retain the control over the new local administration and development projects (AVANCSO 2002: 432; Remijnse 2002: 207; CEH 1999c: 175). These actions constituted a clear blocking to transitional justice initiatives impulse by civil society organizations (Oettler 2004).

While the military commissioners represent the individual representation of the army, the PACs were the collective mechanism for implementing self-defence policing. As it was mentioned before, the PACs implemented self-defence policing against alleged insurgents, the military and common crime. Together with the military commissioners, the PACs transformed the traditional local powers institutions and in the post-war became part of the local authorities and community policing organizations. They also were reorganized as a social movement demanding economic compensation for its service during the internal conflict; finally, they were active in political parties as well (Sáenz de Tejada 2004).

In 1997, just one year after their formal dissolution, the former PACs demanded an economic and moral compensation from the government. This demand was made at the Oil Company Basic Resources in Petén (Sáenz de Tejada 2004: 16). The government of Alfonso Portillo accepted to give the economic compensation in 2001 and following that, the ExPACs initiated a cycle of protest in different parts of the country and with differing intensity. Sáenz de Tejada (2004) examines the ExPACs from a social movements perspective which allows to one observe the mechanisms of reproduction through which an organizational structure created during the internal conflict persisted in the post-war not only as policing organization but also as social movement. The demand for economic and moral compensation allowed the ExPACs to interact with a wide range of actors in society such as political parties which saw opportunities to extend their electoral bases as well as other public institutions and the army (Sáenz de Tejada 2004: 111).

In order to understand the continuity of the communitarian function of the PACs in the post-war it is necessary to distinguish between the counterinsurgency actions conducted by the PACs and directed by the army from those activities implemented in the community flowing directly from the self-defence function they represented. In this respect the PACs were integrated from civilians forced by the army, civilians that participated voluntarily, civilians with previous military experience such as military service or reservist status and also civilians which participated in the insurgent groups or in the Local Clandestine Committees and Local Irregular Forces of the insurgency (CEH 1999b: 181). In other words, the PACs aggregated different communitarian actors into a vigilante organization where the common factor was self-defence policing. It has been estimated that between 1983 and 1984 1.3 million men between the age of fifteen and sixty were part of PACs (Schirmer 2001: 146).

For the military the need of organize PACs during the internal conflict was linked to the need for gaining social support for counterinsurgent actions. However, during the peace negotiation, when the end of the internal conflict was inevitable, the continuity of the PACs was justified by their involvement in development projects and common crime prevention (Gramajo 1995). Thus, the idea was to transform the leaders of the Civil Patrols into local authorities, especially Mayors through the political parties so as to continue supporting their role in the economic development and institutional assistance within communities (Schirmer 2001: 164).[193]

Nonetheless, the demobilization plan of the military had three phases. First, a reorientation phase during which the military should explain to the PACs what was being done. The second phase should be disarmament. The third phase was the preservation of the organization of the PACs for local development goals (Remijnse 2002: 217). Meanwhile, the plan was heavily criticized by national and international human rights organizations which demonstrated on one hand that only the first phase of the demobilization plan was implemented and on the other hand that voluntaristic groups integrated by ExPACs took informal control over local authorities and development programs in different communities (Remijnse 2002; AVANCSO 2002). Hence, The plan represented the continuity of use of local organization for self-defence and local development. As was mentioned in Chapter VI of this study, the civil action of the anti communist strategy implemented by the military with support from USAID introduced the duality of security-development in community life. The army was central to both dimensions and the military commissioners and PACs were the implementation mechanisms for policing and local development programs as strategic action against the insurgency.

While the formal structure of the PACs changed, on the contrary, its functions continued. At the beginning of the transition to democracy the name of the PACs was changed in order to adapt them to the civil political context but without changing its functions and organization. During the government on Mejía Víctores PACs became Civil Defence Committees and a decree was issued wherein they were defined as civil organizations of local security that should be advised by the Ministry of Defence. In order to adapt the PACs to the regulations introduced by the new Constitution of 1985, during the government of Vinicio Cerezo, the name was again changed, introducing the voluntary element and excluding the patrol, thus Voluntary Committees of Civil Defence (*Comités Voluntarios de Defensa Civil*) (Schirmer 2001: 160).

Therefore, changing the name but not the function is one of the elements that explain the continuity of this policing organization in the post-war. The formal dissolution had no impact in changing the self-defence function of the PACs; its

193 In 1993 the PACs were transformed into Peace and Development Committees and the World Bank supported developed programs in rural areas to improve human capital through social inversion such as construction of schools, health centres and roads among others (Schirmer 2001: 172).

role in the collective life of the community and the local networks, leaderships, loyalties and power relations constructed around the PACs were only readapted (Sáenz de Tejada 2004: 68; Remijnse 2002: 208; AVANCSO 2002: 432; Oettler 2004). In fact, there were communities in which the violent actions of the PACs such as killings and extortions continued (Remijnse 2002: 214).

While the transformation of the PACs into the local authorities achieved only limited success, the function of self-defence better explains its continuity. Patrolling was obligatory for all men in the community and this initially caused protests, but it became the most effective mechanism for overcoming threats produced by the military as well as the insurgents (Schirmer 2001: 166). Human rights violations were committed in the name of protecting the community and avoiding insurgent activities because allowing them may incite retribution by the army (CEH 1999b: 188). For Kobrak (1997) this situation led to the formation of local sovereignty feeling based on the local security benefits they provided against the dual threats of soldier and insurgent (Kobrak 1997 and Schirmer 2001: 167).

In this context, the existence of local sovereignties, local networks and the common function of self-defence were the basis of the reorganization of the PACs as a social movement. It is important to mention that the reorganization of the ExPAC was made on the former structures meaning the reproduction of the previous leadership of former military commissioners, chiefs of patrols and former military (Sáenz de Tejada 2004: 85). The self perception of the ExPACs as victims of the internal conflict increased in tandem to its the marginalization in the peace negotiations, the stigmatization as human rights violators and the political opportunity of gaining economic compensation. After the first protest in 1997 the leaders of the ExPACs began contacting other leaders in order to reorganize the PACs in those areas where they were dissolved (Sáenz de Tejada 2004: 73). By 2004 the number of ExPACs requiring compensation was of 493,504 while the CEH reported 274,215 (Sáenz de Tejada 2004: 79).

Likewise, political parties found in the organized ExPACs a possibility to extend their electoral bases. This was especially important for the election of 2003 when the Guatemalan Republican Front (FRG), headed by the former General Efraín Ríos Montt, supported the requirement of compensation as a way to gain electoral preferences. The situation was heterogeneous in each community but the link between political parties and ExPACs was present in the national, departmental and communitarian level. Almost all political parties participating in the elections of 2003 negotiated votes with the different association of ExPACs and all of them offered to make effective the economic compensation that aims to strengthen the organization of the ExPACs (Sáenz de Tejada 2004: 122).

At this point it was clear that both military commissioners and PACs played an important role in the collective life of the communities as mechanisms of self-defence policing. Whether voluntary or compulsory, they were the local authority and official representation of the authority of the military in communities until 1996. However, in the context of a contradictory formal process of dissolution of military commissioners and PACs and different informal mechanisms to promote continuity in the post-war, a set of new programs of community policing from a citizen security approach began to be implemented by the PNC in 1999 called Juntas Locales de Seguridad, the main expression of the post-war non-commercial private policing widely active in the country. As Oettler (2006a) argues, lack of transitional justice policies allowed local Ex-PACs to reinforce in their communities narratives that legitimised both its role during the armed conflict and also its role in the post-war (2006a: 16). Complementarily, the new approaches of democratic security, citizen security and community policing required by the organized civil society with the support of the international cooperation, were implemented superficially by a police institution embedded in a weak reform process. The outcome of this transitional period was the reproduction of the same self-defence function with a new change of name.

7.4 Community Policing in the Context of Self Defence Policing

Parallel to the peace negotiation, a process of dialog was initiated by the Central American Governments so as to find a consensual perspective of security in the democratic context. Thus emerged the concept of democratic security grounded in principles of respect for human rights and democracy (Villalta 2007). In December 1995 the Democratic Security Agreement was signed as a regional security model. This agreement is a normative declaration encompassing the rule of law, the security of persons and goods, regional security and the institutions responsible for its implementation. There is a linkage between security, democracy and development in the norms of the Agreement. The institutional organization stipulated by the Agreement for regional security includes the meeting of Central American Presidents, the meeting of Foreign Affairs Ministers, a Security Commission and an Advisor Board (Villalta 2007: 10).

The main objective of the Democratic Security Agreement is to create a conceptual and normative framework that uses democratic values to overcome the legacy of militarism and the National Security Doctrine. However, the concept of democratic security was useful in the change of the discursive sphere of the political class and was rapidly appropriated by a growing organized civil society interested in the transformation of the security sector. The challenge was to translate the concept into policy at the national and local level.

In order to specify the concept of democratic security and acquire the necessary elements for generating security policies, the concept of citizen security was introduced. Citizen security integrated the preventive element and the evaluation of both objective security and subjective security, namely the facts and their social perception. It also included the notion of protection against risks that threaten the collective welfare (Aguilera 1996: 11). This links the definition of citizen security with the concept of human security proposed by the United Nations Development Program, wherein security is directly correlated with the development context of a country (Aguilera 1996: 12; UNDP 1994). The objective of these approaches was to limit the scope of militaries in public security and so make relevant other factors and actors related to democracy and civil society. Despite the discursive variance in post-war security approaches, the concept of citizen security provided policy tools for public institutions, such as the protection of individual citizens against violent and non-violent crime and the importance of the public space to prevent crime among others. Other crime risks are not directly included in the concept of citizen security, such as domestic and sexual violence or prevention of human rights violations by the state and non-state actors; these are some of the most important deficits of the concept (Peetz 2007: 3).

The vaguely defined concept produced different interpretations and applications. Organized civil society used the concept as a normative framework to evaluate the efficiency of public institutions (De León 2001). The military used the term to refer joint military and civil police operation in urban locations (Dammert and Bailey 2005; Withers *et al.* 2010). Despite various attempts to integrate into the citizen security approach other institutional areas such as the judiciary and the prosecutor office, citizen security policies concentrated almost exclusively in the police institution which, in the context of political transition and weak institutional reform, implemented improvised citizen participation programs in order to fight crime. The politization of the security situation, the increase of crime and the situation of public institutions led to the emergence of the so-called "iron fist" (*mano dura*) policies of massive imprisonment, reduction of the penal guaranties of alleged criminals and death penalty (IIDH 1998). These policies made it difficult to achieve the expected functional differentiation between military and police institutions and civilian participation was promoted through the organized civil society in the discussion of citizen security policies but also through the direct participation in crime prevention.

Parallel, civil society organizations implemented democratic accountability for the police and the military reform and it created institutional mechanisms to improve communication through advice and mediation between the government and organized civil society (Arévalo 2002b and 2005). This was an important change achieved during the transition to democracy because it stimulated the growth of an active civil society focused on accountability in the security sector. The most extensive project implemented to research and design the institutional transformation of the post-war society was the War-Torn Society Project in Guatemala (WSP), which included in the dialogue most representative sectors of society. The main areas of the project were decentralization of state decision-making, fiscal police, rural development, public security and citizen participation and constitutional reforms related to identity and rights of indigenous groups (Torres-Rivas and Arévalo 1999). With respect to citizen security, the group defined the foundation of approach subsequently developed by civil society organizations. This was a perspective in which the police, the prosecutor office and the judiciary should be the institutions responsible for implementing an integral citizen security policy (Torres-Rivas and Arévalo 1999: 219).

Thus, the working group identified a set of weaknesses in the previously mentioned institutions and proposed different solutions such as the implementation of an integral police reform and judiciary institutional reengineering according to that stipulated in the Peace Agreements. The interest here is on whom the working group approached with the concept of prevention and citizen participation. One of the recommendations was the creation of Community Councils of Public Security which should be integrated by five members of the community elected by the Municipal Development Council working together with the police. These Community Councils should propose a list of candidates of the community to get into the Police Academy and once graduated they should be the responsible for the local police station. The members of the Community Boards of Public Security should work *ad honorem* but they could receive pay for the time invested in each session (Torres-Rivas and Arévalo 1999: 231).

As a result, the Community Boards of Public Security were designed according to the international models of community oriented policing implemented in the United States, Great Britain and Chile (Frühling 2003). The critical point of these initiatives is that they are normative models that assume a radical change in the historical trajectories of both public institutions and private policing. In other words, the approach of civil society organizations and international cooperation did not include the political context and the recent existence of large organizations of self-defence community policing. By the time of the transition to democracy the strong legacies of self-defence as both voluntary and compulsory participatory mechanisms was still present in the society (AVANCSO 2002: 446; Remijnse 2002; Popkin 1996).

Complementarily, the police started organizing Juntas Locales de Seguridad in 1999 to accomplish the international requirements as well as the civil society organizations demands. In the formal level, the Juntas were established according to the model of citizen security participation, but they rapidly became vigilante organizations. In spite of the concept of prevention and community policing defined by civil society and international cooperation, the legacies of the self-defence community policing were reproduced and translated in the community according to the policing actions implemented before but against crime as the post-war enemy. Studies of the legacies of the self-defence community policing show how security and development were melded in the actions implemented by PACs (AVANCSO 2002: 448; Remijnse 2002). Other studies also show how the concept of prevention and community policing was implemented by both police agents and civil participants in a direction different from what the international model supported by civil society organizations and international cooperation expected (Savenije 2010; Huhn 2011).

***

The transition to democracy and the liberal peace-building program of pacification, transformation and liberalization contrasted with the strong state institutional trajectories and social and political dynamics. While the military gave up control over the main political institutions, the security sector remained controlled even though some formal reforms were agreed and implemented.

The police institution became the centre of attention for international donors, civil society and the public while other important non-state actors such as private security companies and self-defence organizations remained marginalized from the peace process. This marginalization was exploited by actors interested in the continuity of some of these organizations through different mechanisms such as blocking investigative and internal controls of the police or reintegration of members of the former police forces into the new PNC. On the other side, the police promoted the organization of private policing organizations so as to fulfil the new models of community policing in a context where effective demobilization of the vigilante groups active during the internal armed conflict was absent.

The security sector reform promoted the strengthening of an organized civil society specialized in the accountability of public security institutions. The concept of citizen security was appropriated by this organized civil society and developed as a normative standard to evaluate the efficiency of public institutions which as a response implemented formal preventive programs weakly embedded in the functional role of the police. On the other hand, the security sector reform was implemented in a security vacuum, namely the drastic reduction of the army without oversight over the process and without effective alternatives. The civil authorities were incapable of overcoming the political power of the military and implemented institutional reforms without changing institutional functions. The military rapidly recovered the political capital necessary for participating in public security.

Political transformation processes reinforced the continuity of the strong institutional pattern of displacement of the public security function to the private sector. This derail the democratization process by reinforcing vigilante actions such as lynching and "social cleansing", and by the remilitarization of public security.

8. Private Policing, Militarism, and Vigilantism

The previous chapters explained the social and political process which reinforced the institutional pattern of public security displacement. The trajectories of this institutional pattern are dependent upon changes in the social and political context and a set of reproducing mechanisms including self-defence policing and commercial private security that allowed the strengthening and continuity of this pattern even following important political conjunctures such as the end of the armed conflict. While self-defence policing and commercial private security were analysed as the reproductive mechanisms, that explain private security proliferation as an outcome of historical trajectories, there are other outcomes produced by the displacement of public security to the private sphere. On one hand, during the security sector reform a public security vacuum was created when the military left the security institutions and it was the new police's responsibility to deliver public security in the context of institutional weakness, increased crime and political instability. As it was explained in chapter VII, there was an accelerated discredit of the National Civil Police that complemented the necessary public justification for the re-emergence of the military as the only state institution capable of delivering public security. Rather than a process of re-militarization, what occurred in Guatemala's post-war was the continuity of military control over public security. This continuity allowed the military to readapt its institution to new post-war requirements such as the downsizing of the army and the use of the citizen security concept. Other factors, such as the historic confidence of the United States in the military's role in public security, placed the army at the epicentre of the "Drug Wars" so as to reinforce the police's weakness.

On the other hand, the interaction of a weak demobilization process of self-defence policing organizations (military commissioners and civil patrols), a number of attempts to promote its continuity under different informal mechanisms and the way the police implemented community policing programs (*Juntas Locales de Seguridad)* allowed the reproduction of vigilante actions such as lynching and extrajudicial executions. Self-defence policing actions were reinforced during the post-war, justified by the fight against crime and based on a contextual adaptation of the citizen participation and crime prevention concept. Parallel to this situation, the police legitimized the population's organization for policing without controls over their actions. Vigilantism and militarism are the other outcomes that along with the proliferation of private security explain the institutional pattern of public security displacement.

8.1 *The Post-War Role of Military in Public Security*

The most important criteria of democratic civil-military relations is the political subordination of the armed forces to civilian authorities, which implies the military's acceptance of an institutional framework of civilian supervision over their internal activities; namely, democratic controls (Ruhl 2004: 142). In the Guatemalan case, the proposed civil-military reforms in the Peace Accords were limited due to the internal struggles of the army and the public security crisis. As Petersen (2007) argues, Guatemala's situation shows a conditional subordination of the military to the civil authorities (Petersen 2007: 92). Conditional subordinated military avoids overt intervention in political questions but reserves the right to intervene in a national crisis and exercises indirect influence on non-military policies. The armed forces enjoy a quasi-monopoly on security policy and a high degree of institutional autonomy (Fitch 1998; Petersen 2007). By the time of the Peace Accords, the army was politically discredited but with a high capacity for institutional adaptation to a context where without insurgency the meaning of a counterinsurgency army was highly questioned and questionable (Arévalo 2008: 116). During the first year after the Peace Accords, important advances for transforming the army's role in the post-war society were made due to the existence of a legitimized civilian power, a plan to implement the AFPC and a military leadership committed to the reform of the army (Petersen 2007; Arévalo 2008). However, after a short time, the committed military leadership was dismissed and in its place President Arzú appointed new leadership without committeemen opposed to the reform process and even to some reforms included in the AFPC (Petersen 2007; Arévalo 2008).

Failure to limit the historic institutional autonomy of the military was reinforced negatively by the Constitution's reform in 1999; other factors include the indifference of civil political actors (Petersen 2007: 36). A civil political class, indifferent to implementation of the AFPC and incapable of implementing effective policies to the military, complement the context of limited application of the military reforms and explain the wide margin in handling the military conservatives (Arévalo 2008: 123). The military reform was especially attractive to civilians when it was centred on the reduction of the formal political power of the military; once the political influence of the military was reduced, civil politicians and organizations lost interest in its continuity of requiring military reform (Ruhl 2008: 149). The army's political power allowed a controlled implementation of some reforms such as downsizing of military personnel, which improves the international image of the institution. Petersen argues that the army's political power, especially some particular units like the *Estado Mayor Presidencial* (EMP), produced a slow dissolution and allowed its continuity due to the dependence of the civil governments on these units (Petersen 2007: 94). The most important reform related to the civil-military relations was article 224 of the 1985 constitution, which established that the armed forces are responsible for the internal security mission and the obligation to enrol an active-duty officer as the defence minister (Azpurú 2010). The army's reform shows in Guatemala the strategic alliance between civil governments and military to hamper the implementation of the AFPC (Petersen 2007; Schirmer 1998; Gutiérrez 1998).

Based on previous arguments, there are two levels of military role in the post-war. On one hand, the political level at which the alliances between the military, the economic and political elites allowed the preservation of the military prerogatives in the state, meaning continuity of control over security functions. On the other hand, the military's role was reinforced due to the reproducing of military patterns in the state and in the political culture, meaning the transposition of military values and behaviours in other social areas despite this moving away from professional skills (for example citizen security) (Vela *et al.* 2001: 60). This perspective contrasts between political and institutional demilitarization and the continuity of the socio-cultural role of the army and as Gutiérrez (1998) argues, in Guatemala there was no effective process of demilitarization but rather a process for rearranging the civil-military relations (1998: 33).

The first post-war government strengthened the process to consolidate the military on public security. President Alvaro Arzú reproduced the traditional role of "the military men of confidence" posted in the EMP. Parallel to this, President Arzú took a strong position against the wave of kidnappings by establishing a dedicated anti-kidnapping elite unit. The EMP had the necessary information about the kidnapping gangs and implemented effective counter kidnapping operations which led to public recognition of the army's role in the fight against crime (Schirmer 1998: 27; Vela *et al.* 2001).

The post-war crime increase generated a political crisis for Alvaro Arzú's government. Some military officers argued that most of the kidnappings and assaults were so organized and there was no doubt they were demobilized soldiers, military commissioners, demobilized mobile military police agents and PACs (Schirmer 1998: 30). The military also argued that during the peace negotiations, the economic and social situation of the country worsened and so further increased post-war violence (Schirmer 1998: 30). In this situation the president ordered to organize joint patrols of the police and military; later on, the Minister of Interior publicly accepted the police's incapability of addressing crime (Schirmer 1998: 28; Glebbeek 2001; WOLA 2000).

As Schirmer argues (1998), the decision of President Arzú to strengthen the role of the military in public security was interpreted in different ways. First, as a necessity, due to the ill-equipped and incapable civil security institutions dealing with public security problems; second, the choice of civilians to leave the dirty work of fighting crime to the military; third, the military elite saw the possibility of moving back to a central position in the control of delinquency and intelligence matters and forth, the personal and professional agendas of the president and chief of staff correlated (Schirmer 1998: 29). Petersen argues that both the military and civilian authorities benefited from the army's public security participation. Civilian authorities achieved a stronger grasp on the security situation while the army also benefited because their institution was preserved, developed a post-war identity and received continued budget allocations (Petersen 2007: 98).

Based on the police's trajectories and the role of the military within the institutional framework of the security system in Guatemala, it is possible to argue that a combination of both the necessity produced by historic marginalization of the police from its public security functions placed the institution in a situation of incapacity against post-war crime and the political power of the military, which was not reduced during the security sector reform, led to continued military control of the public security function. This is the basis for the use of the military to accomplish the responsibilities the civil governments are not capable to address but governability crises and the lack of state controls could lead to authoritarian responses to social problems such as crime. The continuity of a relative autonomy for the army in the context of a weak state is a threat to the sustainability of the democratization process (Arévalo 2008: 124).

Combined Patrols: Military on the Streets

The first joint operations implemented in the post-war were ordered by president Arzú in the context of increased crime and political instability. In this context and based on the historical trajectories of the security institutions, Arzú's government took this decision even though it contradicted what was expected from the Peace Agreements (Gutiérrez 1998: 31).

Consequently, combined patrols were supported by a number of regulations. Before the signing of the peace accords, the Congress approved Presidential Accord No. 90-96 that allowed the military to lend support the police in public security matters. In 2000, the Congress approved the law No. 40-2000 which strengthened military support to the police in order to fight against organized crime and common delinquency (Petersen 2007: 41).

Later, during President Berger's government in 2004, it was announced that due to of a "crisis of security" the combined patrols were extended. In that same year, the army received a budget increase, which allowed the military to hire 3,000 personnel for the joined patrols (IEPADES 2010). The personnel hired by the army came from the military reserves and from military personnel downsized that year. To avoid criticism by civil society organizations and international donors, the rehired personnel was not integrated into the work sheet of the army and because the official military budget should not be increased as stipulated in the Peace Agreements, the pay of the rehired military personnel was taken from the police budget (*Prensa Libre* 03/31/08). A Special Commando of Reserve for the Citizen Security was created (*Comando Especial de Reserva para la Seguridad Ciudadana)*. The Commando was allowed to carry firearms but not fire them and also they were not allowed to arrest people and conduct raids (*Prensa Libre* 04/07/06). Parallel to the implementation of more combined patrols, the civil security authorities allowed the reintroduction of military personnel into the police institution for functions of training and advisory (Arévalo 2008: 120).

There was a disproportion in the combined operations as for each police officer there were almost ten military foot-mobiles. The combination was made on the grounds that the military presence on the streets was a deterring tactic (Gutiérrez 1998: 34). There were various examples showing that parallel to the implementation of combined operations and the expansion of the military presence in Guatemala's post-war, different crime groups were active under the military coverage: military detachments in Escuintla, Cobán, Quiché and Petén acting as operation centres for kidnappers, raiders and car theft (Gutiérrez 1998: 35). One of the concerns of human rights organizations was that due to the size of the military and the weakness of the police institutions most of the joined patrols would be conducted only by the military; additionally, there were concerns about the prolongation of the combined patrols even though it was originally intended to be a temporary solution (MINUGUA 2000a; Amnesty International 2003).

Parallel, there were some doubts within the military about the implementation of combined patrols with the police. Some officers argued that soldiers were trained for different tasks than the police, they were trained to kill and not to protect the city and it was possible that these technical differences would produce a difficult security situation in urban areas (Schirmer 1998: 31). However, the use of combined patrols increased in each post-war government and as Arévalo (2008) argues, the civil authorities were the ones who called on the military to implement combined patrols and participate in public security (Arévalo 2008: 125).

This fact reinforced the historic police's subordination under the military based on the alleged military efficiency in public security. In 2008, the budget to pay the soldiers participating in combined patrols was again taken from the police institution and it was known that soldiers participating in the combined patrols received a higher salary than police agents (*Prensa Libre* 03/31/08).

Although the ineffectiveness of the combined patrols in the reduction of crime in different countries and especially in Guatemala was clear, the military presence in public security increased and it extended to specific criminal areas and violent actors such as youth gangs, organized crime, border controls and drug trafficking (FLACSO 2007: 81). As Arévalo argues, the military participation in public security has been useless with respect to the alleged solution that justified the combined patrols, namely crime reduction; on the contrary, crime rates continued increasing and as Arévalo argues (2008), especially violent crime was not reduced but continued to increase (2008: 125). Beyond the crime reduction results, the military participation in public security gave the army a significant influence in domestic politics (Ruhl 2008: 148). To the civilian authorities, the use of the military for public security had become the mechanism with which to respond to the public demand for security at which the police institution was clearly incompetent.

Military Deployment in Post-War

Parallel to the use of the military for combined patrols, their participation in public security included the reorganization of the former deployment of military detachments and bases in urban as well as in rural areas. After the dismantling of much of the counterinsurgency distribution of the military personnel there was an increased wave of requirements for more military presence coming from both civil authorities and individuals. It began parallel to the demobilization process as the population experimented feelings of insecurity after the withdrawal of soldiers from those areas covered by the system of military detachments. The system covered almost the whole country and especially the area without police coverage (*Prensa Libre* 02/07/00). MINUGUA reported that before the peace accords the army had 104 military detachments in the country and in 1999 continued to have 95. Since then, the creation of new military detachments was justified due the need to protect natural resources and to prevent crime.[194] It has been observed that the military deployments during the first post-war years were made in order to gain leadership in public security against the new Civil National Police (MINUGUA 1999).

Based on the alleged citizen demand for military participation in public security the military continued expanding its territorial coverage during the next years. In 2008, there were more than 45 requests for the installation of military zones, detachments and task forces for patrolling and surveillance in different parts of the country. The requests were made by individuals, congressmen, judg-

194 In 1998, in the department of Petén 14 military detachments were created, five of them were completely new and the rest was re-created. In the same year another military detachment in the department of Alta Verpáz and another one in the department of Quiché (MINUGUA 1999) were also created.

es and also mayors who argued that the military would be more effective in deterring criminals than the police (*El Periódico* 12/15/08).[195] However this kind of requirement had a strong discursive content which the media exploited, it contributed to reinforcing the idea that the military was the only institution capable of dealing with public security while the police was ineffective.

Although the military presence was expanded in the last years, there are some complaints and distrust by the specific population that suffered military repression during the internal conflict. This is the case of Rabinal in the department of Quiché where there were high levels of violence and even genocide (Oettler 2006b). People who were interviewed by an investigative reporter said the military presence on the streets reminded them of the time of the internal conflict and rather than feeling secure they felt fear; for others, the military generated peace and protection (Sandoval 2010).

In a country where no effective reconciliation process and justice over the war crimes took place, the military's presence reactivated the cultural confrontation which existed during the internal conflict between those who supported the military and those who neglected its presence (Sandoval 2010; Oettler 2004).[196]

It is important to mention that the repressive role of the military during the internal conflict was complemented by a strong program of civil action especially in those areas with high insurgent activity. The role of the military created a conflictive situation between the acceptance of their role due to the fear of repression (Schirmer 2001; AVANCSO 2002; Reminjense 2002). In the post-war, the situation seems to be similar but with the added fear stemming from pervasive insecurity.

The military authorities made a clear differentiation between the military detachment for crime prevention and the hiring of military personnel for the combined patrols. This differentiation was made in order to respond to the different requests that justified its role in public security. The first was a response to a state requirement based on the inefficiency of the police and the increase on crime. The second was the response to citizen requests for military presence as the only representatives of state authority able to deliver protection, and the third element that contributes to explaining the role of the military in public security is

195 The mayor of Mixco in the department of Guatemala even requested the militarization of the municipality (*Prensa Libre* 01/12/09). At the same time the department of Escuintla requested the instauration of a military platoon to increase the confidence of the people and to prevent crime (*Prensa Libre* 05/25/09).

196 However, the military detachment was installed after the mayor made a popular consultation in which an overwhelming majority (90 per cent) voted for a military presence. In Rabinal there are 96 villages which requested military presence in a department which simultaneously has the lowest crime rates in the country (Sandoval 2010).

its participation in the "war on drugs" spearheaded by the United States, as the military is the central institution to implement a reactive strategy against violent actors involved in drug trafficking. This complements the necessary international legitimization of the post-war role of the military.

The Post-war Role of Guatemalan Military in the "War on Drugs"

Together with the combined patrols and the territorial restructure coverage of the military, this study identifies the participation of the military in the "war on drugs" sponsored by the United States as having strengthened their role as the sole provider of public security and reinforced the displacement of private security from the police institution.

The participation of the military in the fight against drug trafficking began in the 80's, when the Reagan administration in the United States began using the military in counter drug trafficking operations and changed the orientation of its military support to the control of drug trafficking (Dammert and Bailey 2005: 149; Marcy 2010: 83). The "war on drugs" thus became an issue of national security and this allowed the military the use of their operational infrastructure built up during the counterinsurgency to displace the police and take control of the fight against drugs (Tokatlian 2010: 45; Marcy 2010: 84). During the internal conflict there was no functional differentiation between the military and the police; as a result, the police became a subordinated institution, which marginalized its public security role of participation in counterinsurgency operations. The "war on drugs" thus relocated the military to the centre stage of the country's security strategy, again placing the police in a subordinate role. The reproduction of the counterinsurgency infrastructure in the "war on drugs" was a consequence of the unification made by the Reagan administration of the Cold War fight against communism in Latin America with the fight against drug production in the region (Marcy 2010: 84). Consequently, the participation of countries involved in the "war on drugs" included policies such as eradication of prohibited plants, disbandment of drug trafficking organizations, militarization of the fight against drugs, extraditions and the rejection to any initiative against drug prohibition (Tokatlian 2010: 44). However the role of the United States was decisive to the participation of countries like Guatemala in the "war on drugs" as there were several internal factors that benefited the expansion of the military in the post-war (Tokatlian 2010).

At the onset of the 90's, there were concerns in the U.S. Government about possible involvement of military personnel in drug trafficking. This included high-ranking officials as well as local military, military commissioners, border agents and police agents among other state actors (Martínez 2011). Nevertheless, the participation of the military in drug trafficking was tolerated by the U.S. government in the context of the counterinsurgency operations in Central America and especially with respect to covert CIA operations related to the situation of the *Contras* in Nicaragua and the possibility that Colombian drug cartels were operating in the country (Marcy 2010: 101; Martínez 2011). Even so, in the context of a reduction of U.S. financial support for counterinsurgency, the military made different requests for technical support and equipment justified through its participation in the "war on drugs". The requests were oriented to control airstrips both to military units and to the Mobile Military Police commanded by Colonel Francisco Ortega Menaldo (DNSA 1989c and 1990a).

Even though the military was significantly involved in drug-trafficking and weapon trafficking there were few criminal investigations over these actions and did not represent a limit to the national and international support of the military (DNSA 1990b; 1992 and 1995j). On the contrary, the military's participation in drug trafficking control was extended to other alleged criminal activities such as youth gangs. Accordingly, U.S. support to this participation has increased in the last ten years especially with the benefits of the Mérida Initiative and the Central American Regional Security Initiative. However, these aspects require deeper analysis and it is important to mention they are the main international support to the military's role in public security. It must be analysed as the outcome of a long trajectory of military participation in public security and not only as a recent phenomenon.

The Mérida Initiative was approved in June 30, 2008 between the United States, Mexico and the countries of Central America and it was initially planned to run three years. It covered areas such as support activities for law enforcement, border security, firearms interdiction assistance, prosecutor capacity building, vetted police units and information exchange programs amongst others. The Mérida Initiative identified drug and arms trafficking, gangs and other criminal organizations which undermine and intimidate government institutions in Mexico and Central America as the prime threat to U.S. regional security (SICA 2008). The Mérida Initiative was designed around the consequences of drug consumption from a national security perspective. The main criticism of the implementation of the Mérida Initiative rests on its focus on the national policies rather than regional efforts which led to the strategy's inability to address what is a transnational problem (Rodríguez 2010: 66). Although there are some positive results related to drug decommission and imprisonment of drug dealers, the punitive perspective of the Mérida Initiative in the end resulted in the radicalization of criminal organizations and an increase in drug trafficking, especially in Mexico (Rodríguez 2010: 66).

Nonetheless, Central America received only a reduced part of the financial support of the Mérida Initiative and for this reason the Central American Regional Security Initiative was created with the aim of concentrating financial resources for specific threats located in the Central American region. For 2010 $55 million were assigned to the Central American Initiative, combining technical assets and training for anti-drugs and anti-gang operations with border and maritime control.[197]

More than an analysis of these initiatives and their effect, the main interest lies in the reinforcement of the militaristic perspective of the "war on drugs".[198] The role of the military in the post-war was legitimized by the institutional trajectories of the police which produced a weak institution and parallel with the increasing on common crime and the involvement in the "war on drugs" restructured the military's central role in public security. While during the internal conflict public security was displaced to the private sphere, in post-war the militarization of public security and its privatization are the two main outcomes of an historic institutional pattern.

In summary, the role of the military in the post-war is an outcome of the historical displacement of public security reinforced by the request for the military made by public authorities, citizenry and international security programs. Aside from these institutional outcomes, there are also social effects that are expanded through policing organizations. "Social cleansing" and lynching are two expressions of the reinforcing of vigilante policing organizations produced by the displacement of public security.

8.2 Vigilante Policing

It is difficult to make a clear-cut division between state and non-state violent actors when looking at extrajudicial executions and collective violence in Guatemala. The institutional trajectories studied here show how private policing turned into vigilante actions when the population implemented self-defence actions with support from state institutions against contextual threats. During the internal conflict, vigilante organizations were only partially controlled by state security institutions and so held a high degree of autonomy. The state delegated the responsibility for the communal security both against insurgents and criminals. In the

197 For the drug war it was assigned also to Mexico, 248 million, Colombia, 160.5 million, Caribbean Basin Security Initiative (CBSI) ($30 million). Congressional Budget Justification, Vol II, Foreign Operations, Department of State, United States of America.

198 The militaristic side of the "war on drugs" and its lack of positive outcomes has been criticized by the Global Commission on Drugs Policy demanding a change of perspective over the drug policies because the failure of the global "war on drugs", see more in www.globalcommissionondrugs.org.

end, self-defence organizations also existed to avoid the repressive actions of the army. After the end of the war, there was no effective disbanding of self-defence organizations and no criminal investigation of death squads and other extrajudicial execution groups. However, the army was reduced and the new civil security institutions were incapable to control the security structures created by the army, which due to the general demobilization process became free of any state control.

The worsening crime situation and the reorganization of community policing organizations under the new concept of civil security and preventive community participation reactivated former organizational structures dormant within communities. There were no controls over who managed these organizations and additionally, the police had no capabilities to implement the necessary collaboration mechanisms with the community as expected by the citizen security model promoted by civil authorities, international donors and civil society.

Thus, vigilante policing as an outcome of the historical institutional pattern of public security displacement was reproduce through two mechanisms, extrajudicial executions and collective violence.

Extrajudicial Executions: "Social Cleansing"

The term "social cleansing" refers to a mechanism of arbitrary and selective repression conducted in a systematic fashion by state related actors or by individual acting under the voluntary or wilful acquiescence of the authorities. Actions are directed against groups or individuals considered "undesirables" (PDH 2006). The term "social cleansing" refers to extrajudicial executions and implies the "cleansing of the society from those undesirable elements". The term implies some level of acceptance of these killings nevertheless is widely used in the media (Amnesty International 2009). "Social cleansing" killings implies the use of torture, tied hands and feet, shot in head after death, the use of different places to commit each killing, mutilation, the use of bags to leave the bodies, and the signing of messages to the group to which the alleged criminal is related with, among others (PDH 2006).[199] Victims of extrajudicial executions are predominantly young and many have come into contact with the criminal justice system and either have a criminal record or are suspected of involvement in crime by local security forces (Amnesty International 2009). Other common features are that most victims appear to have been targeted because they are in some way associated

199 Extrajudicial execution groups were also examined in chapter VI of this study.

with people suspected of involvement in crime and come from some of the most marginalized and deprived neighbourhoods (Amnesty International 2009: 2).

In 2000, MINUGUA reported the participation and cover-up of "social cleansing" operations conducted by public officers (MINUGUA 2000a). The investigations identified how some of the killings were made by police officers with the aim to cover-up the participation of police agents in criminal acts. The MINUGUA reported the existence of almost three different extrajudicial execution groups operating in Escuintla; police agents and a former military commissioner were identified to belong to one of them. The other structure operated under the support of strong economic groups linked with the agribusiness export in that department. The last group operating in Escuintla was composed of elements of the military detachment and local assassins (MINUGUA 2000a). It was also reported in La Libertad in the department of Petén, the extrajudicial executions were conducted by a group of former military commissioners and treasury police elements (MINUGUA 2000a).

Between 2002 and 2003, 16.5 per cent of reported killings presented signs of extrajudicial executions (PDH 2004). In 2004, 23 cases of extrajudicial execution were reported and in 2005 the number rose to 403 cases (PDH 2006). The analysis of the conditions of death allows for identification of the necessity for extrajudicial executions groups to have an operative infrastructure and organization that enables the use of different locations to commit crimes. In 2005 it was reported that in 648 of the 5,338 cases of homicide the body was found in a location different from site of death (PDH 2006).[200]

Extra-legal Collective Violence

Lynching has been identified as one of the main forms of extra-legal collective violence in Guatemala's post-war (Mendoza and Torres-Rivas 2003; MINUGUA 2000a; Godoy 2006; Oettler 2004). The dominant explanation of lynching was oriented to make an association of this collective violent practice with the traditional indigenous justice system recreated in the communal life after the internal conflict (Oettler 2005: 229). However, this perspective is present in the public debate today, and some studies show lynching is not part of the traditional communal justice systems but rather a legacy of repressive practices introduced in collective life during the internal armed conflict (UNDP 2003; MINUGUA 2004b). On the contrary, other studies argue the use of public punishment, in-

200 Chapter V showed the relation between extrajudicial executions and JLS and chapter VI showed who extrajudicial execution were part of a top-down vigilante policing.

cluding the use of violence, is part of most traditional justice systems in indigenous communities (Mendoza 2008: 47). However, political violence during the internal conflict cannot be a key variable in explaining the occurrence of lynching, as Mendoza argues (2008: 47).

The introduction of new transmission mechanisms for this type of violence inside communities is an important cause of lynching; this can include the self-policing organization as transmission mechanisms of the use of violence. Mendoza argues how empirical data shows that most cases of lynching occurred in communities with relatively high indigenous population.[201] In this perspective the *Juntas Locales de Seguridad* became a mechanism for the transmission of traditional public punitive systems, implying physical punishment.[202]

Nonetheless, lynching is identified as a form of collective violence, which whether guided or not exists for the punishment of alleged criminals in a context of impunity (Oettler 2005: 229). This explains how this practice is located in a field between the production and the erosion of security (Oettler 2005: 229). In other words, structural deficiencies in the provision of security by the state and lack of the rule of law explain lynching; as a social phenomenon it provides security through repressive measures, but simultaneously it establishes an atmosphere of insecurity in society (Oettler 2005: 246).

Empirical qualitative data allows identification of key variables for explaining lynching in Guatemala. Violence during the armed conflict is a variable which lost its explanatory potential to the extent of which the number of cases increased in current times (Mendoza 2008: 47). However, the ethnic variable is important to the collective component of lynching because communities with strong social ties seek to procure through collective action those aspects the state fails to provide; in this case, the administration of justice and protection (Mendoza 2008: 49).[203]

201 Mendoza (2008) criticizes MINUGUA's perspective regarding lynching, arguing that the ethnic variable was given a secondary place in the research method when compared with the armed conflict violence variables due to the political problem the former would present so early in post-war (Mendoza 2008 and 2007). In fact, few authors argue that lynching can be understood as a mechanism for indigenous communities to deal with local security issues (Adams and Bastos 2003).

202 Empirical evidence analysed in that chapter shows the way the *Juntas Locales de Seguridad* are used as a mechanism to implement vigilante actions including lynching. For example, the Security Committee of Nahualá, department of Sololá, applied a communitarian punishment to an alleged robber consisted of kneeling on stones for one hour and walking through the town with hands tied (*Prensa Libre* 07/20/10).

203 There is a debate about variables explaining the occurrence of lynching. Extreme poverty and internal conflicts are argued to be the main variables that explain lynching in Guatemala (Mendoza 2007: 40). The qualitative analysis shows that vi-

The existence of planning in the conduction of a lynching and the participation of former PACs and Military Commissioners was observed by MINUGUA in different reports (MINUGUA 2000a; 2004a).[204] However the level of participation of this actors was low (only in 5 cases of 133 reported by MINUGUA between 1996 and 2002) and it probably has been reduced currently; the focus here is not on the continuity of actors but on the continuity of self-defence mechanisms which reproduce the actions of former policing organizations with or without direct participation of the same actors. As it is argued in this study, this constitutes the functional dimension of private policing in the context of public security displacement to the private sphere. The existence of planning represents the informal institutionalisation of functions and represents also that its acceptance as a mechanism that through collective violence creates protection and justice against threats and the absence of state policies. In other words, it represents an outcome of public security displacement.

While lynching can be explained by the lack of justice and security institutions, the introduction of citizen participation in crime prevention included the

olence during the internal armed conflict does not explain the formation of mobs against alleged criminals but it statistically explains the cases in which there are fatal victims. In other words, in those municipalities in which there were human rights violations between 1960-1995 it is probably because a lynching took place (Mendoza 2007: 43). Second, extreme poverty does not explain the occurrence of collective violence but the per cent of indigenous population is statistically significant to the occurrence of an act of collective violence with or without fatalities. The greater the presence of the state is and the more urbanized areas are, the lower is the probability of lynching (Mendoza 2007: 47). Poverty as causal variable of the occurrence of lynching has been also discarded through ethnographic research which observes that whenever cases of lynching occurred in poor indigenous communities, the people lynched were not poor (López and Juárez 2009: 227). Finally, the main variable that explains the occurrence of lynchings is the presence and efficiency of state institutions, specifically of justice administration (Mendoza 2008: 49).

204 From the beginning of observations of the lynching phenomenon in Guatemala, contrary to the idea of a spontaneous action, MINUGUA reported the presence of some level of planning and local authorities tolerance (MINUGUA 2000a: 6). The lynching planning includes the detention of the alleged criminal, his interrogation, a "communal trial", physical punishment and finally probably killing (MINUGUA 2000a). It also includes the participation of armed organizations, some of which include state agents, the search for the criminal in his home and interrogation to identify other alleged participants in criminal acts which then also might be lynched. There is a set of previous actions such as the preparation of ambushes to avoid the escape of the alleged criminals, the previous sharing of information on the victims and their movements, the abduction of the victims from local jails or homes, the creation of rumours, previous threats against the victims and the presence of agitators inside the mob (MINUGUA 2004b: 14).

citizen responsibility for the fight against threats in the same way as it was reinforced during the internal conflict from the self-defence perspective. Popular justice or private justice is legitimized by both institutional inefficiency and the reinforcement of the role of vigilante and judge whether the policing organization has been taken against an enemy constructed by the community or not.

Community policing programs presuppose the local definition of threats and local security management (Savenije 2010). The outcome of this construction, meaning the defined enemy, depends on historical trajectories and contexts rather than objective crime threats (Huhn 2011). The post-war tendency towards the iron fist *(mano dura)* approach which implies the stigmatization of particular groups, authoritarian social control measures, supposes also support for private acts of vigilantism by citizens and the construction of a common enemy (Peetz 2011; Huhn, Oettler and Peetz 2006a; Godoy 2006).

More than just the search for direct participation of former participants in counterinsurgency organizations in post-war community policing organizations, the point to be emphasized here is the functional aspects of self-defence, meaning the fight against alleged threats by means which are not provided by the state but by the community itself.[205] Responsibilization strategies imply that modern society delegates responsibility for security among other aspects on its own citizens (Garland 2005) this element and the meaning of the historical reproduction of self-defence explain collective violence such as lynching. During the internal conflict civil participation was the mechanism for protecting the community against the state and the insurgents, and during the post-war it functioned against crime and also against the inefficiency of public institutions. In Guatemala's case, lynching is an act intended to bring the community together against crime, for this reason solidarity ties are important to the conduction of collective action (Godoy 2006: 117; Mendoza 2004).

However, lynching is not an exclusively post-war phenomenon; the record of lynching in Guatemala began in 2000 when MINUGUA reported them from 1996 to 2000. In this first approach to the phenomenon MINUGUA made a difference between lynching, lynching attempts, people dying through lynching and people injured by lynching. These differences are important due to the lack of a clear definition of lynching in the national regulations (MINUGUA 2004b). The

205 Godoy (2006) identified that not all lynchings are instigated by ex-military or paramilitary, but for all investigated lynchings the view of the residents is that lynchings are an unfortunate but necessary form of self-defence against crime (2006: 93). The author points out that the community's perception of lynchings during the internal conflict was negative but lynching to prevent crime is perceived as positive because the community has no other way of applying justice (Godoy 2006: 93; Zinecker 2005: 146 and 2009: 95).

data shows how the number of cases of lynching increased from 35 cases reported in 1996 to 103 in the first nine month of September 2010.

While the number of lynchings per year varies, the cumulative number increases in the post-war. Due to the lack of criminal investigation it is difficult to identify the reasons for the motives that trigger a lynching. More important is to identify the meaning of the violent collective action and through this the mechanisms through which it functions and reproduces (López and Juárez 2009: 227).

As was mentioned previously, there are general explanations about collective violence and the legacies of the internal war but there is no information available about the relation between crime rates and the occurrence of lynching. It is only possible to describe that while homicide rates have a constant upwards trend, the number of lynchings varies but with an upwards trend as well. Figure 13 shows that only in 1998 there was an equivalent number of dead and injured by lynching. After this year the number of injured increased meaning that not all people lynched have also been murdered. This can explain how the planning of the lynching, which includes the trial of the victims, stipulates different punishments and not invariably the death penalty. The existence of different punishments allows for the argument that vigilante actions are made in the framework of an informal justice and security systems with different categories of protection, trial, punishment and targets.

Vigilante actions as a result of the displacement of public security lead to the extension of informal appropriation for other public functions, in this case the administration of justice. In the same way that the police institution is only one part of the system of security and justice linked with the administration of justice, the informal institutions reproduce the sequence of patrolling, catching and judging alleged criminals. In the context of displaced state functions, the informal administration of justice by the own community is part of the communal autonomy to protect and punish. There is a self-reinforcing dynamic in which the state has informally delegated its functions to the community and the implementations of communal actions increase the distrust in the state due to its lack of institutional efficiency.

Another aspect that the data shows is the distribution of lynching in the departments. In 2010, the department of Guatemala held the majority of lynchings that occurred in the country while the departments with most indigenous population such as Quetzaltenango, Quiché, Sololá, Huehuetenango, Alta Verapaz, San Marcos and Totonicapán reported more cases of lynching than the other departments. As it was mentioned in chapter V and VI those were also the departments with strong presence of self-defence policing organizations. There is a combination of factors such that the level of institutional presence of the state, the efficiency of justice and security institutions and past violent trajectories that mixed within the context of historical displacement of public security to citizens enables extra legal collective violence to become mechanisms of protection

Figure 13: Number of Lynching Per Year and Cumulative

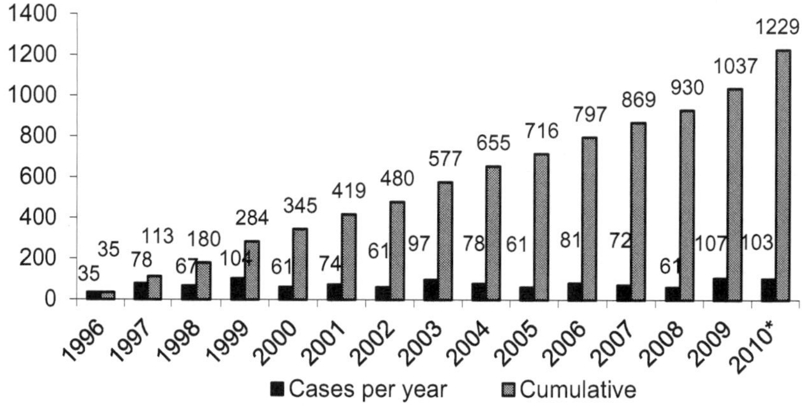

Source: Mendoza 2008 and PDH 2010. *Until September.

.

The necessary coordination and information sharing that collective action requires was restructured through the adaptation of preventive crime measures that made the community responsible for its own security. For some authors the concept of community implies a set of actions that reaffirm the idea of autonomy and communitarian cohesion: expulsion of the state security forces, communal organization for security matters through the creation of security committees, and mechanisms of social control and installation of security checkpoints among others (López and Juárez 2009: 231). However, these actions were part of the self-defence policing program created during the internal conflict and they were reintroduced under the concept of community policing and crime prevention in the post-war.

As it was mentioned before, the legacies of the internal conflict in the postwar society must be sought in the reproduced functions and mechanisms more than in the direct actors. In the ethnographic narrative of the lynchings in Camotán and Jocotán in the department of Chiquimula in 2007, it becomes clear that there exists a planning component to the collective action and that security oganization exists under the form of *Juntas de Locales de Seguridad* (Juárez 2009: 265).[206]

Figure 14: Number of Cases of Lynching, Dead and Injured (different years)

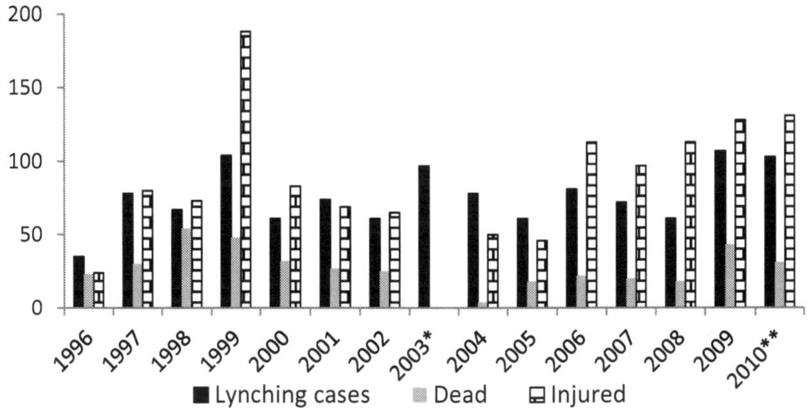

Source: Own elaboration with data from MINUGUA 2004b; PDH 2010. *Incomplete data. **Until September.

The interest here is to highlight that the actions that enable the organization of a lynching and the justification it requires are reproductions of the vigilante actions and justifications (the defence against alleged threats) which supported the existence of self-defence policing organizations during the internal conflict and that those functional mechanisms were reproduced in the discursive form of crime prevention and community policing during the post-war.[207]

206 A member of the National Commission of Lynching Prevention identifies the proliferation of *Juntas Locales de Seguridad* without control has become the main reason for the increase in planned lynchings that incorporate the shot in the head and the elaboration of documents in which the whole community consents to the lynching (Interview with Mildred Luna, Coordinator of the Lynching Prevention Program, 10/15/10).

207 As a vigilante organization, self-defence policing is oriented towards more than merely fighting against crime. In chapter V it was explained how the Juntas Locales de Seguridad implement actions against drunks, *roqueros,* prostitutes, and drug consumers among other alleged cultural deviations of the communal values. In chapter VI it was shown that the main function of the PACs was the social control over deviant behaviours in the communities. MINUGUA identified that an important proportion of the lynchings committed between 1996 and 2002 were conducted for alleged witchcraft acts or due to religious differences; there were cases

Another element that contributes to the legitimization of lynching is its toleration by of local authorities. It was explained in chapter VII how former PACs and military commissioners continued exercising local power through reincorporation into the post-war local authority design. In this context, the creation of community policing organizations reproduced the same social control structures created during the internal conflict and included the use of collective violence as part of the local security strategies. Parallel to the tolerance of local authorities, other local representatives such as church leaders, the media and justice institutions contributed to the legitimization of the lynching (MINUGUA 2004b: 27).

Figure 15: Lynching Per Department in 2010

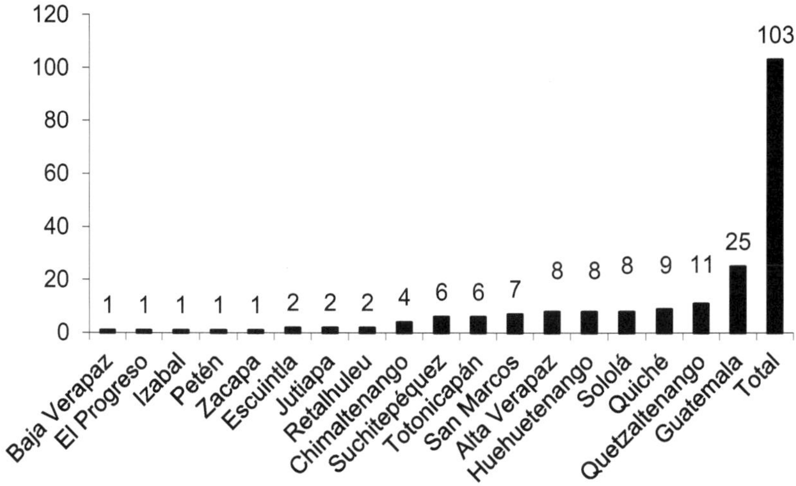

Source: PDH 2010. Data until September 2010.

While the state gave some level of legitimacy to the vigilante action through the organization of *Juntas Locales de Seguridad*, collective violence is also legitimized by the inefficiency of state security and justice institutions. Thus the state plays an active role in promoting self-defence policing and through the converse inactivity gives the necessary justification for the use of violent action. This situ-

where the reason for the lynching were territorial conflicts or disagreements with the decisions of the authorities and state institutions or due to the actions made by a drunk police officer (MINUGUA 2004: 18).

ation can be observed after a lynching; the community does not require the investigation of the perpetrators.[208]

This double role of the state in actively promoting self-defence organizations or inactively due to the lack of institutional presence and efficiency leads to an extension of lynching from the alleged criminals to the destruction and expulsion of public security and justice institutions.[209] In many cases other public institutions expelled from the communities after a lynching are the police, whether due to its alleged participation in crimes but also due to its alleged inefficiency or attempts to halt a lynching.[210]

As the main expression of collective violence in Guatemala, lynching shows how the historical institutional displacement of public security has reinforced violent outcomes that attempt against the already weak democratic institutions, the rule of law and the human rights. This institutional pattern triggers paths that put institutional trajectories in different directions related to normative and formal institutional models. In other words, the outcomes of unchanged historical trajectories challenge alternative political options.

***

This chapter analysed two outcomes of the institutional pattern of public security displacement, namely the strengthening of the post-war role of the military in public security on one hand and the reproduction of vigilante actions such as extra-legal executions ("social cleansing") and collective violence (lynching) on the other. While the proliferation of private security is the main outcome observed in this study, militarization and vigilante actions also proliferated as an expression of the absence of the police's public security role. This is a historical process in which the three outcomes are interrelated in a self-reproducing sequence of the observed institutional pattern.

208 In Quiché in 2000, representatives of 30 communities of Chichicastenango demanded in a meeting with the President of the Republic Alfonso Portillo that no more police investigations would be conducted for the lynching of eight alleged criminals in the community Xalbaquiej a few weeks before and if this demand was not met, there would be reprisals by the communities involved (*Prensa Libre* 07/29/00).

209 In 2006 the justice office in Sumpago, department of Sacatepéquez was closed after the community's protest against the capture of three alleged perpetrators of two lynchings occurred in the community (*Prensa Libre* 07/13/06).

210 For example in La Libertad, department of Quetzaltenango, the community expelled 13 police agents accused of being protectors of delinquents after avoiding the lynching of an alleged delinquent (*Prensa Libre* 02/11/09).

In this perspective, the military did not interrupt its role in public security with the reforms included in the Peace Accords. There existed a set of mechanisms to guarantee formal and informal military controls over security institutions and policing organizations. The military became the institutional support of governments against the lack of capabilities of the new police institution to fight post-war crime. In parallel, the post-war role of the military was also reinforced by an international context where the United States placed the military at the centre of the "war on drugs" justified though citizen security demands and regional threats. Thus the military adapted the institution to the formal requirements to be a post-war army and at the same time reproduced its historical supremacy over the police through the expansion of combined patrols and military detachments.

On the other hand, while it is difficult to explain extra-legal executions and collective violence through the direct participation of actors involved in political violence during the internal conflict, it is possible to argue that the reproduction of self-defence policing occurs at a functional level when the mechanism of community protection against crime or other threats was reintroduced in the post-war. Self-defence policing is the mechanism through which the displacement of public security operates in the community. In different sequences vigilante actions were justified on the basis of the community protection and local security. In the case of lynching the possible causes vary but the important element here is the interaction of collective violence with self-defence policing organizations. Thus lynching can be explained as a consequence of the reintroduction of vigilantism and self-defence policing in the post-war. The displacement of public security is expressed here as the commission of extra-legal actions in the name of an alleged ineffectiveness of public institutions and the argument of the community as the only protection and the only estate to be protected.

The objective here is not to identify causal relations between the proliferation of private security, the role of military and vigilante actions because they are interplaying processes that are linked with the political and social context in a temporal perspective. The three are outcomes of a reinforced institutional pattern of public security displacement to the private sphere in which the acceptance of private security, militarization and vigilante actions came from the historical absence of the role of the police institution in public security. In this perspective lynching is only one expression of the variety of private appropriations of the state functions in which the community closes itself against other communities, the society and the state to guaranty its own security.

9. Conclusions

The central argument of this research suggests that the explanation for private security proliferation in post-war societies is strongly related to the historical trajectories of public security institutions rather than crime rates and state capabilities. This research has shown that in the case of Guatemala, this is a historical process in which public and private security services interplay within the political context. Under this perspective, private security is considered as an outcome of reproductive sequences that reinforce private security as a social function.

The analysis of the current situation of private security reveals a set of formal and informal mechanisms through which different forms of private security reproduce over time and within changing political contexts. Before addressing the development of the historical explanation of private security, this research examined the current situation of commercial and non-commercial private security.

On the side of commercial private security, the lack of control over the number, personnel, and activities of private security companies was identified more as part of the informal rules that define the relation between state and private actors than a problem of state capabilities. There are different mechanisms that allow operations outside the formal regulations, and even as legal companies under other state controls. Chapter IV explains how private security companies avoid the controls of the Ministry of Interior and at the same time however being registered as a company they can avoid some specific taxes. The chapter analyses also the informal existence of the so-called "ghost" companies.

The lack of state controls not only facilitates the operation of non-authorized companies but also increases the profitability of the private sector. This situation is reflected in tax evasion, the payment of low salaries, ignoring labour guarantees, and a lack of investment in professional training for personnel. The diversification of the private security sector and the provision of services without legal support allowed the emergence of a dynamic and adaptive sector able to absorb the excessive oversupply of former military and police officers demobilized after the end of the internal war. In this context, the local private sector expanded throughout the country and even the Central American region. This expansion meant at the same time the strengthening of the informal mechanisms and political controls over public institutions that the private sector had exercised for decades. That explains why international private security companies have no important quotas of the private security market in Guatemala and also why the few international companies that operate in the country have to adapt their services to the dominant informal rules of the private sector. As it was analysed in chapter

IV, the operations of international security companies do not show important differences from those local companies. Different interviewees coincide in the fact that it is explained through the existence of strong informal rules in the local private security sector.

The existence of these informal rules and the lack of state controls over the private security sector are related to the existence of links between private security companies and criminal organizations. As it will be mentioned later, this relation is part of the historical trajectories of private and public security institutions; however, this fact contributes to the debate about the benefits of private security as a means of preventing crime. The increase in private security companies occurred parallel to the increase in crime rates and there is no evidence that the proliferation of private security has led to a reduction of crime. In fact, private security proliferated before the post-war increase in crime. The number of authorizations of private security companies per year shows a link with political changes such as the demobilization of state security forces and the security sector reform rather than a connection to an increase in crime rates.

The non-commercial side of private security was analysed through the current situation of the Juntas Locales de Seguridad. This study addressed non-commercial private security from the beginning of the Juntas Locales de Seguridad in 1999 to its situation in 2010. During the post-war period, the JLSs were introduced as a top-down community-policing model. The political context in which community-policing models were introduced was characterised by the implementation of the security sector reforms and the formal dissolution of an extended network of civil patrols and military commissioners, among other vigilante organizations created during the years of the internal conflict. The analysis of the operations, types of organizations, operational targets, and reproducing sequences showed that the JLSs became a mechanism to reproduce self-defence policing and vigilante actions rather than the democratic security policies proposed by international models of community policing implemented in the post-war. Different factors interacted to produce this outcome. First, the long trajectory of collaborative and repressive mechanisms between state and society reinforced self-defence as a functional social control relation that changed in order to readapt its operations to different contexts. Second, during the post-war years, public security institutions implemented a set of reforms in order to meet international requirements and national political demands but without changing historical institutional patterns. For example, community policing models were implemented through an ambiguous institutional framework in the Ministry of Interior and the National Civil Police. There were different programs supported by international financial organizations which made community policing a mechanism to become financial resources to the police. This situation produced the emergence of different community policing organizations promoted by different state institutions. This ambiguity reinforced the idea of autonomy in the JLSs and also the absence of the state in security matters.

Thus, the formal demobilization of civil patrols and military commissioners did not prevent the reintroduction of self-defence policing as a social function in community life. Community policing models reinforced a set of concepts and actions, such as crime prevention, citizen participation, and organization for protection and surveillance, that due to the political context and the history of the institutional pattern of public security displacement became a legitimate mechanism of vigilantism and collective violence.

The interaction of these elements occurred through a reproductive cycle in which self-defence policing was reintegrated in the collective life of post-war society. This reproductive cycle became evident through the analysis of different cases in which JLSs operate, as follows: first, there was a sense of distrust because JLSs recalled the recently dissolved civil patrols; second, the functional benefit of self-defence started to generate acceptance. Chapter V describes that these functional benefits can be different and range from political power, control of local institutions, economical benefits and to impunity and personal revenge, among others. Third, JLSs proliferated with support by the state and the very communities involved. In Guatemala the difference between top-down and bottom-up private policing is only formal. There is interplay between state and community-motivated organizations which have reproduced the same self-defence function. Fourth, they undertook violent actions such as lynching, vigilantism, and a variety of aggressions; fifth, they deepened public institutional distrust; and sixth, the empowerment of JLSs as repressive and uncontrolled organizations generated fear in the population. As a heuristic resource to examine empirical data, this reproductive cycle indicates that rather than the collaborative relations between community and police for crime prevention, the effects of community policing reinforced the displacement of public security to the private sphere. Parallel to this, JLSs reproduced vigilante actions and the acceptance of the role of the military in public security as a response to the weak institutional capabilities of the police force. The analysis of the JLSs and other community policing organizations in chapter V showed that they preferred the role of the militaries in public security than the police. At the same time, there is evidence of a relation between JLSs and collective violence and extrajudicial executions.

Before analysing the historical institutional pattern of public security displacement as an explanatory framework for the proliferation of private security, this research addressed the relation between crime rates and institutional capabilities and the presence of community policing organizations. The data shows that there is no reliable relation between homicide and other crime rates with the proliferation of JLSs. At the same time other indicators such as poverty rates and state density show no clear relation to the presence or absence of JLSs. The analysis of crime rates, poverty rates and state density showed that there are no clear patterns related to the JLSs and among the indicators. At the same time it is clear that the causes of violence are different to the factors that explain private security proliferation.

As an alternative perspective, this research examined the relation between JLSs and political violence during the internal conflict. The data showed that the departments in which there was an extended presence of vigilante groups are the departments with more active JLSs. More than the acts of political violence that were committed, this research analysed the existence of self-defence organizations during the internal conflict and their functional conversion into community policing organizations during the post-war years. During the internal conflict, political violence against the indigenous population reached the level of an ethnocide in which the participation of self-defence organizations such as civil patrols and military commissioners had a fundamental role due to its membership to the community. The lack of effective policies to deal with the past and transitional justice at the local and national level could be also considered as a strong mechanism that reinforces the reproduction of vigilante policing organizations in the post-war. This field requires a specific research to find the links between lack of transitional justice policies and its effects on the reinforcing of historical institutional patterns of public security displacement.[211]

The analysis of the post-war situation of commercial and non-commercial private security leads into the historical explanation of private security proliferation. Following the logic of historical explanations, this research examined the self-reproducing sequence that reinforced the historical institutional pattern of public security displacement. This process began with a set of initial conditions between 1944 and 1954, a period of social and political reforms that created the context for further structural transformations. This period ended with a critical juncture in which different political options interacted during a short period of structural suspense. The political options selected by different national and international actors triggered a set of institutional arrangements in order to reinforce the established political regime and to avoid competing political options. The 'counterrevolution of 1954' placed in motion a set of reforms in the security forces that, with the support of the United States, reinforced the role of the military in public security and subordinated the role of the police. This meant that the police assumed functions linked to national security while public security was displaced. The initial conditions and the critical juncture explain that private security is the result of a more general political process that has state security insti-

211 For more details about difference between genocide and ethnocide see Oettler 2006b. For details and an extensive analysis about transitional justice and dealing with the past in Guatemala see Oettler 2004 and 2006a and Remijnse 2002.

tutions at its core. At this point the analysis of the origin of the institutional pattern led to the analysis of its development and reproduction.

The institutional pattern of public displacement to the private sphere was reproduced through the interplay of international factors, such as the role of the United States, and also national trajectories such as the role of the military in political and social life. However United States support for Guatemalan armed forces began many years before, from 1954 to 1974 there was implemented a strong program of public safety in which the police was reformed in order to improve its efficiency in the fight against communist organizations and also against insurgents. During this period there was an intensive program of technical and financial support for the investigative and reactive units of the police. The program was oriented to the creation of a police force able to prevent communist activities in the country and to work together with the military, which controlled the security forces. Chapter VI recreates in detail the different paths and reproducing mechanisms of private security proliferation. One of them is the programs supported by the government of the United States. The military program was separated of the public safety program, however the strategic goals were integrated.

A number of security advisors of the USAID worked together with police and military officers in the creation of special units, many of them secret and autonomous. Based on documents of the National Security Archive this research explains the development of the Public Safety Program and the covert and overt units and operations implemented inside the police with the support of U.S. security advisors. The public safety and security program of the United States was complemented with a civil action section with the aim of actively incorporating the civilian population in security operations and development programs. Civil Action programs were part of the U.S. military and police support. These programs were made through the Progress Alliance and also through the organizations of civil groups for security and protection.

The role of the United States was not only limited to the police and military; it also included political influence over other areas of the state and national politics. The existence of the public safety program was an important mechanism that did put the institutional pattern of public security in motion. Parallel to the international factor, there were national institutional trajectories that contributed to reinforcing the displacement of public security, which constitutes the state roots of private security in Guatemala. This research examined the institutional trajectories of the police and its relation with the political context. Chapter VI makes an extensive use of primary sources of the Guatemalan Historical Archive of the National Police. Through this documentations it was possible to identify how the provision of private security services was embedded in the police institution and even with other security forces. At the same time it was possible to identify that private security companies were part of the counterinsurgent strategy during the internal conflict.

The most important institutional trajectory in the police was the Special Service of Surveillance created in 1956. This service consisted in the provision of agents and resources of the police to deliver private security services. Based on this, police officers founded private security companies using state resources provided through the Special Service of Surveillance. Private investors and international security advisors also founded private security companies using the benefits of this institutional service. Finally, there was also a military unit dedicated to deliver private security services that functioned in the same way as that of the police.

Based on the existence of this service, there developed different forms of commercial private security services; because all of them have used the police as a resource for private business, it strengthened the relation between public institutions and private actors. Commercial private security services provided by public institutions filled the public security vacuum created by the excessive concentration of state security forces under the national security strategy. Due to the existence of an anti-communist security strategy and later a counter-insurgent strategy, the police was reformed several times in order to adapt the institution to accomplish political security functions instead of public security function. Thus, the existence of private security services provided by state institutions constitutes one of the causal mechanisms that reinforced the institutional pattern of public security displacement.

The other path that explains a set of reproducing mechanisms of private security proliferation is the existence of top-down vigilante groups that functioned both as political security units and as self-defence civil organizations. Chapter VI examines the origins and evolution of different vigilante groups such as military commissioners, urban and rural civil patrols, scholar patrols, death squads and insurgent irregular forces among others.

The incorporation of civil populations in vigilante actions against communists, insurgents, and alleged criminals activated self-defence as a mechanism to protect individual and community interests against threats. The importance of vigilante groups to explain private security is that the continuity of the self-defence function entailed in these organizations allowed their reincorporation in post-war community policing.

Summarizing, the historical analysis shows that the institutional pattern of public security displacement triggered after the critical juncture of 1954 placed in motion two main causal mechanisms: first, the provision of commercial private services through public security institutions; and, second, the strengthening of civilian self-defence policing through vigilante groups. The significance of the path-dependence approach as an explanation for private policing lies in the reproduction of institutional patterns in a changing political context. In this perspective this research examined how private security was reinforced during the transition to democracy and the post-war security sector reform.

The political context in which the democratisation process began in Guatemala was characterised by the existence of an armed conflict, international pressures, and internal political power struggles, among others. Chapter VII analysed the different approaches to the democratisation process in the country and focuses on the relation between the political context and the security sector reform specifically the police reform. This context and the characteristics of the international models of security sector reform reduced the impact of the reforms contained in the Peace Agreements. A set of short-term policies produced formal reforms with low impacts on the most important security institutional trajectories which, on the contrary, were reinforced. Transitional governments and the first post-war governments implemented the formal dissolution of civil patrols and military commissioners as well as downsizing of the army and depuration of the police. The political context in which those reforms were made and its limitations reinforced the displacement of public security to the private sphere among other outcomes.

This period triggered two main reinforcing mechanisms of private security proliferation. On the one hand, the police reform was implemented in order to guarantee the continuity of the military's role over the security system. The analysis of the police reform during different post-war governments shows that the limited institutional reforms and the continuity of the military control of the police reinforced the subordinated role of this institution in public security. Other elements contributed to this process, such as the proliferation of criminal structures inside the police institution, the absence of political will to strengthen the police, and the absence of a coherent program to orient international support. It was during this period when the commercial private security sector expanded due to the introduction of demobilized military and police officers in the security business. The historical lack of controls over the private security sector was reinforced by the limited police reform. However, the existence of a previous powerful group of security companies that for decades controlled the relation between private sector and public security institutions constrained the authorization of several post-war private security companies. This produced the expansion and strengthening of the informal sector of private security companies and consequently the strengthening of the informal rules that prevail in the commercial private security sector in Guatemala.

On the other hand, the reintroduction of vigilante groups in the form of community policing organizations was undertaken by the police through the organization of Juntas Locales de Seguridad during the post-war years. International models of community policing did not contemplate the historical institutional trajectories. In addition, the context of political instability became a mechanism that rather than legitimising public institutions reinforced the self-defence organization against crime and the absence of effective state security policies. In theoretical terms, the creation of the JLSs in 1999 is an example of how contingent events reinforce institutional patterns when occurred inside a path-dependent process. One characteristic of contingent events is to produce effects that were unpredictable at the moment of its occurrence. For this reason a contingent event can only be identified when the outcome of study is traced back (Mahoney 2000 and 2008).

The institutional pattern of the displacement of public security was reinforced after the transition to democracy and the post-war security sector reform. From a historical institutional perspective, this fact demonstrates that once in motion path-dependent processes increase the probability of being reproduced despite critical junctures. The case of private security in Guatemala shows that regardless of how the end of the war is understood – for example, as a critical juncture that opened up the possibility of liberal peace-building and transformation processes – the continuities of institutional patterns related to security suggest that it might be better understood as a non-critical juncture that rather than produce change, reinforced historical trajectories readapted to the changes in the political and social context. In theoretical terms, a critical juncture is a moment in which there is heightened probability that change can occur but it does not mean that change is bound to occur (Capoccia and Kelemen 2007; Collier and Collier 1991).

While this research focused on one specific outcome of the institutional pattern of public security displacement, it was also possible to identify other outcomes. First, the military's role in public security was triggered during the internal armed conflict and reproduced during the transition to democracy based on the deficiencies of the police and the national and international request for military operations to fight crime. Chapter VIII analyses that however the political transformation of the military, their functions in public security were expanded in the post-war through the implementation of combined patrols with the police and the restructuring of the military deployment throughout the country. This role was legitimised by post-war governments and also by international programs especially supported by the U.S. government such as the "war on drugs". Parallel to this there was an increased citizen demand for military presence on the streets.

From the beginning, the institutional pattern of public security displacement located the military at the centre of the political and functional direction of the security policies and institutions. The continuity of this pattern indicates that what occurred in Guatemala was the reinforcement of a historical role adapted to the democratic framework of the state rather than a post-war militarization of public security.

Second, vigilantism became a strong outcome in the post-war years. This occurred in the form of actions of collective violence such as lynchings and extrajudicial executions. The transition to democracy and the marginalization of non-state violent actors during the security sector reform increased the probability that collective violence became a functional and relational mechanism for the defence of the social order. Vigilante policing is defined in chapter VIII as the existence of a functional reproduction of collective violence and extrajudicial executions in order to protect some specific social order. There are several examples in which it is possible to observe the interaction of community policing organizations, collective violence and the political context in which the legitimation of violent actions is made in order to protect the community against crime and the absence of effective state security policies. Vigilante policing was reinforced through the promotion of local security agendas through which the communities were supposed to identify local threats and propose local preventive solutions. This research identified that the international models of community policing did not have the institutional support of the police which on the contrary delegated in the organized community the responsibility of its own security. This situation gave the community the sufficient autonomy to implement security measures even when they attempt against to the rule of law and human rights.

The contextual political analysis suggests that the aforementioned outcomes of the institutional pattern of public security displacement interact in different temporal sequences. The individualisation of each outcome is only heuristic in order to identify the path dependent process and the particular reinforcing mechanisms. The complexity of this process and the interaction of its different mechanisms and sequences confirm the original argument of this research that private security has to be analysed in a broader perspective based on theoretical assumptions rather than the isolation of crime and state capabilities as explanatory variables. Historical institutionalism provided the theoretical framework to identify how the institutional pattern emerged and changed and even continues today. Based on the results of this research, it is possible to argue that the interaction of contexts and history constitutes a strong analytical basis for the study of private security and the identification of its effects on the more general political context. Thus, this research shows that the increased displacement of public security not only strengthened the proliferation of private security but also the role of the military in public security and the expansion of vigilantism. Based on this, the existence of weak public security institutions and high crime rates rather than causes of the proliferation of private security can be understood as consequences of the reinforcement of outcomes of the historical institutional pattern of public security displacement.

This research identified two theoretical implications. First, historical institutionalism provides security studies with a broader perspective. This theory was used as a framework to construct an argument to explain the links between contexts and historical trajectories related to a particular phenomenon. As it was explained in chapter II, even if historical institutionalism has been developed to explain macro historical processes there are approaches from different subdisciplines such as historical sociology that allow the explanation of particular outcomes embedded in long-term political processes. From a historical institutionalism perspective the temporality of the process depends on the outcome to be explained (Mahoney 2008; Tilly 2008).

Thus, the identification of the institutional pattern, its origin and change as well as its reproducing mechanisms suggests that the explanation of private security requires a broader theoretical perspective than the approach provided by security studies. In chapter II the shortcomings of the different approaches to private security have been analyzed. It can be summarized that most explanations centre only in the present phenomena and the isolation of variables related to crime and state capabilities. Likewise, most security sector reform studies are limited to the inside-sector aspects of the problem. Historical studies, on the other hand, analyse the evolution of private security without systematic analysis of the links between private security and political processes and often also without references to the current situation of private security services.

This research shows that the study of private security should not be limited only to contemporary perspectives because private security is an outcome of political and social processes with a strong historical dimension. In this sense the contribution of this research is to provide security studies with a historical institutional perspective in which contexts and processes have a fundamental explanatory role. The use of a historical approach thereby does not only explain the facts that 'happened' but also provides an explicative framework of the facts that are 'happening'. In other words, private security is considered an outcome of political processes in which a set of reproducing mechanisms triggered a path-dependent institutional pattern with current outcomes. This perspective opens up the explicative spectrum of private security and overcomes the limitations of inside-sector perspectives. Likewise, the study of an institutional pattern allows the identification of other outcomes that are still reproduced and that trigger alternative paths that increase the costs of its transformation and consequently reduce the possibilities of competing options. The case study showed that both private security and militarism and vigilantism are outcomes of an institutional pattern that once in motion increases the political and social costs of its change. The historical trajectory of public security displacement and the presence of strong reproducing mechanisms represent a challenge to the democratization process. From the beginning of the transition to democracy the existence of this institutional pattern has reduced the scope of process of political transformation. Among other factors, the reinforcing of the displacement of public security has reduced the legitimacy and efficiency of public institutions and has reintroduced a violent perspective of conflicts resolution.

The study of private security from the perspective of historical institutionalism contributes to the formulation of theoretical explanations of particular outcomes that are still transforming the political sphere. In this sense, the relevance of developing explanations of particular outcomes within broader theoretical frameworks lies in the possibility of identifying effects and relations that inside-sector analyses would otherwise overlook.

The second theoretical implication is related to the definition of private security for social science research. This research provides an analysis of private security as a social and political function with dynamic and adaptive characteristics. The concept of private policing identified this functional characteristic of private security as well as the interaction of commercial and non-commercial private security. More than the isolation of one particular form of private security, this research defined private security as the social and political interplay of different forms of private policing in a temporal and contextual perspective. The interaction of commercial and non-commercial private security identified the shortcomings of community policing studies and even identified a set of counter-productive effects over the democratic process. The relevance of this perspective on private security lies in the functional interplay of different forms of private policing in particular contexts.

The previous theoretical implications can be considered as a broader field for future research but it is also important to specify some empirical future explorations. The central argument of this research calls for a contextual and historical analysis of current security problems. Militarism and vigilantism in post-war societies open a venue for exploring the persistence of historical patterns related to public security. Those are phenomena linked to increasing crime and weaknesses of public institutions. However, how do institutional trajectories explain the role of the military and vigilantism in a democratic society? What are the consequences of the strengthening of militarism and vigilantism of public security?

This research focused on the historical political processes that triggered an institutional pattern of public security displacement. Still pending is an exploration of the relation between crime and the development of this institutional pattern. To what extend has crime affected the development of the institutional pattern associated with public security displacement? Have discourses about crime functioned as reinforcing mechanisms of the displacement of public security?

The historical and contextual analysis of private security also opened a venue for regional comparative studies. In the case of the post-war context, the Central American region provides a field for comparing the outcomes of public security displacement in the cases of El Salvador, Honduras, and Guatemala. Under this comparative perspective, Nicaragua is a deviant case in which the trajectories of security institutions in a post-war society did not produce the displacement of public security to the private sphere as happened in the other cases. This regional comparative model would be complete with the inclusion of Costa Rica as a case that in the absence of an internal armed conflict presents, nevertheless, a high degree of displacement of public security to the private sphere. The comparison should be made based on the path-dependent processes that shaped long-term institutional patterns that explain contemporary security problems.

The historical trajectories of violence, institutions, and political contexts presented in this research open up venues for future research based on the explicative interaction of history and present outcomes related to security and political processes.

Bibliography

Abrahamsen, R. & Williams, M. (2007). Securing the City: Private Security Companies and Non-State Authority in Global Governance. *International Relations*, 21, 2, 131-253.

Adams, R., Rohe, W. & Acury, T. (2002). Implementing Community-Oriented Policing: Organizational Change and Street Officer Attitudes. *Crime Delinquency,* 48, 3, 399-430.

Adams, R. & Bastos, S. (Ed.) (1993). *Las relaciones étnicas en Guatemala, 1944-2000*. Antigua Guatemala: CIRMA.

Aguilera, G. (Ed.) (1996). *Buscando la seguridad. Seguridad ciudadana y consolidación democrática en Guatemala*. Guatemala: FLACSO.

Alba Vega, C. & Kruijt, D. (2007). Viejos y nuevos actores violentos en América Latina: Temas y problemas. *Foro Internacional*, 47, 3, 485-516.

Alvarenga, P. (1996). *Cultura y ética de la violencia: El Salvador 1880-1932.* San José: EDUCA.

Amnesty International (2003). *Guatemala: Deep cause for concern. Amnesty International's Assessment current human rights situation in Guatemala*. United Kingdom: Amnesty International.

Amnesty International (2009). *Police Involvements in Killings in Guatemala*. United Kingdom: Amnesty International.

Andersen, L. (2006). Security Sector Reform in Fragile States. *DIIS Working Paper*, 15, ‹www.diis.dk/sw104430.asp ›.

Arévalo, B. (1997). *Sobre arenas movedizas: sociedad, Estado y Ejército en Guatemala 1997*. Guatemala: FLACSO.

Arévalo, B. (2002a). *Hacia una política de seguridad para la democracia. Documentos finales*. Guatemala: FLACSO.

Arévalo, B. (2002b). *Hacia una política de seguridad para la democracia. La reforma del sector seguridad en democracias precarias*. Guatemala: FLACSO.

Arévalo, B. (Ed.) (2005). *Hacia un política de seguridad para la democracia en Guatemala: investigación participativa (IAP) y reforma del sector seguridad.* Switzerland: DCAF.

Arévalo, B. (2008). Un problema de Estado. Límites y retos a la subordinación militar en Guatemala. *Nueva Sociedad*, 213, 112-127.

Argueta, O. (2004). *El proceso histórico de estructuración de los mecanismos de control social: patrullas civiles 1930-1944*. Paper presented at the Central American Postgraduate Program of the Latin American Faculty of Social Science, FLACSO Guatemala.

Argueta, O. (2006). La democracia como contingencia y paradoja: Guatemala 1944. *Revista Centroamericana de Ciencias Sociales*, III, 1, 151-171.

Arias, A. (1988). La respuesta del poder: 1982-1986. Población indígena militarizada, acelerada desestructuración de la cultura e identidad étnicas. In CEIDEC (Ed.), *Guatemala, polos de desarrollo: el caso de la desestructuración de las comunidades indígenas*, I. (169-220). México: Praxis.

Arias, P. (2009). Seguridad Privada en América Latina: el lucro y los dilemas de una regulación deficitaria. *Reporte del Sector Seguridad*, 6. Chile: FLACSO.

Arriagada, I. & Godoy L. (2000). Prevention or repression? The false dilemma of citizen security. *CEPAL Review,* 70, 111-136.

AVANCSO (2002). *Se cambió el tiempo. Conflicto y poder en territorio K'iche'.* Asociación para el Avance de las Ciencias Sociales en Guatemala. Guatemala: AVANCSO.

Azpurú, D. *et al.* (2007). *Construyendo la democracia en sociedades posconflicto. Un enfoque comparado entre Guatemala y El Salvador*. Guatemala: F&G Editores.

Azpurú, D. (2010). *Cultura Política de la Democracia, 2010. Consolidación democrática en las Américas en tiempos difíciles*. Vanderbilt: Vanderbilt University.

Ball, N. & Brzoska, M. (2002). *Voice and Accountability in the Security Sector.* Report prepared for Human Development Report Office, Bonn International Center for Conversion, Germany.

Ball, P., Kobrak, P. & Spirer, H. (1999). *State Violence in Guatemala, 1960-1996: A Quantitative Reflection.* Washington, DC: American Association for the Advancement of Science.

Bahbah, B. (1986). *Israel and Latina America: The Military Connection.* New York: St. Martin's Press.

Bastos, S. & Adams, R. (2003). *Las relaciones étnicas en Guatemala, 1944-2000*. Guatemala: Cirma.

Bayley, D. & Shearing, C. (1996). The Future of Policing. *Law and Society Review,* 30, 3, 585-606.

Beck, U. (1998). *World Risk Society*. Malden: Polity Press.

Beit-Hallahmi, B. (1985). U.S.-Israel-Central American Connection. *The Link,* 18, 4, Americans for Middle East Understanding, Inc.

Benavides, E. (2010). *Los desafíos de la prevención de la criminalidad en contextos posconflicto: la experiencia de Guatemala.* Serie Voces Nuevas, 1, Global Consortium on Security Transformation. Chile: FLACSO.

Bernabéu, I. (2007). Laying the Foundations of Democracy? Reconsidering Security Sector Reform under UN Auspices in Kosovo, *Security Dialogue,* 38, 71-92.

Bjune, M. & Petersen, S. (2010). Guarding Privileges and Saving the Day: Guatemalan Elites and the Settlement of the Serranazo. In M. Llanos, & L. Marsteintredet (Eds.), *Presidential Breakdown in Latin America: causes and outcomes of executive instability in developing democracies* (165-180). New York: Palgrave MacMillan.

Blatter, J., Janning, F. & Wagemann, C. (2006). *Qualitative Politikanalyse. Eine Einführung in Methoden und Forschungsansätze.* Hagen: POLIS, Fern Universität in Hagen.

Booth, K. (2005). *Critical Security Studies and World Politics.* London: Lynne Reiner.

Bourne, M. (2002). Security Sector Reform and the Challenges and Opportunities of the Privatization of Security. In D. Lilly, & M. von Tangen Page (Eds.), *Security Sector Reform: The Challenges and Opportunities of the Privatization of Security* (13-30). London: International Alert.

Brachet-Márquez, V. (2001). *El pacto de dominación, Estado, clase y reforma social en México (1910-1995).* México: El Colegio de México.

Branovic, Z. (2011). The Privatisation of Security in Failing States- A Quantitative Assessment, *Occasional Paper,* 24.

Brett, R. (2007). *Una Guerra sin Batallas: Del odio, la violencia y el miedo en el Ixcán y el Ixil, 1972-1983.* Guatemala: F&G Editores.

Brodeur, J. & Shearing, C. (2005). Configuring Security and Justice. *European Journal of Criminology,* 2, 4, 379-406.

Browning, C., Feinberg, S. & Dietz, R. (2004). The Paradox of Social Organization: Networks, Collective Efficacy, and Violent Crime in Urban Neighborhoods. *Social Forces,* 83, 2, 503-534.

Bulmer-Thomas, V. (1989). *La economía política de Centro América desde 1920.* San José: BCIE-EDUCA.

Buzan, B., Waever, O. & de Wilde, J. (1998). *Security, A New Framework for Analysis.* London: Lynne Rienner Publishers.

Byrne, H., Stanley, W. & Garst, R. (2000). *Rescuing Police Reform: A Challenge for the New Guatemalan Government.* Washington: WOLA.

Call, C. (Ed.) (2007). *Constructing Justice and Security After War.* Washington DC: United States Institute of Peace Press.

Camparini, M. (2006). Applying a Security Governance Perspective to the Privatization of Security. In A. Bryden, & M. Camparini (Eds.), *Private Actors and Security Governance* (263-282). Geneva: The Geneva Centre for the Democratic Control of Armed Forces (DCAF).

Capoccia, G. & Kelemen, D. (2007). The Study of Critical Junctures. Theory, Narrative and Counterfactuals in Historical Institutionalism. *World Politics,* 59, 341-69.

Castellanos, J. (2003). Las empresas de seguridad privada y las amenazas a la seguridad. Paper presented at the VI Seminario sobre Investigación y Educación en Estudios de Seguridad y Defensa (REDES), CHDS, Santiago de Chile.

Castillo, M. (Ed.) (2002). *Reforma policial y desmilitarización de la sociedad guatemalteca.* Guatemala: USAC.

CDDHHCEC (2004). *Empresas Privadas de Seguridad.* Guatemala: Coalición de Derechos Humanos contra las Estructuras Clandestinas.

CEH (Ed.) (1999a). Casos Ilustrativos. *Guatemala Memoria del Silencio.* (Tomo VI, Anexo I), ‹http://shr.aaas.org/guatemala/ceh/mds/spanish/anexo1/anexo1.html›.

CEH (Ed.) (1999b). Las violaciones de los Derechos Humanos y los Hechos de Violencia. *Guatemala Memoria del Silencio.* (Cap. II), ‹http://shr.aaas.org/guatemala/ceh/mds/spanish/cap2/cap2.html›.

CEH (Ed.) (1999c). Consecuencias y Efectos de la Violencia. *Guatemala Memoria del Silencio.* (Cap. III), ‹http://shr.aaas.org/guatemala/ceh/mds/spanish/cap3/cap3.html›.

Centro para los Derechos Humanos Robert F. Kennedy (1994). *Violencia Institucional, las Patrullas de Autodefensa Civil en Guatemala.* Washington, DC., ‹www.revistaseguridadydemocracia.org/ediciones/2/indicadores.php›.

CICIG (2011). Comisión antimafias de Naciones Unidas sacude Guatemala, ‹http://cicig.org/index.php?page=comision-antimafias-de-naciones-unidas-sacude-guatemala›.

CIDH (1996). Desarrollo de los Derechos Humanos en la Región: Guatemala. *Informe Anual de la Comisión Interamericana de Derechos Humanos* (Cap. V),‹http://www.cidh.oas.org/annualrep/96span/IA1996CapV3.htm›.

Cleaver, G. (2000). Subcontracting Military Power: the privatization of security in contemporary Sub-Saharan Africa. *Crime, Law & Social Change* 33, 131-149.

Collier, R. & Collier, D. (1991). *Shaping the Political Arena.*Princeton, N.J.: Princeton University Press.

Cullather, N. (2002). *PBSUCCSESS, La operación encubierta de la CIA en Guatemala 1952-1954.* Guatemala: AVANCSO.

Dammert, L. & Bailey, J. (2005). Reforma policial y participación militar en el combate a la delincuencia. Análisis y desafío para América Latina. *Revista Fuerzas Armadas y Sociedad,* 19, 1, 133-152.

Dammert, L. (Ed.) (2007). Reporte del Sector Seguridad de América Latina y el Caribe. Santiago: FLACSO.

Dammert, L. (2010). *Dilemas de la reforma policial en América Latina.* Chile: Red de Policías y Sociedad Civil.

Davis, D. & Pereira, A. (2003). *Irregular Armed Forces and Their Role in Politics and State Formation.* New York: Cambridge University Press.

Davis, R. & James, H. (2001). *The Public Safety History, an informal recollection of events and individuals leading to the formation of A.I. D. Office of Public Safety.* California: The Public Safety Newsletter.

De León-Escribano, C. (Ed.) (2001). Gobernabilidad Democrática y Seguridad Ciudadana en Centroamérica: el caso de Guatemala. *Serie Gobernabilidad Democrática y Seguridad Ciudadana.* Guatemala: CRIES/IEPADES.

De León-Escribano, C. & Sagone, M. (2004). *Presupuesto de defensa en Guatemala, Auditoria Social.* Guatemala: IEPADES.

Demetriou, C. (2009). The realist Approach to Explanatory Mechanisms in Social Science: More than a Heuristic? *Philosophy of the Social Sciences* 39, 440-464.

Diamint, R. (1988). La privatización de la seguridad en Argentina. *Foro Internacional,* 38, 1, 91-113.

Dickins, A. (2001). The Security Guard Industry in Guatemala. Rural Communities and Urban Violence. In K. O'Neill & K. Thomas (Eds.), *Securing the City: Neoliberalism, Space, and Insecurity in Postwar Guatemala* (103-126). Durham: Duke University Press.

Doyle, K. (2007). The Atrocity Files. Deciphering the archives of Guatemala's dirty war. *Harper's Magazine*, 52.

Drouin, M. (2009). *Orígenes y evolución de las estructuras de la Policía Nacional de Guatemala: una aproximación al tema en base a nueve informes del Proyecto de Recuperación del Archivo Histórico de la Policía Nacional (PRAHPAN) de la Procuraduría de los Derechos Humanos de Guatemala (PDH).* Retrieved from Policía Nacional Civil de Guatemala's database.

Dunkerley, J. (1988). *Power in the Isthmus; A Political History of Modern Central America.* London: Verso.

Elsea, J. & Serafino, N. (2007). Private Security Contractors in Iraq: Background, Legal Status and Other Issues. *CRS Report for Congress,* RL32419. Washington: Congressional Research Service.

ENCOVI (2006). *Encuesta Nacional de Condiciones de Vida.* Instituto Nacional de Estadística, Guatemala, http://www.ine.gob.gt/np/encovi/encovi2006.htm

Erdman, G., Elischer, S. & Stroh, A. (2011). Can Historical Institutionalism be Applied to Political Regime Development in Africa? *GIGA Working Papers*, 166, ‹www.giga-hamburg.de/dl/download.php?d=/content/publikationen/pdf/wp166_erdmann-elischer-stroh.pdf›.

Escobar, L. (2008). Más de tres puntos para el futuro. In R. Geramán & O. Rincón (Eds.), *Más allá de víctimas y culpables: relatos de experiencias en seguridad ciudadana y comunicación en América Latina* (137-142). Bogota: FES.

Falleti, T. & Lynch, J. (2009). Context and Causal Mechanisms in Political Analysis. *Comparative Political Studies* 42, 9, 1143-1166.

Figueroa, C. (1994). Centroamérica: entre la crisis y la esperanza (1978-1990). In E. Torres-Rivas (Ed.), *Historia General de Centroamérica,* (35-88). San José: FLACSO.

Fitch, J. (1998). *The armed forces and democracy in Latin America.* Baltimore, MD: John Hopkins University Press.

FLACSO (2002). *Hacia una política de seguridad para la democracia.* Guatemala: FLACSO.

FLACSO (2007). *Reporte del Sector Seguridad en América Latina y el Caribe.* Chile: FLACSO.

FNUD (2008). *Organización Comunitaria para la Seguridad Ciudadana.* Guatemala: Fondo de Naciones Unidas para la Democracia.

Ford, J., Schmitt N., Schechtman S., Hults B. & Doherty M. (1989). Process Tracing Methods: Contributions, Problems, and Neglected Research Questions. *Organizational Behaviour and Human Decision Processes,* 43, 75-117.

Foucault, M. (2003). *"Society Must Be Defended": Lectures at the College the France 1975-1976.* New York: Picador.

Frigio, E. (2006). Seguridad Privada en Latinoamérica: Situación y Perspectivas. *Foro de Seguridad,* ‹www.forodeseguridad.com›.

Frühling, H. (2003). Policía comunitaria y reforma policial en América Latina ¿Cuál es el impacto? *Serie Documentos.* Chile: Universidad de Chile.

Frühling, H. (2007). Dos décadas de reforma policial en América Latina: factores para su éxito o fracaso. In A. Erik & G. Beliz (Eds.), *Cuál es la salida? La agenda inconclusa de la seguridad ciudadana* (281-310). Washington DC: Banco Interamericano de Desarrollo.

Fumerton, M. & Remijnse, S. (2004). Civil Defence Forces: Peru´s Comités de Autodefensa Civil and Guatemala´s Patrullas de Autodefensa Civil in Comparative Perspective. In K. Koonings & D. Kruijt (Eds.), *Armed Actors, Organised Violence and state Failure in Latin America* (52-72). London/New York: Zed Books.

Fundación Arias para la Paz y el Progreso Humano (2003). *La Seguridad Privada en Centroamérica.* Costa Rica: Diálogo Centroamericano.

Gabaldón, L. (2001). Desarrollo de la criminalidad violenta en América Latina: un panorama. In K. Bodemer, S. Kurtenbach & K. Meschkat (Eds.), *Violencia y regulación de conflictos en América Latina* (139-149). Venezuela: Nueva Sociedad.

GAM (2010). *Inform on Human Rights and Violence Situation in Guatemala January to November 2010*, ‹http://www.gam.org.gt/.

García Ferreira, R. (2010). *Guatemala y la Guerra Fría en América Latina 1947-1977*. Guatemala: CEUR-USAC.

Garland, D. (1996). The Limits of the Sovereign State: Strategies of Crime Control in Contemporary Society. *The British Journal of Criminology,* 36, 4, 445-471.

Garland, D. (1997). Governmentality and the Problem of Crime: Foucault, Criminology, Sociology. *Theoretical Criminology,* 1, 2, 173-214.

Garland, D. (2005). *La cultura del control, crimen y orden social en la sociedad contemporánea.* Barcelona: Gedisa.

Garofalo, J. & McLeod, M. (1989). The Structure and Operations of Neighborhood Watch Programs in the United States. *Crime Delinquency*, 35, 3, 326-344.

Gel'man, V. (2004). The Unrule of Law in the Making: The Politics of Informal Institutions Building in Russia. *Europe-Asia Studies*, 56, 7, 1021-1040.

George, A. & Brennett, A. (2005). Case Studies and Theory Development in The Social Sciences. Cambridge: MIT Press.

Gerring, J. (2004). What is a case study an what is it good for? *American Political Science Review,* 98, 2, 341-354.

Gerring, J. (2006). Single-Outcome Studies: A Methodological Primer. *International Sociology*, 21, 5, 707-734.

Gibson, S. (2007). Regulated private security companies versus a professional security sector: A Cautionary Tale. *Journal of Security Sector Management*, 5, 1, n.p.

Giddens, A. (1987). *The Nation-State and Violence*. Berkeley: University of California Press.

Gill, L. (2005). *Escuela de las Américas; entrenamiento militar, violencia política e impunidad en las Américas*. Chile: Cuatro Vientos.

Gillard, E. (2006). Business Goes to War: Private Military/ Security Companies and International Humanitarian Law. *International Review of the Red Cross*, 88, 863, 525-572.

Gills, B., Rocamora, J. & Wilson R. (1993). *Low Intensity Democracy: Political Power in the New World Order*. London: Pluto Press.

Glebbeek, M. (2001). Police Reform and the Peace Process in Guatemala: the Fifth Promotion of the National Civilian Police. *Bulletin of Latin American Research*, 20, 4, 431-453.

Gleijeses, P. (1991). *Shattered Hope: the Guatemalan Revolution and the United States, 1944.1954*. Princeton NJ: Princeton University Press.

Godnick, W. (2009). *Seguridad Privada: Informe preliminar para la segunda reunión del Observatorio del Crimen Organizado para América Latina y el Caribe.* Centro Regional de las Naciones Unidas para la Paz, el Desarme y el Desarrollo en América Latina y el Caribe (UN-LiREC). San José, Costa Rica.

Godoy, A. (2002). Lynching and the Democratization of Terror in Postwar Guatemala: Implications for Human Rights. *Human Rights Quarterly,* 24, 3, 640-661.

Godoy, A. (2006). *Popular Injustice. Violence, community, and Law in Latin America.* Stanford: Stanford University Press.

Goldstein, D. (2005). Flexible Justice. Neoliberal Violence and Self-Help Security in Bolivia. *Critique of Anthropology,* 24, 4, 2389-411.

Gordon, W. (1987). Vigilancia Revolucionaria: A Nicaraguan Resolution to Public and Private Policing. In C. Shearing & P. Stenning (Eds.), *Private Policing,* (147-172). London: Sage Publications.

Gottschalk, K. (2005). Vigilantism v. The State: A case study of the rise and fall of Pagad 1996-2000. *ISS Paper 99*. Pretoria: Institute for Security Studies.

Gramajo, H. (1995). *De la guerra... a la guerra. La difícil transición política en Guatemala.* Guatemala: Fondo de Cultura Editorial.

Grant, E. (1989). Private Policing, *Acta Juridica* (Cape Town), 92-117.

Guerra Borges, A. (1994). El desarrollo económico. In H. Pérez Brignoli (Ed.), *Historia General de Centroamérica* (13-84). San José: FLACSO.

Gumedze, S. (2008). The Private Security Sector in Africa, *ISS Monograph Series*, 146. Pretoria: Institute for Security Studies.

Gumedze, S. (2009). Addressing the Use of Private Security and Military Companies at the International Level. Institute for Security Studies. *ISS Paper,* 206, <http://www.issafrica.org/pgcontent.php?UID=2252>

Gutiérrez, E. (1998). El problema de la desmilitarización en la Guatemala del post-conflicto armado. In R. Sieder (Ed.), *Guatemala after the Peace Accords*, Institute of Latin American Studies (31-41). London: University of London.

Guzmán, A. (1993). Violencia urbana y seguridad ciudadana en Cali. *Revista Foro*, 22, 12-24.

Haas, N. (2010). Representaciones de la violencia en la literatura centroamericana. *GIGA Working Papers*, 148, ‹www.giga-hamburg.de/index.php?file=workingpapers .html&folder=publikationen#148›

Helmke, G. & Levitsky, S. (Eds.) (2006). *Informal institutions and democracy: lessons from Latin America.* Baltimore: The John Hopkins University Press.

Hernández, J. (2005). *Terminar la Guerra, traicionar la paz: Guatemala en las dos presidencias de la paz. Arzú y Portillo (1996-2004).* Guatemala: FLACSO.

Holden, R. (1996). Constructing the Limits of State Violence in Central America: Towards a New Research Agenda. *Journal of Latin American Studies*, 28, 2, 435-459.

Holden, R. (2004). *Armies Without Nations: Public Violence and State Formation in Central America, 1821-1960.* New York: Oxford University Press.

Holmqvist, C. (2005). Private Security Companies: The Case for Regulation. *SIPRI Policy Paper*, 9. Stockholm: Stockholm International Peace Research Institute.

House, J. (2000). *Crime and Policing in Transitional Societies*. Johannesburg: University of Witwatersrand.

Howe, H. (1998). Private Security Forces and African Stability: The case of Executive Outcomes. *The Journal of Modern African Studies*, 36, 2, 307-331.

Huhle, R. (2001). La violencia paramilitar en Colombia: historia, estructuras, reacción del Estado e impacto político. In K. Bodemer, S. Kurtenbach, S. & K. Meschkat (Eds.), *Violencia y regulación de conflictos en América Latina* (171-186). Venezuela: Nueva Sociedad.

Huhn, S., Oettler, A. & Peetz, P. (2006a). Construyendo inseguridades. Aproximaciones a la violencia en Centro América desde la perspectiva del análisis del discurso. *GIGA Working Papers,* 34, ‹www.giga-hamburg.de/dl/download.php?d=/content/publikationen/pdf/wp34_huhn-oettler-peetz.pdf›.

Huhn, S., Oettler, A. and Peetz, P. (2006b). Exploding Crime? Topic Management in Central America News Papers. *GIGA Working Papers*, 33, ‹www.gigahamburg.de/dl/download.php?d=/content/publikationen/pdf/wp33_huhn-oettler-peetz.pdf›.

Huhn, S. (2011). *Kriminalität in Costa Rica: Zur diskursiven Konstruktion eines gesellschaftlichen und politischen Problems.* Baden-Baden: Nomos Verlag.

Hunter, J. (1987). The Israeli Role in Guatemala. *Race Class*, 29, 1, 35-54.

Hurrell, A. (1998). Seguridad y violencia en América Latina: un análisis conceptual. *Foro Internacional*, 38, 1, 19-36.

IEPADES (2010). *Boletín Reforma del Sector Seguridad*, 1, 1, Guatemala: IEPADES.

IIDH (1998). *La Seguridad Ciudadana en Centroamérica: Aspectos Teóricos y Metodológicos*. San José: Instituto Interamericano de Derechos Humanos.

International Crisis Group (2003). The Perils of Private Security: Guards and Militias on Bali and Lombok. *IGC Asia Report, 67*, Jakarta/ Brussels.

Isima, J. (2007a). Regulating the Private Security Sector Governance in Africa: an imperative for Security Governance in Africa. *Journal of Security Sector Management*, 5, 1, n.p.

Isima, J. (2007b). The privatization of Violence and Security Sector Reform in Africa: Nigeria and South Africa Examined. *Journal of Peacebuilding and Development* 3,2, (24-37).

Jaramillo A. (1993). Milicias populares en Medellín entre lo privado y lo público. *Revista Foro*, 22, 25-36.

Johnston L. (1992). *The Rebirth of Private Policing*. London: Routledge.

Johnston L. (1996). What is Vigilantism? *The British Journal of Criminology,* 36, 2, 220-236.

Johnston, L. (1999). Private Policing in Context. *European Journal on Criminal Policy and Research,* 7, 175-196.

Johnston, L. (2001). Crime, Fear and Civil Policing. *Urban Studies,* 38, 959-976.

Johnston L & Shearing, C (2003). *Governing Security: Explorations in Policing and Justice. London: Rutledge.*

Jonas, S. (1981). *Guatemala: plan piloto para el continente.* San José: Editorial Universitaria Centroamericana EDUCA.

Jonas, S. (1990). *Contradictions of Guatemala's Political Opening*. New York: Bergin & Garvey.

Jonas, S. (1991). *The Battle for Guatemala: rebels, death squads, and U.S. Power.* (Latin American Perspectives, 5). Oxford: Westview Press.

Jonas, S. (2000). *Of Centaurs and Doves: Guatemala's Peace Process*. Boulder, Colo.: Westview Press.

Jones, T. (2007). The Governance of Security: Pluralization, Privatization, and Polarization in Crime Control. In M. Maguire, R. Morgan & R. Reiner (Eds.), *The Oxford Handbook of Criminology* (841-865). Oxford: Oxford University Press.

Jones, T. & Newburn, T. (1998). *Private Security and Public Policing*. Oxford: Clarendon Press.

Juárez, L. (2009). Violencias eventuales en la cotidianidad de las violencias. Una etnografía de los linchamientos de Camotán y Jocotán (Julio de 2007). In J. López, S. Bastos & M. Camus (Eds.), *Guatemala, violencias desbordadas* (239-268). Córdoba: Universidad de Córdoba, Servicio de Publicaciones.

Karl, T. (1995). The Hybrid Regimes of Central America. *Journal of Democracy,* 6, 3, 72-86.

Kempa, M., Carrier, R., Wood, J. & Shearing, C. (1999). Reflections on the Evolving Concept of Private Policing. *European Journal on Criminal Policy and Research,* 7, 197-223.

Kempa, M. & Singh, A. (2008). Private Security, Political Economy and the Policing of Race: Probing Global Hypothesis through the Case of South Africa. *Theoretical Criminology*, 12, 3, 333-354.

Klein, L., Luxenburg, J. & King, M. (1989). Perceived Neighborhood Crime and The Impact of Private Security. *Crime Delinquency,* 35, 3, 365-377.

Kilburn, J. & Shrum, W. (1998). Private and Collective Protection In Urban Areas. *Urban Affairs Review,* 33, 790-812.

Kobrak, P. (1997). "Village Troubles: the Civil Patrols in Aguacatán Guatemala". Ph.D. diss., University of Michigan .

Koonings, K. & Kruijt, D. (Eds.) (2003). *Ejércitos políticos: las fuerzas armadas y la construcción. de la nación en la era de la democracia.* (Serie América Problema, 17). Lima: Instituto de Estudios Peruanos.

Koonings, K. & Kruijt, D. (2004). *Armed Actors, Organized Violence and State Failure in Latin America.* New York: Zed Books.

Kraft, D. (2010). Una contrainsurgencia fuera de control. Lyndon B. Johnson y la contrainsurgencia en Guatemala. In R. García (Ed.), *Guatemala y la Guerra Fría en América Latina 1947-1977* (207-221). Guatemala: CEUR-USAC.

Krahmann, E. (2003). Conceptualizing Security Governance. *Cooperation and Conflict: Journal of the Nordic International Studies Association,* 38, 1, 5-26.

Krahmann, E. (2009). Private Security Companies and the State Monopoly on Violence: A Case of Norm Change?, *PRIF Reports,* 88. Frankfurt: Peace Research Institute.

Kruijt, D. (2004). Exclusión social y violencia urbana en América Latina. *Foro Internacional,* 44, 4,178, 746-764.

Kümmel, G. (2004). Die Privatisierung der Sicherheit: Fluch oder Segen? *SOWI-Arbeitspapier,* 137, ‹http://www.sowi.bundeswehr.de ›.

Kumar, S. (1981). *CIA and the Third World, A Study in Crypto-Diplomacy.* New Delhi: Zed Press, New Delhi.

Kurtenbach, S. (2003). El nuevo escenario de (in)seguridad en América Latina: ¿amenaza para la democracia? In K. Bodemer (Ed.), *El nuevo escenario de (in)seguridad en América Latina ¿amenaza para la democracia?* (11-37). Venezuela: Nueva Sociedad.

Kurtenbach, S. (2008). Guatemala's Post-War Development. The structural failure of low intensity peace. *Project Working Paper,* 3. Duisburg: Institute for Development and Peace.

Kurtenbach, S. (2010). Why is Liberal Peacebuilding so Difficult? Some Lessons from Central America. *European Review of Latin American and Caribbean Studies,* 88, 95-110.

Kurtenbach, S. (2011). El lado político de la violencia a-política. In G. Maihold & W. Mackenbach (Eds.), *La transformación de la violencia en América Latina: dinámicas del cambio de la violencia en la sociedad y en la literatura.* (forthcoming).

Lauth, H. (2000). Informal Institutions and Democracy. *Democratization,* 7, 4, 21-50.

Leander, A. & van Munster, R. (2007). Private Security Contractors in the Debate about Darfur: Reflecting and Reinforcing Neo-liberal Govermentality. *International Relations,* 21, 2, 201-216.

Lilly, D. & von Tangen, M. (Eds.) (2002). *Security Sector Reform: The Challenges and Opportunities of the Privatization of Security*. London: International Alert.

Lipson, M. (1988). Private Security: A Retrospective. *American Academy of Political and Social Sciences*, 498, 11-22.

Loader, I. & Walker, N. (2001). Policing as a Public Good: Reconstructing the Connections between Policing and State. *Theoretical Criminology*, 5, 1, 9-35.

Loader, I. & Walker, N. (2004). State of Denial?: Rethinking the Governance of Security. *Punishment Society* 6, 2, 221-228.

López, J. & Juárez, L. (2009). Hacia una deconstrucción del linchamiento como categoría estable. Nuevos contextos, nuevas aproximaciones y nuevas implicaciones para un análisis complejo. In J. López, S. Bastos & M. Camus (Eds.), *Guatemala, violencias desbordadas* (225-237). Córdoba: Univ. de Córdoba.

Luhmann, N. (1998). *Sistemas Sociales. Lineamientos para una teoría general.* Barcelona: Anthropos.

Lyon, D. (Ed.) (2006). *Theorizing surveillance: The panopticon and beyond.* Oregon: Willan Publishing.

Lyon, D. (2007). *Surveillance Studies: An Overview.* United States: Polity Press.

MacDonald, J. (2002). The Effectiveness of Community Policing in Reducing Urban Crime. *Crime Delinquency,* 48, 592-618.

Maguire, E. & King, W. (2004). Trends in the Policing Industry. *The Annals of the American Academy of Political and Social Science,* 593, 1, 15-41.

Mahoney, J. (2000). Path dependence in historical sociology. *Theory and Society*, 29, 507-548.

Mahoney, J. (2001a). *The Legacies of Liberalism. Path Dependence and Political Regimes in Central America.* Baltimore: The John Hopkins University Press.

Mahoney, J. (2001b). Path-Dependent Explanations of Regime Change: Central America in Comparative Perspective. *Studies of Comparative International Development*, 36, 1, 111-141.

Mahoney, J. (2008). Toward a Unified Theory of Causality. *Comparative Political Studies*, 41, 4/5, 412-436.

Mahoney, J., Kimball, E. & Koivu, K. (2009). The Logic of Historical Explanation in the Social Sciences. *Comparative Political Studies,* 42, 1, 114-146.

Mahoney, J. & Schensul, D. (2006). Historical Context and Path Dependence. In R. E. Goodin & C. Tilly (Eds.), *The Oxford Handbook of Contextual Political Analysis* (454-471). Oxford: Oxford University Press.

Mandel, R. (2001). The Privatization of Security. *Armed Forces & Society*, 28, 1, 129-151.

Marcy, W. (2010). *The Politics of Cocaine. How U.S. foreign Policy Has Created a Thriving Drug Industry in Central And South America.* Chicago: Lawrence Hill Books.

Marenin, O. (1982). Parking Tickets and Class Repression: The Concept of Policing in Critical Theorist of Criminal Justice. *Contemporary Crises*, 6, 141-166.

Martínez, O. (2011). Guatemala se escribe con zeta. *El Faro*, March 13, 2011, ‹www.elfaro.net/es/201103/salanegra/3708/›.

Marx, G. (1989). Commentary: Some Trends and Issues in Citizen Involvement in the Law Enforcement Process. *Crime Delinquency,* 35, 3, 500-519.

McCandless, E. & Abu-Nimer, M. (2007). Security for People? The Role of Security Sector Reform in Sustaining Peace. *Journal of Peacebuilding and Development*, 3, 2, 1-6.

McCleary, R. (1999). *Dictating Democracy: Guatemala and the End of Violent Revolution.* Florida: University Press of Florida.

McClintock, M. (1985). *The American Connection, State Terror and Popular Resistance in Guatemala*, II. London: Zed Books.

Melara, L. (2001). Los servicios de seguridad privada en El Salvador. *Estudios Centroamericanos*, 636, 907-932.

Méndez, J., O'Donnell, G. & Pinheiro, S. (1999). *The (Un)Rule of Law and the Underprivileged in Latin America.* Notre Dame: Notre Dame University Press.

Mendoza, C. (2004). *Collective violence in post-conflict Guatemala: Understanding lynch mobs*. Paper presented at the 24th. Meeting of the Latin American Studies Association, Las Vegas, Nevada, October 7-9.

Mendoza, C. (2007). *Ausencia de Estado y violencia colectiva en tierras mayas. Una aproximación cuantitativa al fenómeno de los linchamientos en Guatemala.* Guatemala: FLACSO.

Mendoza, C. (2008). Linchamientos en México y Guatemala: reflexiones para su análisis comparado. *El Cotidiano*, 152, 43-51.

Mendoza, C. & Torres-Rivas, E. (2003). *Linchamientos: ¿Barbarie o justicia Popular?* Guatemala: FLACSO.

Merkel, W., Puhle, H. J. & Croissant, A. (Eds.) (2003). *Defekte Demokratie*, I: Theorie. Opladen: Leske-Budrich.

Ministry of Interior (2011). *Vecinos recibirán apoyo para formar comités de seguridad,* Guatemala, ‹www.mingob.gob.gt/index.php?Option=com_content &view=article&id=591:vecinos-recibiran-apoyo-para-formar-comites-deseguridad&catid=71:eventos&Itemid=54›.

MINUGUA (1997). *Segundo Informe del Secretario General,* A/52/757, United Nations Verification Mission in Guatemala.

MINUGUA (1999). *Cuarto informe del Secretario General*, A/54/526, United Nations Verification Mission in Guatemala.

MINUGUA (2000a). *Eleventh Report on Human Rights,* A/55/174, United Nations Verification Mission in Guatemala.

MINUGUA (2000b). *Los linchamientos: un flagelo contra la dignidad humana*, United Nations Verification Mission in Guatemala.

MINUGUA (2002). *Seguridad Privada en Guatemala. Estudio sobre su control y regulación jurídica*, United Nations Verification Mission in Guatemala.

MINUGUA (2004a). Final Report. The Consultancy of the Strengthening of Civilian Power. In *Ten Years of Work of MINUGUA in Guatemala*, Guatemala: MINUGUA.

MINUGUA (2004b). *Los linchamientos en Guatemala.* Colección Acuerdos de Paz y derechos humanos, Material de formación, United Nations Verification Mission in Guatemala.

MINUGUA (2005). *The Situation in Central America: progress in fashioning a region of peace, freedom, democracy and development.* Report of the Secretary-General to the General Assembly of United Nations.

Moore, B. (1966). *Social Origins of Dictatorship and Democracy.* Boston: Beacon Press.

Moore, R. (1988). Civil Liability for Negligent and Inadequate Training: A Private Security Problem. *Journal of Contemporary Criminal justice*, 4, 2, 106-118.

MUNIGUATE (2000). *Plan Vecino Vigilante, Seguridad Ciudadana 2000-2004*, Municipalidad de Guatemala, Ciudad de Guatemala.

MUNIGUATE (n.d). *Estructura participativa*, <http://mingob.gob.gt/index.php?option=com_content&view=article&id=591:vecinosrecibiranpoyoparaformar-comites-de-seguridad&catid=71:eventos&Itemid=54>.

Murga, J. (1997). Santiago Atitlán. Organización comunitaria y seguridad de los habitantes. Un reto para la paz. In E. Carranza (Ed.), *Delito y seguridad de los habitantes* (124-151). Costa Rica: Siglo XXI.

Müller, M. (2010). Community Policing in Latin America: Lessons from Mexico City. European Review of Latin American and Caribbean Studies, 88, 21-37.

NACLA (1987). *The Israeli Connection: Guns and Money in Central America*, Report on the Americas 21, 2, North American Congress on Latin America.

Nalla, M. & Newman, G. (1990). *A Primer in Private Security.* New York: Harrow & Heston.

Nathan, L. (2004). Obstacles to Security Sector Reform in New Democracies. *Journal of Security Sector Management*, 2, 3, n.p.

National Submit on Intelligence (2008). *Gathering, Sharing, Analysis and Use after 9-11.* Community Oriented Policing Services, U.S. Department of Justice & U.S. Department of Homeland Security.

Neild, R. (2002). *Sustaining Reform: Democratic Policing in Central America. Citizen Security Monitor.* Washington: WOLA.

Newburn, T. & Reiner, R. (2007). Policing and The Police. In M. Maguire, M. Rod & R. Reiner (Eds.), *The Oxford Handbook of Criminology* (910-952). Oxford: Oxford University Press.

OCAVI (2008). Estadísticas criminales del Observatorio Centroamericano sobre Violencia. http://www.ocavi.com/index.php?mod=cats&id=1..

O'Connor, D., Lippert, R., Spencer, D. & Smylie, L. (2008). Seen Private Security Like a State. *Criminology and Criminal Justice,* 8, 2, 203-226.

Ocqueteau, F. (1993). Legitimation of the Private Security Sector in France. *European Journal on Criminal Policy and Research,* 1, 4, 108-122.

O'Donnell, G. (1996). Illusions about Consolidation. *Journal of Democracy,* 7, 2, 32-51.

O'Donnell, G. (1997). *Contrapuntos.* Buenos Aires: Paidos.

O'Donnell, G. (2002). *La (in)efectividad de la ley y la exclusión en América Latina.* Buenos Aires: Paidos.

O'Donnell, G. (2004). Why the rule of law matters. *Journal of Democracy,* 15, 4, 32- 46.

ODHAG (1998a). *Guatemala Nunca Más: los mecanismos del horror*, II, Guatemala: Oficina de Derechos Humanos del Arzobispado de Guatemala.

ODHAG (1998b). *Guatemala Nunca Más: el entorno histórico*, III, Guatemala: Oficina de Derechos Humanos del Arzobispado de Guatemala.

ODHAG (2010). *Violencia en Guatemala: estudio estadístico en cinco departamentos: Chiquimila, Guatemala, Petén, Quetzaltenango y San Marcos*, Guatemala: Oficina de Derechos Humanos del Arzobispado de Guatemala.

OECD (2005). *Security Sector Reform and Governance,* Paris.

Office of the High Commissioner for Human Rights in Guatemala (2010). *Annual Report*, Guatemala.

Oettler, A. (2004). *Erinnerungsarbeit und Vergangenheitspolitik in Guatemala.* Frankfurt: Vervuert.

Oettler, A. (2005). Lynchjustiz in Guatemala. Produktion und Erosion von Sicherheit. In M. Basedau, H. Mattes & A. Oettler (Eds.), *Multiple Unsicherheit. Befunde aus Asien, Nahost, Afrika und Lateinamerika* (229-249). Hamburg: DÜI.

Oettler, A. (2006a). Encounters with History. Dealing with the 'Present Past' in Guatemala. *European Review of Latin American and Caribbean Studies*, 81, 3-19.

Oettler, A. (2006b). Guatemala in the 1980s: A Genocide Turned into Ethnocide? *GIGA Working Papers*, 19, <http://www.giga-hamburg.de/dl/download.php?d=/content/publikationen/pdf/wp19_oettler.pdf>.

Olmo, R. (2000). Ciudades duras y violencia urbana. *Nueva Sociedad*, 167, 74-86.

O'Malley, P. (1997). Policing, Politics and Postmodernity. *Social Legal Studies*, 6, 3, 363-381.

PDH (2004). *Muertes violentas de niñez, adolescencia y juventud y propuestas para su prevención*, Procurador General de los Derechos Humanos, Defensoría de la Niñez y Adolescencia, Guatemala.

PDH (2006). *Las características de las muertes violentas en el país,* Procurador General de los Derechos Humanos, Guatemala.

PDH (2010). *Estadísticas generales sobre linchamientos 2004-2010 (al mes de septiembre)*, Procurador de los Derechos Humanos, Dirección de Estudio, Análisis e Investigación, Guatemala.

Peacock, S. & Beltrán, A. (2004). *Poderes Ocultos. Grupos ilegales armados en la Guatemala post conflicto y las fuerzas detrás de ellos.* Washington: WOLA.

Pearce, J. (2006). *Case Study of IDRC - Supported Research on Security Sector Reform in Guatemala, Final Report.* Peace, Conflict and Development Program, University of Bradford.

Peetz, P. (2007). Innere Sicherheit in Lateinamerika: Probleme und Perspektiven, *GIGA Focus*, 7, ‹www.giga-hamburg.de/dl/download.php?d=/content/publikationen/pdf/gf_lateinamerika_0707.pdf›.

Peetz, P. (2011). *Maras, Medien, Militär: Gesellschaftlicher Diskurs und staatliche Politik gegenüber Jugendbanden in Honduras.* (forthcoming).

Pennell, S., Curtis, C., Henderson, J. & Tayman, J. (1989). Guardian Angels: A Unique Approach to Crime Prevention. *Crime Delinquency,* 35, 3, 378-400.

Pepinsky, H. (1989). Issues of Citizen Involvement in Policing. *Crime & Delinquency* 35, 458-470.

Pereira, A. (2003). Armed Forces, Coercive Monopolies and Changing Patterns of State Formation and Violence. In D. Davis & A. Pereira (Eds.), *Irregular Armed Forces and Their Role in Politics and State Formation* (387-409). New York: Cambridge University Press.

Perrin, B. (2006). Promoting Compliance of Private Security and Military Companies With International Humanitarian Law. *International Review of the Red Cross*, 88, 863, 613-636.

Petersen, S. (2007). *Peacebuilding and Democratic Consolidation in Post-war Guatemala: A Comparative Assessment of the Impact of Civil-Military Reforms in the Guatemalan Peace Accords*, Department of Comparative Politics. Bergen: University of Bergen.

PGDH (2009). *El derecho a saber*, Informe especial del archivo histórico de la Policía Nacional, Procurador General de los Derechos Humanos, Guatemala.

Pierson, P. (2000). Increasing Returns, Path Dependence and the Study of Politics. *The American Political Science Review,* 94, 2, 251-267.

Pierson, P. (2004). *Politics in Time.* Princeton-Oxford: Princeton University Press.

Pierson, P. (2007). The Costs of Marginalization. Qualitative Methods in the Study of American Politics. *Comparative Political Studies*, 40, 2, 145-169.

Pinto Soria, J. (2010). Guatemala: Estados Unidos y la dictadura militar en Guatemala: el derrocamiento de Miguel Ydígoras Fuentes en 1963. In R. García (Ed.), *Guatemala y la Guerra Fría en América Latina 1947-1977* (173-205). Guatemala: CEUR-USAC.

PNC (2008). *Informe Anual de Actividades Realizadas*, División de Relaciones Comunitarias de la Policía Nacional Civil de Guatemala.

PNC (2009). *Informe Anual de Actividades*, Sección de Intervención en Relaciones Comunitarias de la Policía Nacional Civil de Guatemala.

PNC (2010). *Informe de avances*, Sección de Intervención en Relaciones Comunitarias de la Policía Nacional Civil de Guatemala.

Popkin, M. (1996). *Las Patrullas Civiles y su legado: superar la militarización del campo guatemalteco.* Washington D.C.: Centro de Derechos Humanos de la Organización Conmemorativa Robert F. Kennedy.

Pozo, P. (2007). El uso de compañías militares privadas en contextos de contrainsurgencia: problemas de legitimidad, gestión y control. *Athena Intelligence Journal*, 2, 4, 11/11.

PRAHPN (2008). *Informe final: investigación de las estructuras, organización y funcionamiento de la Policía Nacional y el involucramiento del Cuarto Cuerpo en violaciones a los Derechos Humanos, priorizando el período 1975-1985 en el Archivo Histórico de la Policía Nacional*, Procuraduría de los Derechos Humanos.

PRAHPN (2009). *Informe final de investigación: Centro de Operaciones Conjuntas de la Policía Nacional, fondo documental GT PN 51*, Procuraduría de los Derechos Humanos.

Procuraduría de los Derechos Humanos (2006). *Las características de las muertes violentas en el país. Informe del Procurador de los Derechos Humanos de Guatemala.* Guatemala: Procuraduría de los Derechos Humanos.

Remijnse, S. (2002). *Memories of Violence, Civil Patrols and the Legacy of Conflict in Joyabaj, Guatemala.* Amsterdam: Thela Latin America Series.

Richards, A. & Smith, H. (2007). Addressing the Role of Private Security Companies Within Security Sector Reform Programs. *Journal of Security Sector Management*, 5, 1, n.p.

Rights Action (2005). *Masacre en Nueva Linda, caso abierto*, ‹www.rightsaction.org/›.

Riekenber, M. (1996). La policía, la "moral" y el orden public en Guatemala (siglo XIX). In P. Waldmann (ed). *Justicia en la Calle. Ensayos sobre la policía en América Latina*. Medillín: Biblioteca Jurídica Diké

Rodríguez, A. (2010). La iniciativa Mérida y la guerra contra las drogas. Pasado y presente. In R. Benítez (Ed.), *Crimen organizado e Iniciativa Mérida en las relaciones México-Estados Unidos* (31-68). México D.F.: CASEDE.

Rojas Bolaños, M. (1994). La Política. In H. Pérez Brignoli (Ed.), *Historia General de Centroamérica, V: De la posguerra a la crisis* (85-163). San José: FLACSO.

Rosales Sandoval, I. (2011). The Wheels of a Corrupt Machine: Public Officials and the Migration Industries in Guatemala. In T. Gammeltoft-Hansen & N.N. Sørensen (Eds.), *Migration Industries and Migration Management* (Forthcoming).

Ruhl, J. (2004). Curbing Central America's Militaries. *Journal of Democracy,* 15, 4, 137-151.

Sáenz de Tejada, R. (2004). *Víctimas o Vencedores? Una aproximación al movimiento de los ex PAC*. Guatemala: FLACSO.

Salazar J. (1993). La criminalidad urbana: actores visibles e invisibles. *Revista Foro*, 22, 38-44.

Sandoval, M. (2010). Que vengan los soldados. *El Periódico*, January 24.

Savenije, W. (2010). *Persiguiendo Seguridad: Acercamiento de la Policía a las comunidades con problemas de inseguridad en Centro América.* San Salvador: FLACSO.

Schaefer, M. (2008). Understanding Community Policing as an Innovation: Patterns of Adoption. *Crime and Delinquency,* 58, 4, 564-587.

Schirmer, J. (1998). Prospects for Compliance: The Guatemalan Military and the Peace Accords. In R. Sieder (Ed.), *Guatemala after the Peace Accords* (21-32). Institute of Latin American Studies. London: University of London.

Schirmer, J. (1999). Prospects for Compliance: The Guatemalan Military and the Peace Accords. *Working Papers on Latin America*, 98, 99, 1, ‹www.Drclas.harvard.edu/files/98-99-1.pdf›.

Schirmer, J. (2001). *Intimidades del proyecto político de los militares en Guatemala,* Guatemala: FLACSO.

Schlesinger, S. & Stephen K. (1982). *Fruta amarga. La CIA en Guatemala.* México: Siglo Veintiuno.

Schneider, S. (1999). Overcoming barriers to communication between police and socially disadvantaged neighborhoods: a critical theory of community policing. *Crime, Law and Social Change*, 30, 347-377.

Schreier, F. & Camparini, M. (2005). Privatizing Security: Law, Practice and Governance of Private Military and Security Companies. *DCAF Occasional Paper*, 6.

Sedra, M. (2007). Security Sector Reform in Afghanistan and Iraq: Exposing a Concept in Crisis. *Journal of Peacebuilding and Development*, 3, 2, 7-23.

SEESAC (2005). *SALW and Private Security Companies in South Eastern Europe: A Cause or Effect of Insecurity?* South Eastern and Eastern Europe Clearinghouse for the Control of Small Arms and Light Weapons, Belgrade.

SEESAC (2007). *Philosophy and Principles of Community-Based Policing,* South Eastern and Eastern Europe Clearinghouse for the Control of Small Arms and Light Weapons, Belgrade.

Sekhonyane, M. & Louw, A. (2002). *Violent Justice, Vigilantism and the State's Response*. Monograph 72, Institute for Security Studies. Pretoria.

Senechal, R. (1996). Collective Violence and Social Control. *Sociological Forum,* 11, 1, 97-128.

Sereseres, C. (1998). The Interplay of Internal War and Democratization in Guatemala Since 1982. In D. Mares (Ed.), *Civil-Military Relations, Building Democracy in Latin America, Southern Asia and Central Europe* (206-222). Boulder: Westview Press.

Serrano, M. (1998). Orden público y seguridad nacional en América Latina. *Foro Internacional*, 38, 1, 5-18.

Shearing, C. (1992). The Relation between Public and Private Policing. *Crime and Justice*, 15, 399-434.

Shearing, C. (2005). Nodal Security. *Police Quarterly,* 8, 1, 57-63.

Shearing, C. & Kempa, M. (2000). The Role of Private Security in Transitional Democracies. *Crime and Policing in Transitional Societies,* Jan Smuts House, University of the Witwatersrand, Johannesburg, ‹www.kas.de/proj/home/pub/32/2/year-2001/dokument_id-4865/index.html›.

Shearing, C. & Stenning, P. (1983). Private Security: Implications for Social Control. *Social Problems,* 30, 5, 493-506.

Shearing, C. & Stenning, P. (Ed.) (1987). *Private Policing*. London: Sage Publications.

Sherman, J. & DiDomenico, V. (2009). *The Public Cost of Private Security in Afghanistan*. New York: Center on International Cooperation, New York University.

SICA (2008). *The Merida Initiative*, SICA-U.S. Dialogue on Security, U.S. Department of State, Washington D.C.

Sieder, R. (Ed.) (2002). Who Governs? Guatemala Five years After the Peace Accords, *Hemisphere Initiatives*, Cambridge, Massachusetts.

Sieder, R. (2003). Renegociando la ley y el orden: reforma judicial y respuesta ciudadana en la Guatemala de posguerra. *América Latina Hoy. Revista de Ciencias Sociales,* 35, 61-86.

Singer, P. W. (2003). *Corporate Warriors: the rise of privatized military industry*. Ithaca: Cornell University Press.

Singh, A. (2005). Private Security and Crime Control. *Theoretical Criminology,* 9, 2, 153-174.

Skogan, W. (1989). Communities, Crime and Neighborhood Organization. *Crime & Delinquency,* 35, 3, 437-457.

South, N. (1988). *Policing for Profit. The Private Security Sector.* London: Sage Pub.

Stanley, W. (1996). *The Protection Racket State: Elite Politics, Military Extortion and Civil War in El Salvador.* Philadelphia: Temple University Press.

Stanley, W. (2007). Business as Usual? Justice and Policing Reform in Postwar Guatemala. In C. Call (Ed.), *Constructing Justice and Security After War* (113-155). United States Institute of Peace Press, Washington D.C.

Táger, A. & Mérida, M. (2002). The Privatisation of Security in Guatemala. In D. Lilly & M. von Tangen (Eds.), *Security Sector Reform: The Challenges and Opportunities of the Privatisation of Security* (91-119). London: International Alert.

Thelen, K. (1999). Historical Institutionalism in comparative politics. *Annual Reviews of Political Science,* 2, 369-404.

Thelen, K. (2003). How Institutions Evolve: Insights from Comparative Hisotircal Analysis. In J. Mahoney & D. Rueschemeyer (Eds.), *Comparative Historical Analysis in the Social Sciences* (208-240). Cambridge: Cambridge University.

Tilly, C. (1985). War Making and State Making as Organized Crime. In P. Evans, D. Rueschemeyer & T. Skocpol (Eds.), *Bringing the State Back In* (169-187). Cambridge: Cambridge University Press.

Tilly, C. (2001a). Mechanism in Political Processes. *Annual Review of Political Science,* 4, 21-41.

Tilly, C. (2001b). Historical Analysis of Political Processes. In J. Turner (Ed.), *Handbook of Sociological Theory* (567-588). New York: Kluwer Academic / Plenum Publishers.

Tilly, C. (2002). *Coercion, Capital and European States.* Cambridge, Oxford: Blackwell.

Tilly, C. (2003). Armed Force, Regimes, and Contention in Europe since 1650. In D. Davis & A. Pereira (Eds.), *Irregular Armed Forces and Their Role in Politics and State Formation* (33-82). Cambridge: Cambridge University Press.

Tilly, C. (2008). *Explaining Social Processes.* Boulder: Paradigm.

Tilly, C. & Goodin, R. (2006). It Depends. In R. Goodin & C. Tilly (Eds.), The Oxford Handbook of Contextual Political Analysis (3-32). Oxford: Oxford University Press.

Tipografía Nacional (1932). *Reformas para el buen régimen político, económico y administrativo*, decreto no. 1987, Recopilación de leyes vigentes de Gobernación, Guatemala.
Tipografía Nacional (1937). *Leyes vigentes de Gobernación y Justicia*, Secretaría de Gobernación y Justicia, Guatemala.
Tipografía Nacional (1971). *Recopilación de leyes de la República de Guatemala,* Guatemala.
Tischler, S. (2001). *Guatemala 1944: crisis y revolución; ocaso y quiebre de una forma estatal*. Guatemala: F&G Editores.
Tokatlian, J. G. (2010). La guerra antidrogas y el Comando Sur. *Foreign Affairs Latin America*, 10, 1, 34-50.
Torres-Rivas, E. (1994). Introducción a la década. In E. Torres-Rivas (Ed.), *Historia General de Centroamérica* (11-33). San José: FLACSO.
Torres-Rivas, E. & Aguilera, G. (1998). *Del autoritarismo a la paz*. Guatemala: FLACSO.
Torres-Rivas, E. & Arévalo, B. (1999). *Del conflicto al diálogo: El WSP en Guatemala.* Guatemala: FLACSO.
Trevaskes, S. (2007). The Private/Public Security Nexus in China. *Social Justice,* 34, 3-4, 38-55.
Triplett R., Gainey, R. & Sun I. (2003). Institutional Strength, Social Control and Neighborhood Crime Rates. *Theoretical Criminology*, 7, 4, 439-467.
Trudeau, R. (1993). *Guatemalan Politics: the popular struggle for democracy.* Boulder: Rienner.
UDEFEGUA (2010a). *El Acompañante*, 1, 01/10, Unidad de Protección a Defensores de Derechos Humanos de Guatemala.
UDEFEGUA (2010b). *El Acompañante*, 2, 07/10, Unidad de Protección a Defensores de Derechos Humanos de Guatemala.
UNDP (1994). *Human Development Report*. New York, Oxford: UNDP.
UNDP (2003). *La ley de Xibalba o linchamientos*. Guatemala: UNDP.
UNDP (2006). *El costo económico de la violencia en Guatemala,* Programa de Seguridad Ciudadana y Prevención de la Violencia del PNUD Guatemala.
UNDP (2007). *Informe Estadístico de la Violencia en Guatemala*, Programa de Seguridad Ciudadana y Prevención de la Violencia del PNUD Guatemala.
UNDP (2010a). *Informe sobre Desarrollo Humano para América Central 2009/2010*, ‹http://desarrollohumano.org.gt/sites/default/files/ISDH_Americacentral_2009-2010.pdf›.
UNDP (2010b). *Informe Nacional de Desarrollo Humano para Guatemala,* ‹http://desarrollohumano.org.gt/sites/default/files/INDH_2009-2010_0.pdf ›.
UDNP (n.d). *Los Proyectos de Desarrollo y la Colaboración del PNUD,* ‹www.undp.org.gt/frmMapa.aspx›.

Ungar, M. (2007). The Privatization of Citizen Security in Latin America: From Elite Guards to Neighborhood Vigilantes. *Social Justice*, 34, 3-4, 20-37.

UNODC (2007). *Crime and Development in Central America, Caught in the Crossfire*, ‹www.unodc.org/documents/data-and-analysis/Central-america-study-en.pdf›.

UNODC (2008). *Homicide Statistics 2003-2008*, ‹www.unodc.norg/unodc/en/data-and-analysis/homicide.html›.

Van Evera, S. (1997). *Guide to Methods for Students of Political Science*. Ithaca: Cornell University Press.

Van Cott, D. (2006). Dispensing Justice at the Margins of Formality. The Informal Rule of Law in Latin America. In G. Helmke & S. Levitsky (Eds.), *Informal institutions and democracy: lessons from Latin America*. Baltimore: The John Hopkins University Press.

Vaughan, B. (2007). The Provision of Policing and the Problem of Pluralism. *Theoretical Criminology*, 11, 3, 347-366.

Vela, M. (2008). *Masas, armas y elites. Guatemala, 1820-1982. Análisis Sociológico de Eventos Históricos*. Guatemala: FLACSO.

Vela, M., Sequén-Mónchez, A. & Solares, H. (2001). *El lado oscuro de la eterna primavera. Violencia, criminalidad y delincuencia en la postguerra*. Guatemala: FLACSO.

Villalta, A. (2007). *El Tratado Marco de Seguridad Democrática en Centro América.* Seminario La normativa jurídica del SICA y la consulta prejudicial.

Vindevogel, F. (2005). Private Security and Urban Crime Mitigation: A bid for BID's. *Criminal Justice*, 5, 3, 233-255.

Waard, J. (1999). The Private Security Industry in International Perspective. *European Journal on Criminal Policy and Research*, 7, 143-174.

Waldmann, P. (1995). Vigilantismo, democratización y el papel de la policía. In M. Mols & J. Thesing (Eds.), *El Estado en América Latina* (67-106). Buenos Aires: KAS.

Walter, K. (2004). *El régimen de Anastasio Somoza 1936-1946.* Nicaragua: Instituto de Historia de Nicaragua y Centroamérica.

Weber, M. (1969). *The Theory of Social and Economical Organization.* New York: Free Press.

Weisburd, D. (1988). Vigilantism as Community Social Control: Developing a Quantitative Criminological Model. *Journal of Quantitative Criminology,* 4, 2, 137-153.

Weiss, R. (2007). From Cowboy Detectives to Soldiers of Fortune: Private Security Contracting and Its Contradictions on the New Frontiers of Capitalist Expansion. *Social Justice*, 34, 3-4, 1-19.

Wilson, R. (1993). Continued Counterinsurgency: Civilian Rule in Guatemala. In: Gills, B., Rocamora, J. & Wilson R. *Low Intensity Democracy: Political Power in the New World Order* (127-160). London, Pluto Press.

Wisler, D. & Onwudiwe, I. (2008). Community Policing in Comparison. *Police Quarterly,* 11, 4, 427-446.

Withers, G., Santos, L. & Isacson, A. (2010). *Preach What You Practice: The Separation of Military and Police Roles in the Americas*. Washington D.C.: WOLA.

WOLA (2000). *Rescuing the Police Reform: A Challenge for the New Guatemalan Government*. Washington D.C.: WOLA.

WOLA (2009). *Protect and Serve? The Status of Police Reform in Central America*. Washington D.C.: WOLA.

Wulf, H. (2002). Change of Uniform but not Uniform Change in Function: Soldiers in Search of a New Role: In BICC (Ed.), *Conversion Survey 2002* (92-111). Baden-Baden: Nomos.

Wulf, H. (2007). Challenging the Weberian Concept of the State: The Future of the Monopoly of Violence. *Occasional Papers Series*, 9. The Australian Centre for Peace and Conflict Studies.

Wynsberghe, R. van & Khan, S. (2007). Redefining Case Study. *International Journal of Qualitative Methods*, 6, 2, 80-94.

Yin, Robert K. (1981). The Case Study as a Serious Research Strategy. *Science Communication*, 3, 97-114.

Zinecker, H. (1999). Transición incompleta y sociedad civil violenta. In: Hengstenberg, P., Kohut, K. & Maihold, G. (Eds.), *Sociedad civil en América Latina: representación de intereses y gobernabilidad* (183-195). Venezuela: Nueva Sociedad.

Zinecker, H. (2005). Krise in Zentralamerika? In A. Boeck & R. Öhlschläger (Eds.), *Krisenregionen in Lateinamerika. Weingartener Lateinamerika-Gespräche* (129-174). Hamburg: Institut für Iberoamerika-Kunde.

Zinecker, H. (2009). Gewaltkriminelle Ordnungen als Bottom-up-Governance. Das Beispiel Zentralamerika. In H. Weiland, I. Wehr & M. Seifert (Eds.), *Good Governance in der Sackgasse?* (91-106). Baden-Baden: Nomos.

Zirker, D. & Danopoulos, C. (2004). Personal Security, Governability and the Military in Latin America. *Journal of Security Sector Management*, 2, 1, n.p.

Documents of the Digital National Security Archive

DNSA (1953). *Guatemala General Plan of Actions*, September 11, 1953. Collection Guatemala and the U.S., item number GU00003.

DNSA (1954). *Mass arrest of communist peasant leaders*, July 29, 1954. Collection Guatemala and the U.S., item number GU00012.

DNSA (1955a). *Outline Plan of Operations for Guatemala*, June 01, 1955. Collection Guatemala and the U.S., item number GU00015.

DNSA (1955b). *The New Phase in Guatemalan Political Life and its Relation to U.S. Policy,* June 24, 1955. Collection Guatemala and the U.S., item number GU00016.

DNSA (1956a). *Establishment of General Office of National Security*, March 6, 1956. Collection Guatemala and the U.S., item number GU00018.

DNSA (1956b). *Report on the National Police of Guatemala,* April 9, 1956. Collection Guatemala and the U.S., item number GU00019.

DNSA (1956c). *Report of Situation in Guatemala*, June 29, 1956. Collection Guatemala and the U.S., item number GU00020.

DNSA (1956d). *Civil Police Program for Guatemala*, July 31, 1956. Collection Guatemala and the U.S. item number GU00021.

DNSA (1957). *Overseas International Security Program*, June 03, 1957. Collection Guatemala and the U.S., item number GU00022.

DNSA (1959a). *Evaluation of Guatemalan Program*, May 13, 1959. Collection Guatemala and the U.S., item number GU00025.

DNSA (1959b). *Mutual Security Program in Guatemala*, September 21, 1959. Collection Guatemala and the U.S., item number GU00026.

DNSA (1961a). *Internal Security Situation and Needs,* May 22, 1961. Collection Guatemala and the U.S., item number GU00032.

DNSA (1962a). *Military Assistance to Guatemalan Government,* February 10, 1962. Collection Guatemala and the U.S., item number GU00063.

DNSA (1962b). *Riot Control Training Curse Sponsored by USAID,* June 08, 1962. Collection Guatemala and the U.S., item number GU00089.

DNSA (1962c). *Guidelines for Policy and Operations,* September 11, 1962. Collection Guatemala and the U.S., item number GU00093.

DNSA (1962d). *Police Report Program,* September 25, 1962. Collection Guatemala and the U.S., item number GU00095.

DNSA (1963a). *Recognition of Guatemalan Military Government*, April 01, 1963. Collection Guatemala and the U.S., item number GU00130.

DNSA (1963b). *U.S. Posture Toward Colonel Peralta's Government,* April 03, 1963. Collection Guatemala and the U.S., item number GU00131.

DNSA (1963c). *Provisional rule of military government in Guatemala.* April 04, 1963. Collection Guatemala and the U.S. item number GU00132.

DNSA (1963d). *The New Guatemalan Regime and Implications of the Coup for U.S. Policy*, April 05, 1963. Collection Guatemala and the U.S., item number GU00133.

DNSA (1963e). *Internal Defense Plan –Guatemala,* May 28, 1963. Collection Guatemala and the U.S., item number GU00141.

DNSA (1963f). *Public Safety Program Guatemala,* June 17, 1963. Collection Guatemala and the U.S., item number GU00142.

DNSA (1963g). *Internal Defense Plan for Guatemala*, September 07, 1963. Collection Guatemala and the U.S., item number GU00146.

DNSA (1963h). *Civic Actions Assessment*, October 08, 1963. Collection Guatemala and the U.S., item number GU00151.

DNSA (1964). *Police Reorganization Program*, March 10, 1964. Collection Guatemala and the U.S., item number GU00165.

DNSA (1965a). *Report on Public Safety Programs,* June 02, 1965. Collection Guatemala and the U.S., item number GU00206.

DNSA (1965b). *Kidnapping Task Force*, November 24, 1965. Collection Guatemala and the U.S., item number GU00222.

DNSA (1965c). *Public Safety Advisor*, November 27, 1965. Collection Guatemala and the U.S., item number GU00244.

DNSA (1965d). *Subversive Activities*, December 04, 1965. Collection Guatemala and the U.S. item number GU00229.

DNSA (1965e). *Guatemalan Regime in Serious Troubles*, December 07, 1965. Collection Guatemala and the U.S. item number GU00232.

DNSA (1966a). *Police Coordination Efforts*, January 14, 1966. Collection Guatemala and the U.S., item number GU00245.

DNSA (1966b). *Public Safety Report*, January 14, 1966. Collection Guatemala and the U.S., item number GU00246.

DNSA (1966c). *Assistance to Internal Security Forces*, January 20, 1966. Collection Guatemala and the U.S., item number GU00252.

DNSA (1966d). *U.S. Policy Assessment*, February 12, 1966. Collection Guatemala and the U.S., item number GU00255.

DNSA (1966e). *Request for Team to Provide Advice and Training*, March 01, 1966. Collection Guatemala and the U.S., item number GU00259.

DNSA (1966f). *Conversations with Méndez Montenegro*, September 26, 1966. Collection Guatemala and the U.S., item number GU00305.

DNSA (1966g). *U.S. Internal Security Programs in Latin America*, November 30, 1966. Collection Guatemala and the U.S., item number GU00318.

DNSA (1966h). *Request for Assistance in Covert Training*, December 03, 1966. Collection Guatemala and the U.S., item number GU00321.

DNSA (1966i). *Guatemala Police Powers Expanded*, December 24, 1966. Collection Guatemala and the U.S., item number GU00327.

DNSA (1967a). *Vigilantism Poses Threat to Stability*, May 12, 1967. Collection Guatemala and the U.S., item number GU00332.

DNSA (1967b). *Rural Development Advisor*, July 17, 1967. Collection Guatemala and the U.S., item number GU00336.

DNSA (1967c). *Irregular Militias*, July 17, 1967. Collection Guatemala and the U.S., item number GU00340.

DNSA (1967d). *Irregular Militias of the Government,* August 11, 1967. Collection Guatemala and the U.S., item number GU00342.

DNSA (1967e). *A Counter-Insurgency Running Wild?*, October 23, 1967. Collection Guatemala and the U.S., item number GU00348.

DNSA (1968a). *Organization of the Guatemalan Internal Security Forces*, February 05, 1968. Collection Guatemala and the U.S., item number GU00357.

DNSA (1968b). *Assessment of Public Safety Program and Internal Security Situation in Guatemala,* February 07, 1968. Collection Guatemala and the U.S., item number GU00358.

DNSA (1968c). *Country Analysis and Strategic Paper*, March 22, 1968. Collection Guatemala and the U.S., item number GU00364.

DNSA (1968d). *Disarming the right wing vigilantes*, October 21, 1968. Collection Guatemala and the U.S., item number GU00383.

DNSA (1968e). *Armed Civilian Groups*, November 00, 1968. Collection Guatemala and the U.S., item number GU00385.

DNSA (1968f). *Security Forces Reorganization Program*, December 00, 1968. Collection Guatemala and the U.S., item number GU00390.

DNSA (1969). *Progress Report on the Action Plan for Guatemala*, September 10, 1969. Collection Guatemala and the U.S., item number GU00399.

DNSA (1970a). *Assistance to Arana to Cope Urban Terrorism*, March 30, 1970. Collection Guatemala and the U.S., item number GU00410.

DNSA (1970b). *Assistance to Elite Police Corps*, April 20, 1970. Collection Guatemala and the U.S., item number GU00417.

DNSA (1970c). *Ojo por Ojo: a new rightist counter terror organization,* May 19, 1970. Collection Guatemala and the U.S., item number GU00419.

DNSA (1970d). *Counter-Terror Attack Again After Two Year Pause,* May 26, 1970. Collection Guatemala and the U.S., item number GU00420.

DNSA (1970e). *Guatemala's Internal Security Situation,* June 02, 1970. Collection Guatemala and the U.S., item number GU00422.

DNSA (1970f). *Upgrading of Guatemalan Police*, October 30, 1970. Collection Guatemala and the U.S., item number GU00430.

DNSA (1970g). *Extra Legal Activities of Members of the Government*, December 01, 1970. Collection Guatemala and the U.S., item number GU00433.

DNSA (1971a). *Request for Equipment*, February 01, 1971. Collection Guatemala and the U.S., item number GU00438.

DNSA (1971b). *New Chief of the National Police*, February 17, 1971. Collection Guatemala and the U.S., item number GU00439.

DNSA (1971c). *Police Morale*, February 22, 1971. Collection Guatemala and the U.S., item number GU00440.

DNSA (1971d). *Expansion of the Role and Mission of the Mobile Military Police,* July 18, 1971. Collection Guatemala and the U.S., item number GU00451.

DNSA(1971e). *Public Safety Program in Guatemala,* September 08, 1971. Collection Guatemala and the U.S., item number GU00455.

DNSA (1971f). *Evaluation of the Public Safety Program in Guatemala*, December 00, 1971. Collection Guatemala and the U.S., item number GU00462.

DNSA (1972). *Military Intelligence Situation*, June 13, 1972. Collection Guatemala and the U.S., item number GU00468.

DNSA (1973a). *Country Analysis and Strategic Paper*, May 30, 1973. Collection Guatemala and the U.S., item number GU00477.

DNSA (1973b). *Arana's Wan on Common Crime*, June 01, 1973. Collection Guatemala and the U.S., item number GU00479.

DNSA (1973c). *Colonel Fernando Romeo Lucas Garcia*, June 28, 1973. Collection Guatemala and the U.S., item number GU00479.

DNSA (1974a). *Death Squad Strikes*, February 04, 1974. Collection Guatemala and the U.S., item number GU00481.

DNSA (1974b). *Termination Phase Out Study Public Security Project Guatemala*, July 00, 1974. Collection Guatemala and the U.S., item number GU00486.

DNSA (1974c). *Military Intelligence Summary,* April 01, 1974. Collection Guatemala and the U.S., item number GU00494.

DNSA (1976a). *Dealing with Political Kidnapping*, September 1976. Collection Terrorism and U.S. Policy 1968-2002, item number TE00550.

DNSA (1976b). *Monthly Report on Political Violence and Human Rights*, December 07, 1976. Collection Guatemala and the U.S., item number GU00502.

DNSA (1979a). *Right Win Terrorism*, April 04, 1979. Collection Guatemala and the U.S., item number GU00574.

DNSA (1979b). *Human Rights in Guatemala*, September 22, 1979. Collection Guatemala and the U.S., item number GU00601.

DNSA (1979c). *Creation of a National Front Against Communism,* November 15, 1979. Collection Guatemala and the U.S., item number GU00620.

DNSA (1980a). *Political Violence and Interagency Rivalry Within Guatemalan Police Forces*, August 28, 1980. Collection Guatemala and the U.S., item number GU00673.

DNSA (1980b). *Military Intelligence Summary (MIS), Volume VIII, Latin America*, September, 1980. Collection Guatemala and the U.S., item number GU00674.

DNSA (1982) *Military Attack Against Civil Population in Ixil Area*, February 00, 1982. Collection Guatemala and the U.S., item number GU00767.

DNSA (1988). *A Business Proposal with Kickbacks*, October 12, 1988. Collection Guatemala and the U.S., item number GU01198.

DNSA (1989a). *Former Members of Guatemalan National Police and Civilians Kill Criminals*, February 00, 1989. Collection Guatemala and the U.S., item number GU01220.

DNSA (1989b). *Low Controls Over Paramilitary Forces*, November 22, 1989. Collection Guatemala and the U.S., item number GU01294.

DNSA (1989c). *Army Strives to Keep Free of Drug Corruption*, February 07, 1989. Collection Guatemala and the U.S., item number GU01221.

DNSA (1990a). *Comments by Senior GT Army Officer Concerning Drugs*, June 08, 1990. Collection Guatemala and the U.S., item number GU01340.

DNSA (1990b). *Mayor of Zacapa Arrested for Drug Trafficking*, December 28, 1990. Collection Guatemala and the U.S., item number GU01420.

DNSA (1992). *Military Officer Involvement in Narcotics Trafficking*, June 15, 1992. Collection Guatemala and the U.S., item number GU01599.

DNSA (1993). *Indigenous pressures against the Army*, December 05, 1993. Collection Guatemala and the U.S., item number GU01783.

DNSA (1994). *Human Intelligence Sources of the D-2,* February 00, 1994. Collection Guatemala and the U.S., item number GU01793.

DNSA (1995a). *Military Commissioners acted as de facto Mayors*, August 01, 1995. Collection Guatemala and the U.S., item number GU02008.

DNSA (1995b). *Demobilization Plan,* August 14, 1995. Collection Guatemala and the U.S., item number GU02011.

DNSA (1995c). *Military Commissioners were not incorporated as military reserves,* August 29, 1995. Collection Guatemala and the U.S., item number GU02014.

DNSA (1995d). *Military Commissioners*, September 06, 1995. Collection Guatemala and the U.S., item number GU02016.

DNSA (1995e). *Militaries Humit Network changed name but not mission*, September 14, 1995. Collection Guatemala and the U.S., item number GU02017.

DNSA (1995f). *Military Commissioners Demobilization*, September 14, 1995. Collection Guatemala and the U.S., item number GU02019.

DNSA (1995g). *Military Commissioners Demobilization,* September 20, 1995. Collection Guatemala and the U.S., item number GU002002.

DNSA (1995h). *Military Commissioners and the N2*, December 07, 1995. Collection Guatemala and the U.S., item number GU02039.

DNSA (1995i). *Police and Military Patrolling*, December 08, 1995. Collection Guatemala and the U.S., item number GU02040.

DNSA (1995j). *Possible Military Connection to Gang Activity in Guatemala*, April 17, 1995. Collection Guatemala and the U.S., item number GU01956.

DNSA (1996). *Former Military Commissioners Working for the DECAM*, January 26, 1996. Collection Guatemala and the U.S., item number GU02049.

Documents of the Historic Archive of the National Police of Guatemala

AHPN (1954/doc1760054). *Ordenes Generales* 1954-01-02-1954-12-31, Fondo GT PN35, Libro 10563, code number 964327916112007.
AHPN (1955). *Memoria de trabajos llevados a cabo por la Policía Nacional en 1955*, GT PN30, Central de Libros, libro 1856.
AHPN (1957/doc1770813). *Ordenes Generales* 1957-01-02-1958-01-01, October 23, 1957, Fondo GT PN35, Libro 10569, code number 434412719112007.
AHPN (1958/doc1747670). *Ordenes Generales* 1958-01-02-1958-12-29, February 10, 1958, Fondo GT PN35, Libro 10576, code number 435639917112007.
AHPN (1959/doc1742190). *Ordenes Generales* 1959-01-02-1959-12-30, January 27, 1959, Fondo GT PN35, Libro 10577, code number 394118813112007.
AHPN (1960/doc592911). *Ordenes Generales* 1960-01-01-1960-12-29, February 05, 1960, Fondo GT PN35, Libro 10579, code number 2244181922007.
AHPN (1969/doc665327). *Ordenes Generales* 1969-01-31-1970-01-01, April 11, 1969, Fondo GT PN35, Libro 10603, code number 1949418132007.
AHPN (1970/doc852624). GT PN30-01 S010, *Memoria de Labores de la Policía Nacional* from July 01, 1969 to June 30, 1970, code number 21145292832007.
AHPN (1971/882301923102007). *Memoria de Labores de la Policía Nacional* from July 01, 1971 to April 30, 1972.
AHPN (1973/doc1926161). GT PN30 S004, *Informe de carácter confidencial*, May 19, 1973, code number 925237142312008.
AHPN (1976/doc2773170). GT PN51-02 S002, September 21, 1979, Oficio No. 1289, code number 112115711222009.
AHPN (1977/doc2765087). GT PN51-01 S007, December 21, 1977, Oficio No. 704/cat.
AHPN (1979/doc1028660). Year 1979-02, box 0002, file 13, April 02, 1979, code number 58562181652007.
AHPN (1979/doc2773753). GT PN51-02 S002, July 04, 1979, Oficio No. 1079, code number 19374891222009.
AHPN (1979/doc2773756). GT PN51-02 S002, July 04, 1979, Oficio No. 1084, code number 19374891222009.

AHPN (1979/doc2773802). GT PN51-02 S002, July 17, 1979, Oficio No. 1313, code number 19374891222009.
AHPN (1979/no.6019). Ref. DAR/sst, October 05, 1979.
AHPN (1979/pro.318). Providencia No. 318/JAG/jrmm, COCP, October 25, 1979.
AHPN (1980/doc2774098). GT PN51-02 S002, June 05, 1980, code number 49155111222009.
AHPN (1980/doc2774071). GT PN51-02 S002, June 09, 1980, code number 49155111222009.
AHPN (1980/doc2774089). GT PN51-02 S002, June 09, 1980, code number 49155111222009.
AHPN (1980/04GX9-101a). *Comunicación CONSESA al Coronel Pedro García Arredondo*, Cuerpo de Detectives, Policía Nacional, November 04, 1980.
AHPN (1980/04GX9-101b). *Comunicación CONSESA al Coronel Germán Chupina Barahona*, Cuerpo de Detectives, Policía Nacional, November 04, 1980.
AHPN (1980/4GX9-101c). Memo to File, ref. IM-801, December 04, 1980.
AHPN (1981/ref4111). GT PN51 S002, box 116, leg. 3, cam. Dic (101).
AHPN (1981/4GX9-101d). Memo to File, January 28, 1981.
AHPN (1981/doc2774125). GT PN51-02 S002, Oficio No. 01222, August 20, 1981, code number 49155111222009.
AHPN (1981/doc2774131). GT PN51-02 S002, October 03, 1981, code number 49155111222009.
AHPN (1982/doc2776364). GT PN51-02 S002, February 11, 1982, code number 65283271322009.
AHPN (1982/pro0046). GT PN51-02 S002, Providencia No. MCP/0046, February 12, 1982, code number 65283271322009.
AHPN (1982/doc2776521). GT PN51-02 S002, March 18, 1982, code number 65283271322009.
AHPN (1982/doc2773268). GT PN51-02 S015, Oficio No. MCP/1770, April 21, 1982, code number 99215271222009.
AHPN (1982/doc2776670). GT PN51-02 S002, Providencia No. 165/HCB, Jun 03, 1982, code number 65283271322009.
AHPN (1982/04GX9-101e). *Comunicación CONSESA al Jefe de Departamento, División de Investigaciones Técnicas de la Policía National, Col. Oswaldo Yat*, June 23, 1982.
AHPN (1982/doc2776733). GT PN51-02 S002, July 06, 1982, code number 65283271322009.
AHPN (1982/doc2770953). GT PN51-02 S015, Oficio No. 08470, July 08, 1982, code number 822434131122009.
AHPN (1982/doc2773398). GT PN51-02, S015, Oficio No. MCP/1989, July 19, 1982, code number 99215271222009.

AHPN (1982/doc3151861). GT PN51-02 S002, August 02, 1982.
AHPN (1982/doc2776800). GT PN51-02 S002, August 02, 1982, code number 65283271322009.
AHPN (1982/doc2776805). GT PN51-02 S002, August 19, 1982, code number 65283271322009.
AHPN (1982/doc2762896). GT PN51-02 S015, Oficio No. COC-SRIO.2368, October 21, 1982, code number 248289622009.
AHPN (1982/doc2774133). GT PN51-02 S002, Oficio No. 1066, October 31, 1982, code number 491553111222009.
AHPN (1982/doc2776868). GT PN51-02 S002, Providencia No. COC/SRIO.335, November 08, 1982, code number 65283271322009.
AHPN (1982/doc2774135). GT PN51-02 S002, Oficio No. 1119, November 16, 1982, code number 491553111222009.
AHPN (1982/doc2774137). GT PN51-02 S002, Radiograma, November 28, 1982, code number 491553111222009.
AHPN (1982/doc2774136). GT PN51-02 S002, Radiograma, November 28, 1982, code number 491553111222009
AHPN (1982/doc2774139). GT PN51-02 S002, Oficio No. 1,200, November 30, 1982 code number 491553111222009.
AHPN (1982/doc2776896). GT PN51-02 S002, Providencia No. COC/sm/406, December 12, 1982, code number 65283271322009.
AHPN (1982 /doc2774144). GT PN51-02 S002, Oficio No. 1264, December 21, 1982, code number 491553111222009.
AHPN (1983 /doc2774145). GT PN51-02 S002, Oficio No. 080, January 18, 1982, code number 491553111222009.
AHPN (1983/doc2774148). GT PN51-02, S002, Oficio No. 581, May 16, 1983, code number 491553111222009.
AHPN (1983/doc2774156). GT PN51-02, S002, 01, June 17, 1983, code number 491553111222009.
AHPN (1983/doc2776352). GT PN51-02, S002, Oficio No. 1129, July 27, 1983, code number 491553111222009.
AHPN (1983/doc2766782). GT PN51-01, S007, August 01, 1983, code number 1000313922009.
AHPN (1983/of1163). Oficio no. COC/sm/1163, September 23, 1983, code number n.s.
AHPN (1983/ref4245). September 23, 1983, Ref. No. 4245.
AHPN (1984/doc277350). GT PN51-02, S015, Providencia No. 1015, January 17, 1984, code number 82243431122009.
AHPN (1984/doc2773354). GT PN51-02, S015, January 17, 1984, code number 82243431122009.

AHPN (1984/doc2773370). GT PN51-02, S015, January 17, 1984, code number 82243431122009.

AHPN (1984/doc2764806). GT PN51-01, S007, January 18, 1984, code number 2739177922009.

AHPN (1984/doc2777049). GT PN51-02, S002, Providencia No. 054/COC-SRIO, April 03, 1984, code number 634942111322009.

AHPN (1984/doc2777096) GT PN51-02, S002, Providencia No. 122, June 18, 1984, code number 634942111322009.

AHPN (1984/doc2773122). GT PN51-02, S002, June 22, 1984, Oficio No. 2954, code number 82243431122009.

AHPN (1984/doc2770950). GT PN51-02, S015, Oficio No. 207-84, September 12, 1984, code number 822434131122009.

AHPN (1984/doc2777132). GT PN51-02, S002, Providencia No. 186, September 18, 1984, code number 634942111322009.

AHPN (1984/doc2773434). GT PN51-02, S002, Providencia No. 31432, November 12, 1984, code number 61274871222009.

AHPN (1984/doc2762837). GT PN51-01, S007, December 04, 1984, code number 9819529622009.

AHPN (1985/doc2765346). *Policías particulares que operan en la República*, GT PN51-01, S007, code number 10003139222009.

AHPN (1985/doc2765022). GT PN51-01, box 510040.

AHPN (1985/doc2767903). GT PN51-01, S007, February 02, 1985, code number 8042527922009.

AHPN (1985/doc2767786). GT PN51-01, S007, April 22, 1985, code number 75465012622009.

AHPN (1985/doc2767792). GT PN51-01, S007, May 14, 1985, code number 75465012622009.

AHPN (1985/doc2764907). GT PN51-01, S007, May 28, 1985, code number 8042527922009.

AHPN (1985/doc2767786). GT PN51-01, S007, May 24, 1985, code number 75465012622009.

AHPN (1985/doc2767767). GT PN51-01, S007, July 02, 1985, code number 75465012622009.

AHPN (1987/doc2773360). GT PN51-02, S002, January 17, 1987, code number 82243431122009.

Documents of the General Archive of Central America

AGCA (1933). Comunicación de la Comandancia Departamental de Huehuetenango a la Secretaría de Guerra, 1933, L 81, R 8.

AGCA (1938). *Revista Militar*, XV, 5, June & August 1938.

Interviews

Alex Valdez. Current Institution: Security manager of ASEGURI. November 3, 2009. Guatemala.

Álvaro Hernández. Current institution: Security Advisory of the Division de supervision y control de empresas, entidades y personas individuales de seguridad privada of the PNC, Ministry of Interior. March 12, 2009. Guatemala.

Axel Romero. Current institution: Chief of Communal Organization of the Ministry of Communal Affairs. March 12, 2009. Guatemala.

Byron Heredia. Current institution: Consejo de Seguridad Hotelera de Guatemala. February 24, 2009. Guatemala.

Carlos Quintanilla. Current institution: Owner of SERPROP. March 17, 2009. Guatemala.

Carlos Maldonado. Current institution: Cámara de Empresas de Seguridad de Guatemala. March 10, 2009. Guatemala.

Edgar Herrera. Current institution: Security Advisor of EMISA. March 23, 2009. Guatemala.

Fernando Girón. Current institution: Myrna Mack Foundation. March 13, 2009. Guatemala.

Ivan García and Arturo Matute. Current institution: Citizen Security Programme, PNUD. March 5, 2009. Guatemala.

Jorge Sierra. Current Institution: Grupo Almo (Private Security Company). March 2, 2009. Guatemala.

Jorge Sierra. Current Institution: Grupo Almo (Private Security Company). March 9, 2009. Guatemala.

Manfredo Chocano. Current institution: Director of Institutional Planning and Development, Superintendencia de Administración Tributaria -SAT-. February 19, 2009. Guatemala.

Mario Mérida. Current institution: Former Vice Ministry of Interior and former Colonel of the Guatemalan Army. May 5, 2009. Guatemala.

Mildred Luna. Current institution: Coordinator of the Lynching Prevention Program of the Judiciary. October 15, 2010. Guatemala.

Priscila de Narciso. Current institution: Auxiliary Mayor of District 9 of the metropolitan area. March 18, 2009. Guatemala.

Rodolfo Muñoz Piloña. Current institution: Owner of the Unidad de Servicios Integrales de Seguridad. March 17, 2009. Guatemala.

Rubén Darío Martínez. Current institution: Auxiliary Mayor of District 1 of the metropolitan area. March 23, 2009. Guatemala.

Anonymous Interviews

Interview with a security advisor of the Division for Supervision and Control of Private Security Companies, Entities, and Individuals. March 12, 2009. Guatemala.

Interview with intelligence analyst of the State Intelligence Agency (SIE). March 5, 2009. Guatemala.

Interview with a police officer of the Sección de Intervención en Relaciones Comunitarias de la Policía Nacional Civil. October 22, 2010. Guatemala.

Newspapers

Prensa Libre

(02/07/2000). Pánico colectivo en la aldea El Güiscoyal.
(05/16/2000). *Comités de seguridad crean temor entre indígenas.*
(05/29/2000). *Juntas de seguridad en Quiché.*
(07/29/2000). *Linchamientos: se oponen a capturas.*
(09/20/2001). *Intimidan a contralores in Occidente.*
(10/10/2004). ¿Están ellos preparados?
(05/04/2005). *Pobladores patrullarán.*
(06/28/2005). *Capitalinos se unen contra la delincuencia.*
(07/07/2005). *Municipios sin protección.*
(07/27/2005). *Piden a PNC que no los dejen solos.*
(09/01/2005). *Frente contra la violencia.*
(09/07/2005). *Municipios sin Protección.*
(09/27/2005a). *Piden a PNC que no los dejen solos.*
(09/27/2005b). *Rechaza Patrullaje.*
(11/23/2005). *Se unen para protegerse.*
(01/19/2006). *No creen en PNC.*
(01/20/2006). *Crece venta de seguridad privada.*
(04/07/2006). *Fuerza militar y civil a la calle.*
(05/06/2006). *A los pueblos regresa la calma.*
(05/15/2006). *Pésimas condiciones.*
(07/13/2006). *Cierran juzgado en Sumpango.*
(07/14/2006). *Pandilleros pretenden ser guardias.*
(07/16/2006). *Ejército de guardias sin control.*
(08/20/2006). *Vecinos se cuidan por su cuenta.*
(09/27/2006). *Amenazan con desterrar a presuntos delincuentes.*

(05/21/2007). *Huyen de las exPAC.*
(11/07/2007). *Linchan a cinco en dos meses.*
(12/12/2007). *Muere por violar toque de queda.*
(03/10/2008). *DOAN llegó a ser un cartel.*
(03/31/2008). *Policía Pagará Q120 millones por soldados.*
(05/05/2008). *El esquivo sucesor de Víctor Rivera.*
(05/13/2008). *Vecinos se unen contra la violencia.*
(05/16/2008). *Queman a presuntos ladrones en Sololá.*
(06/27/2008). *Ex asesores de Policía ultimados.*
(10/16/2008). *Vecinos patrullarán las calles.*
(12/12/2008). *Imponen trabajos forzados a mareros.*
(01/04/2009). *Justicia Indígena; crimen y castigo.*
(01/12/2009). *Piden militarizar el municipio de Mixco.*
(01/30/2009). *Empresarios utilizan Q4 millones para cuidar buses.*
(02/11/2009). *PNC expulsada de municipio La Esperanza, Quetzaltenango.*
(03/27/2009). *Vecinos de Santiago Atitlán exigen justicia.*
(04/28/2009). *Investigan a patrulleros ciudadanos por denuncias de agresiones.*
(04/29/2009). *Investigan a ocho grupos de vecinos que brindan seguridad.*
(05/25/2009). *Patrullarán calles; Ejército apoyará tareas de PNC en Escuintla.*
(06/10/2009). *Rondas ciudadanas reducen crímenes.*
(08/11/2009). *Juntas de seguridad actúan al margen de la ley.*
(11/11/2009). *Vecinos de San Martín Jilotepeque linchan a policía.*
(12/04/2009). *Justicia sin control en Huehuetenango.*
(03/01/2010). *Juntas de seguridad abusan de funciones.*
(07/20/2010). *Aplican castigo comunitario a presunto ladrón.*
(10/11/2010). *Policía y Ejército redoblan vigilancia.*
(10/22/2010). *Vecinos contra la violencia.*
(01/08/2011). *Panajachel frente a Panajachel.*

El Periódico

(09/24/2007). Limpieza social en Santiago Atitlán.
(02/14/2008). *Colom pide que se retome el control en San Juan Sacatepéquez.*
(06/27/2008). *Asesinan a los Hermanos Benítez.*
(09/08/2008). *Buscan a Carlos Quintanilla en Taxisco.*
(10/26/2008). *Vecinos de Muxbal con seguridad de soldados.*
(11/14/2008). *A los pobladores de Palín les salió el tiro por la culata.*
(12/15/2008). *Más de 45 solicitudes piden seguridad al Ejército.*
(02/02/2010). *Asesinato de pilotos: conteo para 2010 lleva 14 víctimas.*

(04/13/2010). *Agentes privados solo podrían portar armas si tienen 25 años o más.*
(07/22/2010). *Encuesta empresarial refleja incremento de la violencia en el país.*
(08/22/2010). En la pequeña Amsterdam.

Annexes

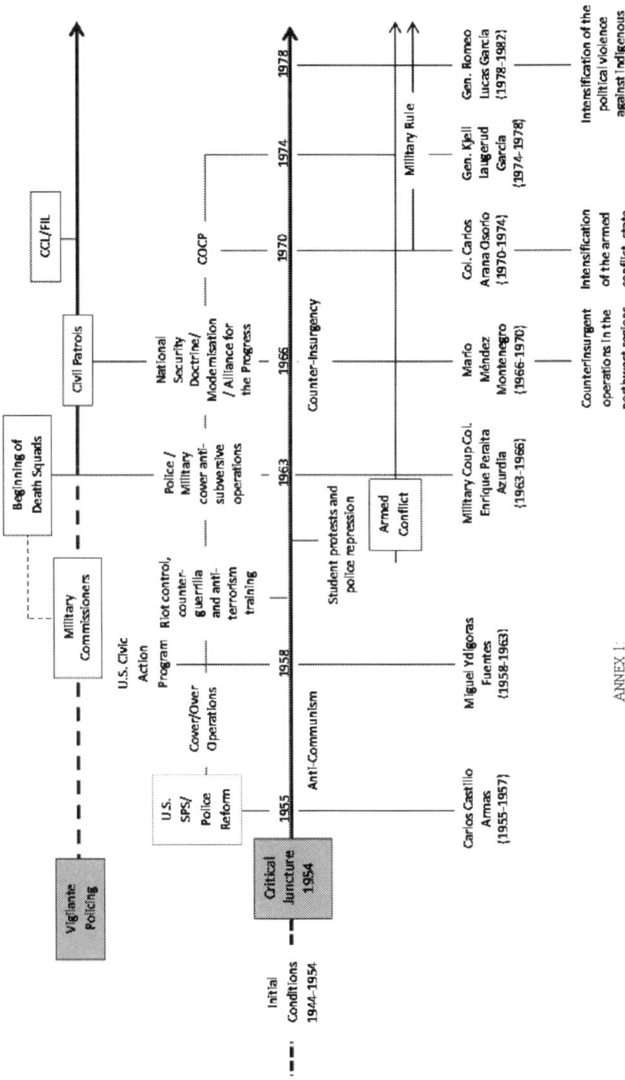

ANNEX 1:
THE INSTITUTIONAL PATTERN OF PUBLIC SECURITY DISPLACEMENT

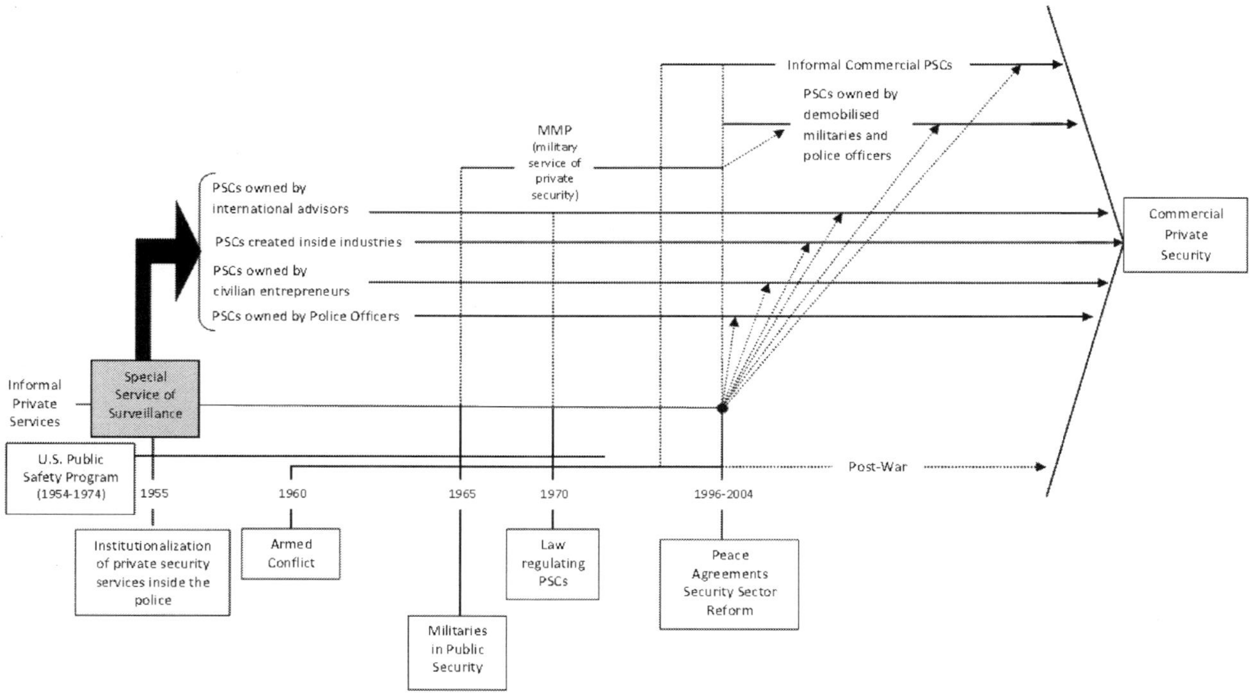

ANNEX 2:
PATHWAY OF COMMERCIAL PRIVATE SECURITY PROLIFERATION